Unleashing the Crowd

"A book that describes how to manage crowds collectively innovating is badly needed. I know through personal experience that it's a competitive advantage to unleash the crowds not simply to get their ideas, but to have them collaborate and collectively produce. Majchrzak and Malhotra aptly fill this gap."

—Dirk Ahlborn, *Founder and CEO of Hyperloop Transportation, Technologies Inc and Jumpstart, Inc*

"The principles for crowdsourcing laid out in this book are simple yet highly effective. I have witnessed them at work first hand. After seeing many crowdsourcing events prior to using the principles in this book, I completely agree with their approach. These are really two books in one. One written for the academician and the other for a crowd-sourcing practitioner, but also important for the social scientist and philosopher. The book is a description of innovative research describing the necessary steps to fully release the innovation power of the crowd and also an exploration into the nature of human creativity that is stimulating well beyond the world of business."

—William Bonfield M.D., P.H., life fellow A.A.P.L., *Chief Medical Officer Optum Behavioral Health*, retired

"In this expertly researched book, Ann and Arvind offer a refreshing look at crowdsourcing: Drawing upon sharp examples and insights, the authors build a roadmap for organizations to develop crowdsourcing as a key capability for collectively producing innovation among the crowds. A timely and important reading, particularly in the age of technology platforms and big data organizations."

—Dr. Konstantinos Trantopoulos, *Accenture Growth & Strategy*

"Majchrzak and Malhotra show us that we can advance crowdsourcing the same way we can advance innovation itself: by opening it up! Open crowds have surprising capabilities to tackle even wicked problems, and anyone seeking to gain new innovative insights from diverse knowledge sources will find this book a stimulating and invaluable reference."

—Henry Chesbrough, Professor, *UC Berkeley, USA*; author of the award-winning book, *Open Innovation: The New Imperative for Creating and Profiting from Technology*

"Majchrzak and Malhotra have authored a ground-breaking book of how crowds can be deployed to solve complex and difficult problems. Based on hands-on research, inventing a new method on organizing crowds and careful reflective analysis they show the five practices needed to achieve high-value solutions collaboratively from the crowd. This book is a must read for practitioners in all types of organizations who want to achieve breakthrough innovations by using both internal and external crowds. Scholars will appreciate the book for its rigor and creative theorizing on crowd innovation."

—Karim R. Lakhani, *Charles E. Wilson Professor of Business Administration, Harvard Business School, USA*; author, *Revolutionizing Innovation*

"Ann and Arvind have done a fine service for both the innovation research community and practitioners of innovation. Crowds and open innovation are a crucial innovation logic that contrasts with traditional closed logics. Yet research and practice on the effectiveness of crowd-based innovation is equivocal. This book both reviews the literature in this space and makes concrete and bold suggestions on when, where, and how to use crowds to solve wicked societal and organizational problems. This is a well conceptualized and well written book on this crucial innovation mode. Well done."

—Michael Tushman, *Baker Foundation Professor*, Paul R. Lawrence MBA Class of 1942 Professor of Business Administration, Emeritus, Charles B. (Tex) Thornton Chair of the Advanced Management Program, *Harvard Business School, USA*; Author, *Lead and Disrupt: How to Solve the Innovator's Dilemma*

"Tackling wicked problems is not just for individuals and teams. Majchrzak and Malhotra's theory of collective innovation offers a breakthrough that provides five practices to design on-line 'crowd' platforms for superior innovation performance. The theoretical and practical insights from their impressive field research make for a winning combination. I highly recommend this book."

—Jackson Nickerson, *Frahm Family Professor of Organization and Strategy, Olin Business School, Washington University in St. Louis, USA*; Nonresident Senior Fellow in Governance Studies, *Brookings Institution*

"How to extract wisdom from the crowd to solve humanity's hardest problems, is critically important but poorly understood. Majchrzak and Malhotra offer a seminal treatise on crowd-based problem solving, deeply rooted in outstanding empirical research on a variety of collaborative projects. A must-read for any innovation scholar!"

—Georg von Krogh, *Professor and Group Head, Strategic Management and Innovation, ETH Zurich, Switzerland*

"This book offers an original approach to how individuals and organizations can develop and collaborate with communities for idea generation. The book skillfully demonstrates how communities have unique properties that enable them to generate and share knowledge that can solve specific types of problems better than other organizational forms. As such the book is a valuable resource for managers as well as for researchers."

—Lars Frederiksen, *Professor of Innovation, Entrepreneurship and Strategy at Dept. of Management, School of Business and Social Sciences, Aarhus University, Denmark*

"In an age where we are often so dismissive of the ideas and opinions expressed by others, this book reminds us how much more productive we can be, when in addition to questioning others, we are willing to challenge our own assumptions and beliefs. We can do so much more when we remain open to the possibilities we can create together."

—Ray Eugene Reagans, *Alfred P. Sloan Professor of Management and Professor of Organization Studies, MIT Sloan School of Management, USA*

"This book is a unique and timely contribution to the study of crowdsourcing. Ann Majchrzak and Arvind Malhotra combine with unusual astuteness conceptual analysis with practical relevance to produce a book of great interest to researchers and practitioners of crowdsourcing, crowd-based knowledge development and digital innovation more widely."

—Jannis Kallinikos, Professor, *London School of Economics, UK*

"The promise of open crowds for dealing with wicked problems is unprecedented. Majchrzak and Malhotra's novel yet actionable approach makes essential reading for anyone dealing with the big business societal challenges of our time"

—Ola Henfridsson, *Professor of Information Systems and Management, Warwick Business School, The University of Warwick, UK*

"Getting people who don't know each other and who will likely never meet to come up with solutions to society's biggest problems seems like a pipe dream. Yet it is the driver behind most crowdsourcing initiatives. In Unleashing the Crowd, Malhotra and Majchrzak take one of the biggest steps ever toward turning this dream into a reality. Their recommendations—drawn from impressive data collection—are imminently practical and provide the wisdom we need to use crowds effectively".

—Paul Leonardi, *Duca Family Professor of Technology Management, UC Santa Barbara, USA*

"Ann Majchrzak and Arvind Malhotra are exactly the right people at the right time to help us leverage crowdpowered innovation. In *Unleashing the Crowd: Collaborative Solutions to Wicked Business and Societal Problems*, they share results of their research and show that unconstrained, unleashed, crowds (very different from most current strategies) are powerful contributors to solving today's biggest problems."

—Terri L. Griffith, *Keith Beedie Chair in Innovation and Entrepreneurship, Simon Fraser University, USA*

Ann Majchrzak • Arvind Malhotra

Unleashing the Crowd

Collaborative Solutions to Wicked Business and Societal Problems

palgrave
macmillan

Ann Majchrzak
University of Southern California
Los Angeles, CA, USA

Arvind Malhotra
University of North Carolina
Chapel Hill, NC, USA

ISBN 978-3-030-25556-5   ISBN 978-3-030-25557-2 (eBook)
https://doi.org/10.1007/978-3-030-25557-2

© The Editor(s) (if applicable) and The Author(s), under exclusive licence to Springer Nature Switzerland AG 2020

This work is subject to copyright. All rights are solely and exclusively licensed by the Publisher, whether the whole or part of the material is concerned, specifically the rights of translation, reprinting, reuse of illustrations, recitation, broadcasting, reproduction on microfilms or in any other physical way, and transmission or information storage and retrieval, electronic adaptation, computer software, or by similar or dissimilar methodology now known or hereafter developed.

The use of general descriptive names, registered names, trademarks, service marks, etc. in this publication does not imply, even in the absence of a specific statement, that such names are exempt from the relevant protective laws and regulations and therefore free for general use.

The publisher, the authors and the editors are safe to assume that the advice and information in this book are believed to be true and accurate at the date of publication. Neither the publisher nor the authors or the editors give a warranty, expressed or implied, with respect to the material contained herein or for any errors or omissions that may have been made. The publisher remains neutral with regard to jurisdictional claims in published maps and institutional affiliations.

Cover illustration: © hoperan / shutterstock.com

This Palgrave Macmillan imprint is published by the registered company Springer Nature Switzerland AG.
The registered company address is: Gewerbestrasse 11, 6330 Cham, Switzerland

Executive Summary

Crowdsourcing and Use of Open Crowds to solve big societal and business problems—wicked problems—is receiving growing attention among business practitioners and academics. This book is for both reflective practitioners and researchers, balancing practical needs for advice, with the precision of scholarly research backing up that advice. We build this book on a series of five case studies as well as 20 crowdsourcing events in which innovative outcomes were achieved in the field of health-care insurance, toy industry, entertainment industry, software industry, and societal change. These crowds created new business models, new product lines, new strategies for growth, solving global transportation problems, and even suggesting ways to solve New Zealand's pest problem. By innovative solutions, we mean solutions that are novel to the organization sponsoring the crowdsourcing event, implementable by the sponsoring organization, and useful (e.g., for a business, usefulness means the solution provides a competitive advantage). Our data collection, analysis, and field observations demonstrate that traditional forms of crowdsourcing and crowds are greatly under-leveraged for solving wicked problems due to some key assumptions made and approaches taken by practitioners and propagated by researchers today. The crowdsourcing process and platforms of today end up restraining or "mind-cuffing" the crowd. As a result, the crowd is only encouraged to offer ideas (an Idea-Sharing approach), with the expectation that only close-knit teams with strong social bonds can solve wicked problems.

We find that when the design of platform and the crowdsourcing process "unmindcuffs" the crowd from a focus on Idea-Sharing, the ideas the crowd collectively produces are more innovative and produced more efficiently compared to those produced by crowds restricted to an Idea-Sharing crowdsourcing process. A deep analytical examination of the trace data left by the 20 crowds led us to find 5 practices the crowds used when they are "unmindcuffed". These five practices make it possible for crowd participants to learn about all the various issues involved in solving the wicked problem in easily consumable and inspiring sound-bites that take little time of any single individual. It is truly a collective experience. The five practices are as follows:

Practice 1: Minimally committed knowledge baton passers. A crowd responding to an innovation challenge question offers less than two posts per participant, with virtually no dialogue, and little time in social support. They do not "collaborate" in a traditional sense. *Rather, such crowds collaborate by passing bits of knowledge as short batons specially conceived to inspire, not simply inform others.*

Practice 2: Sharing a variety of knowledge types matters more than any specific knowledge shared. We coded the traces of knowledge sound-bites shared for different types of knowledge shared about the problem description and solution. The types we looked at were whether the knowledge contained facts about the problem, examples and personal experiences of how the problem in other contexts known to a participant, paradoxes in objectives that need to be considered for solving the problem, and ideas for solving the problem. We then quantitatively analyzed if an innovative idea was more likely to be posted after posts with any of these specific types of knowledge sharing. What we found was that no single specific type of knowledge—including prior ideas—affected whether an innovative idea was posted. What mattered was the variety of the knowledge types. In other words, more ideas do not breed better solutions, which is what most of the literature emphasizes. *Rather, it was the variety of types of knowledge that matters.*

Practice 3: Amplifying Creative Associations. Just mimicking others' ideas or knowledge does not make the crowd more likely to innovate. Instead, participants use the creative associations shared by others as jumping off points, to think about other associations they might have in their own memory about the problem. *Individuals then post these associations, which serve to inspire others to post associations, which starts a positive feedback loop providing more fodder for creative discovery.*

Practice 4: Reconstructing Problem-Associated Needs to Spark Creative Associations. The crowd cannot simply accept needs or solutions offered by others if the crowd wants to collectively produce innovative solutions. If they simply accepted others' professed needs, the best the crowd could do would be to treat the needs as requirements and generate a solution that is more expansive or inclusive of those needs. That is counterproductive to an innovation agenda as all that this accomplishes is that new solutions suggested by the crowd are merely a refinement and broadened version of initially proposed solutions, with little collective co-generation. Instead, Collective Production of innovation requires that the crowd *reformulates the* *initial needs to spark others to explicate their creative associations.* The crowd reformulates others' initial professed needs—either by offering personalized and concrete examples of the need in a different context to create an analogy for others to build upon, or to abstract the initial need to apply to societal issues and corresponding human action. *This then, in turn, inspires others in the crowd to strive to achieve solutions that address new more value-based goals than simply meeting professed requirements.*

Practice 5: Enacting self-selected innovation-enabling roles. We find that the crowd is composed of not just mere ideators. Rather, in more innovation-producing crowds, individuals perform a range of innovation-enabling roles other than ideation. Some individuals engage in need elicitation, others offer need reconstruction, others offer creative associations, and yet others offer basic knowledge facts about the problem. Then, there are those individuals who generate new solutions specifically by using (integrating or reshaping) the knowledge provided by others. *None of these roles are simply providing social support since the more social support offered in posts, the less innovative the crowd. Rather, the crowd gives everyone a voice about the problem, in their own preferred way of sharing that voice.*

These five practices lead us to offer a new theory of Collective Production of innovative ideas: a theory of fragments of associations and association-amplification. The theory is briefly described in the illustrative figure here, which is elaborated in the book.

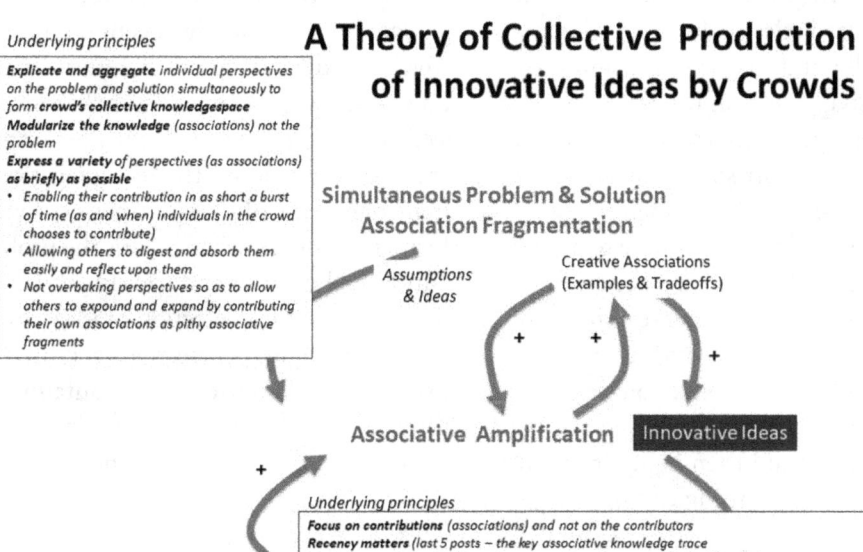

Our theory differs from traditional Idea-Sharing theories of innovation in the following ways:

1. Participants do not need to commit to spending significant time in the innovation process socializing with others and trying to create a shared understanding before making an important contribution.
2. Instead of attempting to understand each other's perspective, participants are allowed to express their diverse perspectives as short statements of fragments of their knowledge—creative associations, facts, and unconstrained ideas. Therefore, no single person's complete perspective matters as much as a varied collage of pieces or fragments of perspectives are shared.
3. The fragments of knowledge thus shared serve to simultaneously provide elaborated definitions of the problem and exposure to a range of possible solutions. There is no constraint on the crowd to reach a consensus about the problem definition prior to generating solutions. As such, solutions shared can spark creative associations that then lead to a redefinition of the initial problem itself.
4. Having some participants offer creative associations, in conjunction with other knowledge types offered, will stimulate others to contribute more creative associations, leading to a positive network effect—amplification—which eventually leads to a creative discovery of innovative ideas.

The theory of Collective Production we put forth in this book is one where paradoxically disaggregation and re-aggregation of knowledge occur continually and in parallel, leading to collectively producing innovative ideas. The disaggregation occurs as people break down their causal models, their coherent perspectives, their proposals of need-solution pairs into factual assumptions, short statements of ideas, and creative associations. The re-aggregation occurs as a "co-mingling" of the different fragments of different perspectives that help the collective to appreciate the many issues associated with the problem, which a more comprehensive solution will need to and should strive to address. Instead of searching and selecting ideas from a collection of ideas and instead of working in a team to create a coherent perspective, a crowd's Collective Production centers on continuously adding to traces containing fragments of knowledge and creative associations, observing patterns in those traces, and then being inspired to add more to the traces, including creative ideas of co-mingled knowledge.

Our theory—derived from our field-intensive research findings—is that any single individual in the crowd spends so little time contributing to the wicked problem, that the more the crowd, on the whole, can effectively elicit each other's disaggregated knowledge to creatively stimulate each other in a virtuous cycle, the more likely that the crowd will successfully produce innovative solutions. In sum, the knowledge that is desired from the crowd is *not* "individually constructed" coherent perspectives of needs and solutions to the problem, or causal models of assumptions, but disaggregated cause-effect models so they can be reconsidered creatively.

Our theory and the five practices have implications for both practitioners and researchers. For practitioners, specific implementation issues are raised, including how to design the software platform to support the Collective Production of innovation practices and how to prepare the organization for the often path-breaking ideas that result. For researchers, we suggest that our theory of Collective Production should lead to the reconsideration of assumptions underlying existing theories not just about crowdsourcing, but about how innovation is achieved. Thus, we offer to spark creative association through our theory in the spirit of the Collective Production process we have described here. In this spirit, we do not profess that our theory is in anyway summative. Rather, we believe it is the first spark in the reconsideration of assumptions of traditional innovation idea-search-centric process.

Teams are increasingly looking more like crowds, and therefore, traditional team-based practices should be reconsidered as potentially benefiting from these crowd-based practices and from our theory of Collective Production. Additionally, organizational boundaries are increasingly porous, requiring new theories of organizational design that take the openness of the crowd into account. A new conceptualization of innovation processes is needed that finally stops assuming that people have straightforward conversations like they used to and instead considers how digital artifacts can now be used to support innovation when accompanied by a process of disaggregation, reflection, patterns in the traces of artifacts, and re-aggregation. Organizational researchers studying how the "augmented workforce" is used will find our theory of Collective Production to be useful. For example, instead of considering the workforce as a set of people or skills or recipients of tasks and rewards, as is done in traditional theories of organizational design, or people as contributors and consumers of knowledge, as is done in the knowledge-based theory of the firm, our theory of Collective Production places the role of the traces of artefacts left by both humans and tools as the fodder from which innovation is stimulated, if allowed to be appropriately disaggregated, shared for creative associations, and comingled. As organizations are increasingly managed by digital artifacts and artificial intelligence, our Collective Production theory explains how to ensure that innovative outcomes will result from their use. Disaggregation of the knowledge embedded in artificial intelligence as well as embedded in the human partner to the AI tools is needed for creative associations to be developed by the human partner.

How is the book unique? Our book differs from prior research and books on crowdsourcing. Most management scientists and practitioners think of crowdsourcing as a way to get individuals from inside or outside the organization to provide ideas from which the organization can select the "best" ideas. This prevailing practice of crowdsourcing relies on the assumption that restraining crowds to offering ideas for well-defined problems will surface the few brilliant individuals ("experts") who can solve the problem. The prevailing practice has been further expanded such that when the problem is overly complex (i.e., "wicked") as big problems facing society and business are, the problem cannot be solved by the crowd because the crowd cannot possibly understand the complex interdependencies well enough to offer creative solutions.

We believe that restraining the crowd in this way oppresses the value of the individual in society, keeps individuals from having a role in helping to solve wicked problems, and keeps organizations from exposure to truly innovative ideas that require new ways of thinking. We will present examples showing that crowds are able to collectively solve complex wicked problems when allowed to do so without mindcuffs. Such crowds have been able to offer ways for an organization to strategically differentiate itself from competitors, suggest novel ways to reduce a country's pest problems, develop new work practices for a global firm, design new delivery methods for health care, pivot an industry's widely practiced business model, change a company's culture, and suggest novel initiatives for a government agency to spend development dollars in developing countries—*all of this with no single individual offering more than two posts on the average and no one moderating the crowdsourcing process*! These are not "small" well-defined problems typically given to crowds. These crowds are able to derive these innovative solutions because they are not embedded in the practices of yesteryear and thus able to challenge assumptions about the problem that have kept organizations from the breakthrough thinking they need. These crowds are able to simultaneously resolve complex paradoxical objectives not because they are experts, but precisely because they are nonexperts, listening and reading as they all share sound-bites of their many different perspectives held not only because of their formal job roles (e.g., suppliers, potential customers, media, influencers, researchers, managers, policymakers, citizens, current customers, competitors, advocacy groups), but more importantly, because of their observations of life. It is how the crowd resolves this paradox of solving big problems through little efforts (pieces of knowledge and time) that we unlock in this book, which makes this book unique.

The series of research studies presented throughout this book demonstrates how innovative and useful solutions can be generated by crowds of people who individually only spend a few minutes, receive minimal financial incentives, use only simple technology platforms, do not know each other, and have little in common with each other. Our rigorous but highly practical research that we present here should raise the hope of those practitioners who had given up on crowdsourcing because they told us that the current way of Idea-Sharing was generating ideas that were "not really innovative". For those who think that crowdsourcing is simply a marketing and a public relations campaign, this research is intended to convince them that crowds can do more: they can help co-produce ideas that can be usefully implemented to change the world. Finally, for the researcher who does not see a connection between research on crowds and research on organizations, this book is intended to show you how the study of crowds leads to modern theories of modern organizations.

Acknowledgments

We would like to first thank the National Science Foundation for supporting our research (Grant Award number 53-4200-348.). With that initial funding, we were able to attract and run the crowdsourcing events which provided us the data that are central to the findings in this book. This NSF-supported research taught us so much about how to not constrain crowds so they can effectively and efficiently produce innovative and useful ideas in order to solve some of the most wicked problems facing society and businesses alike.

Our sincerest gratitude also goes to Henry Chesbrough, Solomon Darwin, and Sirkka Jarvenpaa, who opened up their Open Innovation Industry-University Centers to allow us to partner with their corporate sponsors to run the crowdsourcing events.

We'd like to thank Paul Tran at Brightidea for providing us with access to Brightidea's crowdsourcing software platform so we could run the crowdsourcing events, configure the software, and obtain the data for analysis. He also stayed up late one night when we were doing an international crowdsourcing event and helped us troubleshoot! True customer service!

We'd like to thank our research students over the years who helped us see what the crowds were trying to tell us: Jeremiah Johnson, Albert Armisen, Yao Sun, and Andrew Mertens.

We thank our academic colleagues who, just by being willing to work with us, helped us build our confidence that we were truly doing something new: Michael Zaggl, Aron Lindberg, Oliver Alexy, Philipp Tuertscher, Luca Giustiniano, Esteve Almirall.

We thank the incredible people at Landcare Research Inc.—Andrea, Bruce, and at the time, Rebecca Niemiec—who took a chance on us to run a crowdsourcing event on pest-free New Zealand.

We thank Esteve Almirall who gave us access to the data on the US AID international innovation jam session.

We want to thank Alph Bingham at Innocentive who engaged with Arvind in countless discussions regarding where crowdsourcing should go in the future. All those discussions inspired us to keep pushing toward better uses of the crowd.

We thank our reflective practitioners, especially Bill Bonfield and Steve Meyers at Optum and Sean Looram at Li & Fung, who during the events worked tirelessly to teach us how to make what we're doing practical and useful.

We thank the many academic colleagues who provided us feedback during presentations we have given over the years on our crowdsourcing research: all those who attended our Harvard Digital Innovation Lab presentation, Boston College's Social 2.0 workshops, participants at Eric von Hipple's MIT Innovation Lab, all those attending the 2018 Org Sci Winter Conference, all those attending the 2019 Utah Winter Strategy Conference, and those attending the 2017 Open Innovation and Lead User Conference. We have also benefited from senior editors handling our academic papers over the years, including Richard Whittington, David Seidl, Terri Griffith, and Samer Faraj.

We thank people to whom we have reached out who were willing to review earlier versions of the book chapters and who pushed us to explain better, reach further, and try to make a difference: Bill Bonfield, John Wentworth, John Mullins, Christiana Hills. Of course, we take full responsibility for all content!

Finally, we'd like to dedicate this last decade of research to our families—Peter, Jared, and Becky, Claudia, Sebastian and Benjamin—who put up with our downs and ups of breaking new ground, helping us especially to overcome the downs. Your tireless dedication and continual encouragement are the bedrock of the effort resulting in this book.

October 1, 2019   Ann and Arvind

Contents

Part I	**Introduction**	1
1	**What Is Crowdsourcing for Innovation?**	3
1.1	What Is a Wicked Problem?	3
1.2	What Is a Crowd?	4
1.3	Where Does Crowdsourcing Fit in an Organization's Innovation Strategy?	5
1.4	What Is the Traditional Idea-Sharing Process to Crowdsourcing for Innovation?	7
1.5	What Are the Assumptions Underlying Idea-Sharing?	10
1.6	How Did the History of Crowdsourcing Make Idea-Sharing So Popular?	14
1.7	Why Is Idea-Sharing with Crowds Suboptimal?	18
1.8	What Is the Evidence Concerning Outcomes of Crowdsourcing for Idea-Sharing?	20
1.9	Could These Current Disappointments Be Because of the Idea-Sharing Process Itself?	23
1.10	Could Questioning Traditional Crowdsourcing's Idea-Sharing Process Also Nudge Changes in the Use of Teams for Solving Wicked Problems?	25
1.11	How Do We Address the Idea-Sharing Process' Suboptimality?	27
1.12	Overview of Chapters	28
	References	39

Contents

2	**Our Research on Comparing Idea-Sharing Versus Unmindcuffing the Crowd**	47
	2.1 Figuring Out How We Were Going to Compare Idea-Sharing Versus Unconstraining the Crowd	49
	2.2 How We Created the Crowds and Data	53
	2.3 Details About the Field Research Study	54
	2.4 Why Anonymity and Persistent Visibility Matters in Creating the Right Online Environment for Unmindcuffed Crowds	58
	2.4.1 Why Anonymity Matters in Unmindcuffed Crowds	58
	2.4.2 Why Persistent Visibility of Knowledge Matters in Unmindcuffed Crowds	60
	2.5 How Outcomes from Crowdsourcing Field Events Were Analyzed	61
	2.6 Results of the Analysis: Does Unmindcuffing Crowds Lead to More Innovative Outcomes?	63
	2.7 How Do Unmindcuffed Crowds Innovate: Using Trace Data to Reveal What Was Previously Hidden	64
	2.7.1 Teaser: Example from Trace Data of One Revelation About How Crowds Innovate	65
	References	73
Part II	**How Do Crowds Innovate?**	77
3	**Practice 1: Minimally Committed Knowledge Baton Passers**	83
	3.1 A Story of Innovation Arising from a Minimally Committed Crowd: USAID's Global Pulse Innovation Crowdsourcing Event	85
	3.2 Are All Crowds Minimally Committed to the Crowdsourcing Event?	90
	3.3 How Do Our Findings Align with Current Research on Online Crowds?	95
	3.4 Summary of Practice 1: Minimal Commitment to Crowdsourcing Event	96
	3.4.1 What Is a Crowd?	96
	3.4.2 What Is Collaboration in a Crowd?	96
	3.4.3 How Does a Crowd Interpret Others' Knowledge?	97

	3.4.4	How Does a Crowd Create Consensus?	97
	3.4.5	Are Crowds Influenced by Others in the Crowd?	99
	3.4.6	Summary of Participation Differences	99
3.5		What Does This Mean for Future Research on Innovation and Mass Collaboration?	100
3.6		What Does This Mean for Practice?	102
References			105

4 Practice 2: Crowds Offering a Variety of Types of Knowledge Are More Innovative Than Crowds Suggesting More Ideas — 109

- 4.1 Stories from "Our Ocean's Challenge" and the MIT Climate Change Crowdsourcing Lab: Importance of Knowledge Type Variety — 110
- 4.2 Overcoming Harmful Representational Gaps in Crowds Through Diverse Knowledge Sharing — 113
- 4.3 Sharing a Variety of Ideas May Not Lead to More Innovative Ideas — 114
- 4.4 Evidence from Our 20 Field-Research Crowdsourcing Events on the Effects of Variety of Knowledge Types Shared by Crowds on Innovation — 116
- 4.5 Exploring Alternative Influences on Innovative Ideas — 119
- 4.6 How Do Our Findings Align with Current Research on Online Crowds? — 120
  - 4.6.1 Developing the Notion of Knowledge Diversity in Crowds — 121
  - 4.6.2 Developing the Notion of Knowledge Diversity Evolution — 122
- 4.7 What Does This Mean for Future Research? — 122
- 4.8 What Does This Mean for Practice? — 125
- References — 130

5 Practice 3: Amplify Creative Associations of Knowledge Fragments — 135

- 5.1 A Case of Creative Associations: A Story at Novell — 137
- 5.2 Triggering the Start of a Creative Process with the Wicked Problem — 139
- 5.3 What Are Creative Associations and How Can They Be Inspired? — 140
- 5.4 Summary of the Process of Creative Associations — 144

5.5	What Is the Evidence for the Effects of Creative Associations on Innovativeness of Ideas?	145
5.6	Exploring If Other Alternative Explanations for Creative Association Influence Co-production of Innovative Ideas	146
5.7	Is There Evidence for How Creative Associations Are Inspired?	150
5.8	Summary of the Process of Creating and Using Creative Associations	151
5.9	How Do Our Findings Contribute to Current Research on Online Crowds?	153
5.10	What Do These Findings Mean for Practice?	154
References		160

6 Practice 4: Reconstructing Needs for Creative Associations — 165

6.1	The Story of Optum Behavioral Health Care's Crowdsourcing for Innovation	165
6.2	Relevant Literature on How Discussion Threads Lead to Innovative Ideas	169
6.3	How Can Discussions Capture Crowd Attention to Be Potentially Generative?	172
	6.3.1 Ruling Out Alternative Plausible Causes of Number of Replies	175
6.4	Was There Something About Follow-on Comments During Collective Production that Led to Innovative Ideas?	176
6.5	Summary of Findings of Practice 4	185
6.6	How Our Findings Align with Existing Research on Crowdsourcing	186
6.7	What Does This Mean for Future Research?	191
6.8	What Does This Mean for Practice?	192
References		196

7 Practice 5: Allowing the Crowd to Play Any Innovation-Enabling Roles They Choose — 201

7.1	What Is a Role to a Crowd?	202
7.2	A Story About Different Roles Played by Crowd Participants in the Predator-Free New Zealand Challenge	203
7.3	Collective Production Roles Found Across the 20 Field Crowdsourcing Events	207

7.4	How Do the Roles We Find Align with Existing Research?		212
7.5	What Does This Mean for Future Research?		215
7.6	What Does This Mean for Practice?		216
7.7	Summary of Our Practices		216
	7.7.1	Practice 1: Minimally Committed Knowledge Baton Passers	217
	7.7.2	Practice 2: Sharing a Variety of Knowledge Types Matters More Than any Specific Knowledge Shared	217
	7.7.3	Practice 3: Amplification of Others' Creative Associations	218
	7.7.4	Practice 4: Reformulating Problem-Associated Needs to Spark Creative Associations	218
	7.7.5	Practice 5: Crowd Enacts Self-selected Innovation-enabling Roles	218
References			220

Part III What's Next: Implications for Research, Technology Platforms, and Managers — 223

8 Tying It All Together: A Theory of Collective Production of Innovation to Inspire Future Research — 225

8.1	Theory of Collective Production of Innovation	226
8.2	Time for a New Perspective to Understanding Online Innovation	228
8.3	Implications of Our Theorizing for Research on Innovation	234
8.4	Implications of Our Theorizing for Innovation Potential of New Organizational Forms	237
8.5	Conclusion About the Research Implications	238
References		245

9 Designing Technology Platforms for Collective Co-Production: Advice When Selecting Crowdsourcing Platforms — 251

9.1	Designing Technology Platforms for Collective Production in Innovation Crowdsourcing Events		252
	9.1.1	Design Principle 1: You Can't Make Crowds Do Anything, But Prime Them and Some Will Follow	253

	9.1.2	Design Principle 2: Incentivizing "Coopetition" for Sharing and Reusing Knowledge	253
	9.1.3	Design Principle 3: Surface Differences	256
	9.1.4	Design Principle 4: Encourage Surfacing Different Problem Descriptions	257
	9.1.5	Design Principle 5: Making Knowledge-Sharing Easier	257
	9.1.6	Design Principle 6: Enhance Crowd's Knowledge Evolution Transparency	258
9.2	Designing a Platform for a Crowd-Powered Organization		259
	9.2.1	Design Principle 7: Design for Fast Event Spinups	260
	9.2.2	Design Principle 8: Maintain History Despite Fluidity	260
	9.2.3	Design Principle 8: Manage the Nuanced Need to Share Sensitive Information	261
	9.2.4	Design Principles 9: Use Performance Assessment for Multiple, Non-people, Purposes	262
9.3	Conclusion		262
References			263

10 Unleashing the Crowd: Overcoming the Managerial Challenges — 265

10.1	Action Steps to Overcome the Challenge of Myopic Incremental Improvement Focus		269
	10.1.1	Who Should Be the Sponsor of the Crowdsourcing Event?	269
	10.1.2	How Should the Innovation Crowdsourcing Event Be Sold Internally?	270
	10.1.3	What Types of Wicked Problem Should Be Posed to the Crowd?	272
	10.1.4	What Is the Role of the Planning Committee in Managing the Crowdsourcing Event?	274
10.2	Action Steps to Overcome the Challenges of Collaboration Disincentives and Grandstanding in the Crowdsourcing Event		275
	10.2.1	How Should Crowds Be Identified and Encouraged to Participate in Crowdsourcing Events?	276
	10.2.2	What Incentives Encourage the Crowd to Collectively Produce Innovative Solutions?	279

	10.3	Action Steps to Overcome the Challenge of Domination by Experts	281
		10.3.1 Should Crowds Be Monitored and Moderated? If So, How?	281
	10.4	Action Step to Overcome the Challenge of Outcome Uncertainty	284
		10.4.1 What Criteria Can Be Used to Select the Innovative Solutions Posed by the Crowd?	284
		10.4.2 What Should Be Done with the Best Solutions?	286
	10.5	How to Manage Innovation in Organizations: Learning from Crowdsourcing	288
		10.5.1 Closing Inspiration for Executives (Especially Those Wanting to Use Internal Crowdsourcing)	292
	References		293
11	**What's the Future? Managing Organizations as Crowds Enabled by Super-Connectivity and Big Data**		**295**
Index			**299**

List of Figures

Fig. 1.1	Where crowdsourcing for innovation fits in an organization's innovation strategy	6
Fig. 1.2	Screenshot of an Idea-Sharing crowdsourcing website	10
Fig. 1.3	The funnel model to innovation providing initial inspiration for the Idea-Sharing process to using crowds	11
Fig. 1.4	Two dimensions of the growth of crowdsourcing	15
Fig. 1.5	Scale, scope, and shape to solve wicked problems using crowdsourcing	24
Fig. 2.1	The three dimensions of crowdsourcing	51
Fig. 2.2	How the different crowds were instructed	57
Fig. 2.3	Sequence of posts in some crowds identified from trace data (adapted Majchrzak and Malhotra 2016)	66
Fig. II.1	A graphical depiction of the Collective Production process for crowd innovation	78
Fig. II.2	How Collective Production of knowledge occurs	79
Fig. II.3	Framework: The 5 Characteristics of an unconstrained crowd's innovation process	82
Fig. 3.1	Practices of Collective Production	84
Fig. 3.2	(**a**) Discussion topics (**b**) Discussions within topic	86
Fig. 3.3	Do participants show a preference about when they participate?	92
Fig. 4.1	Practice of Collective Production	110
Fig. 5.1	Practices of Collective Production	136
Fig. 5.2	A process of creative associations used by crowds	144
Fig. 5.3	Model of crowd's creative association process	152
Fig. 6.1	Practices of Collective Production	166
Fig. 6.2	Crowdsourcing event webpage	168
Fig. 6.3	Summary of second form of collective creativity	186

Fig. 7.1	Practices of Collective Production	202
Fig. 7.2	Topic cloud of posts from the Predator-Free New Zealand innovation crowdsourcing	205
Fig. 7.3	Roles placed in the collaborative production process	212
Fig. 8.1	Theory of Collective Production of innovative ideas by crowds	227
Fig. 9.1	Leaderboard	254
Fig. 9.2	Semantic network for first, second, and third of contributions for NZ Pest Event. (**a**) First third of contributions. (**b**) Second third of contributions. (**c**) Final third of contributions	259
Fig. 10.1	Value of internal crowdsourcing for employees	290
Fig. 10.2	Personal benefits from the crowdsourcing event at Optum	291

List of Tables

Table 1.1	Tradeoffs of crowd versus team to solve structured versus ill-structured problems	26
Table 1.2	Brief comparison of traditional to the Collective Production process	29
Table 2.1	Summary constraints imposed by Idea-Sharing process	48
Table 2.2	Example of wicked problems from the organizations in our field research	54
Table 2.3	Summary of allocation to conditions	56
Table 2.4	What's the same across the crowdsourcing events	59
Table 2.5	Results of effect of unconstraining crowds on innovativeness of ideas generated	63
Table 3.1	Ideas identified by USAID as most innovative for the topic: exercising political and civil rights	88
Table 3.2	What the 20 crowds look like in terms of commitment	91
Table 3.3	Summary of commitment differences between teams, online communities, and collectively producing crowds for innovation	99
Table 4.1	Knowledge categories	117
Table 4.2	Example of a trace with coded knowledge sharing in posts in a trace	118
Table 4.3	Results of knowledge variety in traces and relationship with innovativeness of ideas	119
Table 5.1	Results of patterns of knowledge traces and their relationship with innovativeness of ideas	147
Table 5.2	Knowledge traces affecting posting of creative associations	151
Table 5.3	How patterns in posts influence participants	153
Table 6.1	Expectations from literatures about what drives crowd attention to ultimately affect emergence of innovative ideas	171
Table 6.2	Coding of the 75 discussion thread starters	173

List of Tables

Table 6.3	Predictors of number of replies to a discussion thread starter ($N = 75$)	175
Table 6.4	Example of need-solution match followed by a discussion supporting initial solution idea	177
Table 6.5	Coding for changes to initial solution-ideas in replies	178
Table 6.6	Content discussed during Collective Production sequences	179
Table 6.7	Determinants of new solutions during Collective Production	181
Table 6.8	Coding for posts offering new customer needs	182
Table 6.9	Test for impact of need-solution pair start on DVs when dialogue occurs	184
Table 6.10	Expectations from literature and findings about what drives crowd attention and ultimately affects the emergence of innovative ideas	187
Table 7.1	Roles enacted by participants in the 20 crowdsourcing events	208
Table 7.2	Distribution of roles played in Idea-Sharing versus Unmindcuffed events	211
Table 8.1	Comparison of open crowd conditions and cognitive behavior of stigmergic actors	231
Table 8.2	Comparison of findings with explanations by cognitive stigmergy	232
Table 10.1	Managerial challenges in conducting collectively productive crowdsourcing challenges and steps for overcoming challenges	266
Table 10.2	Checklist for actions to be taken by organizations using crowdsourcing to solve wicked problems	288

List of Boxes

Textbox 1.1	Research: Pervasiveness of VSR Model in Management, Organizational, and Information Systems Research Topics	13
Textbox 1.2	Practice: Pervasiveness of VSR Assumptions on How Managers Manage Innovation	14
Textbox 2.1	How the 20 Field Crowdsourcing Events Were Assigned to Different Conditions	55
Textbox 2.2	How We Measured and Analyzed Innovativeness of Ideas Emerging from Crowds	62
Textbox 2.3	Why and How We Constructed and Used Trace Data	64
Box 6.1	Measuring Persuasive Tone of a Starter Poster	176
Box 6.2	Multinomial Linear Regression	183

Part I

Introduction

The book is divided into three parts. The first part lays out our vision for the book. In Chap. 1 we explain how the type of crowdsourcing we are talking about is different from past versions of crowdsourcing. In Chap. 2, we provide evidence that this new form of crowdsourcing outperforms past versions of crowdsourcing.

Part II describes in detail the precise characteristics of this new form of crowdsourcing, with each chapter describing another characteristic we discovered.

Part III focuses on the future: how should the software look to foster this new form of crowdsourcing? What should practitioners do to implement this new form? Can we get rid of the Stage-Gate models, the funnel approach to innovation, current team approaches to collaborative innovation? Finally, since our findings call into question much of the previous research on how to foster innovation in teams and organizations, we talk about the implications for future research and theory-building on innovation.

1

What Is Crowdsourcing for Innovation?

This book is about how crowds can help to innovatively solve wicked problems: problems that are vexing to companies as well as problems that have an existential impact on societies. In this chapter, we first explain what we mean by a wicked problem and what we mean by a crowd, then discuss what is meant by crowdsourcing for innovation. Then we discuss the traditional model of crowdsourcing: the Idea-Sharing process. We discuss the basic theoretical assumptions of this process and how it historically evolved. We describe the evidence for and against this process indicating why we believe this process is "mindcuffing" the crowds from offering innovative solutions to wicked problems. We introduce our competing process—Collective Production—which serves as the basis for the remainder of the book.

1.1 What Is a Wicked Problem?

Wicked problems are the kind of problems that are difficult or near impossible to solve by an individual or small group of individuals. Wicked problems are not well-understood and are uniquely context-dependent, with a myriad of interdependent considerations.[1] Wicked problems as such do not have pre-ascertainable criteria for optimal solutions as there are countless tradeoffs and contingencies that unfold as the problem is being solved. Wicked problems are so ill-structured problems[2] that they cannot be turned into structured problems,[3] in contrast to structured problems which can be decomposed into neat narrow modularizable components which the crowd is often used to solve. Wicked problems have often been seen as grand societal challenges[4] such as solving homelessness, global warming, water resource management, natural resource management. However, wicked problems are found in most organizations and governments today, ranging from achieving sustainability, involving stakeholders in formulating new strategic initiatives,[5] identifying which new markets to pursue and what new offerings to bring to market, and finding ways for an organization to help reduce global warming.[6]

1.2 What Is a Crowd?

There are many definitions of crowds used when the term "crowdsourcing" is considered.[7] For many, the notion of a "crowd" can solicit negative connotations such as Anonymous crowds pursuing their anti-corporate stance or Digg crowds boycotting Digg because of policy changes made by Digg administrators.[8] This notion of crowds as unruly multi-headed monsters ready to chop off any executive's head is an image often described.[9] But many crowds are not like that.

A crowd can be a broad mass of individuals with ideas.[10] Crowds can be open (meaning anyone can join them) or closed (meaning that there is a vetting process to join the crowd). Crowds can be physically collocated as when a crowd of people attends a stockholders' meeting in-person, or online as when a crowd of people uses the Internet to interact with each other. Crowds can be temporary as when they are brought together exclusively to solve a particular problem, or long-term as when they are part of a community such as a user innovation group focused on enhancing medical devices.[11]

While there are these many variations on a crowd, we focus on open, online, temporary crowds of people interested in helping to solve a problem. "Open" is a relative term. While crowds outside of organizations are often completely open to anyone who wants to participate, some organizations prefer to "open" to just employees. Having a degree of openness is meant explicitly to allow for serendipity in who participates and how they participate. When a crowd is opened to all employees of a large organization, the janitor can have enormous impacts even if the janitor may not have been initially expected to attend.[12] The crowds we focus on are explicitly temporary because we want people helping to solve problems who are busy, have other activities in their life that they can draw from, and are interested only in solving the problem, not in joining a community. The crowds we focus on are online because we believe that participation should be based on having an interest in participating even if the individual has minimal time and is not located near the center of the action. Therefore, our definition of a *temporary crowd* involved in solving a wicked problem is:

> *A set of individuals who cannot be a priori grouped with certainty, but, who self-select to pursue the same problem working together anonymously, asynchronously and whose knowledge is more important than who they are. Each individual in the crowd is free to decide if they want to contribute and what they want to contribute without being explicitly controlled by a central mechanism. It is the knowledge that is contained in their contribution that is critical to the greater cause of solving the wicked problem, not who they are. The collaboration, therefore, cannot be mandated, contracted or expected a priori; rather collaboration emerges through the crowd responding to, reacting to, and building on others' contributions. It is through this emergent collaboration in crowds that the wicked problem gets solved; therefore, the expectation is not that any single individual solves the problems but rather it is the crowd that solves a wicked problem.*[13]

Note that a crowd is *not* by definition a community because community members share a social identity (e.g., I am a Salesforce.com developer) and repeatedly engage with the community so that online identities of individuals emerge.[14] There are generally norms of reciprocity and a shared social fate in communities, as exemplified in the ideologies fundamental to communities of Wikipedia, user innovation communities, LEGO developers, Nine Sigma, and open source software.[15]

1.3 Where Does Crowdsourcing Fit in an Organization's Innovation Strategy?

We define Crowdsourcing specifically for Innovation as

> *Events in which a problem an organization is experiencing is openly broadcasted to a large pool of potentially interested people out of which those self-select to participate in offering innovative solutions to the problem.*

Innovative solutions refer to solutions that are novel, implementable, and useful, that is, provide value to the organization.[16] It is important that the solution be novel (i.e., new to the organization); otherwise, the solution would have already been considered within the organization. It is important that the solution be implementable; otherwise, there is no point. Finally, it is important for the solution to be useful to the organization, such as help it to achieve a competitive advantage or help it to achieve a need. Because novel solutions that take implementability and usefulness into account are rarely completely developed during crowdsourcing for innovation, we refer to the solutions obtained from crowds as "solution-ideas", that is, suggestions, paths, and directions to pursue. Novel solution-ideas still must take into account implementability and usefulness to be innovative and therefore worthwhile to the organization sponsoring the crowdsourcing event; however, any solution-idea obtained is likely to need additional work.

Crowdsourcing for innovation is now seen as a complement for internal R&D innovation efforts.[17] It is part of a larger paradigm shift in many organizations today in which R&D is no longer the exclusive holder of ideas. Crowdsourcing is not exclusive for business purposes though. Many non-profit organizations and governments have adopted crowdsourcing.[18] For example, in the Climate CoLab, solutions from 50,000 members are solicited each year for addressing global climate change.[19] An initiative by the maritime industry involving crowdsourcing for actions on environmental sustainability called Our Ocean's Challenges has been conducted each year and recognized by the United Nations for its value to the UN goal of sustainable development.[20] Where crowdsourcing for innovation fits in the organization's innovation strategy is shown in Fig. 1.1.

As shown in Fig. 1.1, organizations have two sets of choices to make when pursuing innovation. First is whether to engage people and organizations they

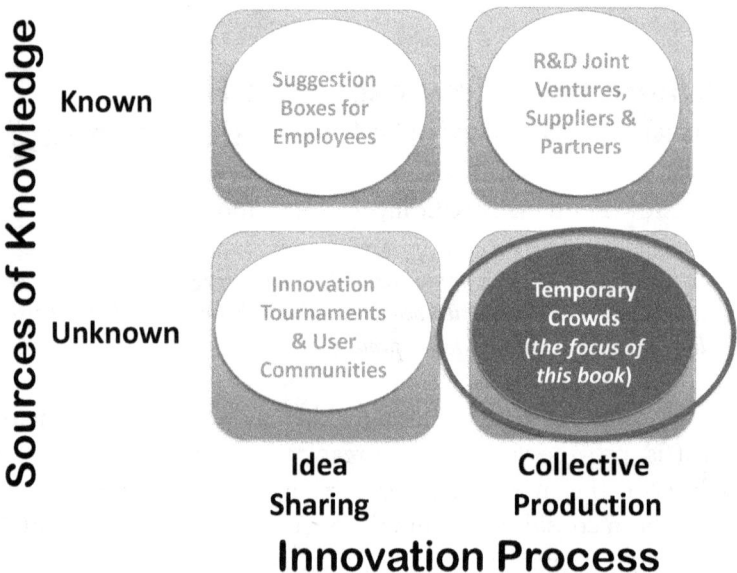

Fig. 1.1 Where crowdsourcing for innovation fits in an organization's innovation strategy

know or come to know in a regulated partnership relationship. Known sources of knowledge could refer to internal employees or to highly trusted value chain actors. Unknown sources of knowledge can refer to outside crowds of consumers, customers, potential customers, user communities, social media influencers, competitors, universities, and governments[21] that might become involved in an innovation tournament. The second decision is which innovation process to follow. The most traditional is to innovate entirely using known parties such as cross-functional teams within the R&D unit using a Collective Production model in which the members of the team collaborate to develop new ideas (upper right quadrant in Fig. 1.1). With a recognition that these ideas may be found outside of the R&D unit but still within the organization, employees of the organization are occasionally engaged in offering individual ideas such as with a suggestion box (upper left quadrant in Fig. 1.1). This quadrant for using known sources in an Idea-Sharing approach is one in which the organization is seeking the best ideas. The organization can apply the same Idea-Sharing approach to unknown sources. The organization may obtain those ideas through competitions, such as Innovation Challenges or Tournaments,[22] or by observing and possibly intervening in user communities, such as Hallmark's user community for the creation of cards, the Lego community for creation of new Lego products, Starbuck's idea community, and Dell's IdeaStorm community of users suggesting improvements to Dell's products[23] (lower left quadrant in Fig. 1.1). We will discuss in the next section precisely what the Idea-Sharing process looks like for crowdsourcing.

The last quadrant discussed is the lower right quadrant in Fig. 1.1. This quadrant is rarely used in organizations today because it expects sources unknown to the organization to become a temporary crowd to collectively produce ideas that are useful, novel, and helpful to the organization. Many organizations don't even know that this option exists. This book is intended to change that.

We spend the rest of the chapter describing the difference between the traditional Idea-Sharing approach to innovation crowdsourcing and our proposed new approach: Collective Production among the crowds.

1.4 What Is the Traditional Idea-Sharing Process to Crowdsourcing for Innovation?

The traditional approach to crowdsourcing for innovation—whether using crowds of known partners or unknown crowds—is the Idea-Sharing process.[24] This process—which we can also call the "highly constrained process"—

imposes control on a crowd in a manner we argue stifles the creative latitude of the masses, that is, "mindcuffs the crowd". The crowds are told what to say ("give us ideas"), how to say it (by minimizing knowledge exchange), what knowledge to use (your own "ideas"), and about what (modularized problems such as creating an advertising campaign, or narrowly defined aspects of rather complex problems).

The Idea-Sharing process is defined as one in which the crowd is provided a well-defined decomposed problem and asked to provide only their highest quality, most innovative solution-idea. Another name for crowdsourcing in the academic literature is "broadcast shar",[25] indicating that the expectation for an organization engaged in such a process is to "shar-and-find" the best idea.

The process begins by managers in an organization (generally executives) taking a problem they are experiencing and turning it into a structured, well-defined, often-times decomposed problem with specific criteria for solving the problem and then broadcasting the problem to a crowd in the hopes that one person in the crowd will know the answer.[26] They offer to the crowd only decomposed problems since those problems are easier for evaluating the right solutions and easier for one person to solve.[27] This way of crowdsourcing is essentially a shar process, locating solution-ideas.[28] The consequence of such a process is that the crowd is best used only to solve problems of limited scope. This leads to leveraging crowds in a very limited way to solve narrowly pre-defined problems. The problems are crafted in a manner that one individual located somewhere in the crowd will have the individual creativity to solve the problem with limited contextual knowledge.[29]

In most cases, the Idea-Sharing process is structured so that individuals in a crowd privately and independently offer their solutions without interacting with others in the crowd.[30] That is, in many crowdsourcing processes, individuals in the crowd do not see others' solutions because the shar is for the individual with the right perspective (as in most innovation competitions/tournaments such as on Kaggle or Top Coder). Even when crowds can see each other's solutions, crowds are asked to focus their contributions to refining and improving others' ideas, not collectively producing the idea.[31] As a result, the Idea-Sharing process narrows the use of crowds as a vehicle for locating the one individual with the right solution.

With such a limited view, it is pre-ordained that there are many things that crowds are unable to do. Crowds are unable to suggest that maybe the wrong problem is being solved, to begin with. Crowds cannot suggest that maybe a larger, more complex problem should be solved instead. Crowds are not

1 What Is Crowdsourcing for Innovation?

enabled and encouraged to openly collaborate. In some cases, they are allowed to react to others' ideas but only in highly restricted ways such as refining someone else's idea or drawing attention to ideas by voting on them. Crowds are not given ways to express or be aware of what others in the crowd may know that can help define the problem to be the right problem to be solved and bring knowledge that can alter perspectives and lead to breakthroughs. Consequently, crowds are not allowed to collectively produce solutions.

Collective Production of innovative ideas builds on the notion that "no one knows everything, everyone knows something, [and] all knowledge resides in humanity"; consequently, digitization and communication technologies must become central in this coordination of far-flung genius.[32] However, our notion of Collective Production of innovative ideas is not to be confused with what the academic literature is currently referring to as "collective intelligence", defined as the general ability of the group to perform a wide variety of tasks[33] or the ability of the group to do better than any individual alone.[34] While these definitions generally apply to our work, a key difference between our view of Collective Production and the literature's notion of collective intelligence is that researchers working on collective intelligence tend to focus on the particular social interaction processes such as social sensitivity and convergence and explicit coordination practices that occur within bounded groups.[35] For example, work on temporary crowds as having formal organizational structures—roles, teams, and hierarchies—that encode responsibilities, interdependencies, and information flow.[36] In contrast, our view of Collective Production of innovative ideas does not require any social interaction, sensitivity, convergence, or explicit coordination in the collective; all that is required is temporary participants in an unbounded crowd releasing their knowledge about the problem and possible solutions into a common knowledge pool. Similarly, our view of Collective Production is not what has been popularized as the "wisdom of the crowds"[37] since we are focused on how innovative ideas are collectively co-produced, not on how individual ideas are simply offered (as in the Idea Shar approach) or how individual estimates are aggregated (as in averaged predictions about the weight of a bull or who will win the World Series). By "production" we mean that the outcomes emerged as a result of knowledge transfer and transformation within the crowd. The key in our focus is that the crowd is co-producing innovative ideas, but not through interacting socially.

Take a look at Fig. 1.2. There are several ways, intended or unintended, in which the crowds are not allowed to do anything else than follow an Idea-Sharing process:

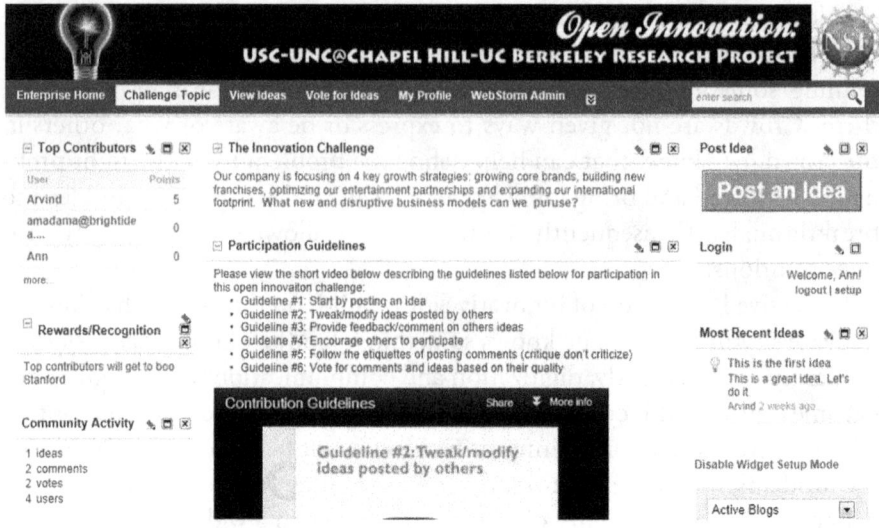

Fig. 1.2 Screenshot of an Idea-Sharing crowdsourcing website

- Oversimplified problems (or pieces of the wicked problem) are presented to the crowds.
- Individuals in the crowds are asked only for ideas to solve the problems. Sometimes these ideas are not even made visible to others in the crowd.
- When the ideas are made transparent, the crowd can only refine others' ideas.
- No other (besides ideas) knowledge related to the problem is invited.
- The crowd is told what problem it should solve and is provided the definition of the problem.
- Those who are considered the top contributors are measured as those who contribute the most ideas (with the intent of increasing the number of ideas that an organization using crowdsourcing can select from).
- Finally, one (or few) individuals are rewarded/recognized for their individual "best" idea, thereby, turning the crowd into a competitive rather than collaborative crowd.

1.5 What Are the Assumptions Underlying Idea-Sharing?

Idea-Sharing crowdsourcing for innovation came about as an outgrowth of the more general term of Crowdsourcing made popular by Howe in a Wired Article's blog.[38] He wrote that "crowdsourcing represents the act of a company or institution taking a function once performed by employees and outsourcing it to an undefined (and generally large) network of people in the form of an open call". An open call is a message broadcasted to a large audience over the Internet in the form of advertisements and announcements. Usually, the message broadcast contains the pre-defined problem that an organization has and requests the help of anyone interested to solve. Many times the message also advertises the prize money associated with winning ideas for the innovation contest or tournament.[39]

This definition has little in it about how innovation should be achieved. Crowdsourcing has become associated with non-innovative activities such as outsourcing and microtask platforms such as Amazon Mechanical Turk. Crowdsourcing has also become associated with the aggregation and coordination of developers in the production of software, such as with open source software and the aggregation and coordination of information, such as Wikipedia or Wikitravel.

While this definition did describe the early forms of crowdsourcing, such a definition created an assumption that crowdsourcing for innovation is simply performing an outsourced function. As such, this led to the notion that the way in which ideas are collected in internal R&D units should be used for crowdsourcing.

Idea solicitations in traditional R&D units in organizations are based on the "funnel" model, with stage gates working through each stage of the funnel.[40] The funnel model is shown in Fig. 1.3. A manager drafts a problem

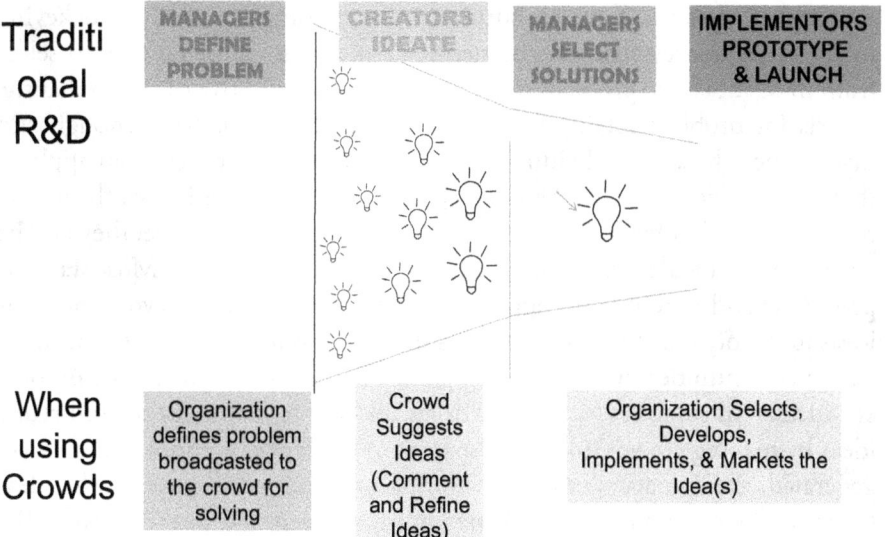

Fig. 1.3 The funnel model to innovation providing initial inspiration for the Idea-Sharing process to using crowds[41]

statement with explicit criteria that forms the basis for idea generation (e.g., the product must be user-friendly and have a number of functions that allow navigation). Then, typically R&D or different units are responsible for generating a variety of ideas. Then managers apply the criteria to select the best ideas. The best ideas are then further developed. These assumptions have not changed over the decades. Figure 1.3 only shows a couple of stage gates, but in some companies, the stage gates can number 15 or 20, each bifurcating the process and passing on further downstream the ills of any badly considered problem statement.

This funnel model is based, theoretically, on the variance-selection-retention theory of innovation.[42] This theory was developed from the biological Darwinian evolutionary epistemology paradigm in which only the best [ideas] survive.[43] In this paradigm, in order for creative evolution to occur, there must exist cognitive mechanisms that encourage and support a great range of diverse variation. For innovation, there must be initially a well-defined problem for which a diverse range of ideas exist which can potentially innovatively solve the problem (Variation). The problem must be defined sufficiently so that criteria can be applied to select a subset of those ideas (Selection). Finally, there must be a mechanism for retention of that one idea to develop and implement (Retention).

When innovation is opened[44] to allow the potential of new ideas coming from outside the organization, crowds can become a source of new ideas, just as a supplier or customer might.[45] Since the funnel model is structured to expect that ideas will fight for survival, ideas become the warriors jockeying for position as they fight the battle. Since managers must be able to select from these ideas, the problem must be sufficiently well-structured, so that the criteria for problem-solving will be clear. If the crowd is large enough and diverse enough, some individuals will recognize how the criteria can apply to their knowledge and thus offer a solution. Another characteristic of the funnel model depicted in Fig. 1.3 is that crowds play one particular role: they are the generators of a wide variety of ideas to a pre-defined problem. Most state-of-practice crowdsourcing is designed as contests whereby the crowds send their ideas to the organization that sponsors the crowdsourcing challenge, or innovation communities in which participants offer ideas or refinements on others' ideas.[46] In some cases, the crowds are allowed to comment on and refine ideas by making crowds' ideas transparent to all. However, once the ideas are generated, the managers in the sponsoring organization then select the ideas based on the criteria that may or may not have been told to the crowds. The selected ideas are then developed further inside the organization. In many cases, the crowds are not informed as to why the ideas were selected or what happened to them.

The funnel model, and its variance-selection-retention theoretical parent, leads to a number of assumptions that are carried into the Idea Shar process. First is that problems need to be specified well enough to choose between all the ideas and know how to proceed through the stage gates. Second is that there are distinctively different roles, responsibilities, and expertise between the problem-generators, the idea-generators, the idea-selectors, and the idea-implementers. Third is that the crowd is the idea-generator only, not engaged in defining the problem or thinking through the implementation. Sometimes crowd members vote on the ideas, but organizations rarely exclusively use the crowd's votes since there are internal issues the idea must be aligned with.[47] Fourth is that ideas are individualized, owned by the individual who proposes them and are only combined inside the organization.

In many ways, the variance-selection-retention theory permeates scholarly management research such as in strategic, organizational, and information systems on innovation (see Textbox 1.1). Additionally, the theory permeates how innovation in practice is managed (see Textbox 1.2). If we are able to demonstrate that the variance-selection-retention theory on which today's Idea-Sharing process is based under-leverages the crowd, could it be possible that it is under-leveraging how organizations are designed, managed, and researched?

Textbox 1.1   Research: Pervasiveness of VSR Model in Management, Organizational, and Information Systems Research Topics

- Search, governance, social capital, team problem-solving, problem-based view of firm, strategy, innovation stage gate models, separation of functions by expertise, open source software development.
- Separation of duties: problem definer vs. problem solver vs. solution selector vs. solution implementers (e.g., typical stage gate process, R&D functions vs. marketing managers).
- Separation of expertise (expertise diversity, "shared understanding" within expertise, need to build "shared understanding" when multiple areas of expertise are brought to bear).
- Entities have ideas (individuals, teams, & organizations have behaviors which are likely to repeat) and managers can define the problem that these entities can solve.
- Problems need to be defined before they are solved (technology adoption, ROI/investment decisions).
- Innovative ideas need to come from diverse sources in large numbers (knowledge management systems, knowledge-creating online communities, generative collectives, design communities, user communities, innovation challenges, open source development).

> **Textbox 1.2 Practice: Pervasiveness of VSR Assumptions on How Managers Manage Innovation**
> - Experts are the best ones to solve difficult problems.
> - Bringing people of diverse expertise together is the best way to innovatively solve difficult problems.
> - Brining people into teams that work together on the problem over time is the best way to solve difficult problems.
> - Innovation is more likely to be achieved with clear problem statements and customer needs.
> - Managers should define the problem that others solve.

In summary, the Idea-Sharing process assumes that innovation with the crowd:

1. Is all about collecting a variety of ideas,
2. Only the companies can define the problem that the crowds then solve,
3. The crowds then follow the process of ideation and then companies do the selection and retention, and
4. Crowds may sometimes be allowed to even select the ideas, but most of the time it becomes an idea popularity contest.

1.6 How Did the History of Crowdsourcing Make Idea-Sharing So Popular?

The advent of the Internet has enabled companies to broadcast their problems to large groups of people: what we call the crowd. The crowd is no single entity but in its idealistic unconstrained form, it can be anybody in the general public. Early on, crowdsourcing branched into two dimensions: (1) *Scale*: broadcast problems to anyone in the world or crowdsource to a selected subset such as a community or selected teams, and (2) *scope*: broadcast problems to solve grand challenges or to solve decomposed problems. These two dimensions are shown in Fig. 1.4.

The first dimension is along the bottom, *the scale*. Crowdsourcing for Innovation is not new, and can be traced back to Archimedes Principle, Longitudinal Prize, and GoldCorp.[48] Technology problems such as the Longitudinal prize were crowdsourced. With the advent of the Internet, it is easy to broadcast to the "world". The growth in terms of scale was accompanied by a reduction in the complexity (scope) of the problem. It was thought that describing complex problems to a crowd is hard, so why not break the

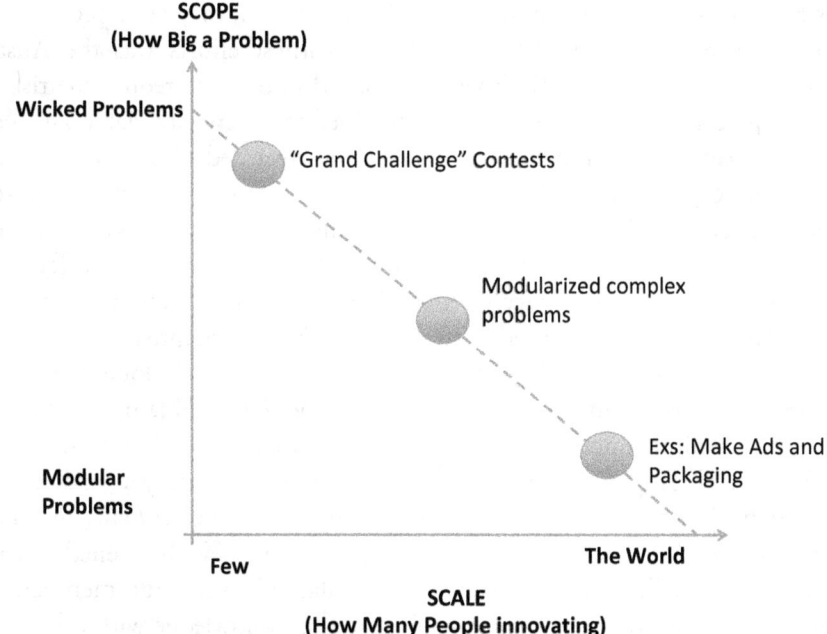

Fig. 1.4 Two dimensions of the growth of crowdsourcing

problem down into pieces that can be solved by a few "individual" brilliant people world over. In October 2006, Netflix offered crowds the "The Netflix Prize", to make the company's recommendation engine 10% more accurate. Attracting over 44,000 submissions. The crowds were not asked to solve a more complex problem as to how to entertain the viewers of Netflix or to use recommender engines to educate viewers. Rather, managers defined the problem as making the recommendation engine 10% better since they thought that a better recommender engine might make Netflix customers more satisfied. It is useful to note that Netflix never used the recommender engine that performed the best from the crowd because the proxy question they identified for the crowd to answer was selected because it was easier to judge solutions proposed by the crowd but, as a result, the solutions were less useful.[49]

The second dimension along which crowdsourcing changed over the years was in increasing the *scope* of the problem. A number of attempts have been made to have teams of experts respond to an organization's "grand challenge". The problem is certainly of the wicked or ill-structured type, but the grand challenges were always structured as Idea-Sharing: entrants offered their idea as the solution and then the organization selected the idea they preferred. In this case, the entrants are rarely an individual; instead, they are typically self-defined teams of experts. One of XPrize's earliest efforts was the Ansari XPRIZE.[50] The Ansari XPRIZE was established in order to reduce the risk of space exploration by developing a sustainable, commercially viable and safe form of space travel. Ten million dollars was awarded to a single winner (albeit an organization), Mojave Aerospace Ventures, who designed the Spaceship One. GE each year consistently offers grand challenges in which the winner is often a company they acquire. DARPA continues to offer such challenges often, as does SpaceX for the hyperloop. XPrize continues to run crowdsourcing in this grand-prize-winner-takes-all manner, giving out $140 million in prizes for different contests. Each time this is done, the crowd is being told in substantial detail about what is the right problem to be solved, and given minimal opportunity to share their knowledge with others.

The Idea-Sharing process to crowdsourcing is not inherently a "bad" use of the crowd. *We propose and find evidence that it is just under-utilizing the intellectual power of the crowd.* Who knows what would have happened during these XPrize challenges if the teams were enlarged to include members of other teams or encouraged to cross-pollinate their knowledge with others, or encouraged to include the public to figure out ways for this level of scientific exploration to have spin-off value for down-to-earth type societal problems such as water resource reallocation?

At the opposite extreme on the scope dimension is the decomposed problems. Decomposing a problem before it is broadcast to the crowd serves several purposes for the organization. First, it ensures that the organization protects sensitive information. An organization may be hesitant to expose their commercial problems as a whole to crowds, lest competitors may become aware of the organization's problems or strategic interests.[51]

Second, decomposing the problem ensures that no single individual will have all the answers to the entire more aggregated problem and thus can replace or compete with the organization. Third, by decomposing the problem, the organization needs to spend fewer resources in sharing tacit knowledge about the problem to the crowd.[52] Fourth, because the criteria are clear about how to evaluate a solution, the many solutions that are provided can be easily sorted and discarded leaving only the traditional top 10% of the most innovative solutions worthy of review by management. Fifth, in a complex problem which is likely to be misunderstood or responded to out of context (such as a design charrette for a waterfront), decomposing may help participants focus on that part of the problem for which the organization wants input and avoid the chaos and emotional dynamics that may come about by allowing an in-person crowd to congregate.

Over the years, decomposing problems came with more complexities than initially anticipated such as protecting the organizations' strategies and dealing with intellectual capital issues. As such, organizations began turning for help on how to decompose problems for crowds to third-party innovation platform providers (e.g., Nine Sigma, Incentive, BrightIdeas, etc.).[53] The crowd, formed by the use of third-party intermediaries, is removed even further from the organization they are trying to affect, and even more unable to question how the problem was scoped, to begin with.

Companies also started to use menial-task platforms for crowdsourcing, making crowdsourcing less about innovation and largely about outsourcing-for-cheap-on-a-large-scale. Amazon's Mechanical Turk is an example of this use of the crowd as simply cheap labor. Although Mechanical Turk claims that it "is a marketplace for work that requires human intelligence" (website), most of the tasks are simple tasks like completing surveys and testing. Crowds are not asked to collaborate to solve wicked problems. Other task-running platforms attracting freelancers or "gig-workers" started to move up the problem complexity scale such as Threadless for T-shirt design, 99designs for graphic design, and Fiverr for a range of human services like lawn-mowing, graphic design or myriad of other tasks.[54] "The number of contests handled by 99designs (a popular crowdsourcing platform) went from about 100,000 in 2012 (Lacy 2012) to 423,000 by July 2015 (99designs.com). Roth et al. (2016) report that Unilever's Foundry IDEAS, a hub to organize Unilever's crowdsourcing briefs, will 'increase its use of crowdsourced ideation tenfold by 2020'".[55] Some[56] have touted these uses of crowdsourcing since they give freelancers a shot at complex projects (which are not so complex after all) while others[57] complain that crowdsourcing is just another method for cost-cutting and under-paying society in general.

Marketers were not far behind this cost-cutting bandwagon by using crowdsourcing as a way to decompose and outsource marketing tasks. Marketers looked at the scale and thought, "Wow! If we get crowds (our brand fans) to solve our marketing (advertising and packaging) problems, not only would we save money, we'd build buzz at cheap. We would let loose an army of brand advocates". This wave brought us crowd-made advertising campaigns: VitaminWater used the crowds to get suggestions for new flavors and also gave out $5000 for designing a new label for the new flavor. Doritos has been using crowd-generated ads for multiple Super Bowls. These were again structured as a competition between individuals in crowds rather than collaborators collectively producing the best ad. Over a ten-year period, Doritos' ads have always been in the Top 5 of *USA Today's* ad meter metric.

If the purpose is to run an ad campaign cheaply, crowdsourcing seems to work. That's an unfortunate under-utilization of the crowd.

The two dimensions of scale and scope generally settled somewhere in the middle: decomposed problems at a moderate scale of deployment using the Idea-Sharing process.

1.7 Why Is Idea-Sharing with Crowds Suboptimal?

We present our case in this book that using a crowd constrained in the Idea-Sharing manner is a suboptimal use of crowds. In the following paragraphs, we lay out in some detail what is the current process for using crowds, the Idea-Sharing process. We describe the assumptions underlying that current process (Sect. 1.1) and how those assumptions have framed how crowds have been used as far back as crowdsourcing event in 1714[58] (Sect. 1.2). We describe the anecdotal and systematic research (Sect. 1.3) indicating that while there are many significant successful new innovations as a result of the current process underlying crowdsourcing, many outcomes have been disappointing. We suggest that suboptimal outcomes may be because of the underlying assumptions of what crowds are, what they do, and how they should (or should not) collaborate. We then explain our concept of Collective Production for using crowds to solve wicked problems (Sect. 1.4). We raise some provocative questions to extend beyond just crowdsourcing to include how innovation is managed in organizations today (Sect. 1.5). We end with an overview of the chapters of the book (Sect. 1.6).

The Idea-Sharing process is suboptimal because more often than not, crowds are not allowed to tackle the most important problems of today—big societal problems such as water shortage, global warming, homelessness, racism, the digital divide, and so on. Similarly, neither are crowds asked to help formulate strategic directions nor are they asked to suggest new business opportunities for organizations. Instead, crowds are highly constrained to modularized problems, or parts of complex wicked problems, such as an improved recommender engine for Netflix or the design of a beer container for Heineken.[59] As such, crowds start out being under-leveraged and consequently have minimal influence and, as a self-fulfilling prophecy, are deemed ineffective to innovatively solve problems.

To expect that any individual in a crowd is creative alone with an answer that matches the needs of the managers is not borne out by the evidence.[60]

Moreover, when crowds are asked to generate lots of ideas, this requires that managers must find that one idea among many—a large nearly impossible task if the crowd is large.[61] Finally, since it is frequently the case that none of the ideas are the right ones or are comprehensive enough, managers must take on the task of combining the many ideas into a comprehensive solution—a nearly impossible task if the number of ideas is large. Moreover, for managers to combine the crowd's ideas requires managers to have a broad enough unvested and creative perspective to identify, choose, and combine the solution-ideas that often times may challenge the managers' own existing paradigms, perspectives, and ways of doing things. Again, this is a tall order and difficult expectation[62] since it asks managers to operate against their own biases, to select and combine truly innovative ideas that break the existing managerial and organizational paradigms.[63]

By treating the crowd as nothing more than an assortment of individual ideas, the true wisdom of crowds[64] is under-capitalized (if not grossly ignored). The central theme of this book is that the true wisdom of the crowd emerges when the crowd is able to share knowledge about the problem as they attempt to combine their knowledge to solve the problem. Such a transparent sharing of knowledge becomes the basis for ***powerful combinations and recombinations that can result in much better solutions to wicked problems***. These novel and powerful combinations may come from creative abrasion[65] in which the disagreements over perspectives yield a novel third perspective. The new combinations of knowledge may be triggered by creative stimuli embedded in the knowledge shared by the crowd in the form of metaphors or analogies that spin off new thoughts.[66] New combinations may also come from little idea seeds or knowledge built into a bigger idea.[67] Limiting the way in which a crowd solves problems is forgetting that true innovation often comes from different pieces of knowledge shared, where the knowledge represents unexpected and multiple perspectives, and in which it is through powerful combinations of these perspectives that big ideas result.[68] By constraining the crowd to solve only highly defined, decomposed problems, the crowd is not being allowed to unleash this power of combining and recombining its intellectual capital.

Finally, while Idea-Sharing crowdsourcing has led to some anecdotal successes, we will show below that there is a growing set of research evidence indicating that it is not as beneficial for innovation as desired. In this book, we offer a way to increase the chances that crowdsourcing will consistently yield more innovative solutions.[69]

1.8 What Is the Evidence Concerning Outcomes of Crowdsourcing for Idea-Sharing?

The Idea-Sharing process has led to some brilliant successes. Dell's IdeaStorm has been a hotbed for allowing customers to voice their opinions and ideas for product improvements and new products. Over 10,000 relatively mundane ideas have been suggested by individuals in the crowd and Dell has gone on to implement almost 1000 of those. Offering Linux on Dell's hardware was one of those ideas.[70] In one study it was found that when problems are well-defined, solutions provided by users can outperform those developed by company experts.[71] NASA has been an avid user of crowdsourcing principles, having held repeated innovation challenges. NASA established a NASA Tournament Lab in a joint effort with Harvard Business School in 2011, running several Idea-Sharing crowdsourcing challenges on decomposed problems.[72] DARPA has also been active in crowdsourcing with its DARPA FANG challenge awarding $1 million to a design team for innovation in Marine swimming tanks. The design offered by a three-person team outperformed DoD's requirements.[73] GE's Data Science Innovation Challenge geared toward solving scarcity through water reuse was won by an individual from an Indian Institute of Management.[74] Companies like Volkswagen have used the third-party platform HYVE to generate ideas for new businesses. The Mayor of Bandung in Indonesia also used the HYVE platform to identify ways to improve living conditions for citizens in the municipality.[75] "According to a survey conducted by the Marketing Executive Networking Group in 2009,[76] 75 percent of company executives think that crowdsourcing is highly effective with respect to new product and service development.[77] Ten out of the eleven top global brands [in 2015] use crowdsourcing communities to find solutions for their business problems."[78]

Clearly, there are raging successes. These examples were successful in part because they either reduced the scope of the problem to make it simpler for an individual to solve, or they fostered expert teams to solve the larger scoped problem. And in all cases, they simply asked the crowd for ideas. These successes, however, are not the norm. In one survey, 80% of the Web 2 implementations (of which crowdsourcing was one) were considered disappointing for generating innovative ideas to complex problems.[79] We identify three of the several types of anecdotal disappointments reported in the popular press.

First is what we call Trivial Questions May Yield Trivial Answers. There are many examples in which the crowd provides trivial answers when asked simply to name something. When NASA asked the crowd to choose the name of the International Space Station, they chose Colbert as their option over NASA's own options of Serenity, Legacy, Earthrise and Venture. Yet the most popularly voted was "Colbert" (after the popular late-night comic Stephen Colbert). When Natural Environment Research Council (NERC) launched a crowdsourcing campaign Name Our Ship, the expectation was that names would be in line with the prestigious scientific mission the ship was designed for (e.g., Falcon and Endeavour.). Instead, the crowd favorite turned out to be *RRS Boaty McBoatface*.[80]

A second anecdotal disappointment with Idea Shar crowdsourcing is that only obvious answers are offered, rather than solution-ideas that consider the comprehensive range of issues. For example, California Governor Arnold Schwarzenegger set up MyIdeas4CA.com to crowdsource ideas to fix the problems that the state was facing. The most popular idea was—"Legalize Marijuana". Similarly, when a crowd was asked to identify solutions to the racial police brutality on black young males in Ferguson, Ohio, 104 recommendations were offered with none touching on the most foundational root causes of the problems in Ferguson.[81]

A third anecdotal disappointment with Idea Shar crowdsourcing is that the organization may not be ready for the radical solutions offered by crowds when the crowds are allowed to collective produce. For example, when Iceland decided to redraft its constitution through crowdsourcing[82] to create a system of transparency and engaging the citizens, the crowd succeeded at creating a constitution. However, the Althing (Iceland's parliament) found the constitution too radical to implement.[83]

In addition to this anecdotal evidence, there is more systematic academic evidence and scholarly discussions about the disadvantages of the Idea-Sharing Process. This research says the following:

- Participants in Idea-Sharing competitions are engaged in withholding their best ideas purely to protect their intellectual property.[84]
- Although studies have demonstrated that Idea-Sharing for well-defined problems leads to innovative ideas,[85] the assumption in the Idea-Sharing literature is that it cannot be used for wicked and strategic problems[86] because there are no experts on these problems, participants won't share, and the problems are too complex and take too much of a participant's time. However, some scholars have recently started to question why crowds can't be used for wicked problems[87] and there is a recent move in the strategy literature toward open strategy formulation for which crowdsourcing as Idea-Sharing doesn't work.[88]

- One study[89] examined the results of the 13 NASA Idea Searching type crowdsourcing events in which NASA used Innocentive, Yet2.com, and Topcoder. The open calls asked the crowd to improve barrier layers keeping food fresh in space, better forecasting of solar events, better tracking of medical consumables, and the creation of a simple microgravity laundry system, among others. What the researcher found was that, out of the 13, only 2 were completely solved, 6 were partially solved, and 5 were not solved—a pretty poor success rate.
- The often-presumed efficiency of participants' self-selection processes (i.e., that the right types of people join a given contest) has been called into question.[90] The concept that, through self-selection, the most creative individuals enter the competition has been shown to not be accurate based on a competition with Porsche.[91] Similarly, the motivations that people have determine the degree they attend to implementability of their ideas; as such, it is impossible to know why people are participating in crowdsourcing events.[92] Research of over 300+ ideas implemented found that the intrinsic motivation of the ideator was *not* related to whether the idea was implemented but rather whether the ideator paid attention to others' ideas.[93] Another study finds that the originality of any ideators' idea in Idea-Sharing competitions is largely random.[94] As such, using individuals' characteristics as criteria for determining if an Idea Shar crowdsourcing event will successfully yield innovative ideas is random.
- Few ideas obtained during Idea-Sharing crowdsourcing are implemented.[95] In an empirical study on ideas for solving a well-defined problem concerning baby products, the ideas of ordinary users when submitted individually lacked feasibility.[96] In a review of Idea-Sharing crowdsourcing research, it was found that crowdsourcing typically yields a large number of contributions that only have limited value for organizations and that co-created ideas in crowdsourcing are of higher quality than those autonomously submitted by individuals.[97] It is generally accepted in the literature on crowdsourcing that there are scant findings describing the value of crowdsourcing and how to increase the quality of participant contributions.[98]
- Extended rivalry can prevent potential preferable participants from joining an Idea-Sharing crowd innovation contest,[99] calling into question the value of putting crowd participants into rivalrous situations if innovations are preferred.
- In a study of a "community-based innovation contest" in which students could discuss ideas, they found that degree of cooperation among students had a U-shaped relationship with the degree of innovativeness: very high cooperation or very low cooperation led to a high degree of innovative-

ness.[100] Thus, cooperation is not necessarily a good or bad thing (cooperation defined in this study as students discussing others' ideas).
- Within crowds engaged in Idea-Sharing—especially when voting and feedback by crowd participants are permitted—domination by a few can occur. In a study of the Local Motors open source car development platform, all 10,000 posts were examined, and it was found that over time, a small group of participants became more dominant in providing feedback, but these dominant individuals were not the ones providing the most successful submissions.[101] In a detailed analysis of four failed crowdsourcing events, the authors found that a dominant few "hijacked" the purpose of the event as well as engaged in what they called "crowdthink".[102]
- In a 2018 review of Idea-Sharing crowdsourcing, problem over-specification was found in many cases, leading to detrimental outcomes. The authors discuss how Isaac Newton's limitation that solutions to finding longitude at sea be based only on astronomy principles delayed finding the eventual solution which used principles of clockwork. As another example, an optimal solution for a problem in toxicology did not come from toxicology as the sponsors expected but came from protein crystallography.[103] They conclude: "To accommodate for the impossibility of predicting the possible origins of a solution, it is important not to impose any more restrictions … on a task than necessary".[104]

In sum, both systematic research and anecdotes seem to suggest that the Idea-Sharing process to crowdsourcing maybe most successful only when problems are well-defined and even then, may be disappointing.

1.9 Could These Current Disappointments Be Because of the Idea-Sharing Process Itself?

What would happen if we removed the requirement from the crowd to just post ideas? In a study of the 1700 participants joining the Swarovski Enlightened jewelry Idea-Sharing design competition, the researchers found that co-creation experience with other participants directly impacted the number of contributions participants made as well as the quality of submitted designs.[105]

Therefore, suppose we allowed the crowd to share whatever knowledge members wanted to share, asking them to not simply post an idea but col-

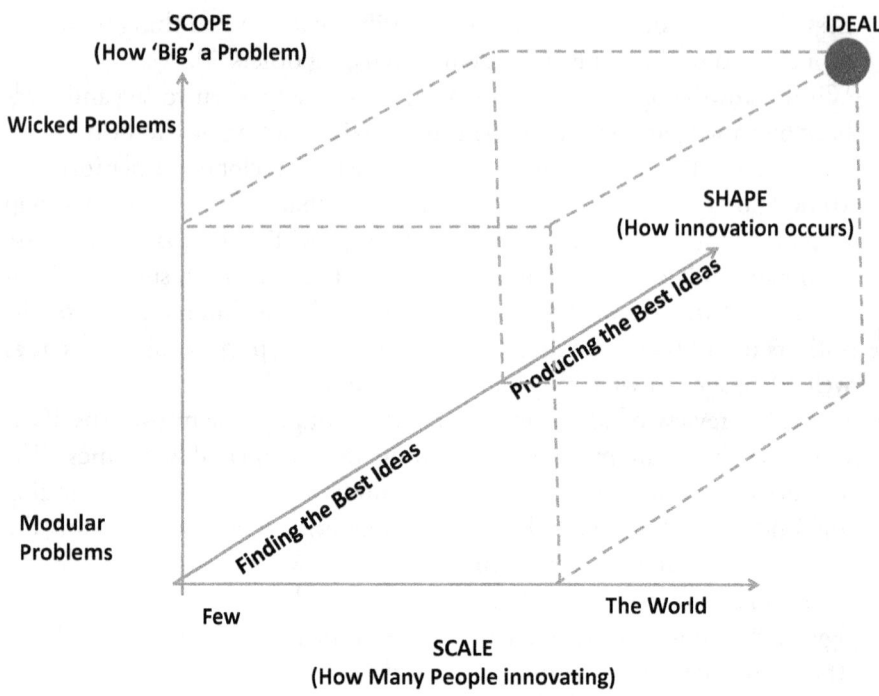

Fig. 1.5 Scale, scope, and shape to solve wicked problems using crowdsourcing

lectively produce (or co-create) a range of ideas to solve the wicked problem in its entirety. We thought that maybe if we release the crowd from the Idea-Sharing process, this will allow the crowd to shape its own way of innovating. Self-shaping implies that crowd members can share whatever knowledge they want to share in whatever ways they want without focusing on who has the best idea to be refined and selected later. Self-shaping applies to not only producing the solutions but more importantly defining and redefining the problem itself (often in parallel with producing solutions). Self-shaping is shown in the upper right quadrant of Fig. 1.5.

This vision of self-shaping is not achievable with the Idea-Sharing specification imposed on the crowd. In fact, prior to this book, no one knows what the crowd will do if they aren't required to offer ideas; what will the crowd's self-shaping process look like? What we do know is that, if left to self-shape, the collective will not be constrained to offer the one best idea, but has the opportunity to collectively produce an idea. Whether the crowd uses that opportunity of being freed from the "mindcuffs" of focusing on ideas to co-produce more innovative ideas, and how they would go about doing that, is the discovery which we share with you in this book.

The book will show that when crowdsourcing allows people to self-shape the way they want to in order to solve the wicked problem, they will offer more innovative solutions than with the Idea-Sharing requirements imposed. And this book will show you what we unearth, through our data forensics, about how they shape their Collective Production.

1.10 Could Questioning Traditional Crowdsourcing's Idea-Sharing Process Also Nudge Changes in the Use of Teams for Solving Wicked Problems?

When one allows a crowd to collectively produce rather than shar for an innovative solution to wicked problems, the crowd begins to compete against the traditional way in which wicked problems are solved: by teams of the privileged, powerful, and prominent rather than by the masses. Using teams to solve wicked problems has certain advantages as shown in the upper right-hand quadrant of Table 1.1. You can dialogue, resolve, and integrate differences between team members in the hopes of generating a more innovative and implementable solution. With a team of "insiders", you can also keep knowledge private to the organization. But there are distinct disadvantages with using a team to solve a wicked problem. There are many people and perspectives not represented in the team, no matter how large and diverse the team. There are many social influences that harm a team's process. Since team members were chosen specifically to solve a problem, it is hard for that team to envision an alternate framing of the problem. Crowds can overcome those disadvantages, as shown in the lower right-hand quadrant of Table 1.1, but only if the crowds are allowed to collectively produce.

As we become more knowledgeable about how to help crowds collectively produce innovative solutions—and this book is a step in that direction—we can rethink how decisions should be made in our organizations. Rather than having the top management team or top team of the most senior people be the first-used resource when "tough" wicked problems surface, maybe crowds should be the first-used resource. In such a new world, the use of teams may become anachronistic since they limit the achievable possibilities. Executives may be expected in the future to manage crowds, not teams where the crowds consist of employees, outside contributors, and ecosystem players.

We do not simply see our mission as one of improving crowdsourcing but rather one of improving the way in which innovation emerges today. We

Table 1.1 Tradeoffs of crowd versus team to solve structured versus ill-structured problems

		Type of problem needing to be solved	
		Structured[a]	Wicked[a]
Organizational mechanism to solve problem	Teams of privileged, powerful, and prominent	Advantages of a team: Can create a mental model of what team members credibly know, and then aggregate—assuming that interfaces between modules are well-defined. Disadvantages: An individual might be sufficient but yet the individual may not be on the team	Advantages of a team: Dialogue, resolve and integrate differences in a planned approach; private knowledge in organization can remain private Disadvantages: Hard to know the right expertise needed in advance to know who to include in the team; likelihood of negative social influences harming innovation: Anchoring, dominance, fault lines, too early convergence. Reduces chance of serendipity when using team members only
	Online open crowd solving problem	With the *Idea-Sharing* process: Advantage: By casting net widely, can increase the chance that the right individual with the right solution can be found Disadvantage: The crowd does not know the full scope of the problem and thus offer a solution that sub-optimizes the full problem, so depends on how the problem was decomposed and the interfaces between the decompositions	With the *Collectively Produce* process: Advantage: Since don't know expertise needed in advance, casting net wide increases the chance of a range of expertise of varying types to be offered. Less likely for negative social influences; unexpected alternative problem formulations may emerge from serendipity Disadvantage: Need to be careful about what private knowledge to share with crowd; may obtain unexpected solutions; crowd may become chaotic or emotional; potential for information overload; challenges in governing the crowd.

[a]Complex, ill-structured/wicked problem: Cannot specify evaluation criteria in advance; cannot specify how to achieve innovative solutions in advance since they may come unexpectedly; has many interdependent elements for which dependencies can't be predicted in advance so can't be decomposed. In contrast, structured problems are decomposable. Thank you to Jackson Nickerson for his inspiration for this table

believe crowds allow for the "little guy" to have some way to help in solving wicked problems. We believe crowds allow for little pieces of knowledge from unknown corners to be surfaced which may—just maybe—offer the innovative spark to solve what appears to be intractable. As such, we believe that crowds allow for a future of inclusiveness, expansiveness, and perspective sharing in how wicked problems are solved, and how twenty-first-century organizations function.

1.11 How Do We Address the Idea-Sharing Process' Suboptimality?

It's time the "mindcuffs" (intellectual handcuffs) and all the requirements of the Idea-Sharing process are taken off the crowds to leverage their true potential. The research done by us (and several others we refer to in this book) indicates that the way "crowdsourcing" is being conceptualized and used today does not leverage the crowds' knowledge to solve wicked problems. Recently, a few forward-thinking organizations have become to engage in open strategy formulation, which refers to the inclusion of a variety of stakeholders in formulating new strategic initiatives for the organization.[106] Examples of such strategic wicked problems[107] concern identifying which new markets to pursue, what new offerings to bring to market, how to remove invasive species in a societally acceptable manner, and how an organization can help in reducing global warming.

It is time to reconceive how companies, organizations, and governments should use crowds. If we free crowds from the mindcuffing constraints placed on them, crowds can help impact the strategies of companies as they seek to manage the upheavals in markets due to tectonic digital disruptions. They can help organizations and governments do good for the world and come up with creative ways to solve water rights issues, refugee crises, global warming, and the like. Along this journey, crowds can help organizations to restrategize to become more socially responsible, protect our data, and find the will to reallocate resources. While we may be wildly optimistic, we demonstrate our enthusiasm about the true potential of the crowds with findings from data we systematically collected and also supported by research from others.

We are writing this book for both practitioners and researchers, balancing practical needs for advice with the precision of scholarly research backing up that advice. This mixed audience process is not a writing style commonly seen. While researchers would like to see the rigor, the practitioners want immediate relevance. Those practitioners who are particularly in a hurry can simply skip to the chapter on Management Implications toward the end. This chapter provides very specific practical guidance on how to use crowds to solve wicked problems summarized from the rigorous research presented throughout.

For the practitioners who want to reflect, muse, and chew on how we arrived at the practical guidelines, and those academic scholars interested in this stream of research, theory, and implications for future research, we have organized each chapter as a series of stories and the learning that is derived from the stories. The stories are not "applied business fiction" but rather stories of application in-field research. Some of the stories focus on people in the crowd. Some of the stories have data that allude to crowds' behaviors. The antagonist in all the stories is the current Idea-Sharing process to using crowds, providing the evidence for the alternative, Collective Production process.

We realize that practitioners and researchers have two different objectives when they read stories of our research. To make our stories relevant for both, we separate out the learnings for research from the learnings for practice. Moreover, when we anticipate our two audiences to have specific and different questions, we present stand-alone story boxes that can be quickly glanced over. All the references to relevant research by others have been presented as endnotes so as not to disturb the reading flow.

1.12 Overview of Chapters

In the next chapter, we first answer the question of whether removing the Idea-Sharing process' limits on the crowd facilitates the crowd when attempting to solve wicked problems. In the following five chapters, we then go further by looking deeply into how crowds generate innovative solutions when they are allowed to develop their own innovation process. We find that they behave in ways that current research and practice would not have expected. We refer to this crowd-based innovation process they use as "Collective Production" since it requires only a minimum investment of time but maximally inclusive knowledge transformation. Table 1.2 briefly characterizes the Collective Production process we will be explaining in more detail throughout the book.

Finally, after describing the Collective Production process, in the last part of the book, we describe implications for how technology platforms for Collective Production need to be redesigned, how research on innovation and crowdsourcing needs to be redirected, and how managers need to reconsider how they use the crowds.

Table 1.2 Brief comparison of traditional to the Collective Production process

Idea-Sharing(traditional) process	Collective Production process
• Crowd **not allowed to redefine problem**; problem to be solved as posed by the organization (managers)	• Crowd **can redefine problem** by sharing multiple perspectives
• **Ideas are generated by individuals themselves** prior to joining the crowd; ideas may be then shared (or not) with the crowd	• **Ideas are developed by combining a variety of knowledge** that acts as stimuli for the crowd as to what and why to combine
• Ideas may be only thing crowd shares with others (if allowed to)	• Crowd is not restrained to just sharing ideas
• Shared ideas may or may not be refined by others in the crowd, **crowd does not share any other knowledge** (other than individuals' ideas) pertaining to the problem	• Crowd **goes beyond by sharing a variety of knowledge** that may further elaborate the problem or alter the problem to be solved (not sticking to the initial formulation of the problem)
• The assumption is **that the more idea contributors the better** as a range of ideas are available making it easier to locate the truly exceptional ideator	• The fundamental belief is that **more knowledge shared, the better**. A range of knowledge can stimulate the crowd in a range of ways to combine and recombine knowledge to redefine the problem and collaboratively develop new solutions
• **Process is imposed** by the explicit rules of crowdsourcing (as laid out by managers or platforms)	• **Process emerges** from the crowd (i.e., self-shaping of crowd) as crowd members based on knowledge already shared, autonomously decide what else needs to be shared
• **Individuals in crowd spend significant time** ruminating on the posed problem outside of the crowd and self-formulating solution-ideas to the problem	• Each crowd member **spends minimal slivers of their own time**, contributing whatever knowledge they deem pertinent when they can in short bursts of engagement

Notes

1. Ackoff, R. L. (1974). *Redesigning The Future: A System Approach to Societal Problems.* John Wiley and Sons, NY.
2. Simon H. A. 1973. The structure of ill-structured problems. *Artificial Intelligence*, 4 (3–4): 181–201.
3. Ibid.
4. George, G., Howard-Grenville, J., Joshi, A., & Tihanyi, L.(2016). Understanding and tackling societal grand challenges through management research. *Academy of Management Journal*, 59(6): 1880–1895; George, G. (2014). Rethinking management scholarship. *Academy of Management Journal*, 57(1): 1–6.

5. Hautz, J., Seidl, D., & Whittington, R. (2017). Open strategy: Dimensions, dilemmas, dynamics. *Long Range Planning*, 50(3), 298–309; Whittington, R. (2019) *Opening Strategy: Professional Strategists and Practice Change, 1960 to Today*, Oxford Press; D. Seidl, R. Whittington, G. Von Krogh (2018) *Cambridge Handbook of Open Strategy*.
6. Camillus, J. C. (2008). Strategy as a wicked problem. *Harvard business review*, 86(5), 98.
7. Esteles-Arolas, E & Gonzalex-Ladron-de-Guevara, F. (2012). Towards an integrated crowdsourcing definition. *J Inf Sci*, 38, 189–200; West, J. & Sims, J. (2018) How firms leverage crowds and communities for open innovation. In Tucci, C. L., Afuah, A., & Viscusi, G. (Ed) *Creating and Capturing Value through Crowdsourcing*. Oxford University Press.
8. https://www.popsci.com/scitech/article/2007-05/digg-mutiny%E2%80%94censored-users-get-their-way.
9. Wilson, M., Robson, K., & Botha, E. (2017). Crowdsourcing in a time of empowered stakeholders: lessons from crowdsourcing campaigns. *Business Horizons*, 60(2), 247–253.
10. Adamczyk, S., Bullinger, A. C., Möslein, K. M., (2012). Innovation contests: a review, classification and outlook. *Creat. Innovat. Manag.* 21(4), 335–360; Mack, T., & Landau, C. (2015). Winners, losers, and deniers: Self-selection in crowd innovation contests and the roles of motivation, creativity, and skills. *Journal of Engineering and Technology Management*, 37, 52–64.
11. Von Hippel, E. (2005) Democratizing Innovation. MIT Press; von Hippel, E. (1986) Lead users: A source of novel product concepts. *Management Science*, 32(7), 791–805; Von Hippel, E. (2016) *Free Innovation*, MIT Press.
12. Crockett, Z. (2017) How a janitor at Frito-Lay invented Flamin' Hot Cheetos: Richard Montañez went from cleaning toilets to being one of the most respected execs in the food industry. *The Hustle*, November 29.
13. Others have proposed similar definitions: Afuah, A. (2018). Crowdsourcing: A Primer and Research Framework. In Creating and capturing value through crowdsourcing. In Tucci, C. L., Afuah, A., & Viscusi, G. (Eds.), *Creating and Capturing Value through Crowdsourcing* Oxford University Press, pp. 39–57; Afuah, A., & Tucci, C. L. (2012). Crowdsourcing as a solution to distant search. *Academy of Management Review*, 37(3): 355–375; Dahlander, L. & Piezunka, H. 2014. Open to suggestions: How organizations elicit suggestions through proactive and reactive attention. *Research Policy*, 43(5), 812–827; Ghezzi, A., Gabelloni, D., Martini, A., & Natalicchio, A. (2018). Crowdsourcing: a review and suggestions for future research. *International Journal of Management Reviews*, 20(2): 343–363. Felin, T., Lakhani, K. R., & Tushman, M. L. (2017). Firms, crowds, and innovation. *Strategic organization*, 15(2), 119–140. Howe, J. (2006). The Rise of Crowdsourcing. *Wired magazine*, 14(6): 1–4.; Viscusi, G. & Tucci,

C.L. 2018. Three's a Crowd. In Tucci, C. L., Afuah, A., & Viscusi, G. (Eds.) *Creating and capturing value through crowdsourcing*, Oxford University Press, pp. 39–57.
14. West, J & Sims, J. (2018). How firms leverage crowds and communities for open innovation. In C. Tucci, A. Afuah and G. Viscusi (Ed) *Creating and Capturing Value through Crowdsourcing*. Oxford.
15. Boudreau, K. J., & Lakhani, K.R. 2009. How to manage outside innovation. MIT Sloan Management Review, 50(4), 69–76; Franke, N. & Shah, S. 2003. How communities support innovative activities: an exploration of assistance and sharing among end-users. *Research Policy* 32, 157–178; Fuller, J., Jawecki, G., & Muhlbacher, H. 2007. Innovation creation by online basketball communities. *Journal of Business Research*. 60, pp. 60–71; Fuller, J., Hutter, K., Hautz, J., and Matzler, K. 2014. User roles and contributions in innovation-contest communities. *Journal of Management Information Systems*, 31(1), 273–307.
16. Amabile, T. M. 1996. *Creativity in Context: Update to the Social Psychology of Creativity*. Westview Press, Boulder, CO; Amabile, T. M., & Pratt, M. G. 2016. The dynamic componential model of creativity and innovation in organizations: Making progress, making meaning. *Research in Org Behavior* 36,157–183; Mack, T., and Landau, C. ibid.
17. Chesbrough, H. 2003. *Open Innovation: The New Imperative for Creating and Profiting from Technology*. Boston, MA: Harvard Business School Press; Chesbrough, H. 2006. "Open Innovation: A New Paradigm for Understanding Industrial Innovation." In H. Chesbrough, W. Vanhaverbeke, and J. West (ed) *Open Innovation: Researching a New Paradigm*, 1–12. Oxford: Oxford University Press; Chesbrough, H. 2011. *Open Services Innovation: Rethinking Your Business to Grow and Compete in a New Era*. San Francisco, CA: Jossey-Bass; Chesbrough, H., and M. Bogers. 2014. "Explicating Open Innovation: Clarifying an Emerging Paradigm for Understanding Innovation." In H. Chesbrough, W. Vanhaverbeke, and J. West, (ed) *New Frontiers in Open Innovation*, 3–28. Oxford: Oxford University Press; Chesbrough, H., S. Kim, and A. Agogino. 2014. "Chez Panisse: Building an Open Innovation Ecosystem." *California Management Review* 56 (4): 144–171. Chesbrough, H., and M. M. Appleyard. 2007. "Open Innovation and Strategy." *California Management Review* 50 (1): 57–76. Chesbrough, H., and R. S. Rosenbloom. 2002. "The Role of the Business Model in Capturing Value from Innovation: Evidence from Xerox Corporation's Technology Spin-off Companies." *Industrial and Corporate Change* 11 (3): 529–555; West, J. & Sims, J. (2018). How firms leverage crowds and communities for open innovation. In C. Tucci, A. Afuah & G. Viscusi (Ed) *Creating and Capturing Value Through Crowdsourcing*. Oxford Press.
18. Brabham, D. C. (2013). *Crowdsourcing*. MIT Press; Zhao, Y & Zhu, Q. 2014. Evaluation on crowdsourcing research: Current status and future

direction. *Information Systems Frontier*, 16, 417–434; Clark, B. Y., Zingale, N., Logan, J., & Brudney, J. (2019). A framework for using crowdsourcing in government. In *Social Entrepreneurship: Concepts, Methodologies, Tools, and Applications* (pp. 405–425). IGI Global; Mechant, P., Stevens, I., Evens, T. & Verdegem, P. (2012) E-deliberation 2.0 for smart cities: A critical assessment of two "idea generation" cases. *International Journal of Electronic Governance*, 5(1), 82–98; Saebo, O., Rose, J & Flak, L. S. (2008) The shape of eParticipation: Characterizing an emerging research area. *Government Information Quarterly*, 25(3), 400–428; Price, V. (2009) Citizens deliberating online: theory and some evidence. In T. Davies & S. Noveck (Eds). *Online Deliberation: Design, Research & Practice*. University of Chicago Press; Porter, A. J., Tuertscher, P. & Huysman, M. 2019 Saving Our Oceans: Tackling Grand Challenges Through Crowdsourcing, *Journal of Management*.
19. Malone, T., Nickerson, J.V., Laubacher, R. J., Fisher, L. H., de Boer, P., Han, Y., Towne, W. B. (2017). Putting the pieces back together again: Contest webs for large-scale problem solving. *CSCW*, 2017.
20. Porter, A. J., Tuertscher, P., and Huysman, M. (2019) Saving our oceans. Tackling grand challenges through crowdsourcing. *Journal of Management*.
21. Laursen, K., Salter, A., 2006. Open for innovation: the role of openness in explaining innovation performance among UK manufacturing firms. *Strategy Management. J.* 27, 131–150.
22. Innovation contests such as those regularly hosted on the platform Innocentive.com represent the dominant form of crowd innovation contests according to Mack, T., & Landau, C. (2015). Winners, losers, and deniers: Self-selection in crowd innovation contests and the roles of motivation, creativity, and skills. *Journal of Engineering and Technology Management*, 37, 52–64; Terwiesch, C. & Ulrich, K. T. (2009). Innovation tournaments: Creating and selecting exceptional opportunities. *Harvard Business Review*; and Terwiesch, C. & Xu, Y. 2008. Innovation contests, open innovation, and multiagent problem solving. *Management Science*, 54(9), 1529–1543.
23. The following are papers describing online user communities: basketball community in Franke, N. & Shah, S. (2003). How communities support innovative activities: an exploration of assistance and sharing among end users. *Research Policy* 32, 157–178 and Fuller, J., Jawecki, G., & Muhlbacher, H. 2007. Innovation creation by online basketball communities. Journal of Business Research. 60, pp. 60–71; Dell's Idea Storm in Di Gangi, P. M., Wasko, M. M., & Hooker, R. E. (2010). Getting customers' ideas to work for you: learning from dell how to succeed with online user innovation communities. MIS Quarterly Executive, 9(4); LEGO's communities in El Sawy, O. A., Kræmmergaard, P., Amsinck, H., & Vinther, A. L. (2016). How LEGO Built the Foundations and Enterprise Capabilities for Digital Leadership. MIS Quarterly Executive, 15(2); and a variety of lead user innovation communities in both Von Hippel, E. (2005) *Democratizing*

Innovation. MIT Press and Von Hippel, E. (2016) Free Innovation, MIT Press.
24. Dahlander, L., Piezunka, H., & Jeppesen, L. 2018. How organizations manage crowds: Define, broadcast, attract and select. In J. Sydow and H. Berends (eds.) *Managing Inter-organizational collaborations—Process View. Part of a series: Research in the Sociology of Organizations.* They review the crowdsourcing literature and confirms that Idea searching is the current dominant form of crowdsourcing for innovation.
25. Lakhani, K. R., Lifshitz-Assaf, H., & Tushman, M. (2013). Open innovation and organizational boundaries: task decomposition, knowledge distribution and the locus of innovation. *Handbook of Economic Organization: Integrating Economic and Organizational Theory*, 355–382; Jeppesen, L. B & Lakhani, E. R. 2010. Marginality and problem-solving effectiveness in broadcast search. *Organization Science*, 21(5), 1016–1033; Nickerson, J A., T. R. Zenger. 2004. A knowledge-based theory of the firm: The problem solving perspective. Organ. Sci. 15(6), 617–632.
26. West, J., Bogers, M., 2014. Leveraging external sources of innovation: a review of research on open innovation. J. Prod. Innov. Manag. 31 (4), 814–831.
27. Afuah, A., & Tucci, C. L. (2012). Crowdsourcing as a solution to distant search. Academy of Management Review, 37(3): 355–375; Vukovic M., Mariana L., Laredo, J. PeopleCloud for the globally integrated enterprise. In: Asit D et al. (eds) Service-oriented computing. Berlin/Heidelberg: Springer-Verlag, 2009; Heer J., Bostock M. Crowdsourcing graphical perception: using mechanical turk to assess visualization design. In: Proceedings of the 28th international conference on human factors in computing systems, CHI'10, ACM, New York, 2010, pp. 203–212; Esteles-Arolas, E. & Gonzalex-Ladron-de-Guevara, F. (2012). Towards an integrated crowdsourcing definition. J Inf Sci, 38, 189–200; Dahlander, L., Piezunka, H., & Jeppesen, L. 2018. How organizations manage crowds: Define, broadcast, attract and select. In J. Sydow and H. Berends (eds.) *Managing Interorganizational collaborations—Process View.* Part of a series: Research in the Sociology of Organizations.
28. Lopez-Vega, H., Tell, F., & Vanhaverbeke, W. (2016). Where and how to search? Search paths in open innovation. Research Policy, 45(1), 125–136.
29. Mack, T., & Landau, C. (2015). Winners, losers, and deniers: Self-selection in crowd innovation contests and the roles of motivation, creativity, and skills. *Journal of Engineering and Technology Management*, 37, 52–64.
30. Jeppesen, L. B & Lakhani, E. R. 2010. Marginality and problem-solving effectiveness in broadcast search. Organization Science, 21(5), 1016–1033.
31. See review of crowdsourcing processes by Dahlander, L., Piezunka, H., Jeppesen, L. B. 2018. How organizations manage crowds: Define, broadcast and select. In J. Sydow & H. Berends (Eds) *Research in the Sociology of Organizations*, Sept 2018.

32. Lévy, P. (1997 [1995] pp. 13–14) *Collective Intelligence: Mankind's Emerging World in Cyberspace* (R. Bononno, Trans.) New York: Plenum. Cited in: Brabham, D. C. (2008). Crowdsourcing as a model for problem solving: An introduction and cases. Convergence, 14(1), 75–90.
33. Woolley, A. W., C. F. Chabris, A. Pentland, N. Hashmi, T. W. Malone. (2010). Evidence for a collective intelligence factor in the performance of human groups. Science 330(6004) 686–688.
34. Malone, T. W., & Bernstein, M. S. (Eds.). (2015). *Handbook of collective intelligence.* MIT Press.
35. Malone, T. W., & Bernstein, M. S. (Eds.). (2015). Handbook of collective intelligence. MIT Press;.Woolley, A., & Fuchs, E. (2011) Collective Intelligence in the Organization of Science OrganizationScience, 22(5), 1359–1367.
36. Valentine, M. A., Retelny, D., To, A., Rahmati, N., Doshi, T., & Bernstein, M. S. (2017, May). Flash organizations: Crowdsourcing complex work by structuring crowds as organizations. In Proceedings of the 2017 CHI conference on human factors in computing systems (pp. 3523–3537). ACM.
37. Surowiecki, J. (2004) *The Wisdom of Crowds.* NY: Random House.
38. J. Howe (2006). The rise of Crowdsourcing. Wired, Issue 14.06. Over 40 of these more general definitions of crowdsourcing were reviewed and integrated by Esteles-Arolas, E & Gonzalex-Ladron-de-Guevara, F. (2012). Towards an integrated crowdsourcing definition. J Inf Sci, 38, 189–200.
39. Esteles-Arolas, E & Gonzalex-Ladron-de-Guevara, F. (2012). Towards an integrated crowdsourcing definition. J Inf Sci, 38, 189–200.
40. See review on crowdsourcing by Dahlander, L, Piezunka, H., Jeppesen, L.B. 2018. How organizations manage crowds: Define, broadcast and select. In J. Sydow & H. Berends (Eds) Research in the Sociology of Organizations, Sept 2018.
41. The Well-Known Variation/Selection/Retention Model to Innovation has been discussed in: classic texts in psychology, sociology, management, business strategy, economics, and organization studies. See for example: Campbell, D. T. (1960). Blind variation and selective retention in creative thought as in other knowledge processes. Psychological Review, 67, 380–400; Simonton, D. K. (2011). Creativity and discovery as blind variation: Campbell's (1960) BVSR model after the half-century mark. Review of General Psychology, 15(2), 158–174; Staw, B. M. 1990. An evolutionary approach to creativity and innovation. In M. West & J. L. Farr (Eds.), Innovation and creativity at work: Psychological and organizational strategies: 287–308. Chichester, UK: Wiley; Nelson, R. R., & Sidney, G. (1982). Winter. 1982. An evolutionary theory of economic change, 929–964.
42. Hobday, M. (2005). Firm-level innovation models: perspectives on research in developed and developing countries. Technology analysis & strategic management, 17(2), 121–146.

43. Harvey, S. (2014). Creative synthesis: Exploring the process of extraordinary group creativity. Academy of Management Review, 39(3), 324–343; Staw, B. M. 1990. An evolutionary approach to creativity and innovation. In M. West & J. L. Farr (Eds.), Innovation and creativity at work: Psychological and organizational strategies: 287–308. Chichester, UK: Wiley; Chen, J., & Adamson, C. (2015). Innovation: Integration of random variation and creative synthesis. Academy of Management Review, 40(3), 461–464.
44. Chesbrough (2003, 2006, 2011).
45. Laursen and Salter (2006).
46. See for example a recent study by Hwang, Elina H., Param Vir Singh, and Linda Argote. "Jack of all, master of some: Information network and innovation in crowdsourcing communities." *Information Systems Research* (2019), which focuses on idea-generators within a community.
47. Lifshitz-Assaf, H. (2018). Dismantling knowledge boundaries at NASA: The critical role of professional identity in open innovation. Administrative science quarterly, 63(4), 746–782.
48. Suriowiecki, *Wisdom of the Crowds*. 2004.
49. "We conducted this competition to find new ways to improve the recommendations we provide to our members, which is a key part of our business. However, we had to come up with a proxy question that was easier to evaluate and quantify: the root mean squared error (RMSE) of the predicted rating." https://medium.com/netflix-techblog/netflix-recommendations-beyond-the-5-stars-part-1-55838468f429.
50. https://www.xprize.org/prizes/ansari; https://www.xprize.org/about/people/the-ansari-family; https://science.howstuffworks.com/x-prize1.htm.
51. Dahlander et al. (2018); Henkel, J., Schöberl, S., & Alexy, O. (2014). The emergence of openness: How and why firms adopt selective revealing in open innovation. Research Policy, 43(5), 879–890.
52. Afuah and Tucci (2012).
53. Lopez-Vega, H., Tell, F., & Vanhaverbeke, W. (2016). Where and how to search? Search paths in open innovation. Research Policy, 45(1), 125–136.
54. Riedl, C., & Seidel, V. P. (2018). Learning from mixed signals in online innovation communities. Organization Science, 29(6), 1010–1032.
55. Quote from P919 in Mo, J., Sarkar, S., & Meno Mo, J., Sarkar, S., & Menon, S. (2018). Know when to run: recommendations in crowdsourcing contests. MIS Quarterly Vol. 42 No. 3, pp. 919–944.
56. Altman, E., Nagle, R. & Tushman, M. L. (2015) Innovating without information constraints: organizations, communities, and innovation when information costs approach zero In C. Shalley, M. Hitt, and J. Zhou (Ed) The Oxford Handbook of Creativity, Innovation, and Entrepreneurship.
57. Bauer, R. M., & Gegenhuber, T. (2015). Crowdsourcing: Global search and the twisted roles of consumers and producers. Organization, 22(5), 661–681.

58. https://longitudeprize.org/about-us/history.
59. What is referred to as task decomposition in Lakhani, K. R., Lifshitz-Assaf-H & Tushman, M. L. (2013) Open innovation and organizational boundaries: task decomposition, knowledge distribution and the locus of innovation. Handbook of Economic Organization.
60. Mack and Landau (2015).
61. Dahlander, L., and Gann, M.D. (2010) "How open is innovation?", *Research Policy*, Vol. 39(2010) 699–709.
62. Henkel, J., Schöberl, S., & Alexy, O. (2014). The emergence of openness: How and why firms adopt selective revealing in open innovation. Research Policy, 43(5), 879–890.
63. Venkataramani, Elad N. Sherf, Subra Tangirala, Vijaya. "Research: Why Managers Ignore Employees' Ideas." Harvard Business Review. April 08, 2019.
64. Surowiecki, J. 2005. *The Wisdom of Crowds* NY: Anchor.
65. Leonard-Barton, D., & Swap, W. C. (1999). When sparks fly: Igniting creativity in groups. Harvard Business Press.
66. Finke, R. A. Ward, T. B. & Smith, S.M. 1996. Creative Cognition: Theory, Research and Applications. MIT Press.
67. Grant, R. M. 1996. Prospering in dynamically competitive environments: organizational capability as knowledge integration. Organization Science 7(4): 375–387; Kogut, B., & Zander, U. (1992). Knowledge of the firm, combinative capabilities, and the replication of technology. Organization science, 3(3), 383–397; Fleming, L. (2001). Recombinant uncertainty in technological search. Management science, 47(1), 117–132.
68. Jeppesen, L. B & Lakhani, E. R. 2010. Marginality and problem-solving effectiveness in broadcast search. Organization Science, 21(5), 1016–1033.; and Dahlander, L., Piezunka, H., & Jeppesen, L. 2018. How organizations manage crowds: Define, broadcast, attract and select. In J. Sydow and H. Berends (eds.) Managing Inter-organizational collaborations—Process View. Part of a series: Research in the Sociology of Organizations.
69. Lifshitz-Assaf, H. (2018). Dismantling knowledge boundaries at NASA: The critical role of professional identity in open innovation. Administrative science quarterly, 63(4), 746–782.
70. Di Gangi, P. M., Wasko, M. M., & Hooker, R. E. (2010). Getting customers' ideas to work for you: learning from dell how to succeed with online user innovation communities. MIS Quarterly Executive, 9(4), as well as https://www.informationweek.com/10-crowdsourcing-success-stories/d/d-id/1096464?page_number=2.
71. Poetz, M. K., & Schreier, M. 2012. The value of crowdsourcing: Can users really compete with professionals in generating new product ideas? Journal of Product Innovation Management, 29(2) 245–256.

72. Lifshitz-Assaf, H. (2018). Dismantling knowledge boundaries at NASA: The critical role of professional identity in open innovation. Administrative science quarterly, 63(4), 746–782.
73. https://newatlas.com/darpa-fang-winner/27213/.
74. https://geinnovationlab.com/10eqs/solvingscarcitythroughwaterreuse?1.
75. https://www.hyve.net/en/.
76. Cited in Dissanayake, I., Zhang, J., & Gu, B. (2015). Task division for team success in crowdsourcing contests: Resource allocation and alignment effects. Journal of Management Information Systems, 32(2), 8–39.
77. Sullivan, E. A group effort: More companies are turning to the wisdom of the crowd to find ways to innovate. Marketing News, 44, 2 (2010), 22–28.
78. Crowdsourcing.org. 10 of the 11 best global brands use creative crowdsourcing. http://www.crowdsourcing.org/editorial/10-of-the-11-best-global-brands-use-creative-crowdsour cing-/16935 (accessed on March 20, 2015).
79. McKinsey Quarterly Reports (2009). How Companies are Benefiting from Web 2.0. September.
80. Wilson, M., Robson, K., & Botha, E. (2017). Crowdsourcing in a time of empowered stakeholders: lessons from crowdsourcing campaigns. Business Horizons, 60(2), 247–253.
81. Williams, M. (2010) California Crowdsources Ideas for Replacing Legacy Systems: P. K. Agarwal, director of the Office of Technology Services, launches a crowdsourcing tool where users can submit ideas for improving and replacing California's legacy IT systems. Government Technology, February 8.
82. https://qz.com/68910/icelands-experiment-with-crowd-sourcing-its-constitution-just-died/.
83. Landemore, H. (2014) We, All of the People: Five lessons from Iceland's failed experiment in creating a crowdsourced constitution. *Slate*, July 31.
84. Foege, J. N., Lauritzen, G. D., Tietze, F., & Salge, T. O. (2019). Reconceptualizing the paradox of openness: How solvers navigate sharing-protecting tensions in crowdsourcing. *Research Policy*.
85. Boudreau, K. J., Lacetera, N., & Lakhani, K. R. 2011. Incentives and problem uncertainty in innovation contests: An empirical analysis. Management Science, 57(5): 843–863; Dahlander, L, Piezunka, H. and Jeppesen, L. (2018) How organizations manage crowds: Define, broadcast, attract and select. Research in the Sociology of Organizations; Poetz, M. K., & Schreier, M. 2012. The value of crowdsourcing: Can users really compete with professionals in generating new product ideas? Journal of Product Innovation Management, 29(2) 245–256; Felin & Zenger 2014. Closed or open innovation? Problem solving and the governance choice. Research Policy, 43(5), 914–925; Lakhani, K. R., Lifshitz-Assaf, H., & Tushman, M. (2013). Open innovation and organizational boundaries: task decomposition, knowledge

distribution and the locus of innovation. Handbook of Economic Organization: Integrating Economic and Organizational Theory, 355–382.
86. Afuah, A., Tucci, C. L. (2012) Crowdsourcing as a solution to distant search. Academy of Management Review, 37(3), 355–375; Pollok, P., Luttgens, D., Piller, F. T. (2019) Attracting solutions in crowdsourcing contests: The role of knowledge distance, identity disclosure, and seeker status, Research Policy, 48, 98–114.
87. Nickerson, J. A., Wuebker, R., & Zenger, T. (2017). Problems, theories, and governing the crowd. Strategic Organization, 15(2): 275–288; Viscusi, G. & Tucci, C. L. Three's a Crowd? In C. L. Tucci, A. Afuah & G. Viscusi (Ed) creating and Capturing Value Through Crowdsourcing. Oxford Press.
88. Hautz, J., Seidl, D., & Whittington, R. (2017). Open strategy: Dimensions, dilemmas, dynamics. Long Range Planning, 50(3), 298–309.
89. Lifshitz-Assaf, H. (2018). Dismantling knowledge boundaries at NASA: The critical role of professional identity in open innovation. Administrative science quarterly, 63(4), 746–782.
90. Franke, N., Keinz, P., Klausberger, K., 2012. "Does this sound like a fair deal?" Antecedents and consequences of fairness expectations in the individual's decision to participate in firm innovation. Organ. Sci. 24, 1495–1516; Fuller, J., Jawecki, G., & Muhlbacher, H. 2007. Innovation creation by online basketball communities. Journal of Business Research. 60, pp. 60–71.
91. Mack and Landau (2015).
92. Acar, O.A., (2019) Motivations and solution appropriateness in crowdsourcing challenges for innovation. Research Policy.
93. Schemmann, Brita et al. (2016) Crowdsourcing ideas: Involving ordinary users in the ideation phase of new product development. Research Policy. [Online] 45 (6), 1145–1154.
94. Franke, N., Lettl, C., Roiser, S., Tuertscher, P., 2013. Does god play dice? Randomness vs. deterministic explanations of idea originality in crowdsourcing. In: 35th DRUID Celebration Conference 2013, Barcelona, Spain.
95. Dahlander, L. & Piezunka, H. 2014. Open to suggestions: How organizations elicit suggestions through proactive and reactive attention. Research Policy, 43(5), 812–827.
96. Poetz, M. K., & Schreier, M. 2012. The value of crowdsourcing: Can users really compete with professionals in generating new product ideas? Journal of Product Innovation Management, 29(2) 245–256.
97. Blohm, I, Bretschneider, U., Leimeister, J. M., Krcmar, H. 2011. Does collaboration among participants lead to better ideas in IT-based idea competitions? An empirical investigation. International J of Networking and Virtual Organizations, 9(2), pp. 106–122.
98. Nambisan, S., Baron, R. A., 2010. Different roles, different strokes: Organizing virtual customer environments to promote two types of cus-

tomer contributions. Organ. Sci. 21, 554–572; Franke, N., Keinz, P., Klausberger, K., 2012. "Does this sound like a fair deal?" Antecedents and consequences of fairness expectations in the individual's decision to participate in firm innovation. Organ. Sci. 24, 1495–1516; Adamczyk et al. (2012), Mack and Landau (2015).
99. Boudreau, K. J., Lacetera, N., & Lakhani, K. R. 2011. Incentives and problem uncertainty in innovation contests: An empirical analysis. Management Science, 57(5): 843–863.
100. Bullinger, A. C., Neyer, A. K., Rass, M. & Moeslein, K. (2010) Community-based innovation contests: Where competition meets cooperation. Creativity and innovation management, 19(3), 390–303.
101. Mattarelli, E., Schecter, A., Hinds, P. Contractor, N., Lu, C., Topac, B. (2018). How co-creation processes unfold and predict submission quality in crowd-based open innovation. Thirty-Ninth International Conference on Information Systems, San Francisco.
102. Wilson, M., Robson, K., & Botha, E. (2017). Crowdsourcing in a time of empowered stakeholders: lessons from crowdsourcing campaigns. Business Horizons, 60(2), 247–253.
103. Example originally provided by Jeppesen, L. B. & Lakhani, K. R. (2010) Marginality and problem-solving effectiveness in broadcast search. Org Sci, 21(5), 1016–1033.
104. Quote in Dahlander, L, Piezunka, H., Jeppesen, L. B. 2018. How organizations manage crowds: Define, broadcast and select. In J. Sydow & H. Berends (Eds) Research in the Sociology of Organizations, Sept 2018.
105. Fuller, J., Hutter, K., & Faullant, R. Why co-creation experience matters? Creative experience and its impact on the quantity and quality of creative contributions. R&D Management 41(3), 2011, pp. 259–273.
106. Whittington (2011, 2015); Seidl et al. (2018).
107. Camillus (2008, HB).

References

Ackoff, R. L. (1974). *Redesigning the Future: A System Approach to Societal Problems*. New York: John Wiley and Sons.

Adamczyk, S., Bullinger, A. C., & Möslein, K. M. (2012). Innovation Contests: A Review, Classification and Outlook. *Creativity and Innovation Management, 21*(4), 335–360.

Afuah, A. (2018). Crowdsourcing: A Primer and Research Framework. In C. L. Tucci, A. Afuah, & G. Viscusi (Eds.), *Creating and Capturing Value Through Crowdsourcing* (pp. 39–57). Oxford: Oxford University Press.

Afuah, A., & Tucci, C. L. (2012). Crowdsourcing as a Solution to Distant Shar. *Academy of Management Review, 37*(3), 355–375.

Altman, E., Nagle, R., & Tushman, M. L. (2015). Innovating Without Information Constraints: Organizations, Communities, and Innovation When Information Costs Approach Zero. In C. Shalley, M. Hitt, & J. Zhou (Eds.), *The Oxford Handbook of Creativity, Innovation, and Entrepreneurship*. Oxford: Oxford University Press.

Amabile, T. M. (1996). *Creativity in Context: Update to the Social Psychology of Creativity*. Boulder, CO: Westview Press.

Amabile, T. M., & Pratt, M. G. (2016). The Dynamic Componential Model of Creativity and Innovation in Organizations: Making Progress, Making Meaning. *Research in Organizational Behavior, 36*, 157–183.

Amatriain, X., & Basilico, J. (2012, April 6). Netflix Recommendations: Beyond the 5 Stars (Part 1). Medium. Retrieved April 29, 2019, from https://medium.com/netflix-techblog/netflix-recommendations-beyond-the-5-stars-part-1-55838468f429

Bauer, R. M., & Gegenhuber, T. (2015). Crowdsourcing: Global Shar and the Twisted Roles of Consumers and Producers. *Organization, 22*(5), 661–681.

Berthon, P. R., Pitt, L. F., McCarthy, I., & Kates, S. M. (2007). When Customers Get Clever: Managerial Approaches to Dealing with Creative Consumers. *Business Horizons, 50*(1), 39–47.

Blohm, I., Bretschneider, U., Leimeister, J. M., & Krcmar, H. (2011). Does Collaboration Among Participants Lead to Better Ideas in IT-Based Idea Competitions? An Empirical Investigation. *International Journal of Networking and Virtual Organizations, 9*(2), 106–122.

Bogers, M., & West, J. (2012). Managing Distributed Innovation: Strategic Utilization of Open and User Innovation. *Creativity and Innovation Management, 21*, 61–75.

Boudreau, K. J., Lacetera, N., & Lakhani, K. R. (2011). Incentives and Problem Uncertainty in Innovation Contests: An Empirical Analysis. *Management Science, 57*(5), 843–863.

Boudreau, K. J., & Lakhani, K. R. (2009). How to Manage Outside Innovation. *MIT Sloan Management Review, 50*(4), 69–76.

Brabham, D. C. (2008). Crowdsourcing as a Model for Problem Solving: An Introduction and Cases. *Convergence, 14*(1), 75–90.

Brabham, D. C. (2013). *Crowdsourcing*. Cambridge, MA: MIT Press.

Buchanan, R. (1992). Wicked Problems in Design Thinking. *Design Issues, 8*(2), 5–21.

Bullinger, A. C., Neyer, A. K., Rass, M., & Moeslein, K. (2010). Community-Based Innovation Contests: Where Competition Meets Cooperation. *Creativity and Innovation Management, 19*(3), 390–303.

Camillus, J. C. (2008). Strategy as a Wicked Problem. *Harvard Business Review, 86*(5), 98.

Campbell, D. T. (1960). Blind Variation and Selective Retention in Creative Thought as in Other Knowledge Processes. *Psychological Review, 67*, 380–400.

Casey, K. (2011, March 4). 10 Crowdsourcing Success Stories. *InformationWeek*. Retrieved April 29, 2019, from https://www.informationweek.com/10-crowdsourcing-success-stories/d/d-id/1096464?page_number=2

Chen, J., & Adamson, C. (2015). Innovation: Integration of Random Variation and Creative Synthesis. *Academy of Management Review, 40*(3), 461–464.

Chesbrough, H. (2003). *Open Innovation: The New Imperative for Creating and Profiting from Technology*. Boston, MA: Harvard Business School Press.

Chesbrough, H. (2006). Open Innovation: A New Paradigm for Understanding Industrial Innovation. In H. Chesbrough, W. Vanhaverbeke, & J. West (Eds.), *Open Innovation: Researching a New Paradigm* (pp. 1–12). Oxford: Oxford University Press.

Chesbrough, H. (2011). *Open Services Innovation: Rethinking Your Business to Grow and Compete in a New Era*. San Francisco, CA: Jossey-Bass.

Chesbrough, H., & Bogers, M. (2014). Explicating Open Innovation: Clarifying an Emerging Paradigm for Understanding Innovation. In H. Chesbrough, W. Vanhaverbeke, & J. West (Eds.), *New Frontiers in Open Innovation* (pp. 3–28). Oxford: Oxford University Press.

Chesbrough, H., & Appleyard, M. M. (2007). Open Innovation and Strategy. *California Management Review, 50*(1), 57–76.

Chesbrough, H., & Rosenbloom, R. S. (2002). The Role of the Business Model in Capturing Value from Innovation: Evidence from Xerox Corporation's Technology Spin-off Companies. *Industrial and Corporate Change, 11*(3), 529–555.

Chesbrough, H., Kim, S., & Agogino, A. (2014). Chez Panisse: Building an Open Innovation Ecosystem. *California Management Review, 56*(4), 144–171.

Dahlander, L., & Piezunka, H. (2014). Open to Suggestions: How Organizations Elicit Suggestions Through Proactive and Reactive Attention. *Research Policy, 43*(5), 812–827.

Dahlander, L., & Gann, M. D. (2010). How Open Is Innovation? *Research Policy, 39*, 699–709.

Dahlander, L., Piezunka, H., & Jeppesen, L. (2018). How Organizations Manage Crowds: Define, Broadcast, Attract and Select. In J. Sydow & H. Berends (Eds.), *Managing Inter-organizational Collaborations – Process View*. Part of a Series: Research in the Sociology of Organizations. UK: Emerald Publishing.

Di Gangi, P. M., Wasko, M. M., & Hooker, R. E. (2010). Getting Customers' Ideas to Work for You: Learning from Dell How to Succeed with Online User Innovation Communities. *MIS Quarterly Executive, 9*(4), 213–228.

Dissanayake, I., Zhang, J., & Gu, B. (2015). Task Division for Team Success in Crowdsourcing Contests: Resource Allocation and Alignment Effects. *Journal of Management Information Systems, 32*(2), 8–39.

El Sawy, O. A., Kræmmergaard, P., Amsinck, H., & Vinther, A. L. (2016). How LEGO Built the Foundations and Enterprise Capabilities for Digital Leadership. *MIS Quarterly Executive, 15*(2), 141–166.

Esteles-Arolas, E., & Gonzalex-Ladron-de-Guevara, F. (2012). Towards an Integrated Crowdsourcing Definition. *Journal of Information Science, 38*, 189–200.

Estellés-Arolas, E., & González-Ladrón-de-Guevara, F. (2012). Towards an Integrated Crowdsourcing Definition. *Journal of Information Science, 38*(2), 189–200.

Felin, T., & Zener, T. R. (2014). Closed or Open Innovation? Problem Solving and the Governance Choice. *Research Policy, 43*(5), 914–925.

Felin, T., Lakhani, K. R., & Tushman, M. L. (2017). Firms, Crowds, and Innovation. *Strategic Organization, 15*(2), 119–140.

Finke, R. A., Ward, T. B., & Smith, S. M. (1996). *Creative Cognition: Theory, Research, and Applications*. Cambridge: MIT Press.

Fleming, L. (2001). Recombinant Uncertainty in Technological Shar. *Management Science, 47*(1), 117–132.

Franke, N., & Shah, S. (2003). How Communities Support Innovative Activities: An Exploration of Assistance and Sharing Among End Users. *Research Policy, 32*, 157–178.

Franke, N., Keinz, P., & Klausberger, K. (2012). 'Does This Sound Like a Fair Deal?' Antecedents and Consequences of Fairness Expectations in the Individual's Decision to Participate in Firm Innovation. *Organization Science, 24*, 1495–1516.

Franke, N., Lettl, C., Roiser, S., & Tuertscher, P. (2013). Does God Play Dice? Randomness vs. Deterministic Explanations of Idea Originality in Crowdsourcing. In *35th DRUID Celebration Conference 2013*, Barcelona, Spain.

Fuller, J., Hutter, K., & Faullant, R. (2011). 2011 Why Co-creation Experience Matters? Creative Experience and Its Impact on the Quantity and Quality of Creative Contributions. *R&D Management, 41*(3), 259–273.

Fuller, J., Hutter, K., Hautz, J., & Matzler, K. (2014). User Roles and Contributions in Innovation-Contest Communities. *Journal of Management Information Systems, 31*(1), 273–307.

Fuller, J., Jawecki, G., & Muhlbacher, H. (2007). Innovation Creation by Online Basketball Communities. *Journal of Business Research, 60*, 60–71.

Garriga, H., Von Krogh, G., & Spaeth, S. (2013). How Constraints and Knowledge Impact Open Innovation. *Strategic Management Journal, 34*(9), 1134–1144.

George, G. (2014). Rethinking Management Scholarship. *Academy of Management Journal, 57*(1), 1–6.

George, G., Howard-Grenville, J., Joshi, A., & Tihanyi, L. (2016). Understanding and Tackling Societal Grand Challenges Through Management Research. *Academy of Management Journal, 59*(6), 1880–1895.

Ghezzi, A., Gabelloni, D., Martini, A., & Natalicchio, A. (2018). Crowdsourcing: A Review and Suggestions for Future Research. *International Journal of Management Reviews, 20*(2), 343–363.

Grant, R. M. (1996). Prospering in Dynamically-Competitive Environments: Organizational Capability as Knowledge Integration. *Organization Science, 7*(4), 375–387.

Harvey, S. (2014). Creative Synthesis: Exploring the Process of Extraordinary Group Creativity. *Academy of Management Review, 39*(3), 324–343.

Hautz, J., Seidl, D., & Whittington, R. (2017). Open Strategy: Dimensions, Dilemmas, Dynamics. *Long Range Planning, 50*(3), 298–309.

Heer, J., & Bostock, M. (2010). Crowdsourcing Graphical Perception: Using Mechanical Turk to Assess Visualization Design. In *Proceedings of the 28th International Conference on Human Factors in Computing Systems, CHI'10* (pp. 203–212). New York: ACM.

Henkel, J., Schöberl, S., & Alexy, O. (2014). The Emergence of Openness: How and Why Firms Adopt Selective Revealing in Open Innovation. *Research Policy, 43*(5), 879–890.

Howe, J. (2006). The Rise of Crowdsourcing. *Wired Magazine, 14*(6), 1–4.

Jeppesen, L. B., & Lakhani, E. R. (2010). Marginality and Problem-Solving Effectiveness in Broadcast Shar. *Organization Science, 21*(5), 1016–1033.

Kogut, B., & Zander, U. (1992). Knowledge of the Firm, Combinative Capabilities, and the Replication of Technology. *Organization Science, 3*(3), 383–397.

Kristensson, P., Gustafsson, A., & Archer, T. (2004). Harnessing the Creative Potential Among Users. *Journal of Product Innovation Management, 21*, 4–14.

Lacy, S. (2012). Get Over It, Haters: 99designs Has Tipped. Retrieved from http://pando.com/2012/01/24/get-over-it-haters-99designs-hastipped/.

Lakhani, K. R., Lifshitz-Assaf, H., & Tushman, M. (2013). Open Innovation and Organizational Boundaries: Task Decomposition, Knowledge Distribution and the Locus of Innovation. In *Handbook of Economic Organization: Integrating Economic and Organizational Theory* (pp. 355–382). Cheltenham, UK: Edward Elgar.

Laursen, K., & Salter, A. (2006). Open for Innovation: The Role of Openness in Explaining Innovation Performance Among UK Manufacturing Firms. *Strategy Management Journal, 27*, 131–150.

Leonard, D. (1995). *Wellsprings of Knowledge*. Boston: Harvard Business School Press.

Levinthal, D. A., & Posen, H. E. (2007). Myopia of Selection: Does Organizational Adaptation Limit the Efficacy of Population Selection? *Administrative Science Quarterly, 52*(4), 586–620.

Lévy, P. (1997 [1995]). *Collective Intelligence: Mankind's Emerging World in Cyberspace* (R. Bononno, Trans.). New York: Plenum Trade.

Lifshitz-Assaf, H. (2018). Dismantling Knowledge Boundaries at NASA: The Critical Role of Professional Identity in Open Innovation. *Administrative Science Quarterly, 63*(4), 746–782.

Lopez-Vega, H., Tell, F., & Vanhaverbeke, W. (2016). Where and How to Shar? Shar Paths in Open Innovation. *Research Policy, 45*(1), 125–136.

Mack, T., & Landau, C. (2015). Winners, Losers, and Deniers: Self-selection in Crowd Innovation Contests and the Roles of Motivation, Creativity, and Skills. *Journal of Engineering and Technology Management, 37*, 52–64.

Magnusson, P. R. (2009). Exploring the Contributions of Involving Ordinary Users in Ideation of Technology-Based Services. *Journal of Product Innovation Management, 26*, 578–593.

Malone, T. W., & Bernstein, M. S. (Eds.). (2015). *Handbook of Collective Intelligence*. Cambridge, MA: MIT Press.

Malone, T., Nickerson, J. V., Laubacher, R. J., Fisher, L. H., de Boer, P., Han, Y., et al. (2017). Putting the Pieces Back Together Again: Contest Webs for Large-Sale Problem Solving. CSCW, 2017.

Mattarelli, E., Schecter, A., Hinds, P., Contractor, N., Lu, C., & Topac, B. (2018). How Co-creation Processes Unfold and Predict Submission Quality in Crowd-Based Open Innovation. *Thirty Ninth International Conference on Information Systems*, San Francisco.

Mechant, P., Stevens, I., Evens, T., & Verdegem, P. (2012). E-deliberation 2.0 for Smart Cities: A Critical Assessment of Two 'Idea Generation' Cases. *International Journal of Electronic Governance, 5*(1), 82–98.

Mirani, L. (2013, March 29). Iceland's Experiment with Crowd-sourcing Its Constitution Just Died. *Quartz*. Retrieved April 29, 2019, from https://qz.com/68910/icelands-experiment-with-crowd-sourcing-its-constitution-just-died/.

Mo, J., Sarkar, S., Meno Mo, J., Sarkar, S., & Menon, S. (2018). Know When to Run Recommendations in Crowdsourcing Contests. *MIS Quarterly, 42*(3), 919–944.

Nambisan, S. (2002). Designing Virtual Customer Environments for New Product Development – Toward a Theory. *Academy of Management Review, 27*, 392–413.

Nambisan, S., & Baron, R. A. (2010). Different Roles, Different Strokes: Organizing Virtual Customer Environments to Promote Two Types of Customer Contributions. *Organization Science, 21*, 554–572.

Nickerson, J. A., & Zenger, T. R. (2004). A Knowledge-Based Theory of the Firm: The Problem Solving Perspective. *Organization Science, 15*(6), 617–632.

Nickerson, J. A., Wuebker, R., & Zenger, T. (2017). Problems, Theories, and Governing the Crowd. *Strategic Organization, 15*(2), 275–288.

Piezunka, H., & Dahlander, L. (2015). Distant Shar, Narrow Attention: How Crowding Alters Organizations' Filtering of Suggestions in Crowdsourcing. *Academy of Management Journal, 58*(3), 856–880.

Piller, F. T., & Walcher, D. (2006). Toolkits for Idea Competitions: A Novel Method to Integrate Users in New Product Development. *R&D Management, 36*, 307–318.

Pisano, G. P., & Verganti, R. (2008). Which Kind of Collaboration Is Right for You? *Harvard Business Review, 86*(12), 78–86.

Poetz, M. K., & Schreier, M. (2012). The Value of Crowdsourcing: Can Users Really Compete with Professionals in Generating New Product Ideas? *Journal of Product Innovation Management, 29*(2), 245–256.

Porter, A. J., Tuertscher, P., & Huysman, M. (2019). Proceedings of the 34th European Group for Organizational Studies (EGOS) Colloquium, 2018.

Prahalad, C. K., & Ramaswamy, V. (2000). Co-opting Customer Experience. *Harvard Business Review, 78*(1), 79–87.

Price, V. (2009). Citizens Deliberating Online: Theory and Some Evidence. In T. Davies & S. Noveck (Eds.), *Online Deliberation: Design, Research, and Practice*. Chicago: University of Chicago Press.

Riedl, C., & Seidel, V. P. (2018). Learning from Mixed Signals in Online Innovation Communities. *Organization Science, 29*(6), 1010–1032.

Ranade, G. V., & Varshney, L. R. (2018). The Role of Information Patterns in Designing Crowdsourcing Contests. In C. Tucci, A. Afuah, & G. Viscusi (Eds.), *Creating and Capturing Value Through Crowdsourcing*. Oxford: Oxford Press.

Rittel, H. W., & Webber, M. M. (1973). Dilemmas in a General Theory of Planning. *Policy Sciences, 4*, 155–169.

Roth, Y., Petavy, F., & de Matos, M. B. (2016). The State of Crowdsourcing in 2016. eYaka 2016 Crowdsourcing Report (eyaka.com).

Saebo, O., Rose, J., & Flak, L. S. (2008). The Shape of eParticipation: Characterizing an Emerging Research Area. *Government Information Quarterly, 25*(3), 400–428.

Sawhney, M., Verona, G., & Prandelli, E. (2005). Collaborating to Create: The Internet as a Platform for Customer Engagement in Product Innovation. *Journal of Interactive Marketing, 19*(4), 4–17.

Schemmann, B., Herrmann, A. M., Chappin, A., & Heimeriks, G. J. (2016). Crowdsourcing Ideas: Involving Ordinary Users in the Ideation Phase of New Product Development. *Research Policy, 45*(6), 1145–1154.

Seidl, D., Whittington, R., & Von Krogh, G. (Eds.). (2018). *Cambridge Handbook on Open Strategy*. Cambridge: Cambridge University Press.

Simon, H. A. (1973). The Structure of Ill-structured Problems. *Artificial Intelligence, 4*(3–4), 181–201.

Simonton, D. K. (2011). Creativity and Discovery as Blind Variation: Campbell's (1960) BVSR Model After the Half-Century Mark. *Review of General Psychology, 15*(2), 158–174.

Staw, B. M. (1990). An Evolutionary Approach to Creativity and Innovation. In M. West & J. L. Farr (Eds.), *Innovation and Creativity at Work: Psychological and Organizational Strategies* (pp. 287–308). Chichester, UK: Wiley.

Sullivan, E. (2010). A Group Effort: More Companies Are Turning to the Wisdom of the Crowd to Find Ways to Innovate. *Marketing News, 44*(2), 22–28.

Surowiecki, J. (2005). *The Wisdom of Crowds*. New York: Random House.

Terwiesch, C., & Ulrich, K. T. (2009). *Innovation Tournaments: Creating and Selecting Exceptional Opportunities*. Boston, MA: Harvard Business Review Press.

Terwiesch, C., & Xu, Y. (2008). Innovation Contests, Open Innovation, and Multiagent Problem Solving. *Management Science, 54*(9), 1529–1543.

Tucci, C. L., Afuah, A., & Viscusi, G. (2018). Introduction to Creating and Capturing Value Through Crowdsourcing. In C. L. Tucci, A. Afuah, & G. Viscusi (Eds.), *Creating and Capturing Value Through Crowdsourcing*. Oxford: Oxford Press.

Venkataramani, V., Sherf, E. N., & Tangirala, S. (2019, April 8). Research: Why Managers Ignore Employees' Ideas. *Harvard Business Review*. Retrieved from https://hbr.org/2019/04/research-why-managers-ignore-employees-ideas.

Viscusi, G., & Tucci, C. L. (2018). Three's a Crowd. In C. L. Tucci, A. Afuah, & G. Viscusi (Eds.), *Creating and Capturing Value Through Crowdsourcing* (pp. 39–57). Oxford: Oxford University Press.

Von Hippel, E. (1986). Lead Users: A Source of Novel Product Concepts. *Management Science, 32*(7), 791–805.

Von Hippel, E. (2005). *Democratizing Innovation*. Cambridge: MIT Press.

Von Hippel, E. (2016). *Free Innovation*. Cambridge: MIT Press.

Vukovic, M., Mariana, L., & Laredo, J. (2009). PeopleCloud for the Globally Integrated Enterprise. In D. Asit et al. (Eds.), *Service-Oriented Computing*. Berlin; Heidelberg: Springer-Verlag.

West, J., & Bogers, M. (2014). Leveraging External Sources of Innovation: A Review of Research on Open Innovation. *Journal of Product Innovation Management, 31*(4), 814–831.

West, J., & Sims, J. (2018). How Firms Leverage Crowds and Communities for Open Innovation. In C. Tucci, A. Afuah, & G. Viscusi (Eds.), *Creating and Capturing Value Through Crowdsourcing*. Oxford: Oxford Press.

Whittington, R. (2015). The Massification of Strategy. *British Journal of Management, 26*(S1), S13–S16.

Whittington, R., Cailluet, L., & Yakis-Douglas, B. (2011). Opening Strategy: Evolution of a Precarious Profession. *British Journal of Management, 22*(3), 531–544.

Valentine, M. A., Retelny, D., To, A., Rahmati, N., Doshi, T., & Bernstein, M. S. (2017, May). Flash Organizations: Crowdsourcing Complex Work by Structuring Crowds as Organizations. In *Proceedings of the 2017 CHI Conference on Human Factors in Computing Systems* (pp. 3523–3537). New York: ACM.

Whittington, R. (2019). *Opening Strategy: Professional Strategists and Practice Change, 1960 to Today*. Oxford: Oxford Press.

Wilson, M., Robson, K., & Botha, E. (2017). Crowdsourcing in a Time of Empowered Stakeholders: Lessons from Crowdsourcing Campaigns. *Business Horizons, 60*(2), 247–253.

Woolley, A., & Fuchs, E. (2011). Collective Intelligence in the Organization of Science. *Organization Science, 22*(5), 1359–1367.

Woolley, A. W., Chabris, C. F., Pentland, A., Hashmi, N., & Malone, T. W. (2010). Evidence for a Collective Intelligence Factor in the Performance of Human Groups. *Science, 330*(6004), 686–688.

Zhao, Y., & Zhu, Q. (2014). Evaluation on Crowdsourcing Research: Current Status and Future Direction. *Information Systems Frontier, 16*, 417–434.

2

Our Research on Comparing Idea-Sharing Versus Unmindcuffing the Crowd

In this chapter, we describe our field research in which we compare the rated innovativeness of crowds who were exposed to the Idea-Sharing process against "unmindcuffed" crowds. To just collect the data, we had to embark on a painstaking five-year effort of data collection and analysis because all third-party vendors were using the Idea-Sharing process. We describe details about how we ran the 20 crowdsourcing events in the field with partner organizations, making changes to third-party software to create the condition of unmindcuffing the crowd. We randomly assigned events to either the Idea-Sharing or the Unmindcuffed condition. We had executives rate the ideas for their novelty, implementability, and competitive advantage. We found that the unmindcuffed crowds produce more innovative solutions than the more traditionally used Idea-Sharing process.

In Chap. 1, we contended that the current Idea-Sharing process of crowdsourcing is inadequate, especially for crowds asked to solve wicked problems. We suggested that the current approach is "mindcuffing" crowds by not allowing them to offer alternatives to the initial problem, to share their entire gamut of knowledge about the problem (not just ideas for solving the problem), and to learn from each other to collectively produce new solution-ideas. In Table 2.1, we remind the reader of the limits imposed by the Idea-Sharing process.

We had two Research questions in our Research. The first was simply:

Question 1: If we remove the constraints (i.e., mindcuffs) of the Idea-Sharing Process, will a crowd be able to generate more innovative solutions than a crowd using the Idea Sharing process, especially when the problem is wicked?

Table 2.1 Summary constraints imposed by Idea-Sharing process

Crowd does not redefine problem to increase chance of an innovative solution
Crowd's role is to offer ideas they conceived of prior to posting, limiting any innovation possibilities created by interacting with diverse perspectives
Crowd only shares refinements of others' ideas if allowed, limiting possibilities of new ideas when synthesizing from multiple ideas
Crowd does not integrate others' ideas into a new idea
Crowd does not share personal knowledge they have about the problem unless it is part of an idea

With this question we ascertain whether taking off the mindcuffs of the Idea-Sharing Process leads to chaos and unbridled useless dribble from the crowd as some Researchers have suggested. Inversely, we explore whether taking off the mindcuffs leads to more innovative solutions with wicked problems, despite those who would say that it cannot be done.

If Question 1 shows that taking off the mindcuffs leads to more innovative solutions, the obvious next question we address is:

Question 2. How? What exactly does the crowd do to generate these more innovative ideas when they're not told what to do?

In this chapter, we take the reader down the journey of how we answered the two questions. To just collect the data, we had to embark on a painstaking five-year effort of data collection and analysis because all third-party vendors were constraining the crowds like that in Table 2.1.[1] We had to first design a platform that did not mindcuff the crowd. Then we had to convince organizations to conduct a crowdsourcing event in which participants were asked to provide innovative solutions to wicked problems (even though most organizations do not normally use crowds for that purpose). We assigned some organizations to the unconstrained (or "unmindcuffed") way of doing crowdsourcing and others to the traditional Idea-Sharing process. We had to have many instances of each of the two types of crowds that would allow rigorous comparison with objective data collection. Finally, we had to successfully obtain enough people to contribute to the crowdsourcing event.

To do all this, we partnered with two business schools' open innovation centers to find organizations willing to sponsor innovation crowdsourcing events with us. For crowdsourcing events that followed the Idea-Sharing process, we obtained software from a third-party innovation provider (Brightideas, Inc.) and used the default configuration since most customers use the software for Idea-Sharing crowdsourcing. For innovation crowdsourcing events in which crowds were unmindcuff, we had to redesign the software and user interface to remove the constraints and yet kept the software looking as similar as possible to Idea-Sharing.

Finally, when all the crowdsourcing events—Idea-Sharing and Unmindcuffed—were completed, the data regarding how the crowd behaved and what the crowd produced were compared across these two types. We conducted a simple comparison: which crowds produced more innovative ideas? Did those crowds unconstrained from the Idea-Sharing process generate more innovative ideas?

Answering these questions was just the first step. Our real quest was taken up if the unconstrained crowds produced more innovative solutions: how did they do it? The "How?" was the key question that we were after and what we describe in the chapters to follow. This exploration of the "how" uncovered for us what the crowds were contributing differently in terms of knowledge and how was that leading to the emergence of innovative solutions. This required that we get into the details of reading and understanding the actual posts made by crowd members, what are referred to as "**trace data**". This data forensics gave us a fine-grained view of how crowds behave in terms of the knowledge they share in their posts, as a result, how innovative ideas emerge.

In this chapter, we begin by describing the field Research we ran to test the hypothesis that crowds not constrained to the Idea-Sharing process will outperform crowds constrained by an *Idea-Sharing* process. Then, we explain how we construct our trace data and the analyses we did. As a teaser, we describe one example of our findings already published. In each chapter in the rest of the book, we unfold each new finding based on our trace data analysis that allows us to understand better **how** the crowd behaves to create innovative ideas when they are allowed to do so.

2.1 Figuring Out How We Were Going to Compare Idea-Sharing Versus Unconstraining the Crowd

We initially thought that we could simply access data from one of the third-party innovation-platform vendors since each of them already uses software platforms to conduct their crowdsourcing events for a multitude of clients. Our thinking was that a vendor might have run a number of different types of crowdsourcing events such that some of the events were conducted with the mindcuffs removed so we could compare the results of the different types of crowdsourcing. The comparison we were interested in was ratings (on a

1-to-7 scale) of the ideas proposed by the crowd indicating, for each idea, how the idea was judged by executives on each of three key dimensions of innovativeness: if the idea was novel for their organization's industry, feasibly implemented, and useful, that is, likely to lead to a competitive advantage or support outcomes important to the organization. We also thought that most vendors must have run a substantial number of crowdsourcing events explicitly to solve wicked problems.

We approached the six largest third-party innovation-platform vendors and obtained their permission to look at lists of crowdsourcing events they had run in the past. We were stunned (and severely disappointed) to discover that *none* of the third-party vendors had run crowdsourcing events for organizations in which the crowds were asked to solve wicked problems and allowed to do so without the mindcuffs imposed by following Idea-Sharing process. Moreover, rarely were ideas formally evaluated with ratings along the three key dimensions of innovativeness: novelty, implementability, and utility. In fact, we found that almost all of the crowdsourcing events presented problems that were componentized or purely art-based (e.g., beer bottle designs), and thus not wicked. And, on top of that, in all the crowdsourcing events that had been run by the vendors, the crowd was instructed and limited to only offering ideas or commenting on others' ideas with little leeway to share any knowledge they wanted in any form they wanted. We recognize that solving independent components of a problem can and may be done using the Idea-Sharing process since objective criteria (such as speed of an algorithm) can be used. However, we are focused at the other end of the spectrum with wicked problems which are ill-structured, ill-defined and with a multitude of interdependent components and conflicting objectives that need simultaneous consideration. For solving such wicked problems we suggest that the ideal point shown in Fig. 2.1 requires ensuring as many people as possible feel able to contribute in a way that allows them to collectively produce the most innovative solutions.

As shown in Fig. 2.1, crowdsourcing events conducted to this point in public as well as with organizations were not near the *ideal* point (green dot) for solving wicked problems to allow us to even begin to determine how crowds unmindcuffed shape their own Collective Production to generate more innovative ideas.

Disappointed with our first foray into locating existing data on past crowdsourcing events from third-party innovation-platform vendors, we broadened our shar for other sources of such data. We looked at websites used by companies to run their own crowdsourcing for innovation. We also sought out user-innovation communities and online communities and discussion forums in

2 Our Research on Comparing Idea-Sharing Versus Unmindcuffing...

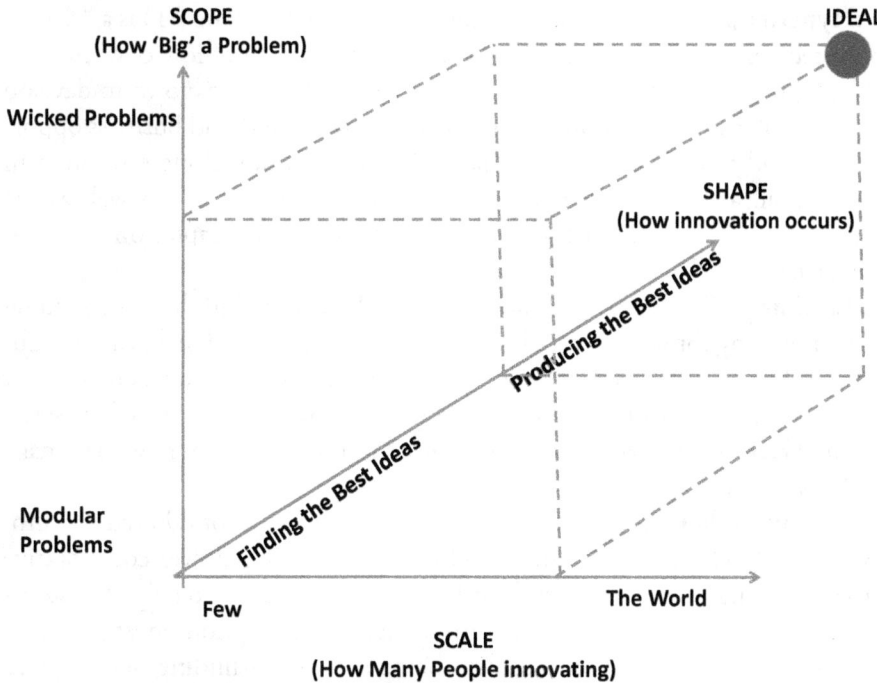

Fig. 2.1 The three dimensions of crowdsourcing

which hobbyists share creative ideas (e.g., Youtube, Thingiverse, Propellerhead, etc.). We found that there was little collective solving of a wicked problem in such contexts. Even in online "knowledge production" communities like Wikipedia and Open Source Software, innovative problem-solving is a small part of the communities' task. These knowledge production communities are focused on work division and aggregation of knowledge from different sources and rationalizing the aggregated knowledge.[2] Therefore, once again, the data wasn't available to allow us to determine if releasing crowds from the Idea-Sharing mindcuffs could enhance the innovativeness of the solutions for wicked problems. In effect, we found that all the crowds representing state-of-practice were in the lower left-hand corner of Fig. 2.1—presenting a very limited set of invited crowds to contribute ideas to solve simpler problems.

We did find exciting one-off case studies where participants weren't as restricted as in Idea-Sharing crowdsourcing. These we bring to bear at various points throughout the book to illustrate what is possible with these crowds. Such cases serve as rich anecdotes that are then followed by more rigorous evidence for how unconstrained crowds with no mindcuffs behave. These case studies will be used to illustrate some of our points:

Hyperloop Transportation Technology, Inc. (HyperloopTT) is a "crowd-powered" organization working on the wicked problem of low-cost, sustainable, high-speed transportation systems. They are using the crowd to develop the technology (a hyperloop), open up new markets, and find business opportunities and new partners, in exchange for stock options.[3] Here we look in some detail at the roles that HTT crowds serve for Chap. 7 as well as the unique ways in which HTT manages the crowd in our chapter on "How to Manage Crowds".

Li&Fung. Fashion and retail company Li&Fung Ltd has been doing crowdsourcing for wicked problems for years. We described in an earlier publication how Li&Fung describe six different criteria for employees to attempt to meet when suggesting solutions to internal crowdsourcing problem statements.[4] Here we use Li&Fung to provide additional details on how to manage an internal crowd.

Optum Behavioral Health Care. Optum is part of United Health. Working closely with Optum, we helped them run a first-ever collaborative crowdsourcing event with their health care practitioners who helped customers match behavioral health needs with service delivery options meeting insurance guidelines. The wicked problem being solved was finding new ways to better serve their customers. The event helped the executive committee identify seven new approaches to better serve the customer in ways that had not been considered previously. We have published parts of this case in an article in *Human Resources Management*[5] but in this book, we dive deeply into the data of how discussions evolved, described in Chap. 7.

The United States Agency for International Development (USAID) ran a large crowdsourcing event in 2010, the first-ever global IBM Innovation Jam. The wicked problem was to help identify ways in which USAID should offer development support to those in developing countries. We were able to obtain the actual discussion threads, the final report which detailed what the USAID staff had learned and found innovative, as well as interviews with those involved in the planning. This is the first time these data are presented; see Chap. 3.

New Zealand Landcare Research Inc. (Landcare) is responsible for helping the country remove the threat posed by pests, such as possums and rats, who have decimated the native species in the country. We worked with Landcare personnel to prepare and offer a collaborative crowdsourcing event with the public, and then had a variety of stakeholders provide the innovation forecasting of the ideas produced. We have written a case study about this event.[6] In Chap. 7, for the first time, we are able to present a detailed analysis of how the discussion ensued to lead to innovative ideas.

2.2 How We Created the Crowds and Data

Because the crowds didn't exist, we had to actually create the crowds to generate the data to test our hypothesis. It took us almost five years to create the crowds to have enough data to test our hypothesis. All the crowds needed to come from real-world field settings to ensure practical implications. So, we worked with multiple and diverse organizations.

We ran 20 real-world Innovation Crowdsourcing Events with 20 different organizations. For each event, we worked with the organization's chief executive to identify a strategic problem that was "wicked" in the sense that it was hard to ascertain the correct answer beforehand (if at all). The problem also needed to be one that the organization had tried to address previously but had been unsuccessful to do so. This meant that the organization's appetite for solutions from the crowd would be such that crowds' solutions would not be rejected outright with creative solutions welcome.

For each strategic "wicked" problem to be solved for each organization, we then helped to identify ten online interest groups which formed the starting basis for identifying crowds interested in solving the problem. In other words, we had to identify the potential crowd unique to each wicked problem in order to ensure that diverse perspectives were brought to bear. The wicked problem statement was then broadcast to each online interest group with the permission of the administrator of the interest group. The message that was broadcast was the problem statement with a solicitation to join the crowdsourcing event, with a link to the website to register for the crowdsourcing event. We assigned each crowdsourcing event to one of two websites, where one website described the Idea-Sharing process the crowd should follow and the other website provided instructions that were much less constrained.

We made sure that all the crowdsourcing events, regardless of the process they followed, were consistent in their duration window (7–10 days) in order for us to avoid any effects of different durations on the innovativeness of the solutions. After each event ended, we gave the ideas generated by the crowd, to the executive at the organization who offered the wicked problem that was posed to the crowd. The executives were not aware of whether the crowd that had generated these ideas in response to their problem had followed the Idea-Sharing process or the unconstrained unmindcuffed process. We requested each of the executives to forecast to what extent each idea they received was: (a) novel (i.e., hadn't been tried by the organization previously), (b) feasible, and (c) provided a competitive advantage in the marketplace. The "innovativeness" score used in our analysis is an aggregate of these three measures.

Table 2.2 Example of wicked problems from the organizations in our field research

How do we remove the pests in New Zealand?
How should we spend our USAID funds for next year to have the greatest impact on developing countries?
What are some of the services-led strategies that our company can adapt to transition from a hardware and software-centric business to a services-centric business that creates new markets and new customers?
What novel solutions can an international courier service provider offer US-based small businesses to support their worldwide shipping, logistics, and business needs?
What new value/services can the company offer on its new platform to create new market segments?
How might mobile technology be used to improve the employee and client experience?
How do we become more effective as a managed care company focusing on improving the member experience?

From running the 20 different crowdsourcing events, we had compiled an extensive log database about actions crowd participants take during the events, specifically, the knowledge they contribute and when they contribute. It is this data we analyze when we speak about the trace data, examining differences in the trace data before ideas judged as more or less innovative.

In addition to the 20 Crowdsourcing Events from which we derived the quantitative actions and results data, the qualitative data from the five longitudinal case studies of crowd participation mentioned above help to round out the results. We use these case studies to deepen our understanding of what crowds do when they are unconstrained. These crowds help us tell you stories of what happens when the mindcuffs are removed from the crowds. All said, we had the opportunity to observe, collect data from, and analyze the knowledge behaviors of 25 different crowds solving a variety of wicked problems pertaining to society and business. A few specific examples of these wicked problems are shown in Table 2.2.

2.3 Details About the Field Research Study

To test our hypothesis for comparing the constraints of Idea-Selecting against the unmindcuffed condition, we were connected to 20 organizations primarily from open innovation Research centers at several universities. We partnered with the faculty at the Research centers who were engaging their students in doing open innovation projects with the companies. We asked the faculty if we could add an additional open innovation aspect to the project the students were doing. Normally, in such projects, a company executive prepares a wicked-type problem and the faculty assigns the problem statement to a team of business students who learn more about the company on their own, brainstorm in their teams, and then present a single suggested solution to the problem at the end of the semester. We asked the faculty to add in a crowdsourcing component early in the team's work. The teams were informed that the crowdsourcing was to be used as additional input for their project. For us, the student project engagement permitted us the entry point to conduct a crowdsourcing for innovation event for each organization. The teams were not required to use the input as part of their own project solution. We shared the idea solutions with each executive in a separate spreadsheet.

We worked with the organization executives to ensure that all the problems identified by the executives were wicked problems they were currently struggling with and required multiple perspectives to solve since there were so many different interdependent elements. Also, we asked that these problems were ones for which they had tried to solve internally and for which they were still struggling to obtain innovative solutions. In crafting the problem statement, we always tried to ensure that the organizations did not ask questions that were subproblems of a larger problem. For example, instead of asking how can we sell existing products to particular market segments, the executives asked what future strategic markets should they address. We then designed the crowdsourcing events to be alike in all aspects except for whether the crowd was asked to follow the Idea-Sharing process or were allowed to share knowledge in an unlimited way. Condition 1 was the control condition which followed the Idea-Sharing process. Condition 2 was our "treatment" condition which we call the Unmindcuffed Condition in which participants were not constrained to post ideas and could share whatever knowledge they wanted, and consider others' knowledge and ideas when formulating their own ideas. How we assigned organizations to the two conditions to remove as much as possible contaminating factors not related to the process is described in Textbox 2.1.

Textbox 2.1 How the 20 Field Crowdsourcing Events Were Assigned to Different Conditions

We collected data over three semesters of classes. In the first year, the faculty member provided us access to six organizations. We assigned them all to the Idea-Selecting condition so we would have a baseline. We had to drop one of the companies because no crowds joined the crowdsourcing event.

(continued)

Textbox 2.1 (continued)

> In the second semester of classes (at a different university), the faculty member provided us with access to six organizations. We had to drop three of the organizations because of the lack of crowd interest. The remaining three were assigned to the Unmindcuffed, Unconstrained condition.
>
> In the third semester, we had access to 14 organizations across two classes. We assigned two to the Idea-Selecting condition based on a coin toss, and the rest to the Unconstrained condition. One from the Idea-Selecting and one from the Unconstrained were dropped for lack of interest.
>
> To control for any selection bias, we control for observable covariates in a (multilevel) regression design.[7]

By the end of our data collection, we had a total of 1720 registered participants across the 20 events, making a total of 2428 contributions. The number of participants for each of the events across the two conditions was about the same (i.e., not statistically significantly different). See Table 2.3 for a summary of allocation for the two conditions.

How the two conditions looked on each of their condition's website are shown in Fig. 2.2.

The interface you see in Fig. 2.2 is for the Unmindcuffed, Unconstrained condition with the yellow balloons highlighting differences with the Idea-Sharing interface. The key differences in the interfaces are:

1. The traditional Idea-Sharing software has *post ideas*. Participants were asked to "post ideas", which fixates them on "ideas" as the only contributable knowledge; in the Unconstrained Condition, a button indicating *post* is attempting to turn the attention of participants away from just ideas.
2. Idea-Sharing condition did not have a Post Types list since only ideas or comments on ideas were allowed; Post Types was introduced in the Unconstrained condition to encourage participants to post other knowledge than just ideas.

Table 2.3 Summary of allocation to conditions

Control/Condition 1	Treatment/Condition 2
Idea-sharing: Crowd limited to posting ideas and comments on ideas	Unmindcuffed: 1's constraints removed and added suggestions to post knowledge about the problem as well as own ideas and integrative ideas
$N = 7$ crowdsourcing events	$N = 13$ crowdsourcing events
Avg number of participants per event: 93.42 (standard deviation = 12.98)	Avg number of participants per event: 82.00 (standard deviation = 9.52)
Total across both conditions: 1720 registered actors making a total of 2428 posts	

2 Our Research on Comparing Idea-Sharing Versus Unmindcuffing...   57

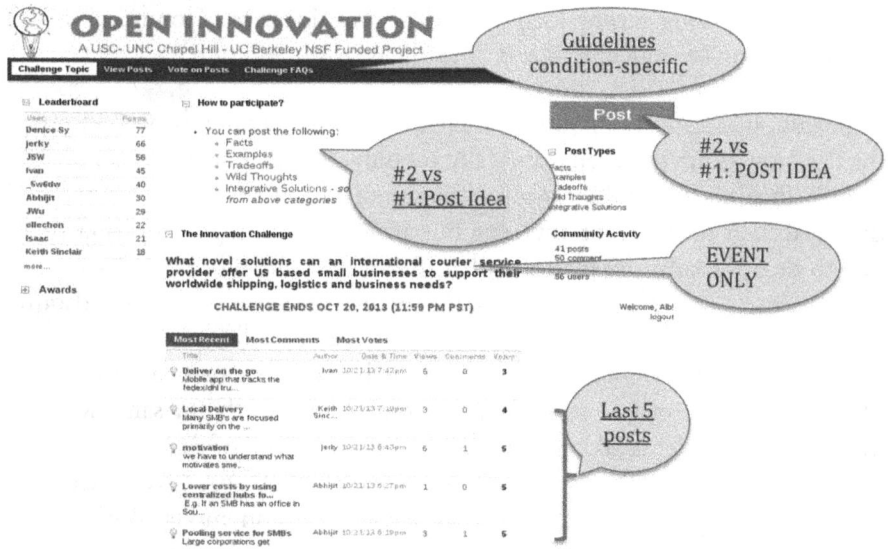

Fig. 2.2 How the different crowds were instructed

3. Correspondingly, the instructions on how to participate are different. For, Idea-Sharing process, the instructions were:

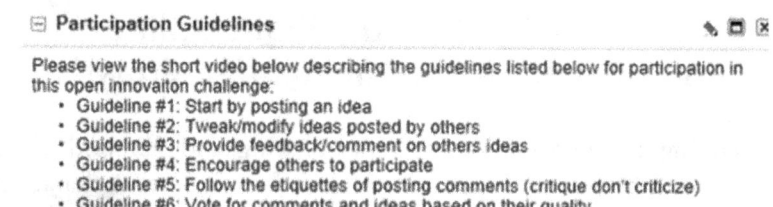

4. In contrast, the instructions for the Unconstrained condition specify that they can post any of the following: facts, examples, tradeoffs, wild thoughts, and integrative solutions. We pilot-tested these instructions to make them as simple as possible to capture the participants' attention to consider posting *any other knowledge* than ideas.
5. For both conditions, there was a leaderboard listing indicating individuals who had the most points where points were based on posting ideas in Condition 1 and posting ideas and commenting on others' threads in Condition 2. The highest ranked at the end of the challenge received a small award such as corporate swag. Challenge FAQs were the same for

both conditions except focusing on posting ideas for Condition 1 and focusing on sharing any type of knowledge for Condition 2.

In sum, it is critical to point out that we had to configure the web interface for the crowdsourcing events specially to allow for the unconstrained condition 2 since *none* of the innovation vendors (e.g., Hyve, Spigit, BrightIdea) designed their software for anything but an Idea-Sharing process. That is, we had to design a software platform that didn't exist, in addition to partnering with business schools and helping the organizations run the crowdsourcing events.

While we have focused on the differences between the two conditions, the 20 crowdsourcing events were in most respects run exactly the same way (see Table 2.4). The events all lasted about the same amount of time (7–10 days). All participants were asked to limit their post length to 142 characters to foster skimming by others. All participants were anonymous. Both conditions allowed for the knowledge shared to be transparent in a way to influence others' in the crowd. Finally, incentives were similar. Because of the extensive similarities among the 20 events, crowd participants, MBA students, and the executives did not report on differences between the events.

2.4 Why Anonymity and Persistent Visibility Matters in Creating the Right Online Environment for Unmindcuffed Crowds

In describing the two conditions—Idea-Sharing and Unmindcuffed—we have indicated how the instructions differed. Two important characteristics, though, were the same: anonymity and persistent visibility. We explain below why we believe these are particularly important for the unmindcuffed crowds. While Idea-Sharing crowdsourcing events usually have these two characteristics, we argue that these two characteristics take on extra importance for unmindcuffed crowds.

2.4.1 Why Anonymity Matters in Unmindcuffed Crowds

Crowds need to feel psychologically safe to contribute anything and everything with a promise of quasi—(if not full) anonymity.[12] Anonymity is the ability of members of a group to contribute comments without being identified.[13] Researchers have shown that anonymity matters in online

Table 2.4 What's the same across the crowdsourcing events

Screening criteria for organizations	Geographically distributed, **Prior experience with crowdsourcing** so would find the idea of applying Crowdsourcing to Wicked Problems an interesting one, and Willing to follow the guidelines below. Many identified by reaching out to Open Innovation classes taught at other universities over a two-year period.
Incentives	**Coopetition**: Small in-kind brand or impact awards for (1) top ideas as judged by sponsor ($300) and (2) posting on others' posts.[8]
Crowdsourcing event problem statement	CEO or chief innovation officer in each company asked to identify a "**strategic problem** benefiting from multiple perspectives on the problem and involving consideration of a wide range of issues for implementation and competitive advantage".
Procedural guidance	Detailed info about strategic problem was included in an FAQ. Instructions about how to post, what leaderboard meant, rewards, and how innovative ideas would be rated. Each condition had more detailed explanations for additional suggestions provided such as what to post, e.g., different ways to describe problem as you see it.
Participants	10 Listserves identified by executive with people likely to be passionate about topic; event announced on each listserve with permission of listserve administrators with a link to the event.[9]
Registration	Anonymity and pseudo-anonymity were encouraged during registration.[10]
Short length of event	7–10 elapsed days to promote urgency.
Easy engagement	**Standardize** user interface on BrightIdeas.com platform **Limited ALL post lengths to 142 characters** Crowd asked to post ideas for solutions, not necessarily a complete proposal As posts made, actors can choose to offer a comment (add to an existing discussion thread started previously) or start a new discussion thread.
Judging innovative posts	Same executive asked to do **creativity forecasting**[11] sent a spreadsheet at end of non-duplicate ideas to mark forecasts on multiple dimensions (Amabile). Spreadsheet blinded to order in which idea was posted, which pseudoanonymous person posted it and # of votes it received

groups tasked with problem-solving including removing individual background characteristics from the knowledge-based interaction[14] which might harm creativity.[15] That is, when participants are aware of the background of the individual who contributes knowledge, biases are introduced based on assessments about knowledge credibility, power, and influence which may affect willingness to contribute new knowledge.[16] These assessments will cause participants to attend to some knowledge and ignore other knowledge, decreasing the likelihood that the participants will attend to new knowledge especially if it pushes or counters their cognitive position.

Moreover, simply because an individual's background indicates a particular expertise (such as advanced technical/educational training or experience with repeatedly solving similar wicked problems) does not necessarily mean that those with less formal expertise about the problem have nothing to contribute. Someone with less formal expertise about the problem is not educated in existing perspectives and thus are more likely to offer knowledge not typically associated with formal expertise.[17] Consequently, innovative thinking can be stimulated possibly even to a greater degree from those without formal expertise in a particular discipline. Sometimes those impacted are more likely to solve the wicked problem due to their expedient and pressing need.[18] Such individuals can provide personal experiences with the problem, wild idea thoughts about solutions without worrying about feasibility, and concerns they have which may raise issues not previously considered by others.

Another advantage of anonymity is that, once knowledge is anonymously shared, that knowledge is disassociated from the individual. In other words, the veracity and usefulness of the knowledge are not associated with who contributes that knowledge. Rather it is about the knowledge content itself, since the contributor is not known personally.[19]

Another value of anonymity is that individuals in the crowd are not compelled to conform to the majority view if they are not inclined to do so.[20] Similarly, anonymity can have the effect of reducing evaluation apprehension. That is, when people are in anonymous contexts, they are less likely to be affected by what others think of them, encouraging them to express their divergent perspectives.[21] Therefore, unmindcuffing of the crowd should be supported by allowing for anonymity.

2.4.2 Why Persistent Visibility of Knowledge Matters in Unmindcuffed Crowds

The knowledge a crowd shares can be made to be "persistently visible", which refers to the ability for all participants to have continuous access to the knowledge shared.[22] The persistently visible knowledge increases the potential for others in the crowd to be influenced and inspired by the knowledge, leading to contributions of new knowledge and novel recombinations of that knowledge.[23] Research has found that persistent visibility allows the knowledge that is shared to take on a life of its own,[24] allowing the crowd to contribute with the audience absent or invisible.[25] This allows the explicated knowledge to be reflected upon and allowed to stimulate others at their own pace and slivers of time.[26] This also allows participants to interpret the knowledge shared in whatever way they prefer, before posting their own contribution.[27] Because the knowledge that has been shared is available for later review, individuals can engage the knowledge shared in a personal mental dialogue to recalibrate their thoughts, compare the knowledge against newly formed conclusions, and reevaluate newly proposed solutions vis-à-vis existing knowledge before posting.[28] Participants do not interact with others personally, rather they "interact" with others' visible knowledge, and as it is persistent, they don't need to be in a hurry to digest it and respond to it. This self-paced asynchronous mental dialogue encourages participants to think of the knowledge they are reading as having partial and provisional interpretations, often fragmentary, and open to change depending on evolving understandings (Baralou and Tsoukas 2015; Ewenstein and Whyte 2009; Nicolini et al. 2012).

Consequently, unlike teams or most conversations for innovation generation, the knowledge content written becomes the primary (and perhaps the sole) crowd input for Collective Production. To be influenced by others' knowledge requires individuals to read them.

2.5 How Outcomes from Crowdsourcing Field Events Were Analyzed

At the end of each innovation crowdsourcing event, we reviewed the list of ideas offered and found many ideas were duplicated. In fact, out of 1198 total ideas, only 297 were non-duplicates or were not greatly semantically overlapping. In other words, we wanted to identify and rate ideas that were very different from each other. For example, early in the event, a participant might recommend that the company should pursue a particular partnership or create an innovation center, or offer customers a particular new line of products, and then later in the event, a different participant offers the same idea. We took only the first idea of the duplicates. In a couple of the events, there were more than 20 non-duplicate ideas. We then randomly selected 20 to cap the number of ideas an executive had to forecast to reduce the crowding effect.[29] In total, we had 297 ideas forecasted for their innovativeness. Textbox 2.2 explains the forecasting process followed by executives to ascertain innovativeness of ideas obtained from the crowds. The box also explains how we analyzed the ideas' innovativeness difference between Idea-Sharing crowds and Unmindcuffed crowds.

Textbox 2.2 How We Measured and Analyzed Innovativeness of Ideas Emerging from Crowds

The traditional way to measure the innovativeness of ideas in the Research is to undertake what is called "forecasting".[30] The executive who constructed the innovation problem is asked to do forecasting—estimate the impact of the idea on the organization—since the executive had personal prior experience attempting to solve the problem and was at a strategic-enough level in the organization to understand the value to the company for solving the problem. Each executive is asked to forecast three aspects of the ideas obtained from the crowdsourcing event related to their wicked problem based on 7-point scales: novelty of the idea relative to prior solutions tried; usefulness of the idea in terms of competitive advantage to the firm if the idea was implemented; and the ease with which the idea could be feasibly implemented.[31] Innovativeness was measured as the aggregate (sum of each raw score weighted by its factor score) so that a low score on any single dimension leads to a low score of innovativeness. The executive is blind to which condition to ensure that there is no potential bias in judgment.

To assess if condition 1 (Idea-Sharing) and condition 2 (Unmindcuffed/Unconstrained) differed in the innovativeness of the ideas posted by the crowds, we used a multilevel modeling statistical technique which allowed us to include variables that might also affect the innovativeness of ideas. We included the amount of participation of the person who posted the idea to control for whether ideas were more innovative just because someone with a lot of activity posted the idea. We controlled for the time order of the idea since ideas posted later might be better, or ideas posted at the beginning of the event might be better. Neither of these control variables was significant. We also controlled for the total number of posts in the event in case events with more posts have more innovative ideas. We controlled for the number of ideas that were rated since, as we mentioned above, some of the events had over 20 non-duplicate ideas. Finally, we controlled for problem complexity or unrestrictiveness of the problem, measured[32] as the degree to which the challenge problem was left unconstrained such that challenge problems were more open if they did not constrain the solution to a particular product and/or market and/or a time frame. It was coded as 0 if time constrained (mostly do immediately) and specific to a product/market (e.g., current cloud offering or for 18–35 years segment), 1 if either time constrained and specific to a product/market, and 2 if problem is *not* time constrained *and* does not specify a particular product or market.

To determine if the results are significant, one first looks at the model fit statistics comparing the controls only model to the model with the controls and the variables of interest—in this case, whether the condition was unmindcuffed or Idea-Sharing. Fit is better with smaller values of the negative log-likelihood or twice the negative log-likelihood (−2 log-likelihood). Akaike's Information Criterion (AICc) is another model fit indicator. The model that has the smallest AICc value indicates the better fit, that is, has better power to explain the variation in the dependent variable (innovativeness of an idea). A difference of ten in AICc between models indicates they are significantly differentiable in their explanatory ability.[33]

2.6 Results of the Analysis: Does Unmindcuffing Crowds Lead to More Innovative Outcomes?

The results of comparing the innovativeness of ideas from the two conditions are shown in Table 2.4. Whether the crowd was in Condition 1 (Idea-Sharing) or Condition 2 (Unmindcuffed) had a significant effect on innovation. The difference is not only statistically significant but a magnitude of difference, that is, the unmindcuffed crowds produced ideas that were discernably more innovative. That is, on the scale of 1 to 7, the improvement of 3.07 in rated ideas is a 42% jump in the innovativeness score.

The way to read Table 2.5 is to first find the variable which is of chief concern: "Was crowd in unmindcuffed condition?" That is, this variable indicates whether the rated idea was generated from one of the 13 crowds that was unconstrained or the 7 which was constrained to the Idea-Sharing process. The positive direction of the estimate of 3.07 indicates that the ideas generated from unconstrained crowds were significantly *more* innovative than the ideas generated in the other condition (the Idea-Sharing condition). Practitioners should note that this means scaling up 3 whole points in

Table 2.5 Results of effect of unconstraining crowds on innovativeness of ideas generated

DV = Innovativeness of the idea after a digital trace (N = 297)[a]	Control model (A)	Effect model (B)
Controls		
Event level		
Number of participants in event	0.02*** (0.005)	0.03*** (0.005)
Problem unrestrictiveness in event	−0.43 (0.32)	0.16 (0.32)
Total rated ideas in event	0.22*** (0.02)	0.005 (0.05)
Rated post level		
Time order of rated idea (log)	0.53 (0.31)	0.13 (0.13)
Activity level of crowd actor posting the rated idea	6.48 (3.39)	5.87 (3.12)
Independent variables (event level)		
Was crowd in unmindcuffed condition?		3.07*** (0.59)
Model fit		
−2 residual log-likelihood	1300.51	1275.95
−2 log-likelihood	1283.49	1259.09
AICc	1295.79	1273.49

*$p < 0.05$; **$p < 0.01$; ***$p < 0.001$
[a]Factor Weighted Innovativeness Score = (*factor weight* for novelty × novelty *raw score*) + (*factor weight* for Implementability × implementability *raw score*) + (*factor weight* for competitive advantage × competitive advantage *raw score*)

innovativeness score of ideas. On a 7-point scale of innovativeness, the estimate means that the innovativeness score jumped a 3 whole points (almost 42% more innovative). This is equivalent to say that instead of a good idea the crowd collectively produced an excellent idea, or instead of a poor idea the crowd produced a good idea. The other variables serve as controls. That is, ideas are more innovative from unmindcuffed crowds even after taking a range of alternative interpretations into account (such as the rated idea collectively produced early or late).

2.7 How Do Unmindcuffed Crowds Innovate: Using Trace Data to Reveal What Was Previously Hidden

Our field research demonstrated that the 13 crowds allowed to share knowledge freely and openly were able to generate more ideas that are more innovative on the average than the 7 crowds using the Idea-Sharing process. However, this analysis didn't answer the question: what did the crowds do in order to generate ideas rated higher in innovativeness by the executives? More specifically, how did the crowds behave when liberated to do so?

To address this question, we engaged in a series of analyses to find out what exactly the crowds were doing to generate these more innovative ideas. We constructed trace data from the log files that recorded the knowledge actions of the crowd, that is, each entry in the log file indicating what was posted, in what order, and by whom. Textbox 2.3 explains the way we used trace data.

Textbox 2.3   Why and How We Constructed and Used Trace Data

Why We Used Trace Data

We are inspired by the career work of Abbott (described most recently in 2001).[34] Abbott argues that there are two ways of seeing historical processes (traces are historical processes since they represent what the crowd did). One way is to see the process as successive outcomes are listed in an effort to find causes for the outcomes. The other "focuses on narratives and aims to find typical patterns" over time such that it has an "implicit logic running from start to finish" with an inherent purpose (p. 164).

In our analysis of trace data, we look for the inherent patterns explaining the logic of the process that the crowds were using when they were allowed to be unconstrained. We anticipate multiple such patterns, with perhaps multiple different logics. We applied a number of different sequence methods looking for these patterns, ranging from Variable Length Markov Models[35] and process

---

(continued)

Textbox 2.3 (continued)

modeling.[36] The most easily interpretable methodology we found was the use of sequence analysis in which we organized the data backward from each of the 297 ideas rated for their innovativeness, and then looked at the sequence of posts that preceded the rated idea. In other words, using each rated idea as the end point (outcome), we look at what knowledge action specifically preceded it in different knowledge-action windows (e.g., posts that immediately preceded the rated ideas). We feel that this unique, temporal, yet ephemeral trace analysis is what gives us unique insights into how ideas that are produced by crowds are more innovative.

How We Constructed Trace Data

For both conditions, the posts were displayed in the same way on the homepage of the crowdsourcing event. The last five posts were summarized as the default. Each individual participant in the crowd could also see the five most commented upon posts or the five posts with the most views by clicking on a hyperlink. Clicking on any of the abbreviated post hyperlinks led the participant to a webpage showing the complete post. Clicking on View Posts in the upper part of the screen showed all the posts organized in Discussion Threads. Online discussions have routinely been organized as threaded discussions. Traditionally, a discussion thread consists of an initial post that starts the discussion, and then a set of posts that may reply to the initial post and follow-on posts in the thread. The choice of whether a participant posts to start a new thread or to reply to a pre-existing post as a comment in an existing thread is up to the participant. In innovation crowdsourcing events following the Idea-Sharing approach as in Condition 1, the thread starter is always an Idea, and comments in the thread are always suggestions relating to that idea. In Condition 2, any post can start a thread or be a comment in a thread.

2.7.1 Teaser: Example from Trace Data of One Revelation About How Crowds Innovate

We have published one of our findings using some of the trace data in an earlier study.[37] We find that in some of the crowds, some posts surface the possibility that there are multiple contradictory objectives that needed to be addressed simultaneously to solve the wicked problem. We call these "tradeoffs" that are captured in a textual contribution of members of the crowd. The posting of a tradeoff starts a chain or sequence of posts that eventually lead to an innovative idea being posted. More specifically, in such a knowledge-action sequence, when the tradeoff was followed by a textual contribution by another participant that provides a factual basis for the tradeoff, and is then followed by a less innovative idea for solving the tradeoff, the result is a subsequent contribution that is an idea that is more innovative. This knowledge action as a textual contribution flow is shown in Fig. 2.3, and it is the

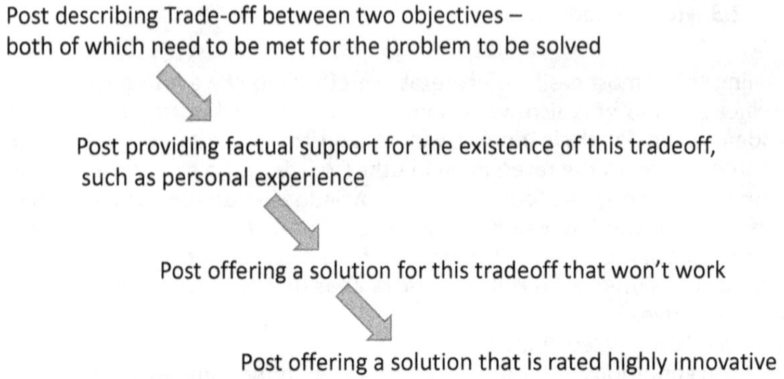

Post describing Trade-off between two objectives –
both of which need to be met for the problem to be solved

⬇

Post providing factual support for the existence of this tradeoff,
such as personal experience

⬇

Post offering a solution for this tradeoff that won't work

⬇

Post offering a solution that is rated highly innovative

Fig. 2.3 Sequence of posts in some crowds identified from trace data (adapted Majchrzak and Malhotra 2016)

fundamental way in which our trace analysis represents the Collective-Production process that we further seek to elaborate in this book.

What is exciting about our use of trace data is that it reveals patterns that previously have not been discovered and highlighted. When a collection of strangers (which is often what open crowds generally are especially if they are scale-free) respond to a wicked problem requiring innovation, and the crowd is allowed to post what knowledge they want, how they want, and when they want to do it, **they don't just post ideas**. They have a lot more to say about the problem and how the solution should be collectively produced. It is clear from our analysis that the crowd pays attention to other posts even when every member of the crowd only participates in a sliver of time. And they aren't just building on others' ideas, by joining their ideas into amalgamated solutions, as many people suggest happens in brainstorming when one builds on others' ideas. They are taking the knowledge content and the way it has been framed (e.g., as facts or as tradeoffs or as metaphors) and being inspired or stimulated or affected in some way by that knowledge content even though they don't know who made the post. They often challenge and redefine the problem itself, not just blindly following what is posed to them. They invoke others to make associations with their memories and challenge prevailing notions. They do so by paying attention to immediate traces rather than the whole knowledge base of the crowd, assuming that the immediate trace contains the evolved knowledge in real time.

This one exemplary trace pattern we have presented inspired us to conduct more exploration to determine if there were other such reinforcing and amplifying patterns, or even innovation-inhibiting patterns. The more we analyzed the trace data, the more we learned about how crowds innovate when allowed to do so. We continue to be amazed at how crowds of relative strangers asynchronously, yet collectively, inspire each other to be innovative. **This is what the rest of the book is about.** With each chapter, we surface another golden nugget of how crowds collectively inspire each other to innovate, when freed from mindcuffs to do so.

Appendix: Detailed List of Participating Organizations in Field Re

Industry of company	Collaborative innovative challenge question	Reg'd Particip	Total posts	# of Ideas	Rated ideas
Software	What technology could [Co. Name] offer its retail and brand clients that would enable consumers to enjoy all the benefits of online shopping?	48	73	37	8
Telecom infrastructure	What are some of the services-led strategies that our company can adapt to transition from a hardware & software-centric business to a services-centric business that creates new markets and new customers?	65	57	25	6
Courier	What novel solutions can an international courier service provider offer US-based small businesses to support their worldwide shipping, logistics, and business needs?	86	91	49	20
Distribution	What new value/services can the company offer on its new platform to create new market segments?	108	47	37	20
Movie studio	How can [the studio] use its animation characters to create a new entertainment experience for you?	50	112	50	20
Data storage/ analysis	How might mobile technology be used to improve the employee and client experience?	106	19	15	3
Telecom	What would the design of a "trusted open space"—virtually and physically—look like so that companies participating in an R&D ecosystem can achieve benefits from the collaboration?	100	61	11	4

(continued)

(continued)

Industry of company	Collaborative innovative challenge question	Reg'd Particip	Total posts	# of Ideas	Rated ideas
Financial services	What new and innovative services can the [company] offer to attract customers from the millennial generation?	179	368	171	20
Telecom infrastructure	What new and innovative services/products can [Co. Name] provide to its customers using new mobile technologies	61	29	19	5
Industrial products	Identify novel business models to generate new revenue streams within and adjacent to our core business areas.	52	93	54	14
Toys	What new and disruptive products, services and/or business models can [Co. Name] pursue to grow its core brands, build new franchises, markets, and customer bases?	89	46	37	9
Pet products	What new and innovative concepts can [Co. Name] develop for eye-health of dogs and cats?	116	206	66	20
Enterprise software	What new business model can [Co. Name] create to attract new application developers to create and deliver "game-changing" applications, on top of [Co. Name]'s strategic technologies and products?	58	54	31	8
Software	Imagine a sports analytic app that would allow you to manipulate and customize sports analytic data of basketball, baseball, and football. What kind of statistical information would you like to get from the app? How would you like to view/use the app?	61	185	100	20
Financial services	What new strategies can [Co. Name] pursue to serve individual and business customers in middle to high-income segments?	124	136	77	20
Auto manufacture	How can [Co. Name] leverage 3D printing to pursue new services and business models for their parts and accessories business?	69	88	43	20
Industrial product	What new business models and revenue streams can [Co. Name] create in the area of remote service offerings?	100	145	54	20

(continued)

(continued)

Industry of company	Collaborative innovative challenge question	Reg'd Particip	Total posts	# of Ideas	Rated ideas
Health care provider	*How might [Co. Name] create incentives for their loyal customers/patients to encourage a healthier lifestyle?*	74	296	136	20
Software	*What new products and business models can [Co. Name] create for its cloud/social/mobile businesses?*	124	264	136	20
Sports association	*What new revenue streams can [Co. Name] develop to generate funds for its central organization?*	50	58	33	20
	Total	1720	2428	1181	297

Notes

1. IBM Innovation Jams doesn't constrain the crowd exactly as in Table 2.1 because they offer to the crowd a wicked question such as helping Royal Bank of Canada articulate a purpose, vision, values, and priorities for a new competitive era but their discussions are highly moderated, heavy involvement of senior management, and not anonymous, which leaves the crowd not constrained to the Idea-Sharing process, but still constrained. In our final chapter when we discuss future Research, we suggest that future Research should begin to assess the degree to which different variations of less constrained instructions affect innovativeness of ideas generated. Additionally, Open Ideo offers the crowd wicked problems but their instructions segment discussions by funnel model stages having the organization to select which ideas they want the crowd to focus on, so we could not use their crowdsourcing events as data. See Bjelland, O. M., & Wood, R. C. (2008). An inside view of IBM's "Innovation Jam". *MIT Sloan Management Review*, 50(1), 32.
2. See table comparing different types of crowdsourcing by their knowledge-sharing properties in Majchrzak, A. and Malhotra, A. (2016). Effect of Knowledge-sharing Trajectories on Innovative Outcomes in Temporary Online Crowds, Information Systems Research, 27(4), 685–703.
3. Information about HyperloopTT can be found on their website and in Majchrzak, A., Griffith, T., Reez, D., Alexy, O. (2018) Organizations Designed for Grand Challenges: Generative Dilemmas and Implications for Organization Design Theory. Academy of Management Discoveries, 4(4), 472–496.
4. Malhotra, A., Majchrzak, A., Kesebi, L., Looram, S. (2017) Developing Innovative Solutions Through Internal Crowdsourcing, Sloan Management Review, 58(4), 73–79. Malhotra et al. MIT Sloan Management Review, 2017.

5. Malhotra, A., and Majchrzak, A. (in press). Engaging Customer Care Employees in Internal Collaborative Crowdsourcing: Managing the Inherent Tensions and Associated Challenges. Human Resource Management.
6. Malhotra, A. Majchrzak, A., and Niemiec, R. (2017) Using Public Crowds for Open Strategy Formulation: Mitigating the Risks of Knowledge Representation Gaps, Long Range Planning, 50(3), 397–410.
7. Shadish, W. R., Clark, M. H., and Steiner, P. M. (2008). Can Nonrandomized Experiments Yield Accurate Answers? A Randomized Experiment Comparing Random and Nonrandom Assignments. Journal of the American Statistical Association 103(484): 1334–1344.
8. Hutter, K., Hautz, J., Füller, J., Mueller, J., & Matzler, K. (2011). Communitition: The tension between competition and collaboration in community-based design contests. *Creativity and innovation management*, *20*(1), 3–21. Luo, X., Slotegraaf, R. J., & Pan, X. (2006). Cross-functional "coopetition": The simultaneous role of cooperation and competition within firms. Journal of Marketing, 70(2), 67–80; Kaufmann, N., Schulze, T., & Veit, D. (2011, August). More than fun and money: Worker Motivation in Crowdsourcing-A Study on Mechanical Turk. AMCIS, 11: 1–11; Leimeister, J. M., Huber, M., Bretschneider, U., & Krcmar, H. (2009). Leveraging crowdsourcing: activation-supporting components for IT-based ideas competition. Journal of management information systems, 26(1), 197–224.; Rogstadius, J., Kostakos, V., Kittur, A., Smus, B., Laredo, J., & Vukovic, M. (2011). An assessment of intrinsic and extrinsic motivation on task performance in crowdsourcing markets. ICWSM, 11, 17–21; Zheng, H., Li, D., & Hou, W. (2011). Task design, motivation, and participation in crowdsourcing contests. International Journal of Electronic Commerce, 15(4), 57–88.
9. For scholarship describing the value of passion over extrinsic motivation, see: Alam, S. L., & Campbell, J. (2017). Temporal Motivations of Volunteers to Participate in Cultural Crowdsourcing Work. Information Systems Research, 28(4), 744–759; Feng, J., Zhang, Y., Liu, X., Zhang, L., & Han, X. (2018). Just the right amount of ethics inspires creativity: a cross-level investigation of ethical leadership, intrinsic motivation, and employee creativity. Journal of Business Ethics, 153(3), 645–658; Lee, J., & Seo, D. (2016). Crowdsourcing not all sourced by the crowd: An observation on the behavior of Wikipedia participants. Technovation, 55, 14–21.
10. Faraj, S., Jarvenpaa, S. L., & Majchrzak, A. (2011). Knowledge collaboration in online communities. Organization Science, 22(5), 1224–1239; Malinen, S. (2015). Understanding user participation in online communities: A systematic literature review of empirical studies. Computers in Human Behavior, 46, 228–238; Massa, F. G. (2017). Guardians of the Internet: Building and Sustaining the Anonymous Online Community. Organization Studies, 38(7), 959–988.

11. Berg, J. 2016. Balancing on the creative high-wire: Forecasting the success of novel ideas in organizations. Administrative Science Quarterly, 61: 433–468.
12. Nembhard, I. M., & Edmondson, A. C. (2006). Making it safe: The effects of leader inclusiveness and professional status on psychological safety and improvement efforts in health care teams. Journal of Organizational Behavior: The International Journal of Industrial, Occupational and Organizational Psychology and Behavior, 27(7), 941–966.
13. Dennis, A. R., Wixom, B. H., & Vandenberg, R. J. (2001). Understanding fit and appropriation effects in group support systems via meta-analysis. MIS quarterly, 25(2), 167–193; McFarland, L. A., & Ployhart, R. E. (2015). Social media: A contextual framework to guide Research and practice. Journal of Applied Psychology, 100(6), 1653.
14. Dennis, A., & Williams, M. (2003). Electronic brainstorming. Group creativity: Innovation through collaboration, 160–178.
15. Tsoukas, H. (2009). A dialogical approach to the creation of new knowledge in organizations. Organization Science, 20(6), 941–957; Fuller, J., Hutter, K., Hautz, J., and Matzler, K. 2014. User roles and contributions in innovation-contest communities. Journal of Management Information Systems, 31(1), 273–307.
16. Pinsonneault, A., & Heppel, N. (1997). Anonymity in group support systems Research: A new conceptualization, measure, and contingency framework. Journal of Management Information Systems, 14(3), 89–108.
17. Jeppesen, L. B., & Lakhani, K. R. (2010). Marginality and problem-solving effectiveness in broadcast shar. Organization Science, 21(5), 1016–1033; Teplitskiy, Misha, Hardeep Ranu, Gary Gray, Michael Menietti, Eva Guinan, and Karim R. Lakhani. "Do Experts Listen to Other Experts? Field Experimental Evidence from Scientific Peer Review." Harvard Business School Working Paper, No. 19–107, April 2019.
18. Von Hippel, E. (2005). Democratizing Innovation. MIT Press; von Hippel, E. (2016). Free Innovation, MIT Press.
19. Tsoukas, H. (2009). A dialogical approach to the creation of new knowledge in organizations. Organization Science, 20(6), 941–957.
20. Hackman, J. R., & Kaplan, R. E. (1974). Interventions into group process: An approach to improving the effectiveness of groups. Decision Sciences, 5(3), 459–480.
21. Nunamaker Jr., J. F., Applegate, L. M., & Konsynski, B. R. (1987). Facilitating group creativity: Experience with a group decision support system. Journal of Management Information Systems, 3(4), 5–19; Pinsonneault, A., & Heppel, N. (1997). Anonymity in group support systems Research: A new conceptualization, measure, and contingency framework. Journal of Management Information Systems, 14(3), 89–108; Rains, S. A., & Scott, C. R. (2007). To identify or not to identify: A theoretical model of receiver responses to anonymous communication. Communication Theory, 17(1), 61–91.

22. Bailey, D. E., Leonardi, P. M., & Barley, S. R. (2012). The lure of the virtual. Organization Science, 23(5), 1485–1504; Treem, J. W., & Leonardi, P. M. (2013). Social media use in organizations: Exploring the affordances of visibility, editability, persistence, and association. Annals of the International Communication Association, 36(1), 143–189. Leonardi, P. M. (2014). Social media, knowledge sharing, and innovation: Toward a theory of communication visibility. Information systems Research, 25(4), 796–816.
23. Nicolini, D., Mengis, J., & Swan, J. (2012). Understanding the role of objects in cross-disciplinary collaboration. Organization Science, 23(3): 612–629.
24. Baralou, E., & Tsoukas, H. (2015). How is new organizational knowledge created in a virtual context? An ethnographic study. Organization Studies, 1–28.
25. McFarland, L. A., & Ployhart, R. E. (2015). Social media: A contextual framework to guide Research and practice. Journal of Applied Psychology, 100(6), 1653.
26. Baralou, E., & Tsoukas, H. (2015). How is new organizational knowledge created in a virtual context? An ethnographic study. Organization Studies, 1–28.
27. Bailey, D. E., Leonardi, P. M., & Barley, S. R. (2012). The lure of the virtual. Organization Science, 23(5), 1485–1504; Baralou, E., & Tsoukas, H. (2015). How is new organizational knowledge created in a virtual context? An ethnographic study. Organization Studies, 1–28; Goffman, E. (1959). The Presentation of Self in Everyday Life. Doubleday, New York.
28. Baralou, E., & Tsoukas, H. (2015). How is new organizational knowledge created in a virtual context? An ethnographic study. Organization Studies, 1–28.
29. Piezunka, H. & Dahlander, L. (2015). Distant shar, narrow attention: How crowding alters organization's filtering of suggestions in crowdsourcing. Academy of Management Journal, 58(3), 856–880.
30. Berg, J. (2016). Balancing on the creative high-wire: Forecasting the success of novel ideas in organizations. Administrative Science Quarterly, 61: 433–468; Mueller, J., Melwani, S., Loewenstein, J., & Deal, J. J. (2018). Reframing the decision-makers' dilemma: Towards a social context model of creative idea recognition. *Academy of Management Journal, 61*(1), 94–110.
31. Amabile, Teresa M. Creativity in context: Update to the social psychology of creativity. Hachette, UK, 1996. This procedure is commonly done for crowdsourcing ideas in which experts are asked to assess for each idea its user-value, producibility, and originality: Mack, T., & Landau, C. (2015). Winners, losers, and deniers: Self-selection in crowd innovation contests and the roles of motivation, creativity, and skills. Journal of Engineering and Technology Management, 37, 52–64; Magnusson, P.R., 2009. Exploring the contributions of involving ordinary users in ideation of technology-based services. J. Prod. Innov. Manag. 26, 578–593; Kristensson, P., Magnusson, P.R. (2010). Tuning users' innovativeness during ideation. Creat. Innov. Manag.

19, 147–159. One way in which our procedure differed from common practice is that we asked each executive to judge each idea independently, giving us an innovativeness rating of all the ideas. Common practice picks the top ten ideas only, turning a continuous outcome variable into a binomial, losing important variability needed for analysis.
32. Malhotra, A., Majchrzak, A., Kesebi, L., Looram, S. (2017). Developing Innovative Solutions Through Internal Crowdsourcing, Sloan Management Review, 58(4), 73–79.
33. Symonds, M. R., Moussalli, A. (2011). A brief guide to model selection, multimodel inference and model averaging in behavioural ecology using Akaike's information criterion. *Behavioral Ecology and Sociobiology*, 65(1), 13–21.
34. Abbott, A. (2001). *Time matters: On theory and method.* University of Chicago Press.
35. Mächler, M., and Bühlmann, P. (2004). "Variable Length Markov Chains: Methodology, Computing, and Software," Journal of Computational and Graphical Statistics, 13(2), 435–455.
36. Van Der Aalst, Wil M. and Ter Hofstede, Arthur H. and Kiepuszewski, Bartosz and Barros, Alistair P. (2003). Workflow Patterns. Distributed and Parallel Databases, 14(1), 5–51.
37. Majchrzak, A. and Malhotra, A. (2016). Effect of Knowledge-sharing Trajectories on Innovative Outcomes in Temporary Online Crowds, Information Systems Research, 27(4), 685–703.

References

Abbott, A. (2001). *Time Matters: On Theory and Method.* Chicago: University of Chicago Press.
Alam, S. L., & Campbell, J. (2017). Temporal Motivations of Volunteers to Participate in Cultural Crowdsourcing Work. *Information Systems Research*, 28(4), 744–759.
Amabile, T. M. (1996). *Creativity in Context: Update to the Social Psychology of Creativity.* Boulder, CO: Westview.
Bailey, D. E., Leonardi, P. M., & Barley, S. R. (2012). The Lure of the Virtual. *Organization Science*, 23(5), 1485–1504.
Baralou, E., & Tsoukas, H. (2015). How Is New Organizational Knowledge Created in a Virtual Context? An Ethnographic Study. *Organization Studies, 36*(5), 593–620.
Berg, J. (2016). Balancing on the Creative High-Wire: Forecasting the Success of Novel Ideas in Organizations. *Administrative Science Quarterly, 61*, 433–468.
Bjelland, O. M., & Wood, R. C. (2008). An Inside View of IBM's' Innovation Jam'. *MIT Sloan Management Review, 50*(1), 32.
Dennis, A., & Williams, M. (2003). Electronic Brainstorming. In *Group Creativity: Innovation Through Collaboration* (pp. 160–178). Oxford: Oxford University Press.

Dennis, A. R., Wixom, B. H., & Vandenberg, R. J. (2001). Understanding Fit and Appropriation Effects in Group Support Systems Via Meta-Analysis. *MIS Quarterly, 25*(2), 167–193.

Ewenstein, B., & Whyte, J. (2009). Knowledge Practices in Design: The Role of Visual Representations as 'Epistemic Objects'. *Organization Studies, 30*(1), 7–30.

Faraj, S., Jarvenpaa, S. L., & Majchrzak, A. (2011). Knowledge Collaboration in Online Communities. *Organization Science, 22*(5), 1224–1239.

Feng, J., Zhang, Y., Liu, X., Zhang, L., & Han, X. (2018). Just the Right Amount of Ethics Inspires Creativity: A Cross-Level Investigation of Ethical Leadership, Intrinsic Motivation, and Employee Creativity. *Journal of Business Ethics, 153*(3), 645–658.

Fuller, J., Hutter, K., Hautz, J., & Matzler, K. (2014). User Roles and Contributions in Innovation-Contest Communities. *Journal of Management Information Systems, 31*(1), 273–307.

Goffman, E. (1959). *The Presentation of Self in Everyday Life*. New York: Doubleday.

Hackman, J. R., & Kaplan, R. E. (1974). Interventions into Group Process: An Approach to Improving the Effectiveness of Groups. *Decision Sciences, 5*(3), 459–480.

Hutter, K., Hautz, J., Füller, J., Mueller, J., & Matzler, K. (2011). Communitition: The Tension Between Competition and Collaboration in Community-Based Design Contests. *Creativity and Innovation Management, 20*(1), 3–21.

Jeppesen, L. B., & Lakhani, K. R. (2010). Marginality and Problem-Solving Effectiveness in Broadcast Shar. *Organization Science, 21*(5), 1016–1033.

Kaufmann, N., Schulze, T., & Veit, D. (2011, August). More Than Fun and Money: Worker Motivation in Crowdsourcing – A Study on Mechanical Turk. *AMCIS, 11*, 1–11.

Kristensson, P., & Magnusson, P. R. (2010). Tuning Users' Innovativeness During Ideation. *Creativity and Innovation Management, 19*, 147–159.

Leimeister, J. M., Huber, M., Bretschneider, U., & Krcmar, H. (2009). Leveraging Crowdsourcing: Activation-Supporting Components for IT-Based Ideas Competition. *Journal of Management Information Systems, 26*(1), 197–224.

Leonardi, P. M. (2014). Social Media, Knowledge Sharing, and Innovation: Toward a Theory of Communication Visibility. *Information Systems Research, 25*(4), 796–816.

Luo, X., Slotegraaf, R. J., & Pan, X. (2006). Cross-Functional "Coopetition": The Simultaneous Role of Cooperation and Competition Within Firms. *Journal of Marketing, 70*(2), 67–80.

Mächler, M., & Bühlmann, P. (2004). Variable Length Markov Chains: Methodology, Computing, and Software. *Journal of Computational and Graphical Statistics, 13*(2), 435–455.

Mack, T., & Landau, C. (2015). Winners, Losers, and Deniers: Self-Selection in Crowd Innovation Contests and the Roles of Motivation, Creativity, and Skills. *Journal of Engineering and Technology Management, 37*, 52–64.

Magnusson, P. R. (2009). Exploring the Contributions of Involving Ordinary Users in Ideation of Technology-Based Services. *Journal of Product Innovation Management, 26*, 578–593.

Majchrzak, A., & Malhotra, A. (2016). Effect of Knowledge-Sharing Trajectories on Innovative Outcomes in Temporary Online Crowds. *Information Systems Research, 27*(4), 685–703.

Majchrzak, A., Griffith, T., Reez, D., & Alexy, O. (2018). Organizations Designed for Grand Challenges: Generative Dilemmas and Implications for Organization Design Theory. *Academy of Management Discoveries, 4*(4), 472–496.

Malhotra, A., & Majchrzak, A. (in press). Engaging Customer Care Employees in Internal Collaborative Crowdsourcing: Managing the Inherent Tensions and Associated Challenges. *Human Resource Management.* https://doi.org/10.1002/hrm.21952

Malhotra, A., Majchrzak, A., Kesebi, L., & Looram, S. (2017a). Developing Innovative Solutions Through Internal Crowdsourcing. *Sloan Management Review, 58*(4), 73–79.

Malhotra, A., Majchrzak, A., & Niemiec, R. (2017b). Using Public Crowds for Open Strategy Formulation: Mitigating the Risks of Knowledge Representation Gaps. *Long Range Planning, 50*(3), 397–410.

Malinen, S. (2015). Understanding User Participation in Online Communities: A Systematic Literature Review of Empirical Studies. *Computers in Human Behavior, 46*, 228–238.

Massa, F. G. (2017). Guardians of the Internet: Building and Sustaining the Anonymous Online Community. *Organization Studies, 38*(7), 959–988.

McFarland, L. A., & Ployhart, R. E. (2015). Social Media: A Contextual Framework to Guide Research and Practice. *Journal of Applied Psychology, 100*(6), 1653.

Mueller, J., Melwani, S., Loewenstein, J., & Deal, J. J. (2018). Reframing the Decision-Makers' Dilemma: Towards a Social Context Model of Creative Idea Recognition. *Academy of Management Journal, 61*(1), 94–110.

Nembhard, I. M., & Edmondson, A. C. (2006). Making It Safe: The Effects of Leader Inclusiveness and Professional Status on Psychological Safety and Improvement Efforts in Health Care Teams. *Journal of Organizational Behavior: The International Journal of Industrial, Occupational and Organizational Psychology and Behavior, 27*(7), 941–966.

Nicolini, D., Mengis, J., & Swan, J. (2012). Understanding the Role of Objects in Cross-Disciplinary Collaboration. *Organization Science, 23*(3), 612–629.

Nunamaker, J. F., Jr., Applegate, L. M., & Konsynski, B. R. (1987). Facilitating Group Creativity: Experience with a Group Decision Support System. *Journal of Management Information Systems, 3*(4), 5–19.

Piezunka, H., & Dahlander, L. (2015). Distant Shar, Narrow Attention: How Crowding Alters Organization's Filtering of Suggestions in Crowdsourcing. *Academy of Management Journal, 58*(3), 856–880.

Pinsonneault, A., & Heppel, N. (1997). Anonymity in Group Support Systems Research: A New Conceptualization, Measure, and Contingency Framework. *Journal of Management Information Systems, 14*(3), 89–108.

Rains, S. A., & Scott, C. R. (2007). To Identify or Not to Identify: A Theoretical Model of Receiver Responses to Anonymous Communication. *Communication Theory, 17*(1), 61–91.

Rogstadius, J., Kostakos, V., Kittur, A., Smus, B., Laredo, J., & Vukovic, M. (2011). An Assessment of Intrinsic and Extrinsic Motivation on Task Performance in Crowdsourcing Markets. *ICWSM, 11*, 17–21.

Shadish, W. R., Clark, M. H., & Steiner, P. M. (2008). Can Nonrandomized Experiments Yield Accurate Answers? A Randomized Experiment Comparing Random and Nonrandom. *Journal of the American Statistical Association, 103*(484), 1334–1344.

Symonds, M. R., & Moussalli, A. (2011). A Brief Guide to Model Selection, Multimodel Inference and Model Averaging in Behavioural Ecology Using Akaike's Information Criterion. *Behavioral Ecology and Sociobiology, 65*(1), 13–21.

Teplitskiy, M., Ranu, H., Gray, G., Menietti, M., Guinan, E., & Lakhani, K. R. (2019, April). Do Experts Listen to Other Experts? Field Experimental Evidence from Scientific Peer Review. Harvard Business School Working Paper, No. 19-107.

Treem, J. W., & Leonardi, P. M. (2013). Social Media Use in Organizations: Exploring the Affordances of Visibility, Editability, Persistence, and Association. *Annals of the International Communication Association, 36*(1), 143–189.

Tsoukas, H. (2009). A Dialogical Approach to the Creation of New Knowledge in Organizations. *Organization Science, 20*(6), 941–957.

Van Der Aalst, W. M., Ter Hofstede, A. H., Kiepuszewski, B., & Barros, A. P. (2003). Workflow Patterns. *Distributed and Parallel Databases, 14*(1), 5–51.

Von Hippel, E. (2005). *Democratizing Innovation*. Cambridge: MIT Press.

Von Hippel, E. (2016). *Free Innovation*. Cambridge: MIT Press.

Zheng, H., Li, D., & Hou, W. (2011). Task Design, Motivation, and Participation in Crowdsourcing Contests. *International Journal of Electronic Commerce, 15*(4), 57–88.

Part II

How Do Crowds Innovate?

Combining the data about participation, the data arranged into traces preceding ideas rated as more or less innovative, and our case studies data, we have developed a ***Theory of the Collective Production*** process. As indicated in Chap. 1, the traditional *Idea Sharing* process is based on the variance-selection-retention theoretical assumptions about how innovation occurs: that by having large crowds required only to share ideas to a well-defined problem, the presumed result will be finding that one individual who has thought about the problem with sufficient intensity and has the right expertise and perspective to offer a solution. As we described in Chap. 2, we find that the Idea Sharing process is less effective when crowds are asked to solve wicked problems compared to a process in which crowds are unmindcuffed by simply asked to share any and all knowledge they have about the problem. What exactly is the crowd doing that leads to more innovative ideas?

We describe what the crowd is doing as our new theory of *Collective Production*. Our theory of *Collective Production* starts with a series of theoretical tenets about the crowd:

1. **There Is No Single Expert**: No single individual in the crowd has that one single idea that is the comprehensive solution to address the complexity of wicked problems. No one has the breadth of experience, sensitivity to issues, and lack of biases to offer the sole right answer. Even Einstein needed his first wife.
2. **Spending More Time on a Problem Doesn't Provide More Innovative Ideas**: It does not take significant time of any single individual for a collectively produced innovative idea to emerge if the time of each individual is used in ways that inspire others.

3. **Perspectives of Others Are Consumable Only in Knowledge Fragments**: Each crowd participant represents a different perspective on the problem, but often those perspectives are not well-articulated and therefore not well-considered. These perspectives are also quite complex, often incorporating a myriad of personal experiences, past associations to the problem, mental models of why the problem exists, idea "seeds" for how the problem might be solved, and specific aspects of the problem which are more or less salient to them. Each of these elements of a perspective can stand on its own in influencing others' perspectives. One does not need to know all the elements of another's perspective. Learning *knowledge fragments* of these perspectives is sufficient for co-producing innovative ideas.
4. **Knowledge Fragments Can Be Creative Associations**: Knowledge fragments need not just be someone's assumptions and facts about the problem; they can be creative associations. Creative associations that one has to a problem, when shared, may stimulate others' creative associations, or inspire others to offer creative associations. Eventually the creative associations will help someone generate a creative discovery articulated as an innovative solution-idea.

Our theory of Collective Production then is a knowledge sharing process in which the crowd shares knowledge fragments which create a knowledge repository which becomes the stimuli for continued sharing of knowledge fragments. This process is in contrast to the Idea Sharing process in which only ideas are the focus. Figure II.1 shows how crowd participants contribute to and draw from the evolving repository.

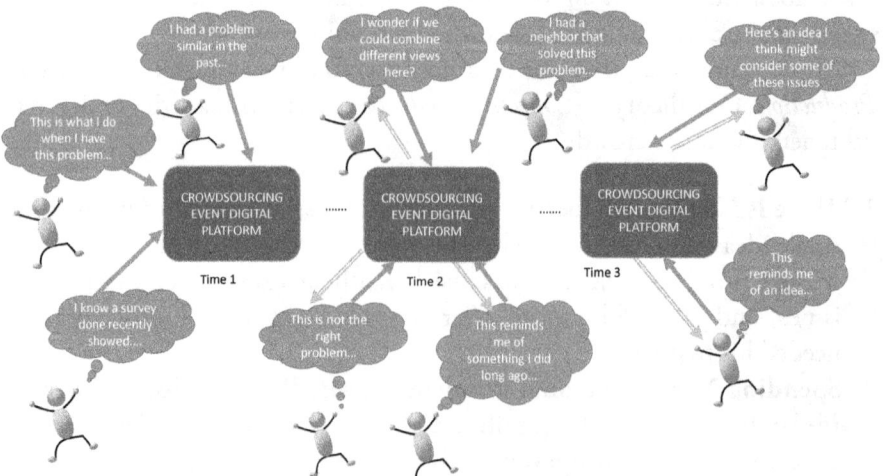

Fig. II.1 A graphical depiction of the Collective Production process for crowd innovation

The traditional Idea Sharing crowdsourcing process reflects the traditional funnel model to innovation: lots of ideas are offered, then winnowed down to a few winners. In contrast, the Collective Production process we discover in our data is closer to cross-functional collaboration in which a collective builds up to ideas by amalgamating their shared knowledge. However, Collective Production is NOT cross-functional collaboration because, during Collective Production, there is NO back-and-forth dialogue, a team doesn't exist, there is no collectively arrived agreement about the goal, and the team members don't participate throughout—from beginning to the end. Instead, individual participants of the collective are minimally engaged, that is, join in and exit when they want, contribute any knowledge when they want (or not). This is why a new theory is needed to explain how crowds produce innovative ideas when not restrained to sharing ideas only.

Our theory of Collective Production draws from a variety of different disciplines. Research on what stimulates people to be creative has helped us to think about crowds' knowledge not as simple chunks of knowledge to be recombined but also as stimulators of additional knowledge production. Research on cross-functional teams has helped us understand how individuals in a team may come to surface their unique knowledge that is not simply ideas and not simply what others suggest. Research on problem-solving helps us think about not simply disaggregating problem-solving from problem definition, but more importantly how both problem definition and problem-solving occur concurrently as two intertwined sub-processes.

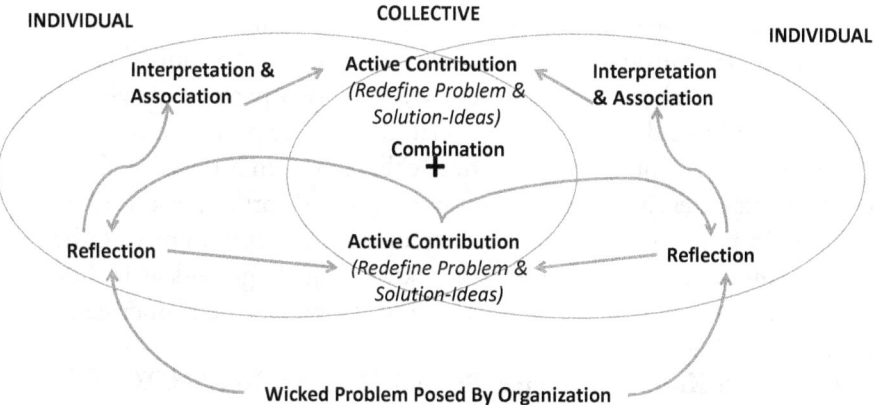

Fig. II.2 How Collective Production of knowledge occurs

In Fig. II.2, we graphically depict and summarize the aforementioned thoughts related to our Collective Production theory. The figure represents the process as evolutionary in that knowledge is accumulated into the crowd's platform over time and participants view this accumulated knowledge to note trends and patterns in the posts of others' that inspire them. The process begins with a wicked problem being posed by an organization. This in turn stimulates individuals in the collective (crowd) to reflect on the problem. Upon reflection, the individuals may either actively contribute knowledge fragments that contain seeds for solution (solution-ideas), creative associations and facts that may help to redefine the problem in inspirational ways. These knowledge fragments may also initiate a reflection process of individuals searching their memories for creative associations and discoveries. Reflections, in turn, lead individuals to interpret the problem based on their own perspective (experiences, contexts, pressing needs, etc.) which stimulate creative associations in their minds. Such creative associations are then contributed as new knowledge fragments which again either contain seeds for solution (solution-ideas) or redefine the problem itself. Overall, the accumulating knowledge fragments then form a collective knowledge base, with each knowledge fragment tacitly containing the evolution of the collective's perspectives. The knowledge fragments then can (1) be combined to form new solutions (more comprehensive and therefore more innovative than the previous ones) and (2) trigger contribution of more knowledge fragments representing how previous knowledge fragments were reflected upon and stimulated new interpretations.

This theorized Collection Production process is practiced by the crowd in five ways. These five practices differentiate between crowds able to generate the most innovative solutions even for wicked problems.

Practice 1: Minimal Commitment Expectation. An individual participant (in our data) on average offers less than two posts, with virtually no dialogue, and spends little time in social niceties like posting how wonderful others' ideas are. The crowd does not "collaborate" in a traditional sense by engaging in extensive socialization and back-and-forth "person addressed" communication as they would in a team or an online community. Rather, the crowds collectively produce by passing knowledge fragments as if they were batons in a foot race. With each passing of the baton, the runner gets closer to the finish line.

Practice 2: Knowledge Types Beyond Ideas Are Needed. We coded the traces of posts leading up to rated ideas for the different types of knowledge shared about the problem description and solution including facts, examples, paradoxical objectives, and ideas for solving the problem. We then analyzed the traces to see if particular types of knowledge were more likely to precede an innovative idea. We found that no specific type of knowledge—including more ideas—preceded innovative ideas. What mattered was that the VARIETY across types of knowledge mattered. In other words, despite much of the basis underlying the traditional Idea Sharing process suggesting the importance of sharing ideas, we found that sharing ideas does NOT lead to more innovative ideas.

Practice 3: Amplification of Creative Associations. The crowd is more likely to innovate when the crowd doesn't just mimic others' ideas, or build upon them or refine them, but rather offers creative associations to the problem and then uses those and others' creative associations as jumping-off points to think about other associations they might have in their memory about the problem. Individuals then post these associations, which serve to inspire others to post associations, which provides more fodder for creative discovery.

Practice 4: Reconstructing Needs to Inspire. The crowd is more likely to innovate not simply by accepting what others suggest are the needs that the problem is implying. Instead, innovation occurs when those needs are reconstructed. The reconstruction occurs first by disaggregating any definition of problem needs from solutions, then reconstructing the problem needs into creative associations. The creative associations are then used to inspire innovative ideas.

Practice 5: Enact Self-Defined Innovation-Enabling Roles. We find that only about 50% of the crowd offer ideas; the others perform a range of what we call innovation-enabling roles. Some individuals exclusively help to reconstruct needs, some offer creative associations, and some offer basic knowledge like facts. Having these roles ensure that there is a place for anyone who wants to contribute. The only role that has a detrimental effect on innovation is the individual who offers social support. As we explain later, social support statements harm innovation.

Figure II.3 graphically depicts the five practices.

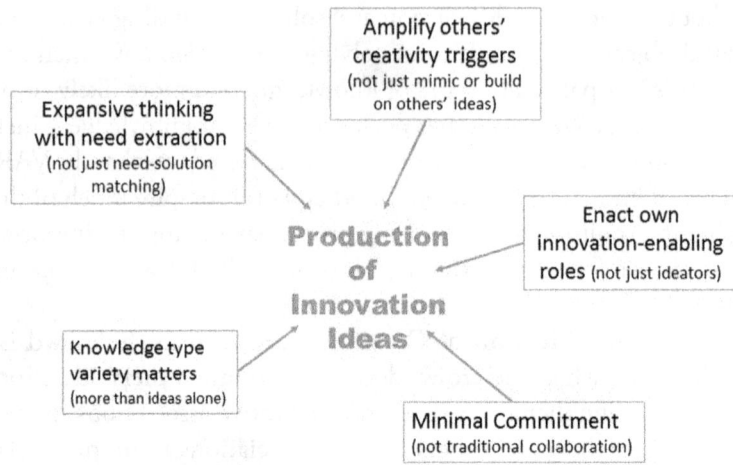

Fig. II.3 Framework: The 5 Characteristics of an unconstrained crowd's innovation process

What follows in the chapters of Part II is a look at each of these practices separately, giving each the attention it deserves. We explain what is conventional practice, from the traditional Idea Sharing process view, and what is the evidence we have to indicate that the traditional process is NOT how crowds actually innovate when given the opportunity to do so for complex wicked problems. In each chapter, we talk about other research related to our findings, and then implications for practitioners and researchers.

3

Practice 1: Minimally Committed Knowledge Baton Passers

This first practice describes how the crowds participated. Our findings indicate that individual participants, on the average, offer fewer than two posts! Their posts are short knowledge fragments (such as only a few sentences). They are not engaged in extensive back-and-forth questioning. They offer minimal social support for others' posts. It is almost as though the posts serve as knowledge batons in a knowledge relay race. The participants will not be the same throughout the race. As in a relay, the knowledge posts act as knowledge batons passed from one leg of the race to another, where the next participant is whomever is interested in getting the baton with no direct communication between the runners themselves. Each participant just takes the baton and keeps the innovation process moving forward.

This chapter only focuses on the first of the five practices shown in Fig. 3.1 below. In this first practice, participants were surprisingly consistent in posting in a way that demonstrated their autonomy in choosing not to spend substantial time with the crowdsourcing event, posting only once or twice rather than posting throughout the event, not following up on their earlier posts, and often not responding to others' comments on their original posts. The crowd exercises expressive freedom coupled with an apparent lack of any mutual commitment to respond to each other or to even arrive at a mutually agreed-upon solution.

In the first section, we describe a story which inspired us to think that, maybe, unmindcuffed could collectively produce innovative ideas without individually spending much time (Sect. 3.1). This inspiration led us to look quantitatively at our data to see if this lack of time commitment observed in the story was repeated in our 20 crowds. We found it was, and found seven

© The Author(s) 2020
A. Majchrzak, A. Malhotra, *Unleashing the Crowd*,
https://doi.org/10.1007/978-3-030-25557-2_3

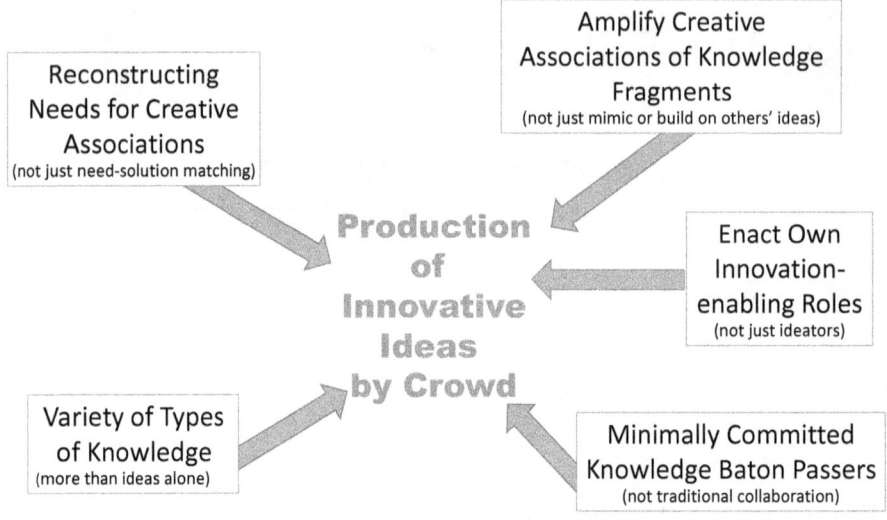

Fig. 3.1 Practices of Collective Production

other interesting results describing the behavior of these crowds (Sect. 3.2). These findings led us to label these crowds not simply as minimally committed, but also as "knowledge baton passers" since they seemed to pick up others' knowledge and continue moving forward to an innovative solution without overt agreements or disagreements about any of the content discussed. We then describe how these findings align with existing research on crowdsourcing and implications for practitioners (Sect. 3.3).

The minimal time commitment combined with the knowledge baton passing makes it possible for the other four remaining practices to exist. As we will discuss in future chapters of the book, the lack of time commitment, the freedom to not agree or disagree, and participants choosing to make their few contributions at any stage of the event means that if a crowd member disagrees with others, he or she can simply choose not to return to make a new post, or choose to make a post in a different discussion thread, or choose to continue to post in the same discussion thread and ignore the prior posts of others. This expressive freedom unbounded from time commitment translates into an ability to focus on offering reflections and creative associations in their posts rather than continuing down any particular conversational path. It allows the crowd to make posts containing only fragments of knowledge for others to pass on rather than completely well-developed proposals which are more difficult to change. This freedom also allows participants to use others' posts—not as explicit knowledge needing to be integrated into a single solution—but rather as touchpoints for inspiring more creative associations which eventually lead to innovative ideas. It is these touchpoints that are passed from one crowd member to another, which is why we refer to crowd participants as knowledge baton passers.

This view of crowd members innovating by reflecting on others' knowledge fragments and adding their own fragments inspired by others is in contrast to cross-functional team research which views the team process of innovation as emerging through extensive, concurrent back-and-forth dialogue among a common core of committed people.[1] Such a practice by unmindcuffed crowds is also in contrast to the Idea-Sharing view that innovation emerges from refining others' ideas since the crowd doesn't appear interested in refining others' ideas. So, asking crowds to provide as many ideas as possible, and then focusing on refining others' ideas (as is the case in Idea-Sharing) does not appear to correspond to how an unmindcuffed crowd emergently operates. In fact, we show that, *while the unmindcuffed crowds offer more innovative ideas, they offer fewer ideas than Idea-Sharing crowds—making them more efficient innovation-producing organisms.* We show in later chapters the practices the crowds use to achieve this efficiency.

3.1 A Story of Innovation Arising from a Minimally Committed Crowd: USAID's Global Pulse Innovation Crowdsourcing Event

This is a story of the United States Agency for International Development (USAID) running a crowdsourcing-for-innovation-event where a crowd with minimal committed ends up producing innovative solutions to a wicked problem. The USAID crowdsourcing planning team chose *not* to use the Idea-Sharing process because they did not want competition between ideators and they thought everyone in the world might have something to contribute, even if that something wasn't necessarily an idea. They called their crowdsourcing Global Pulse 2010 and it was run with the help of IBM using IBM's Innovation Jam software. This software organizes innovation as discussion threads. Figure 3.2 shows screenshots of discussion threads. These screenshots come from a community of USC football fans that one of us owns. Figure 3.2a is an example of discussion topics which are referred to as discussion starters that participants of the community have offered. Figure 3.2b is an example of the replies for one of the topics; all the replies for a particular topic are together referred to as a discussion thread. In a discussion thread, participants can start a topic or reply to a topic started by someone else.

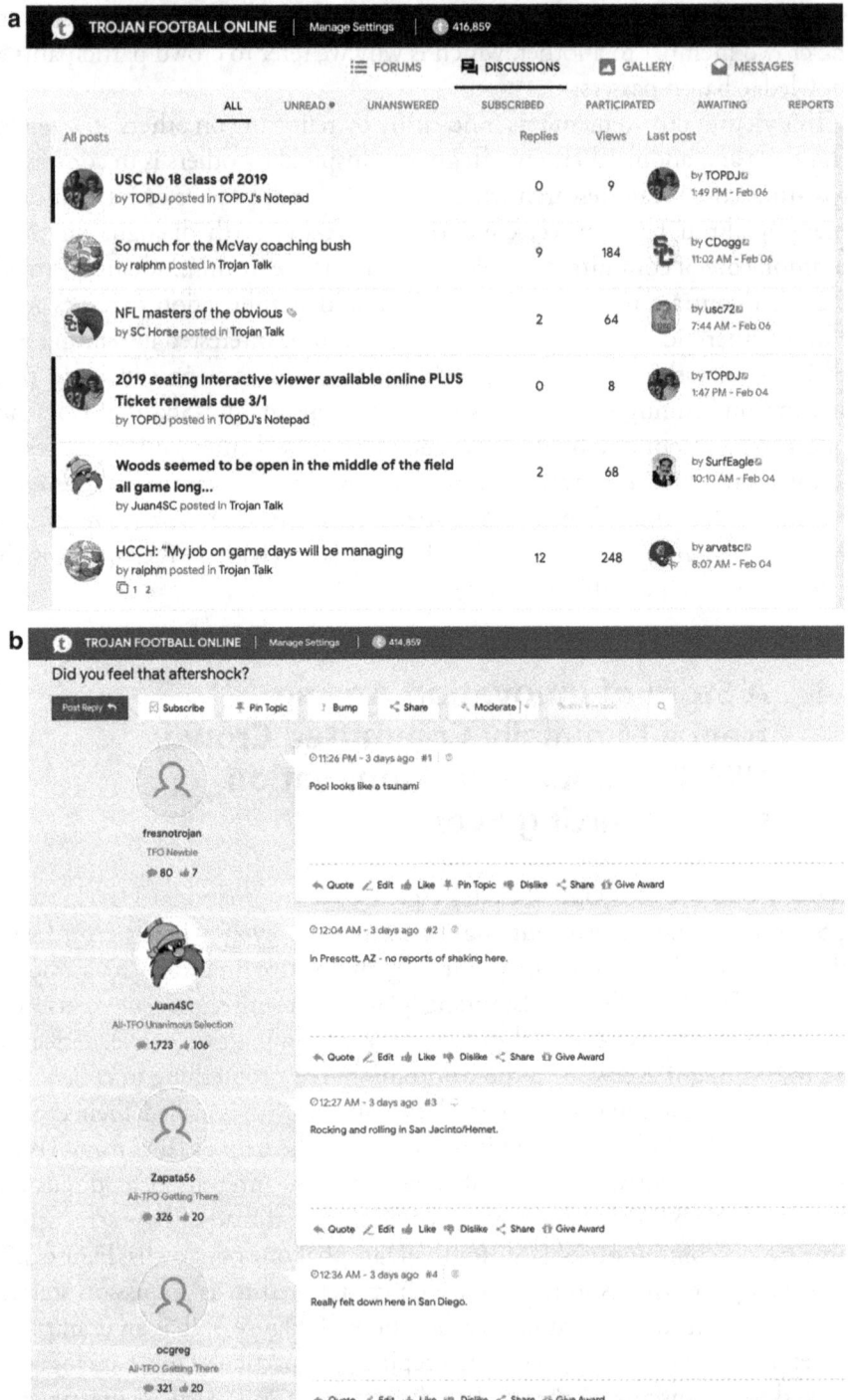

Fig. 3.2 (a) Discussion topics (b) Discussions within topic

The innovation crowdsourcing event was sponsored by the US Department of State with the purpose of helping to define USAID's funding priorities for the coming year. In the past, priorities were established through USAID committees. This time, USAID wanted to hear from "people around the world" about how USAID should spend its development dollars.

The USAID identified ten different topical objectives about which it wanted ideas for funding projects. The topics included improving the use of science and technology in developing countries, improving global health, encouraging small-business entrepreneurship, supporting women empowerment, and encouraging citizens of a country to exercise their political rights. USAID ran ten different crowdsourcing events simultaneously—one for each objective.

To prepare for the events, the USAID planning committee spent months reaching out to over 1000 organizations throughout the world to participate. For each event, a moderator was identified who was willing to spend time during the event encouraging people to participate who had not normally been involved in USAID's priority-setting committees, such as small-business owners, non-governmental organizations, university students, high-school students, activists, health professionals, school administrators, and so on. Global Pulse 2010 was heavily marketed through posters placed in educational and service organizations throughout the world, large email distribution lists, and an active social media presence and a website link. The marketing material emphasized that everyone and anyone should participate because "*each of us is an agent of change for a better tomorrow … in which personal stories and ideas are leveraging our individual and collective power for the greater good*".[2]

All ten events lasted only three days in the hopes that such concentrated time would engender enthusiasm. Across the ten crowdsourcing events, over 10,000 people registered from over 170 countries; 57% were from outside the United States, 47% were youth (under 35), there was gender parity (51% female), and the largest subpopulations were from universities (26%) and NGOs (27%).

Below we focus on the event for one of the ten objectives: **encouraging the exercise of political and civil rights**. This crowdsourcing event was focused on the following problem statement:

Safeguarded rights fuel democracies and allow citizens unfettered participation in the political life. We need to protect individuals from unfair or discriminatory action by anyone or any institution yet recognize that these rights and processes are the domain of a sovereign nation. How do we do that?

Table 3.1 Ideas identified by USAID as most innovative for the topic: exercising political and civil rights

- **Enable government transparency through school signs**—Example of a successful community action: signs were put on the doors of schools saying how much government money was supposed to have been allocated for desks, books, teachers, etc. When parents saw this, they raised the issue with the local officials. It was suggested that mobile phones could help magnify this type of communications effect.
- **Launch pay systems by mobile phone**—Roshan Telecom is testing a system to pay Afghan National Police officers directly by cell phone. This would help eliminate intermediaries tapping into salary funds.
- **Engage youth and student leaders in regional and international initiatives.** This would be an opportunity to exchange experiences and for capacity building. Youth engagement programs need more than "Didactic Civics". As one participant noted, "We can't apply 'typewriter thinking' to the dynamic cultural-social-media-filmic landscape".
- **Leverage mobile phone technology in dealing with situations such as election fraud, corruption, and emergency response**—Two free Internet sites that tie directly into mobile phone use, Ushahidi (www. Ushahidi.com) and FrontlineSMS were singled out in particular for their effectiveness in dealing with situations such as election fraud, corruption, and emergency response.

From Global Pulse report

Over the course of the three days, 625 posts were made to the platform in this event. The USAID planning committee responsible for this objective reviewed the posts and identified several innovative projects to consider for funding which USAID had never previously funded. Some of these are shown in Table 3.1:

Where did these innovative ideas come from? We thought we could easily read the 625 posts and see the emergence of parts of the ideas that would then lead to the building of each of these ideas.

The first surprise to us when reading was the large number of contributors but relatively *few* contributions per contributor. That is, 221 different contributors contributed. Not counting the posts made by the moderator, this meant that, on average, each contributor made less than three posts. This was then not a small crowd of consistently and continually involved participants but a large crowd of participants who made only three posts and left. The second surprise to us was how the textual discussion unfolded. One of the first posts was a discussion thread starter on the use of prediction markets in developing countries:

> *Economists typically believe that in general, the crowds are wiser at predicting future outcomes than individuals. This is why it's so difficult to beat the stock market consistently.*

On reading this, our first thought was: what does this have to do with political and civil rights? But soon, another participant offered a reply that interpreted the post as an idea for using prediction markets to make political and civil rights more transparent, an idea that was not stated by the prior poster:

> *This idea of using predictive markets to hold our governments more accountable for their policy decisions may work. As you would know, the power of a predictive market grows exponentially with the number of people that participate in it. Since predictive markets often work on the premise of "bets" people are making on a specific outcome, why not encourage participation by providing tax benefits for participation in policy-evaluation predictive markets? It creates a win-win-win situation: The government wins, as it gets more visibility of their effectiveness; The citizen wins, as policies with higher social pay-offs will be given more funding over time; and the individual wins by receiving a potential reward through the tax system.*

Thus, our second surprise was that people who post without mindcuffs are not tossing a well-developed idea into the ring and defending it but rather tossing in some knowledge and seeing how others elaborate it.

The third surprise for us was the non-obvious connections between posts even within the same discussion thread. That is, many posts in the same discussion thread did not have clear connections with prior posts. For example, after the first two posts above, a participant started a new discussion thread describing a new aspect of political and civil rights:

> *A key curricular program implemented by Civitas partners is Project Citizen. In over 60 countries worldwide, Project Citizen engages students in hands-on, project-based learning about public policymaking.* (www.projectcitizen.org)

Much later, a reply in this discussion thread was posted:

> *Text Messaging Systems could enable poor people to participate in the evaluation of their own governments on a regular basis in the areas that matter most to them. Text messaging systems could help poor people evaluate government functions that are critical to them such as policing, education, health services, and rural employment. If governments, donors, and/or local NGOs would support bottom-up evaluation systems in the funds already being spent on project evaluation, the activities would provide a greater and longer lasting benefit. Then cell phones can also be used to solve one of the major sources of corruption, the diversion of funds for salaries and supplies for police, education, health, and rural employment if reported by people to an independent NGO that would protect their identity.*

This non-obvious connection between the post about Project Citizen and the follow-on post about the use of cell phones led to what USAID felt was one of the most innovative of the ideas: leveraging cell phones for corruption reporting.

The fourth surprise for us was the many different directions and interpretations of the problem made by participants. While the examples above share a view that the problem of political rights involves citizen participation, the post below describes the problem entirely differently, focusing not on citizens but on politicians:

> *Hi there, I am a Canadian facing incredible global events in that we are "supposed" to be a world leader, however, there is so much complacency, ego-filled need for absolute control and entitlement coming from our politicians of all parties that we are at a severe stalemate and in fact regressing ... How do we deal with politicians globally that when they open their eyes each day are filled with false egos and disastrous ways of dealing with global dysfunction?*

A final surprise was that we expected some back-and-forth dialogue as if crowds were acting like big teams. But, as illustrated in the examples above, there was little back-and-forth exchange. Participants seemed to be using other's posts merely to trigger a thought in their own minds.

3.2 Are All Crowds Minimally Committed to the Crowdsourcing Event?

This story of USAID led us to ask: do all crowds participating in innovation crowdsourcing act in this fashion? So, we looked at all 20 of our crowds from the field research to see what level of time commitment they gave. We thought that maybe only Idea-Sharing crowds would be uncommitted, and that, maybe, unmindcuffed crowds would be more committed because they were allowed to be. We were surprised again.

In Table 3.2, in the first column, one can observe the commitment in terms of participation by all 20 crowds—whether they were constrained to posting ideas as Idea-Sharing Crowds or allowed to be unmindcuffed. Then in the next two columns, we compare the Idea-Sharing crowds versus unmindcuffed crowds using simple statistics to see if there were any obvious differences between the two. The $n = 7$ for Idea-Sharing refers to the seven different Innovation Crowdsourcing Events we ran in which the crowds were instructed in the way it is done today: participants were explicitly asked to offer only

3 Practice 1: Minimally Committed Knowledge Baton Passers

Table 3.2 What the 20 crowds look like in terms of commitment

Type of participation behavior	Overall crowd behavior (n = 20)	Idea-Sharing crowds (n = 7)	Unmindcuffed crowds (n = 13)	t-ratio for difference
Total posts	121.4 (96.10)	100.14 (36.79)	132.84 (27.00)	0.71
Total participants	86 (33.88)	93.42 (12.98)	82.00 (9.52)	−0.71
Posts/participant	1.43 (0.94)	0.96 (0.34)	1.68 (0.25)	1.69
Total threads	50.80 (32.67)	40.85 (12.34)	56.13 (9.06)	0.99
Ideas (% of total posts)	0.53 (0.14)	0.61 (0.05)	0.49 (0.04)	−1.76*
Other knowledge (% of total posts)	0.35 (0.15)	0.23 (0.05)	0.42 (0.04)	3.33**
Questions (% of total posts)	0.15 (0.07)	0.16 (0.08)	0.14 (0.06)	−0.19
Social support (% of total posts)	0.15 (0.07)	0.16 (0.02)	0.14 (0.02)	−0.74

Note: Any post could contain ideas, questions, social support, or other
*$p < 0.05$; **$p < 0.01$; ***$p < 0.001$

ideas or comments on others' ideas. These seven events accounted for a total of 654 registered participants. The $n = 13$ refer to the 13 events in which crowds were allowed to share any knowledge in any way they wanted. The instructions included a suggestion that they could consider posting not just ideas but their knowledge about the problem such as facts, examples, and tradeoffs; however, there was nothing in the platform that forced them to post in that way. These 13 events accounted for a total of 1066 registered participants. Overall, across all 20 crowds there were 1720 registered actors making a total of 2428 posts.

There are several simple, important and interesting findings in Table 3.1.

Finding 1: Unmindcuffed Crowds Are More Efficient than Idea-Sharing Crowds. For the unmindcuffed crowds, 49% of the total number of posts were ideas while, for the Idea-Sharing crowds, 61% of their posts were ideas. Given that the unmindcuffed crowds produced more innovative solutions, these crowds offered more innovative ideas even while contributing a fewer number of ideas. Thus, *unmindcuffed crowds are more efficient at the innovation-production process than Idea-Sharing crowds.* That is, the crowds are able to squeeze more innovativeness into their fewer ideas, making every idea count more than Idea-Sharing crowds.

Finding 2: "Drive-by" Posters. Looking at Table 3.2 (third row: "Posts/Participant"), each participant makes a very small number of posts on the average. More specifically, over the course of each 7–10 day events, partici-

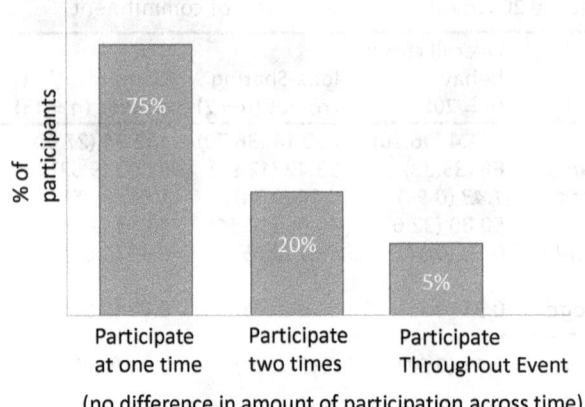

Fig. 3.3 Do participants show a preference about when they participate?

pants in each of those events made less than 2 total posts with little variation, meaning almost all of them made fewer than 2 total posts!

Finding 3: Post at a Single Point in Time. A closer look at the number of posts made during the early, middle, and late phases of the 7–10 events yielded some interesting observations, as shown in Fig. 3.3. First, very few (less than 5%) of the participants made contributions throughout the event (i.e., early, middle, and late). Almost 75% of those participating posted only in *one* of the time periods (early or middle or late). Also, none of the time periods had a significantly larger number of participants (either early, middle, or late). In other words, the participants did not spend their time posting across the entire event but concentrated on a single time period. Fortunately, there was a large enough number of participants choosing to post during different time periods that posts were made throughout the event, just not from the same person. This further exemplifies a knowledge baton-passing view of the crowd.

Finding 4: Minimal Questioning. Much of the literature on innovation says that innovation comes about through extensive and constructive questioning, in an effort to learn from each other; this learning then leads to a better ability to understand differences, understand similarities, and find bridges to cross divides, which then lead to more innovative breakthroughs.[3] Looking at Table 3.2, the proportion of questions that are asked during any event, on the average, is only 15% of all the (total) posts across the 20 events. As there is little back-and-forth dialogue, these questions were rarely directly answered. This means that crowds are not engaging in back-and-forth clarifications, constructive questioning to elicit details, or interacting with others to learn more from each other. Thus the crowds, somehow, are able to innovate without spending time questioning each other. This is quite a different situation for innovation to emerge than in teams where the current literature suggests that, in order to innovate, team members should get to know each other and engage in constructive questioning of each other, and back-and-forth dialogue to clarify each other's positions.[4]

Finding 5: About Half of the Posts Are Still Ideas. Overall, across the 20 events, about half the posts are ideas. This is true even for the crowds allowed to share any knowledge they want. That is, even in unmindcuffed crowds, half of those participating post solution-ideas. Thus, unmindcuffing a crowd does not mean eliminating the ideas; it simply means allowing for the sharing of other types of knowledge.

Finding 6: Both Crowds Have the Same Minimal Commitment YET Different Innovation Potential! Over the 20 different innovation events, the participants did not know about the type of crowd (Idea-Sharing or Unmindcuffed) they were part of, or that other types of crowds were in action. Consequently, there is no reason to believe that participants in the Idea-Sharing crowds were inherently less creative, passionate, expert, or knowledgeable than those in the unmindcuffed crowds. Moreover, according to Table 3.2, there was no difference in the number of posts per participants and the same number of threads (a thread as explained in Chap. 2 is a new topic offered by a participant while a reply to a thread is a participant's reaction to that new topic). Thus, the unmindcuffed crowd was able to generate more innovative ideas from participants with the *same* minimal commitment as with those who were limited to the Idea-Sharing process.

Finding 7: Minimal Social Support. Much of the literature looking at dialogues among crowdsourcing participants describes the importance of a dialogue that is not just polite but openly supportive, affirming others' contributions.[5] Similarly, the literature on innovative groups also calls for the importance of team members offering each other constructive support.[6] For example, one literature review stated that employees who were motivated to help others will not only provide others with helpful feedback but will also be driven to develop ideas that are useful to others.[7]

Social support offers several advantages according to this literature. It creates a condition called psychological safety, in which participants are willing to take "risks". In contexts where we would like innovation, psychological safety means that participants are willing to offer wild and crazier ideas, knowing that others will not scoff at them no matter how wild their ideas are. By having participants repeatedly affirming one's ideas with supportive statements, such as "great idea!", "I like the idea", "Let's do it", a feeling of psychological safety is engendered because you know those around will not reject your ideas and you won't feel personally rejected.[8] Moreover, this literature argues that social support is needed as part of innovation processes because they lead to a social exchange of reciprocity in which people feel that if they are supportive of others, others will be supportive of them, resulting in a quasi quid pro quo.[9] Finally, social support may also be an attention-signaling mechanism, that is, those ideas or other knowledge contributions which are agreed to by others must be worth pursuing further and must have a potential value for the crowds to develop.

Despite all that literature indicating the importance of social support, what we find is that only 15% of all the posts offer social support. This is a relatively small percentage for a large number of total posts. Moreover, this percentage is substantially smaller than the number of ideas posted, which means that most ideas were not supported, suggesting that psychological safety might not have been engendered through social support mechanisms. Moreover, this suggests that the unmindcuffed crowds did not fill in for the lack of cuffs with a new social norm of intensive crowd approval for their ideas. Thus, the literature about how teams innovate may not apply to how crowds innovate.

Finding 8: Other Knowledge. One of the largest differences between the two conditions of crowds was in the "other knowledge" posted as shown in Table 3.2. 42% of the unmindcuffed crowds' posts were not ideas, questions, or social support statements! In contrast, only 23% of the posts of Idea-Sharing crowds were "other knowledge". This difference led us to ask the question: what do these "other" posts pertain to? In later chapters, we show a deep trace analysis of these "other knowledge" posts and how they influenced the emergence of innovative ideas.

Summary Across Findings 1–8: Crowds consist of knowledge relay posters, not collaborators. *The implication across the eight findings is that these crowds are not collaborators in the traditional sense of the term*, that is, with extensive back-and-forth communication. Instead, they offer a post and then leave, with little questioning or agreements about what others have posted. *It is almost as though the posts serve as knowledge batons in a knowledge relay race.* The participants will not be the same throughout the race. As in a relay, the knowledge posts act as knowledge batons passed from one leg of the race to another, where the next participant is whoever is interested in getting the baton with no direct communication between the runners themselves. Each participant just takes the baton and keeps the innovation process moving forward.[10]

Apparent from our findings, as well, is that participants in the crowd are minimally participating regardless if the crowd is using an Idea-Sharing or an unmindcuffed process. They each offer less than two posts. They are not engaged in extensive back-and-forth questioning. They don't spend a great deal of their precious little time in offering social support to others' posts. Therefore no matter which process—Idea-Sharing or unmindcuffed knowledge sharing—they are minimalists in their commitment to spending time posting. Since they equally spend minimal time, the fact that the unmindcuffed collectively produce more innovative ideas than Idea-Sharing crowds is not explained by differences in lack of commitment. In sum, it is not whether the crowd is minimally committed—which they all are—but *how* they use the tiny sliver of time they commit for solving the wicked problem. This is what we turn to in the chapters to follow in the book.

3.3 How Do Our Findings Align with Current Research on Online Crowds?

There has been substantial research on drivers of participation in Idea-Sharing crowds.[11] This research suggests that not everyone acts for purely extrinsic utilitarian purposes such as rewards, especially when ideas are desired, with participants reporting significant benefits from the learning that accumulates from helping others.[12] Moreover, the more challenging the task, the more interest in learning, a finding corresponding to the team literature on the importance of offering challenging open-ended tasks if creativity is desired.[13] However, the role of extrinsic motivation (such as rewards) is not clear.[14] On the one hand, Boudreau and colleagues[15] have revealed the positive influence of expected rewards on the output quality of crowd innovation contests in a software development context. On the other hand, the findings of Frey and colleagues[16] suggest that monetary motivation is related to *non-substantial* contributions to innovation contests, while intrinsic motivation such as a desire to learn leads to substantial contributions. To resolve these differences, another study[17] compared students who chose to participate in a Porsche idea competition against those students choosing not to. It was found that participants show significantly higher levels of domain-relevant skills, creativity-relevant interest, and intrinsic motivation than non-participants.

In sum, the findings from research on Idea-Sharing crowd innovation suggests that intrinsic interest and desire for creativity act as the main driver of participation. Therefore, if these results for Idea-Sharing crowdsourcing apply to unmindcuffed participants, it suggests that the unmindcuffed participants will be curious and interested in creatively solving the problem. Our findings above offer a caveat: *they will be curious and interested as long as it takes mini-*

mal effort. Therefore, the remaining practices we identify in the coming chapters are ones the crowd emergently use to spend as little time as possible with the maximum impact on their learning and ability to creatively solve the wicked problem.

3.4 Summary of Practice 1: Minimal Commitment to Crowdsourcing Event

Based on our research and a review of the literature, we think we can now paint a picture of what participation looks like in crowds focused on innovatively solving a problem when released from traditional Idea-Sharing mindcuffs.

3.4.1 What Is a Crowd?

First, the word *crowd* may be a misnomer. For some, the word "Crowd" implies a single entity, group, or organization which comes together at the beginning to solve the problem and stays together until the end or Event is over. Crowds are not like that. So maybe they should be called fluid crowds?[18] Or maybe open crowds?[19] Or maybe a mass? Or maybe an amoeba? Or maybe a transient collective? Anyway, it is best to think of *the crowd as individual participants coming and going, with the only thing streaming them together over time being the posts they make before they leave. Thus a crowd is not the people, it is the knowledge traces they leave behind.*

3.4.2 What Is Collaboration in a Crowd?

Second, the word "*collaboration*" does not describe the crowd and thus phrases such as "mass collaboration" or "collaborative crowdsourcing" are probably not accurate. Instead of the traditional notion of a people-based collaborative dialogue used in the team research literature, crowds freed from the Idea-Sharing process are engaged in a collaboration that might be more appropriately referred to as "*knowledge baton-passing collaboration*", in which they collaborate not directly with each other but through the posts that others leave. Moreover, the form of collaboration is not back-and-forth dialogue.[20] So we all need to learn more about this new form of collaboration, which is the content of the remainder of the book.

3.4.3 How Does a Crowd Interpret Others' Knowledge?

Since they are engaged in knowledge baton-passing collaboration, *crowd participants can share, interpret and use others' posts in an untold number of different ways which the participants posting the initial knowledge may not have intended.* As a participant reads others' posts, the participant may reuse and build on the other's post, read something that inspires a link with a remembered solution from another domain that can be adapted, learn something new about the problem, reflect on another's idea to see the good and bad points about the idea and how to make it better, notice that the post is something they disagree with and reflect on why they disagree, notice that two posts disagree with each other but both seem right raising the need for a solution to overcome this contradiction, and notice patterns in the post about topics or types of knowledge that inspires sharing similar topics or types of knowledge. All of these different potential actions that a participant might take indicates that each post serves as nothing more than a touchpoint for a highly personalized reflective process. Unmindcuffing the crowd allows for this plethora of personalized reflections to multiply, stimulating more diversity and creative associations. The creation of innovative ideas then may be coming from the opportunity to interpret others' posts freely without regard to what the author of the post intended and regardless of whether the post would be referred to as an idea.

3.4.4 How Does a Crowd Create Consensus?

Because the crowd can interpret others' posts as they want to, "consensus" among participants about problem definitions or solutions is highly unlikely. *Consensus is replaced with parallelism.* As shown in Table 3.2, across the 20 crowds, each event consisted, on average, of about 51 parallel threads among 86 participants. This ratio of threads to participants indicate that participants are rarely engaged in long conversations with the same participants. Being able to start a new thread allows the crowd to avoid consensus and simply engage in parallel discussions about these complex wicked problems. This does not mean that a participant may avoid reading other parallel discussions and learn from them. In a sense, the parallel paths foster a diversity of conversations going on in parallel. Unlike in face-to-face contexts where one individual is rarely able to listen in on parallel conversations, in unmindcuffed online innovation crowdsourcing, participants can listen in and gain diverse perspectives without necessarily engaging in each and every conversation.

Since it is difficult to listen when formulating one's own responses, unmindcuffed participants may be able to be better listeners than they would have been if they had engaged in each conversation themselves. Thus, the parallelism may increase the exposure to diverse knowledge and perspectives being shared in ways not feasible in face-to-face conversations and not feasible if only ideas are allowed to be discussed.

Freeing the crowd from coming up with an agreed-upon consensus of a problem definition allows the crowd to have multiple problem definitions simultaneously, and allowing participants to bleed, integrate, aggregate, select, refine, or disagree with any of the problem definitions. In a sense, the parallelism helps to lay out more clearly the problem definition and requirements space to which solutions are needed. Instead of a sequential problem-definition/problem-solution process, this parallelism fosters integrative critical thinking which leads to more innovative ideas. In an earlier paper,[21] we demonstrated that, when unmindcuffed, crowds' ideas are buried deep into discussion threads and often disconnected from the discussion topic in which they have been posted. It is almost as if participants are reading and reflecting and simply posting where they happen to be in the discussion thread topology.

In place of consensus appears to be attention; attention to each of many different alternative discussions signifies where the crowd energy lies. As thread starters are posted, and replies are posted, the crowd can pursue different aspects of the problem, share in parallel discussions about different interpretations of the problem, and share in parallel discussions of different solutions. If there are only thread starters and no replies, it means that the crowd is so cognitively disconnected that no thread engenders the energy or enthusiasm for a reply. Without replies, knowledge baton passing is more difficult because, even if a reply is only tangentially related to a prior post, there still is a tangent. Without tangents streaming together thoughts made explicit, it is difficult for participants to discern patterns in posts to formulate their own reflections. *Without replies to posts, it is difficult for the participant to discern where the energy, interest, attention, and creativity of the crowd lies—all of which are needed for innovation to emerge.* In unmindcuffed crowds tasked with innovation, the intent of parallelism is to run several relays in parallel, passing knowledge batons as knowledge-containing posts, with each relay potentially ending up at different end points and some winning the race by offering innovative ideas and other relays petering out for lack of energy, interest, attention, and creativity.

3.4.5 Are Crowds Influenced by Others in the Crowd?

Unmindcuffed crowds do not fill the lack of the structure with social hierarchy and norms, based on the few social support posts they make. *It is as if the crowd does not think about the social influence of others.* It is not even like a sports event when crowds can start waves or panic exits and others are influenced by them. These crowds ask few questions of others, they minimize their supportive statements, and we noticed almost no personal attacks. The anonymity appears to lead the crowd to replacing any attention to others as people, with attention exclusively on what was said; *that is, what is said is far more important than who said it.* In the absence of the face-to-face cues and personal profiles, then, the crowd is freed not only from the constraints of the Idea-Sharing but also from the constraints of adhering to what others think.

3.4.6 Summary of Participation Differences

Table 3.3 summarizes the differences between teams, online communities, and crowds engaged in Collective Production in terms of participative commitment behavior.

Table 3.3 Summary of commitment differences between teams, online communities, and collectively producing crowds for innovation

Teams	Online communities	Collectively producing innovation crowds
Agree to a common goal	Agree to a common purpose	No agreement; parallelism
Stay with team until it finishes	Stay on peripheral until allowed to enter core group	Don't stay from beginning to the end; post anytime during the event and leave
Common definition of problem	Generally agreed-upon definition(s) of problem by the core	No common definition of problem, problem interpretable differently, problem redefined continually through knowledge sharing
Care about each other	Care about each other	Don't care about each
Who transmits knowledge is as important as what knowledge is transmitted	Who transmits knowledge is as important as what knowledge is transmitted	Who transmits knowledge doesn't matter. It is the knowledge content that matters.

3.5 What Does This Mean for Future Research on Innovation and Mass Collaboration?

Research on innovation has argued for the importance of focusing on teams or experts to do the work. If innovation, however, can be derived from knowledge baton-passing participants with minimal commitment, we should raise the question: *is innovation generation best done in cross-functional teams as it is done today?* Is it possible to consider that the reason researchers have always assumed that a team is better, especially for ill-structured problems, is because crowds limited to the Idea-Sharing process of giving ideas leads to lots of bad ideas? By removing the limitations, future research on teams should reconsider whether teams, per se, is the right way to achieve innovation.

For future research on crowdsourcing, we must begin to examine the crowd as a phenomenon worthy of study, even as we modify the word crowd to emphasize the fluidity with which participants come and go and knowledge emerges. The conventional assumptions about how a crowd solves a problem are clearly wrong. Crowds don't just post ideas alone if allowed to do otherwise (despite research to the contrary). They don't pay attention to each other if allowed otherwise (despite research to the contrary). They don't engage in dialogue or consensus-building if allowed otherwise (despite research to the contrary). Thus, the interaction we assume crowds engage in is quite different than the interaction we know teams and online communities engage in. We need to study these new forms of "interactions" as they become more prevalent.

These new forms of interactions may increasingly define how "teams" operate, as organizational workers are increasingly members of multiple teams "interacting" over the Internet. In some early research on a completely virtual team, we found that it was only when the teams *stopped* thinking about who was expert in what aspect of the problem and focused exclusively on the designs they were posting regardless of who posted them, that the team was able to achieve an innovative breakthrough for a rocket engine design.[22] Perhaps it is time to supplement the research on the social interactions among members of innovative teams with research on the interactions of teams with the knowledge as it is posted to some common repository of the team. Given the fluidity of the crowd, it is time for those researchers contemplating yet another study on why people participate in crowds, to consider conducting research on why people participate in the way they do: when they make their less-than-two contributions, when they choose to observe versus contribute, and when they decide to build on others' posts versus starting a new discussion thread.

For future research on collaboration in crowds, we must reconsider what "co" means in collaboration. For many researchers of crowds, "co" refers to coordination, which is not collaboration. *Collaboration requires the generation of some concept that was not there previously and that could not have emerged if both parties did not interact. In contrast, coordination refers to agreeing on how work will be done, assigning or self-selecting into tasks to get the work done, and monitoring if the work is done as expected.* With well-defined decomposed problems, as explained in Chap. 1, coordination helps to ensure that individual tasks are completed. Assigning tasks to Mechanical Turk or UpWork or most open source software development projects in which tasks are made clear (such as when bugs need to be fixed or new versions are being planned) are descriptions of tasks to be coordinated, not of collaboration.

Collaboration, however, is needed to generate innovative solutions to complex wicked problems. However, t*he "co" in collaboration does not mean necessarily interaction among people.* In cross-functional teams, this collaboration has typically been accomplished as a dialogue between people. But perhaps, this is how our research is an indication of the future to come. Virtual collaboration of the future may no longer involve people representing disciplinary or functional positions but rather being brought together simply because their perspective is unique in some way from others on the team. As such, such teams may increasingly look like crowds collectively producing innovation in a manner distinctive from the traditional view of teams attempting to cross the divides of different "thought worlds".[23]

People may not need to be in the same place at the same time to "co" innovate. On the contrary, being in the same place may result in people emphasizing social support over pushing others to take on risky alternative perspectives. People may not all need to be involved every day all the time but only when they have something valuable to say. Exactly what they may need to say, and how to say it to stimulate creativity will be discussed in later chapters.

In sum, the "co" of collaboration may signal a new form of collaboration in which people-to-people interactivity becomes less important as organizations and crowds figure out how to interact with each other's knowledge fragments more effectively and efficiently. The fact that the unmindcuffed crowds were able to produce more innovative ideas more efficiently than Idea-Sharing crowds suggests that the following chapters are needed to give us a direction for understanding how to help crowds and team interact with each other's knowledge.

3.6 What Does This Mean for Practice?

Let's play through this scenario for a minute. Suppose a firm could have three functionally distinctive engineers and a marketing staff member working as a team for many months developing an early concept design for a new product to reduce infant mortality rates. Alternatively, the firm could instead have a few hundred people external to the company interested in (and probably experienced with) infant mortality offering their thoughts about a new product over a ten-day period. Which would a practitioner recommend for the firm? The obvious answer is the team. This is because there is the assumption that hundreds of people don't build on each other's posts and redefine the problem in innovative ways; and, besides, what firm wants hundreds of disconnected suggestions from people who don't know the firm's capabilities?

But suppose the crowd didn't act in this way. Suppose the crowd built on each other's posts, learning about various resources needed to implement various product ideas in the process, and identified new ways of thinking about the problem so that changes in the way the firm allocates its resources may be worthwhile? Wouldn't hundreds of participants, working by passing the batons of knowledge about ideas and problem definitions be better than a team? Wouldn't the 15 solution-ideas that emerge from such a crowdsourced process be better than the one solution-idea generated by the team? This is what we found in Chap. 2, with Chap. 3 indicating how minimal that participation can be and still succeed.

This means that, for practitioners to encourage the crowd to innovate, the practitioner must give the crowd what they want: *impact with very little investment*. The crowd is not signing up to work full-time or even part-time over a ten-day period to solve the problem. They are signing up to make a difference with as little effort as possible.

The manager must help them do that. First, the problem needs to be an ill-structured, or "wicked" problem. This means that the problem given to the crowd cannot have a predefined set of criteria for the best idea. A marketing manager for a company's product who asks the crowd to develop a winning commercial which will be shown on Superbowl Sunday is not offering the crowd a wicked problem. The problem is not wicked because the criteria are pretty clear: the solution is a commercial, the solution must be entertaining, and the solution must be in alignment with the product's image. Second, the practitioner must create a technology platform where it is easy for the participants to read others' posts quickly and be encouraged to incorporate that knowledge into their own ideas. Third, the practitioner should not predefine what knowledge the crowd is allowed to share. Finally, remind the crowd that the problem is intentionally ill-structured to allow them to come up with new definitions of the problem and inclusive solutions.

Notes

1. See for example the many reviews on innovation teams: Gong, Y., Kim, T. Y., Lee, D. R., & Zhu, J. (2013). A multilevel model of team goal orientation, information exchange, and creativity. *Academy of Management Journal, 56*(3), 827–851; Amabile, T. M., & Pratt, M. G. (2016). The dynamic componential model of creativity and innovation in organizations: Making progress, making meaning. *Research in Organizational Behavior, 36*, 157–183; Jang, S. (2017). Cultural brokerage and creative performance in multicultural teams. Organization Science, 28(6), 993–1009; Thompson, L. L., & Wilson, E. R. (2015). Creativity in teams. Emerging trends in the social and behavioral sciences: An interdisciplinary, searchable, and linkable resource, 1–14; Sawyer, K. (2017). Group genius: The creative power of collaboration. Basic books; Edmondson, A. C., & Harvey, J. F. (2018). Cross-boundary teaming for innovation: Integrating research on teams and knowledge in organizations. Human Resource Management Review, 28(4), 347–360; Wang, J., Cheng, G. H. L., Chen, T., & Leung, K. (2019). Team creativity/innovation in culturally diverse teams: A meta-analysis. Journal of Organizational Behavior; van Knippenberg, D. (2017). Team innovation. *Annual Review of Organizational Psychology and Organizational Behavior, 4*, 211–233.
2. Quotes are from the USAID's Global Pulse Final Report. Ferguson, D.A. (2010) Global Pulse 2010: Insights and Ideas from Around the World. Washington, D.C., United States Agency for International Development.
3. Harvey, S. (2014). Creative synthesis: Exploring the process of extraordinary group creativity. *Academy of Management Review, 39*(3), 324–343; Carlile, P. R. (2002). A pragmatic view of knowledge and boundaries: Boundary objects in new product development. Organization science, 13(4), 442–455; Carlile, P. R. (2004). Transferring, translating, and transforming: An integrative framework for managing knowledge across boundaries. Organization science, 15(5), 555–568; Mesmer-Magnus, J. R., & DeChurch, L. A. (2009). Information sharing and team performance: a meta-analysis. Journal of Applied Psychology, 94(2), 535–546. Tsoukas, H. (2009). A dialogical approach to the creation of new knowledge in organizations. Organization science, 20(6), 941–957; Nonaka, I., H. Takeuchi. 1995. The Knowledge-Creating Company. New York: Oxford University Press; Nonaka, I., Von Krogh, G., & Voelpel, S. (2006). Organizational knowledge creation theory: Evolutionary paths and future advances. Organization studies, 27(8), 1179–1208.

4. Ibid.
5. Bullinger, A. C., Neyer, A. K., Rass, M. & Moeslein, K. (2010) Community-based innovation contests: Where competition meets cooperation. Creativity and innovation management, 19(3), 390–303.
6. Lovelace, K., Shapiro, D. L., & Weingart, L. R. (2001). Maximizing cross-functional new product teams' innovativeness and constraint adherence: A conflict communications perspective. *Academy of Management Journal, 44*(4), 779–793.
7. Grant, A. M., & Berry, J. W. (2011). The necessity of others is the mother of invention: Intrinsic and prosocial motivations, perspective taking, and creativity. Academy of management journal, 54(1), 73–96.
8. Nembhard, I. M., & Edmondson, A. C. (2006). Making it safe: The effects of leader inclusiveness and professional status on psychological safety and improvement efforts in health care teams. Journal of Organizational Behavior, 27(7), 941–966.
9. Nahapiet, J., & Ghoshal, S. (1998). Social capital, intellectual capital, and the organizational advantage. Academy of management review, 23(2), 242–266.
10. Scott Page has written about the superadditivity of teams with respect to diversity in teams, although his focus is on how the diversity adds together, while our focus is on how the diversity inspires others and creates knowledge that can be passed around as a baton, rather than added together. Page, S. E. (2010). Diversity and complexity (Vol. 2). Princeton University Press; Page, S. E. (2007). Making the difference: Applying a logic of diversity. Academy of Management Perspectives, 21(4), 6–20.
11. Schemmann, B., Herrmann, A. M., Chappin, M. M., & Heimeriks, G. J. (2016). Crowdsourcing ideas: Involving ordinary users in the ideation phase of new product development. Research Policy, 45(6), 1145–1154; Frey, K., Lüthje, C., Haag, S., (2011). Whom should firms attract to open innovation platforms? The role of knowledge diversity and motivation. Long Range Plann. 44 (5–6), 397–420; Muhdi, L., Boutellier, R., (2011). Motivational factors affecting participation and contribution of members in two different Swiss innovation communities. Int. J. Innov. Manage. 15 (3), 543–562., Dahlander, L., Piezunka, H., (2014). Open to suggestions: how organizations elicit suggestions through proactive and reactive attention. Res. Policy 43 (5), 812–827.
12. Leimeister, J. M., Huber, M., Bretschneider, U., & Krcmar, H. (2009). Leveraging crowdsourcing: activation-supporting components for IT-based ideas competition. Journal of Management Information Systems, 26(1), 197–224; Füller, J., Hutter, K., & Faullant, R. (2011). Why co-creation experience matters? Creative experience and its impact on the quantity and quality of creative contributions. R&D Management, 41(3), 259–273.; Jeppesen, L.B., Frederiksen, L., (2006). Why do users contribute to firm-hosted user communities? The case of computer-controlled music instruments. Organ. Sci. 17, 45–64; Stahlbrost, A., Bergvall-Kareborn, B., (2011).

Exploring users motivation in innovation communities. Int. J. Entrep. Innov. Manag. 14, 298–314; Fuller, J., (2006). Why consumers engage in virtual new product developments initiated by producers. Adv. Consum. Res. 33, 639–646; Boudreau, K. J., Lacetera, N., Lakhani, K. R., (2011). Incentives and problem uncertainty in innovation contests: an empirical analysis. Manag. Sci. 57, 843–863.
13. Amabile, T. M., & Pratt, M. G. (2016). The dynamic componential model of creativity and innovation in organizations: Making progress, making meaning. Research in Organizational Behavior, 36, 157–183.
14. Dahlander L, Frederiksen L, Rullani F. (2008). Online Communities and Open Innovation: Governance and Symbolic Value Creation. *Industry and Innovation*, 15: 115–123.
15. Boudreau, K. J., Lacetera, N., Lakhani, K.R., (2011). Incentives and problem uncertainty in innovation contests: an empirical analysis. Manag. Sci. 57, 843–863.
16. Frey, K., Lüthje, C., Haag, S., (2011). Whom should firms attract to open innovation platforms? The role of knowledge diversity and motivation. Long Range Plann. 44 (5–6), 397–420.
17. Mack, T., & Landau, C. (2015). Winners, losers, and deniers: Self-selection in crowd innovation contests and the roles of motivation, creativity, and skills. *Journal of Engineering and Technology Management, 37*, 52–64.
18. Faraj, S., Jarvenpaa, S.L., Majchrzak, A. (2011) Knowledge collaboration in online communities. Organization Science, 22(5), 1224–1239.
19. Tucci CL, Afuah A, Viscusi G, eds. (2018) Creating & capturing value through crowdsourcing. (Oxford, Oxford, UK).
20. Faraj, S., von Krogh, G., Monteiro, E., & Lakhani, K. R. (2016). Special section introduction—Online community as space for knowledge flows. Information systems research, 27(4), 668–684.
21. Malhotra, A. and Majchrzak, A. (2014) Managing crowds in innovation challenges. California Management Review, 56(4), 103–123.
22. Majchrzak, A., Neece, O. E., Cooper, L.P. (2001) Knowledge reuse for innovation—The Missing Focus in Knowledge Management: Results of a Case Analysis at the Jet Propulsion Laboratory. Academy of Management Best Paper, August.
23. Dougherty, D. (1992). Interpretive barriers to successful product innovation in large firms. Organization science, 3(2), 179–202.

References

Amabile, T. M., & Pratt, M. G. (2016). The Dynamic Componential Model of Creativity and Innovation in Organizations: Making Progress, Making Meaning. *Research in Organizational Behavior, 36*, 157–183.

Boudreau, K. J., Lacetera, N., & Lakhani, K. R. (2011). Incentives and Problem Uncertainty in Innovation Contests: An Empirical Analysis. *Management Science, 57*, 843–863.

Bullinger, A. C., Neyer, A. K., Rass, M., & Moeslein, K. (2010). Community-Based Innovation Contests: Where Competition Meets Cooperation. *Creativity and Innovation Management, 19*(3), 390–303.

Carlile, P. R. (2002). A Pragmatic View of Knowledge and Boundaries: Boundary Objects in New Product Development. *Organization Science, 13*(4), 442–455.

Carlile, P. R. (2004). Transferring, Translating, and Transforming: An Integrative Framework for Managing Knowledge Across Boundaries. *Organization Science, 15*(5), 555–568.

Dahlander, L., & Piezunka, H. (2014). Open to Suggestions: How Organizations Elicit Suggestions Through Proactive and Reactive Attention. *Research Policy, 43*(5), 812–827.

Dahlander, L., Frederiksen, L., & Rullani, F. (2008). Online Communities and Open Innovation: Governance and Symbolic Value Creation. *Industry and Innovation, 15*, 115–123.

Dougherty, D. (1992). Interpretive Barriers to Successful Product Innovation in Large Firms. *Organization Science, 3*(2), 179–202.

Edmondson, A. C., & Harvey, J. F. (2018). Cross-Boundary Teaming for Innovation: Integrating Research on Teams and Knowledge in Organizations. *Human Resource Management Review, 28*(4), 347–360.

Faraj, S., Jarvenpaa, S. L., & Majchrzak, A. (2011). Knowledge Collaboration in Online Communities. *Organization Science, 22*(5), 1224–1239.

Faraj, S., von Krogh, G., Monteiro, E., & Lakhani, K. R. (2016). Special Section Introduction – Online Community as Space for Knowledge Flows. *Information Systems Research, 27*(4), 668–684.

Ferguson, D. A. (2010). *Global Pulse 2010: Insights and Ideas from Around the World.* Washington, DC: United States Agency for International Development.

Frey, K., Lüthje, C., & Haag, S. (2011). Whom Should Firms Attract to Open Innovation Platforms? The Role of Knowledge Diversity and Motivation. *Long Range Planning, 44*(5–6), 397–420.

Fuller, J. (2006). Why Consumers Engage in Virtual New Product Developments Initiated by Producers. *Advances in Consumer Research, 33*, 639–646.

Füller, J., Hutter, K., & Faullant, R. (2011). Why Co-creation Experience Matters? Creative Experience and Its Impact on the Quantity and Quality of Creative Contributions. *R&D Management, 41*(3), 259–273.

Gong, Y., Kim, T. Y., Lee, D. R., & Zhu, J. (2013). A Multilevel Model of Team Goal Orientation, Information Exchange, and Creativity. *Academy of Management Journal, 56*(3), 827–851.

Grant, A. M., & Berry, J. W. (2011). The Necessity of Others Is the Mother of Invention: Intrinsic and Prosocial Motivations, Perspective Taking, and Creativity. *Academy of Management Journal, 54*(1), 73–96.

Harvey, S. (2014). Creative Synthesis: Exploring the Process of Extraordinary Group Creativity. *Academy of Management Review, 39*(3), 324–343.

Jang, S. (2017). Cultural Brokerage and Creative Performance in Multicultural Teams. *Organization Science, 28*(6), 993–1009.

Jeppesen, L. B., & Frederiksen, L. (2006). Why Do Users Contribute to Firm-Hosted User Communities? The Case of Computer-Controlled Music Instruments. *Organization Science, 17*, 45–64.

Leimeister, J. M., Huber, M., Bretschneider, U., & Krcmar, H. (2009). Leveraging Crowdsourcing: Activation-Supporting Components for IT-Based Ideas Competition. *Journal of Management Information Systems, 26*(1), 197–224.

Lovelace, K., Shapiro, D. L., & Weingart, L. R. (2001). Maximizing Cross-Functional New Product Teams' Innovativeness and Constraint Adherence: A Conflict Communications Perspective. *Academy of Management Journal, 44*(4), 779–793.

Mack, T., & Landau, C. (2015). Winners, Losers, and Deniers: Self-selection in Crowd Innovation Contests and the Roles of Motivation, Creativity, and Skills. *Journal of Engineering and Technology Management, 37*, 52–64.

Majchrzak, A., Neece, O. E., & Cooper, L. P. (2001). *Knowledge Reuse for Innovation – The Missing Focus in Knowledge Management: Results of a Case Analysis at the Jet Propulsion Laboratory*. Academy of Management Best Paper, August.

Malhotra, A., & Majchrzak, A. (2014). Managing Crowds in Innovation Challenges. *California Management Review, 56*(4), 103–123.

Mesmer-Magnus, J. R., & DeChurch, L. A. (2009). Information Sharing and Team Performance: A Meta-Analysis. *Journal of Applied Psychology, 94*(2), 535–546.

Muhdi, L., & Boutellier, R. (2011). Motivational Factors Affecting Participation and Contribution of Members in Two Different Swiss Innovation Communities. *International Journal of Innovation Management, 15*(3), 543–562.

Nahapiet, J., & Ghoshal, S. (1998). Social Capital, Intellectual Capital, and the Organizational Advantage. *Academy of Management Review, 23*(2), 242–266.

Nembhard, I. M., & Edmondson, A. C. (2006). Making It Safe: The Effects of Leader Inclusiveness and Professional Status on Psychological Safety and Improvement Efforts in Health Care Teams. *Journal of Organizational Behavior, 27*(7), 941–966.

Nonaka, I., & Takeuchi, H. (1995). *The Knowledge-Creating Company*. New York: Oxford University Press.

Nonaka, I., Von Krogh, G., & Voelpel, S. (2006). Organizational Knowledge Creation Theory: Evolutionary Paths and Future Advances. *Organization Studies, 27*(8), 1179–1208.

Page, S. E. (2007). Making the Difference: Applying a Logic of Diversity. *Academy of Management Perspectives, 21*(4), 6–20.

Page, S. E. (2010). *Diversity and Complexity* (Vol. 2). Princeton, NJ: Princeton University Press.

Sawyer, K. (2017). *Group Genius: The Creative Power of Collaboration*. New York: Basic Books.

Schemmann, B., Herrmann, A. M., Chappin, M. M., & Heimeriks, G. J. (2016). Crowdsourcing Ideas: Involving Ordinary Users in the Ideation Phase of New Product Development. *Research Policy, 45*(6), 1145–1154.

Stahlbrost, A., & Bergvall-Kareborn, B. (2011). Exploring Users Motivation in Innovation Communities. *International Journal of Entrepreneurship and Innovation Management, 14*, 298–314.

Thompson, L. L., & Wilson, E. R. (2015). Creativity in Teams. In *Emerging Trends in the Social and Behavioral Sciences: An Interdisciplinary, Searchable, and Linkable Resource* (pp. 1–14). Hoboken, NJ: John Wiley & Sons..

Tsoukas, H. (2009). A Dialogical Approach to the Creation of New Knowledge in Organizations. *Organization Science, 20*(6), 941–957.

Tucci, C. L., Afuah, A., & Viscusi, G. (2018). *Creating & Capturing Value Through Crowdsourcing.* Oxford, UK: Oxford University Press.

van Knippenberg, D. (2017). Team Innovation. *Annual Review of Organizational Psychology and Organizational Behavior, 4*, 211–233.

Wang, J., Cheng, G. H. L., Chen, T., & Leung, K. (2019). Team Creativity/Innovation in Culturally Diverse Teams: A Meta-analysis. *Journal of Organizational Behavior, 40*, 693–708.

4

Practice 2: Crowds Offering a Variety of Types of Knowledge Are More Innovative Than Crowds Suggesting More Ideas

In this chapter, we describe how we coded the knowledge traces contributed by the crowds. We were looking for the presence of any of four different types of knowledge shared about the problem description and solutions: facts, examples, paradoxical objectives, and ideas for solving the problem. We found that innovative ideas were *not* preceded by a larger variety of ideas! Instead, innovative ideas were preceded by the crowd posting a greater variety of different knowledge *types*. Thus, it is not simply diversity of opinions that matter, it is the diversity in how each member frames their knowledge when they are sharing it during the crowdsourcing.

In this chapter, we focus on only one of the practices in Fig. 4.1: the impact of sharing a variety of knowledge types (rather than merely ideas) on the Collective Production of innovative ideas in crowds. First, we scanned the literature for what anecdotal evidence there might be as to the need for and value of diverse knowledge sharing in the crowds (vis-à-vis just sharing of ideas). We present the cases of OOC and CoLab—crowds asked to solve wicked problems of maritime sustainability and global climate change. Next, using our field data from 20 innovation crowdsourcing events, we coded the knowledge traces contributed by the collective for a variety of different types of knowledge shared about the problem description and solution including facts, examples, paradoxical objectives, and ideas for solving the problem. We then explore if just the number of ideas in a trace versus the variety of knowledge types in a trace is more likely to precede an emergent innovative idea at the end of the trace. *We find that variety of knowledge types—not the number of ideas—is more strongly related to the emergence of innovative ideas.* We explain how the sharing of a variety of knowledge types act to better serve crowds than sharing of mere ideas.

© The Author(s) 2020
A. Majchrzak, A. Malhotra, *Unleashing the Crowd*,
https://doi.org/10.1007/978-3-030-25557-2_4

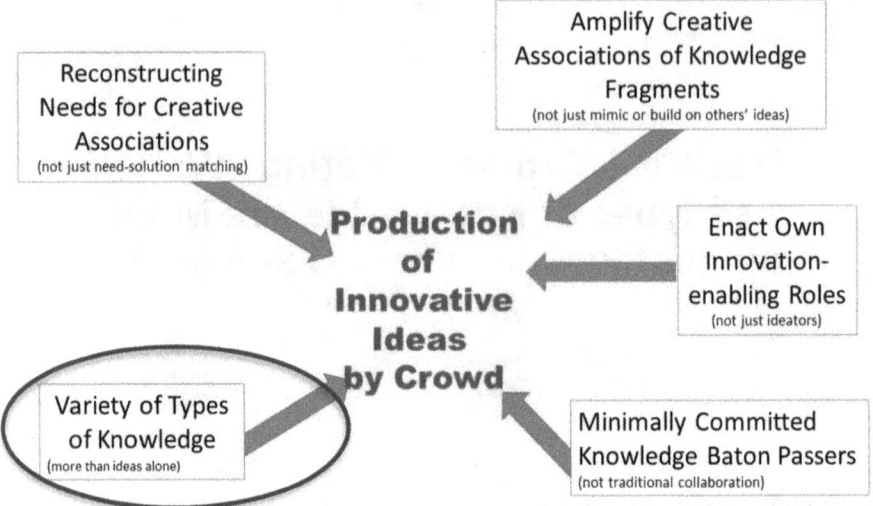

Fig. 4.1 Practice of Collective Production

4.1 Stories from "Our Ocean's Challenge" and the MIT Climate Change Crowdsourcing Lab: Importance of Knowledge Type Variety

Sharing diverse knowledge types was instrumental in tackling the wicked environmental sustainability problem of plastics in the ocean. The annual Our Ocean's Challenge (OOC), aptly described by academic colleagues Amanda Porter, Philipp Tuertscher, and Marleen Huysman[1] was formed to support the maritime industry's development of innovative solutions for sustainable and responsible use of oceans.

OOC was sponsored by a consortium of 12 government research organizations, a network representing 80 firms in the global maritime industry, commercial firms supplying equipment for offshore and onshore maritime operations, a recycler of plastic ocean waste into product development, and a large bank with expertise in sustainable business planning. The challenge sponsors decided to not follow the standard Idea-Search format but instead adopted what is referred to as "robust action", defined as "noncommittal actions that keep future lines of action open in strategic contexts where opponents are trying to narrow them".[2] Robust action is a process in which diverse and heterogeneous actors are encouraged to interact constructively over prolonged timespans, providing different interpretations among various audiences with different evaluative criteria, coordination promoted without requiring explicit consensus, and individuals encouraged to share and engage in the type of experimentation that promotes evolutionary learning while allowing unsuccessful efforts to be abandoned. The types of knowledge encouraged to be exchanged include ideas, questions, general comments, and any knowledge thought to be relevant by the participant. At a philosophical level, "robust action" is very similar to what our unmindcuffed crowds did except that our crowds were all online and did not engage for prolonged periods of time.

The grand challenge question, "How can we use our oceans as a resource for scalable sustainable business?" was split into two subquestions: (1) How do we create a sustainable offshore industry such as minimizing the impact of sedimentation and marine sound? And (2) What new scalable ocean ventures should be considered, such as generating energy from the ocean?

The Challenge was considered highly successful. A number of solutions with business and implementation plans and implementation partners resulted from the effort. For example, a plan for deep sea renewable wave energy was developed among two partners with three other partners reviewing for business and technical support. A plan for slowing and solving corrosion of offshore structures led to the creation of a joint industry project among three organizations.

After initial ideas and knowledge could be offered by anyone in the world, the challenge was closed to outsiders and detailed business and implementation plans and prototypes were developed and then presented to potential investors at an industry event. "OOC partners deemed this a successful challenge and their efforts were recognized in the industry with several prestigious awards (Dupont 2015) and official recognition by the United Nations as frontrunners of Sustainable Development Goal number 14, to conserve and sustainably use the oceans, seas and marine resources for sustainable development (United Nations 2017b). In 2016–2017, OOC hosted a second successful crowdsourcing challenge and it plans to continue hosting annual challenges until it fulfills its vision for a completely sustainable industry."[3]

The researchers interviewed the 12 co-sponsoring organizations and reviewed the 88 ideas and 731 comments offered during the event. From their research, they learned what made the event so successful:

1. Sponsors initially focused the challenge on alleviating the plastic soup problem in the ocean and found much less interest in participation until they expanded the topic to allow for the sustainability of the ocean as a shared resource.

2. Once participants were assured that the contribution of any knowledge—even a non-expert one—was better than no contribution, diversity of expertise on a topic led to substantially enriched conversations and co-created ideas.
3. The involvement of diverse partners enabled each one to align the evolving problem definition with their shared and individual interests, a move which enhanced their commitment to support the idea development later in the process.
4. During ideation, "partner organizations contributed through complementary expertise and divergent perspectives, which often involved rethinking the original problem".[4]

Apparent from the Our Ocean's Challenge was that the challenge succeeded in part because it allowed the participants to maintain and share their diversity of knowledge types and perspectives.

The Climate CoLab was initiated and maintained by Tom Malone at MIT. CoLab is a crowd-based initiative that has a crowd of over 50,000 people, each interested in some aspect of global climate change. Through CoLab crowd experiments it is clear that Collective Production of innovation to address the wicked problem of global climate change is not only possible but is required. As part of the CoLab, integrated crowdsourcing contests are run to encourage Collective Production of solutions from others. For the integration of solutions, diverse knowledge is needed that ensures that solution-ideas are mutually compatible (i.e., similar goals) and that they are collectively sufficient to solve the larger wicked problem. The CoLab experiments show that, for innovative solutions to emerge from Collective Production, sharing of diverse knowledge types such as assumption, solution-ideas, constraints, and objectives are required (we will elaborate further on these knowledge types in later chapters). Such knowledge encourages the integration of idea seeds by allowing participants in the crowd to see that others' knowledge can be reused to obtain more comprehensive solutions (achieving the larger objective of a wicked problem) that meet diverse and sometimes divergent objectives.

These two anecdotes of OOC and CoLab intrigued us to explore the value and impact of sharing diverse types of knowledge in crowds addressing the wicked problem. It is clear that sharing diverse knowledge provides collectives with significant resources from which to create innovative ideas. However, there are also obstacles to such knowledge sharing. Sharing of diverse knowledge types may not be encouraged when organizations put so much emphasis on ideas, ignoring those who don't have ideas but have diverse perspectives on the problem. It may also be the case that when diverse knowledge is shared as part of Idea-Sharing only, the diversity of perspectives may not be easily understood by others. The point of this chapter is that diverse knowledge may be easier to share and understand when it is split into different types of knowledge so that explicit comparisons within a type can be made. For example, one type of knowledge might be assumptions. When each person makes explicit their assumptions, it is easier to compare and discuss those assumptions rather than when an assumption might be buried within a solution.

Following this logic, we argue that enabling and encouraging the crowd to share diverse knowledge types allow them to reconcile, appreciate, and build upon their diverse perspectives and so overcome the problem of "representation gaps". Rather than being impaired by an inability to bridge the cognitive divides imposed by a multitude of perspectives presented in a crowd, sharing of diverse knowledge types in crowds can lead to divergent perspectives enriching the conversation, which can foster the creation of more innovative solutions. These divergent perspectives often can lead to differences in how the same problem can be tacitly conceptualized differently by different individuals—often labeled as representational gaps in groups. In Sect. 4.2, we expound on how we used the theory of representation gaps to suggest how these differences can be overcome. We suggest that when each individual's knowledge is fragmented into knowledge "types" describing one's perspective, then the expression of diverse knowledge through knowledge type fragments helps to overcome misunderstandings and representation gaps. Our basic hypothesis is that the more diverse perspectives are expressed through sharing fragments of knowledge types, the more likely that innovative ideas will be generated. Since ideas are only one type of knowledge shared, the sharing of ideas alone should not lead to more innovative ideas.

4.2 Overcoming Harmful Representational Gaps in Crowds Through Diverse Knowledge Sharing

Crowds of strangers are likely to represent diverse perspectives. By "diverse", we mean differences in formal expertise (such as education and profession), demographic-based experiences (due to differences in geographical regions, ethnicity, and gender), and informal experiences (such as work and non-work activities engaged in). The diversity is a positive aspect of the crowd. Disparate knowledge can challenge others' perspectives in a manner that leads to the creation of new perspectives.[5]

When these strangers interact, though, they are likely to experience "representational gaps". Representational gaps can be thought of as tacit differences as to how shared problems are conceptualized. Such gaps lead to inconsistencies between the individuals in terms of how each of them defines the problem that is being solved.[6] In essence, individuals in collectives construct their own representation of the problem based on the knowledge they hold. Representational gaps, especially when wicked problems are being solved, can cause severe friction amongst individuals when they attempt to understand each other's definition of the problem with different assumptions and with different objectives to achieve. For example, when the crowd is asked to suggest solutions for using technology so that societies can lead a better life, they may each think of the problem from their own, diverse perspective. For some, the problem could be of conceiving technology of the future, and for others, it may be about what technologies are available now. Similarly, some may think of "better life" as a higher standard of living and others may conceive of it as reduced income disparity. Representational gaps create conflict in groups, leading to misattributions, and an inability to understand, appreciate, and build on others' knowledge.

For Collective Production to occur, crowd participants need to be able to understand others' perspectives. Team members decomposing their knowledge into the elements of how they represent the problem can alleviate representational gaps. Knowledge about a problem consists of goals (i.e., objectives), assumptions (i.e., facts about the problem), ideas for solving the problem, and issues to consider when implementing solutions. It is through sharing of these different types of knowledge that representation gaps can be reduced. Crowd participants, who are representative of an infinitely possible diversity, may think of different objectives to solve a wicked problem, they may make assumptions about the problem others do not, and they may have very different perspectives on how a problem can be solved. In crowds, the singularity is impossible nor desired since the singularity, by definition, ignores divergent perspectives. Therefore, in crowds, the sharing of different knowledge types—such as assumptions, objectives, ideas, and implementation issues—may help crowds to understand each other even if they don't agree with each other.

4.3 Sharing a Variety of Ideas May Not Lead to More Innovative Ideas

In the Idea-Sharing crowdsourcing-for-innovation process, the diversity is expressed through ideas, with the more people engaged, the greater diversity of ideas presented. The brainstorming literature[7] on groups has raised the problems with focusing group interactions only on ideas, finding that group members will fixate on a particular idea, or forget about their own ideas as others' ideas capture more attention. More importantly, other researchers have explored the relationship between idea variety and outcomes, finding that, when individuals in a group exclusively focus on offering each other different ideas, the group explores a smaller number of domains, that is, problem search spaces.[8] Using the language of search, ideas may create a fixation effect[9]—a fixation not on any single idea but on the space of possible ideas. As such, a focus exclusively on others' ideas will block or inhibit ideas that may be substantially different or novel.[10] Individuals in a collective may then generate new ideas that are very similar to initial ideas (fixation).

To avoid excessive focus on ideas only, we argue that knowledge types that groups need to share to reduce their representation gaps are their different objectives and assumptions about the problem. Other researchers have similarly suggested the importance of sharing assumptions and objectives to appreciate the differences and similarities amongst individuals and in organizations.[11] In so doing, problem definitions can be elaborated, expanded, or modified in ways that address some of these other definitions. This problem expansion can then potentially lead to new solutions that were not initially considered by the Innovation Crowdsourcing sponsor. A single consensus on the problem definition cannot be expected in crowds and thus the intention of sharing problem definitions is simply for learning and growth, not for agreement.

Moreover, given that the problem is a wicked one, problem definitions are likely to be offered simultaneously with solution-ideas. Participating in a crowdsourcing event, especially one that follows a Collective Production process whereby participants are unconstrained, are very likely to debate and expound on the original wicked problem statement regardless of the solutions being proposed. Moreover, they are not going to wait to define and redefine the problem itself before moving on to generating ideas to solve the problem.

In sum, crowds are more likely to develop innovative solutions when they collectively engage in problem elaboration through sharing knowledge such as assumptions and objectives describing the problem rather than each other's solution-ideas only. This view runs counter to the extensive literature that emphasizes the value of others' ideas in online communities and crowdsourcing.[12] This means that, as participants present their knowledge in terms of problem definitions, they are reducing the representational gaps that exist between diverse participants in the crowd, thus allowing them to understand, absorb, and build on the diverse perspectives to offer a more innovative idea. This was observed in the two examples we presented earlier. We will next test whether this also holds true in the 20 crowdsourcing events that were part of our field research.

4.4 Evidence from Our 20 Field-Research Crowdsourcing Events on the Effects of Variety of Knowledge Types Shared by Crowds on Innovation

We hypothesized that the variety of knowledge types shared by crowds was a more potent predictor of innovativeness of the ideas generated than the number of different ideas shared. To test our hypothesis, we coded the knowledge posts for whether the posts contained different types of knowledge derived from the representational gap theory discussed above. The knowledge categories were developed from the extant literature on archetypes of representational knowledge: ideas, paradoxical objectives, analogies, and assumptions.[13]

Ideas are defined as any solution suggested by the participant. Objectives are defined in terms of tradeoffs between two objectives since the crowd rarely simply restates the objective of the challenge. Finally, assumptions are measured as two forms: *facts* and *examples* as different forms of assumptions about the problem. The knowledge types and how we measured them are shown in Table 4.1 below.

We had two raters code all posts across the 20 innovation crowdsourcing events. In coding, the raters also reviewed both the title of the post and the entire thread prior to coding the post to ensure coding took into account the context of the discussion. A reasonable agreement between the raters was obtained (Cohen's Kappa coefficient $\kappa = 0.74$; $p < 0.001$). Any disagreements were resolved through discussion.

To test our hypothesis, we took each of the 297 ideas rated for innovativeness. We looked at the five most recent posts. An example of a trace with coded posts is shown in Table 4.2.

We counted the number of each knowledge type in the trace. We then constructed a Blau's index of heterogeneity: $1 - \sum_{i=1}^{n} p_i^2$ for each of the traces where p_i is the proportion of posts for each of the i knowledge type. A near zero number for the index indicates that the same type of knowledge was posted by participants who contributed to that trace. A number near 1 indicates that an equal distribution across the four knowledge types is posted. We then look at whether a larger number of knowledge types are more likely to be found prior to ideas rated by the executives as more innovative. To remind the reader, when executives were rating the ideas, they were not aware of or shown the traces that preceded the idea they are rating.

4 Practice 2: Crowds Offering a Variety of Types of Knowledge Are... 117

Table 4.1 Knowledge categories

Coded Stimuli	Short description	Examples of posts	#of posts With	Avg (SD) in a trace
Idea	Statements that present possible solutions to address the problem at hand	"Could we do it this way ...", "I was thinking that maybe we could ...", "I'd like to make a proposal ..."	1181	2.38 (1.47)
Non-idea associations				
Fact	Perceived or objective facts, data, statistics, charts or established practices related to the problem statement	"There are currently 10,000 people who use this tool"; "there will be a new product coming out next year"; "our competitors are doing xxx".	317	0.64 (0.86)
Tradeoff	Identification of issues or conflicting requirements that are difficult or impossible to achieve simultaneously with current known solutions	"How do we sell the software cheaply but don't lose our high-end market, how do we increase the revenue for maintenance and yet not lose clients."	171	0.34 (0.58)
Example	Describe concrete illustrations of cause-effect models of the problem and how the problem may have been solved in another context	"Over at company X they've been doing something like this for years that looks like ..., Could we follow the way that X does it ..."	275	0.55 (0.81)
Agreement	Statements that show agreement with previously stated knowledge	"I agree with what you said"	405	0.81 (0.93)
Non-knowledge contributions	Statements that do not contain any knowledge content, i.e., questions, administrative comments, or others	"Could you please explain this in another way?" "I think the challenge ends tomorrow" "I wish I could get time off"	328	
Total # of codes allocated to 2428 posts			2677	

Table 4.2 Example of a trace with coded knowledge sharing in posts in a trace

1. *If this could be framed to how my bad health affects my kids it would be more powerful. If I were to die early and leave them unsupported it would be terrible or if my bad habits are transferred on to them. An app or website that showed me how my bad habits affect my kids would be a major motivator for me. [Idea]*
2. *I am suggesting that perhaps the rewards/incentives do not always have to address physical or monetary. Maybe, the insurance company could provide me access to counselor or psychiatrist etc. [Idea]*
3. *Fitbit even offers a corporate package to motivate fitness and health around a workplace environment: http://www.fitbit.com/product/corporate-solutions. [Analogy]*
4. *So far the posts have given incentives, rebates, etc. to the loyal customers. What are the revenue streams to offset these costs? Social Impact Bonds? [Paradox]*
5. *Most of the revenue would be cost savings to UnitedHealth. Basically, if you come in for preventative care then High Blood Pressure might be diagnosed earlier and more affordably. Or you could catch cancer at an earlier point, where it is still treatable. It's a better outcome for the patient and for the insurer. [Fact]*

[Rated idea] Building off what a lot of people have been saying. What about a program at work where you tackle your health challenges together? We aggregate the data and in some way we can visualize the future of the average company employee. As the employees go to the gym more, see the doctor, do 5 k runs together, the entire company can see how their community is improving. Sometimes it's hard to motivate to do something on my own. It would help a lot to see all my co-workers doing it, too. I would feel better just knowing that are healthier and happier

The results of the primary analysis are italicized in Table 4.3. The results indicate that posting of an innovative idea at the end of the trace is highly correlated with the presence of a greater variety of knowledge in the five-post trace immediately preceding the idea. Looking at the model fit statistics, it is clear that the model which includes the most recent trace (Control in Table 4.2) shows a better fit to the data, that is, the best explanatory power in explaining the variation in the innovativeness of rated idea. That is, the model that includes our variables of interest (variety of knowledge and proportion of number of ideas in the trace), when compared to model A (controls only model) has smaller values of the negative log-likelihood or twice the negative log-likelihood (−2 log-likelihood), accounting for a significant additional 14% of the variance in innovativeness of the rated idea. The coefficient associated with Proportion of Ideas in the most recent trace does not have a significant relationship with the innovativeness of idea posted after trace, that is, more ideas do not beget a better (innovative) idea.

Table 4.3 Results of knowledge variety in traces and relationship with innovativeness of ideas

DV = Innovativeness of the idea after a digital trace (n = 291)	Control model	Immediate prior trace: Variety effect model
Controls		
Event level	Parameter estimates (SD)	
Number of participants	0.001 (0.004)	0.002 (0.004)
Problem unrestrictiveness	−0.82*** (0.23)	−0.75** (0.24)
Total rated ideas	−0.05* (0.02)	−0.084** (0.24)
Trace level	Standardized variance component estimates (SD)	
Time order of the trace (log)	0.33 (0.21)	0.06 (0.16)
Activity of actor posting idea (log)	0.07 (0.13)	0.02 (0.07)
Independent variables (trace level)		Standardized variance component estimates (SD)
Variety of knowledge types in immediate prior trace		*0.63* (0.31)*
Proportion of ideas in immediate prior trace		0.005 (.013)
Model fit		
Adjusted R^2	0.21	0.35
−2 log-likelihood	1182.92	1150.02

*$p < 0.05$; **$p < 0.01$; ***$p < 0.001$

4.5 Exploring Alternative Influences on Innovative Ideas

We included control variables to rule out alternative explanations for the influence on innovativeness of ideas. We want to demonstrate that our main variable of focus—Variety of Knowledge Types—has a significant effect above and beyond the control variables.

Examining the first column in Table 4.3, the results related to control variables show that number of rated ideas (by an executive sponsor of a challenge) has a relationship with the innovativeness of ideas rated in the challenge. This control variable accounts for the possibility that there may be rating fatigue or comparative high bar for all ideas rated, therefore more the ideas rated more all the ideas are rated lower. The nature of the problem posed to the crowd also seemingly has a relationship with the rating of ideas from the crowd. The more the problem is unrestricted, the higher is the bar of measurement by the executive sponsors. In other words, the more open a problem, the harder it is for the executive raters to assess its innovativeness as there is no precedence or a pre-established bar for what is truly an innovative idea.

What we also find is that increasing the size of the crowd—the greater the number of participants—does not necessarily result in ideas being suggested that are more innovative. It is not the size of the crowd that matters, it is what the crowd does, in terms of contributing a variety of knowledge types that impacts innovativeness of ideas collectively produced by the crowds. Finally, we also controlled for the possibility that the time in the event when an idea is contributed might have an influence on ideas that are collectively produced as there may be learning and more knowledge available to the crowd later in the event. Further, we looked at whether knowledge activity of the individual posting the idea influences whether an idea contributed by the individual is innovative or not.

Finally, we included controls at the knowledge trace level—time order of the trace and activity level of the participant in the crowd who posted the idea. We find that these alternative explanations do not account for the innovativeness of the ideas collectively produced by the crowds. In other words, the time elapsed in the event (group learning effect) or the activity level of the individual contributing the idea (individual learning effect) is not related to the innovativeness of the idea.

4.6 How Do Our Findings Align with Current Research on Online Crowds?

Diversity has been talked about in crowds, whereby it is the long tail of the diversity, that is, outlier expertise, that is the source of innovation.[14] In other words, it is those with peripheral expertise rather than deep and narrow expertise in the topic that bring a new viewpoint that leads to breakthroughs in innovation.[15] These peripherally expert participants are not bound by prevailing assumptions and biases of experts looking at the problem.

However, research has to move beyond the notion of experts versus non-experts in terms of diversity. Building on rich notions of different types of diversity in organizations, our notion of diversity in crowds is different. *Instead of conceptualizing expertise (or lack thereof) as a characteristic of an individual and diversity as the range of expertise represented in the crowd, we characterize expertise as the knowledge fragments contributed and diversity of expertise as the variety of types of knowledge contributed.* Also, by looking at trace-by-trace diversity and impact on Collective Production of innovation, we want to advance research on diversity by focusing on knowledge type diversity that is not "static" but ever evolving. Next, in Sect. 4.6.1, we elaborate on these two notions of knowledge type diversity and evolution knowledge type diversity.

4.6.1 Developing the Notion of Knowledge Diversity in Crowds

The first and foremost way one could think of diversity is how different are crowds' perspective on the wicked problem they are attempting to solve—referred to as separation diversity. Separation diversity is the manifest fault-lines that may develop in attempting to delineate the problem.[16] In some ways having multiple perspectives on the problem may be good as it can be the basis for creative conflict, but in other ways, it can lead to "perspective cliques" in crowd discussions and can lead to fissures that cannot be resolved. A non-productive scenario, from the perspective of the Collective Production by crowds, is the separation between coalesced perspectives of those more familiar with the problem ("experts") and those who are less familiar with the problem ("non-experts"). This leaves unresolvable tensions that are falsely based on "expertise" and lead to a lower probability of innovation occurring. By measuring the amount of separation at the start of the innovation process it may be clear as to whether the crowd is able to produce more or less innovation. Perhaps more separation diversity is better for innovation in crowds. Lack of separation diversity may be an indicator of "group think" about the problem that leads to less creative abrasion in problem definition and therefore less innovation.

The second view of diversity is the one related to dominance (see Note 16). The less is the dominance the more is the diversity. Dominance can be thought of as prevalence of a "single" perspective of the problem or solution, sometimes too soon, in crowd discussions. This view is also symbolic of conformity or group thinking. Too many social affirmations in a discussion can lead to calcification of a single problem or solution viewpoint. In some cases, separation diversity can also lead to dominance, whereby one group of so-called experts organically coalesce and affirm each other's view and drown out others in the discussions. Anonymity is one way to ensure that separation and dominance diversity is well managed.

The third view of diversity is related to the knowledge variety that is expressed in discussions (see Note 16). The greater the variety of knowledge expressed in discussions, the more the perspectives related to the wicked problem. This "knowledge variety" based creative tension can lead to multiple perspectives of the problem that are not based on familiarity with the problem, rather it is based on dissimilarity of knowledge possessed about the problem. Diversity that leads to knowledge variety can, therefore, allow unconstrained crowds.

4.6.2 Developing the Notion of Knowledge Diversity Evolution

Since the crowd is adding to the knowledge continuously, knowledge type diversity is not static as the pattern of the number of types of knowledge seen in a five-post trace will change every time someone contributes. As such, we refer to knowledge type diversity as an evolutionary and iterative notion in the sense of batons being passed, not necessarily in the sense that each new fragment of knowledge literally builds upon all prior knowledge. Knowledge type diversity is self-reinforcing since, at any point, the diversity is influenced by the types of knowledge recently shared by the crowd and will in itself affect the diversity of types available to the crowds at future points in time. The level of diversity changes as the crowd amplifies different knowledge types. Knowledge diversity can also go down if the crowd behaves in a way that privileges one knowledge type over another.

At any given point in time, in crowds, there is a snapshot measure of diversity (static diversity). But, individuals in the crowds, when they are exposed to diversity, evolve their own diversity by contributing different types of knowledge influenced by others' knowledge—either by building on it by contributing similar knowledge or by contributing divergent knowledge. We call this evolutionary diversity.

4.7 What Does This Mean for Future Research?

Much has been written about the role of shared understanding in groups for them to work together effectively.[17] Increasingly there are contexts in which building shared understanding is near impossible either because the group is large or because the group is not a group but is a temporary crowd.

If crowds can innovate without shared understanding, what does this mean for research on creative work teams? Is it possible that team research should be reconsidered in light of our findings? Is it possible that what has been referred to in the past as shared understanding is a different form of shared understanding? In much of the literature, shared understanding means an agreement on the definition of the problem, criteria for evaluating the solution, and the process for solving the problem. Is it possible, though, that shared understanding means, instead, that people have shared their different understandings and a willingness to proceed given these differences? Is it possible that teams do not have to agree, they only have to learn how to share better and listen to each other? In a study of non-governmental agencies after the largest hurricane experienced by New Orleans, the emergent crowd of NGOs swarming on the city to help did not spend time developing a shared understanding of the situation as might be common practice.[18] Instead, they simply exchanged understandings in terms of action steps which worked successfully to extract victims from rising waters and get the victims the help they needed.

For research on teams, then, it may be that teams that appear to achieve a shared understanding prior to suggesting an innovative idea have actually done something quite different. They have disaggregated their knowledge into fragments, they have shared the fragments as types of knowledge, and they have ensured that there is a diversity of knowledge types continuing to be exchanged as the discussions continue. *An innovative idea emerges then not because there was an understanding of the problem in some formal sense but because there was an understanding of everyone else's definition of the problem.* One study specifically on teams has suggested a similar notion when it found that, among highly creative temporary teams, the teams were able to be so creative so quickly because they first shared a collage of different knowledge, posted the knowledge on the walls of their meeting rooms, and then proceeded to try and devise solutions that encompassed the collage of knowledge.[19]

In sum, one implication of our findings described in this chapter is that future research should reconsider the dominant paradigm in the team's literature of an effectively creative team as having a single mental model. Research then would proceed based on this assumption that there is no push toward consensus in effectively creative teams and instead there is only a push to understanding each other's perspective in as simple knowledge bites as possible. This push to understanding each other's perspective may take the form of an iterative creative solution-idea,[20] collages, or parallel paths as crowds do, offering the team's sponsor alternative recommendations rather than one.

Our findings also suggest rethinking what diversity means and what expertise means when both are held at the level of an ever-changing collective. If diversity is achieved not by a person's demographics or a person's industry experience, and instead is reflected in the types of knowledge shared, then theories of diversity need to be modified to account for this new form of diversity.

Finally, the fact that individuals can still offer diverse opinions without spending significant time means that marginalized population with little patience and time for the privileged majority do not need to spend significant time and patience in order to be heard.

In conclusion, future research should focus on how groups and individuals share their understandings of problems so as to increase others' absorption of the shared knowledge. In our research, we have found that submitting a variety of knowledge in easily consumable knowledge chunks influences the collective emergence of innovative ideas in crowds. More research is needed to develop a collective taxonomy of a range of knowledge types, beyond the types we have suggested, which can allow for sharing of perspectives and easy absorption of others' understanding of knowledge. More research is also needed on how such problem understanding should be expressed (what do consumable chunks mean?). Is the length of the contribution (number of words) critical? Is there an optimal size—especially in the age of social media communication? Do linguistics of expression matter, especially when problem perspectives are shared as digital textual artifacts, as is the case in many crowds? Our research is just scratching the surface of what knowledge type variety is and how it is expressed.

As alluded to in the earlier section, our research on the influence of knowledge variety in crowds also has started to scratch the surface of what does expertise in crowds mean. Specifically, what does expertise mean when individuals in the crowd are sharing diverse knowledge perspectives (many of them are not solutions) as chunks? Could expertise be the ability to articulate one's knowledge, in which case experts are less likely to be helpful for crowd innovation? Even though all the crowds we studied are anonymous, does the nature of sharing different types of knowledge lead to the emergence of perception of certain individuals as experts rather than based on their functional tenure or range of experiences. And, does this emergence of a variety of contributor expert lead to certain positive and negative behaviors in the Collective production Process? In other words, if their problem perspective comes to dominate the emergence of new perspectives and ideas, clearly this is a bad outcome no matter how much diversity of knowledge types a person has contributed. Given that in our crowds, on the average, individuals contribute two posts, this "emergent expertise" view is unlikely to occur. But, in other perpetual and highly time-consuming crowds, even though individuals are anonymous, "experts" and "non-experts" can be perceived through the accumulated trajectory of knowledge fragments, especially through what knowledge variety is contributed.

There is also extensive research on how diversity in groups has an influence on the functioning of, and production of, outcomes by groups. Measuring diversity is clearly a subjective and often controversial notion. Researchers have advanced the notion of surface-level and deep diversity.[21] Instead of focusing on the characteristics of the members of the crowd, to ascertain surface-level diversity, we focus on diversity as manifested in a variety of knowledge contributed as a measure of deep-level diversity. Clearly, more research is needed on how "knowledge explicitly expressed" in groups is (or maybe is not) indicative of deep-level diversity. Also, along this path, research is also needed on whether or not explicated diversity of knowledge in a group is indicative of a successful group, both in terms of Collective Production of outcomes and whether these outcomes are useful for organizations that sponsor crowdsourcing events.

4.8 What Does This Mean for Practice?

What are the implications of our discussion in this chapter for managers of crowdsourcing events, especially if they want the crowds to follow the Collective Production process? First and foremost, we reiterate the notion that crowds are more than a source of ideas. Individual are crowds that are wellsprings of diverse perspectives. As a natural tendency, crowds are more likely to contribute ideas rather than the entire gamut of knowledge they possess. This natural tendency is a vestige of the idea-search process they have grown to expect from innovation crowdsourcing.

Managers of crowdsourcing events will have to break this tendency by encouraging the crowds—through instructions and non-monetary awards. As an example, New Zealand Pest Free crowds were instructed to not restrict themselves to technical knowledge (which often is solutions focused) but also to contribute knowledge perspectives related to legal, societal, and political issues related to the wicked problem. These issues were listed on top of instructions that also encouraged the crowds to contribute tradeoffs, examples, facts and rough idea seeds. In the New Zealand case, then, the variety was multilayered: one layer about our knowledge types and one layer about the specific range of content issues to address. Therefore, through carefully thought out instructions, crowds can be encouraged to expand their own view of what is "useful" knowledge in the Collective Production of innovation.

Expressing knowledge variety as specific (and broad) categories helps the crowd understand that in order to participate in the crowd they do not have to cross the high bar of having ideas only to contribute. Suggesting (but not restricting them to) categories of knowledge types desired from them helps them recall their own perspective and encourages them to contribute by explicating any knowledge they may have related to the wicked problem rather than just ideas. Crowds can be encouraged to follow these suggestions with token non-monetary rewards, but crowds need to be allowed to do what crowds want to do. Not everyone will contribute diverse knowledge types; only enough need to do so.

To achieve this, in the initial implementation of the Collective Production process when leveraging crowds, managers may need to train a select few to seed the crowdsourcing platform with diverse types of knowledge. Such seeding of knowledge variety will model for the crowds what knowledge variety contribution is valued and desired. This may be another way that "experts" in the organization can be trained to seed the event, but to do so without emphasizing their own perspective (especially "ideas"). Managers of crowdsourcing events may also want to run pilots, whereby inviting those from outside the organization who are most likely to be pertinent to the problem. The contributions by the "pilot crowd" can be used as seeds for a large-scale main crowdsourcing event.

In sum, managers should expand their horizon in terms of what expertise, at least in the context of crowds, really means. However, even with this broadened view of expertise, managers of crowdsourcing events must realize that expertise is only as good as how it is expressed. The expertise of the crowd is not the expertise of individuals; it is the number of diverse perspectives that are brought to the table for others to view. Some are experts at inculcating creative tension through elicitation of tradeoffs. Others are experts at connecting contexts by providing examples of how a similar wicked problem may have been solved in another context. While others may be good at throwing out rough idea seeds that can be collectively developed by the crowd. What we have shown is that experts of all kinds are needed to have the requisite variety of knowledge available to crowds to collectively produce innovation.

Notes

1. Porter, A. J., Tuertscher, P., & Huysman, M. (2018). Saving our oceans: Tackling grand challenges through crowdsourcing. In *34th European Group for Organizational Studies (EGOS) Colloquium: Surprise in and around Organizations: Journeys to the Unexpected*. EGOS.
2. Padgett, J. F., & Powell, W. W. (2012). The problem of emergence. In J. F. Padgett & W. W. Powell (Eds.), The Emergence of Organizations and Markets (pp. 1–29). Princeton, NJ: Princeton University Press.
3. Porter et al., p. 10
4. Porter et al. p. 24.

5. Frey, K., Lüthje, C., & Haag, S. (2011). Whom should firms attract to open innovation platforms? The role of knowledge diversity and motivation. *Long Range Planning*, 44(5), 397–420; Cohen, W., & Levinthal, D. (1990). Absorptive capacity: a new perspective on learning and innovation. (Technology, Organizations, and Innovation). *Administrative Science Quarterly*, 35(1), 128–152; Tsoukas, H. (2002). Introduction: Knowledge-based perspectives on organizations: situated knowledge, novelty, and communities of practice. *Management Learning*, 33(4), 419–426; Mitchell, R., & Nicholas, S. (2006). Knowledge creation in groups: The value of cognitive diversity, transactive memory and open-mindedness norms. *The Electronic Journal of Knowledge Management*, 4(1), 67–74; Solomon, M. (2006). Groupthink versus the wisdom of crowds: The social epistemology of deliberation and dissent. *Southern Journal of Philosophy*, 44, 28–42; Malhotra, A., Majchrzak, A., & Niemiec, R. (2017). Using public crowds for open strategy formulation: Mitigating the risks of knowledge gaps. *Long Range Planning*, 50(3), 397–410.
6. Cronin, M., & Weingart, L. (2007). Representational gaps, information processing, and conflict in functionally diverse teams. *The Academy of Management Review*, 32(3), 761–773; Baer, M., Dirks, K., & Nickerson, J. (2013). Microfoundations of strategic problem formulation. *Strategic Management Journal*, 34(2), 197–214; Smith, G. (1989). Defining managerial problems: A framework for prescriptive theorizing. *Management science*, 35(8), 963–98; Firth, B., Hollenbeck, J., Miles, J., Ilgen, D., & Barnes, C. (2015). Same page, different books: Extending representational gaps theory to enhance performance in multiteam systems. *Academy of Management Journal*, 58(3), 813–835.
7. Kohn, N., & Smith, S. (2011). Collaborative fixation: Effects of others' ideas on brainstorming. *Applied Cognitive Psychology*, 25(3), 359–371; Smith, S. (2003). The constraining effects of initial ideas. In *Group Creativity: Innovation Through Collaboration* (pp. 15–31). Oxford University Press; Smith, S., Linsey, J., & Kerne, A. (2011). Using evolved analogies to overcome creative design fixation. In *Design Creativity 2010* (pp. 35–39). Springer, London; Michinov, N., Jamet, E., Métayer, N., & Le Hénaff, B. (2015). The eyes of creativity: Impact of social comparison and individual creativity on performance and attention to others' ideas during electronic brainstorming. *Computers in Human Behavior*, 42(C), 57–67.
8. Kohn, N. W., & Smith, S. M. (2011). Collaborative fixation: Effects of others' ideas on brainstorming. *Applied Cognitive Psychology*, 25(3), 359–371.
9. Perttula, M., & Sipilä, P. (2007). The idea exposure paradigm in design idea generation. *Journal of Engineering Design*, 18(1), 93–102; Sio, U., Kotovsky, K., & Cagan, J. (2015). Fixation or inspiration? A meta-analytic review of the role of examples on design processes. *Design Studies*, 39, 70–99; Goldschmidt, G. (2011). Avoiding design fixation: Transformation and abstraction in mapping from source to target. *Journal of Creative Behavior*, 45(2), 92–100; Viswanathan, V., & Linsey, J. (2013). Examining design fixation in engineer-

ing idea generation: the role of example modality. *International Journal of Design Creativity and Innovation*, *1*(2), 109–129.
10. Smith, S. (2003). The constraining effects of initial ideas. In *Group Creativity: Innovation Through Collaboration* (pp. 15–31). Oxford University Press.
11. Harvey, S. (2014). Creative synthesis: Exploring the process of extraordinary group creativity. *Academy of Management. The Academy of Management Review*, *39*(3), 324–342; Putnam, L., Fairhurst, G., & Banghart, S. (2016). Contradictions, dialectics, and paradoxes in organizations: A constitutive approach. *The Academy of Management Annals*, *10*(1), 65–171; Massa, S., & Testa, S. (2008). Innovation and SMEs: Misaligned perspectives and goals among entrepreneurs, academics, and policy makers. *Technovation*, *28*(7), 393–407.
12. Leimeister, J., Huber, M., Bretschneider, U., & Krcmar, H. (2009). Leveraging crowdsourcing: Activation-supporting components for it-based ideas competition. *Journal of Management Information Systems*, *26*(1), 197–224; Poetz, M., & Schreier, M. (2012). The value of crowdsourcing: Can users really compete with professionals in generating new product ideas? *Journal of Product Innovation Management*, *29*(2), 245–256; Bayus, B. L. (2013) Crowdsourcing New Product Ideas over Time: An Analysis of the Dell IdeaStorm Community. (2013). *Management Science*, *59*(1), 226–244; Schemmann, B., Herrmann, A., Chappin, M., & Heimeriks, G. (2016). Crowdsourcing ideas: Involving ordinary users in the ideation phase of new product development. *Research Policy*, *45*(6), 1145–1154; Di, P., Wasko, M., & Hooker, R. (2010). Getting customers' ideas to work for you: Learning from dell how to succeed with online user innovation communities. *MIS Quarterly Executive*, *9*(4), 213–228; Füller, J., Jawecki, G., & Mühlbacher, H. (2007). Innovation creation by online basketball communities. *Journal of Business Research*, *60*(1), 60–71.
13. Carlile, P. (2004). Transferring, translating, and transforming: An integrative framework for managing knowledge across boundaries. *Organization Science*, 15(5), 555–568; Giaccardi, E., & Fischer, G. (2008). Creativity and evolution: a metadesign perspective. *Digital Creativity*, *19*(1), 19–32; Miron-Spektor, E., Gino, F., & Argote, L. (2011). Paradoxical frames and creative sparks: Enhancing individual creativity through conflict and integration. *Organizational Behavior and Human Decision Processes*, *116*(2), 229–240; Montag, T., Maertz, C., & Baer, M. (2012). A critical analysis of the workplace creativity criterion space. *Journal of Management*, *38*(4), 1362–1386.
14. Brabham, D. (2008). Moving the crowd at iStockphoto: The composition of the crowd and motivations for participation in a crowdsourcing application. *First Monday*, *13*(6); Frey, K., Lüthje, C., & Haag, S. (2011). Whom should firms attract to open innovation platforms? The role of knowledge diversity and motivation. *Long Range Planning*, *44*(5), 397–420; Majchrzak, A., & Malhotra, A. (2013). Towards an information systems perspective and

research agenda on crowdsourcing for innovation. *Journal of Strategic Information Systems, 22*(4), 257–268; Prpić, J., Shukla, P., Kietzmann, J., & Mccarthy, I. (2015). How to work a crowd: Developing crowd capital through crowdsourcing. *Business Horizons, 58*(1), 77–85; Stieger, D., Matzler, K., Chatterjee, S., & Ladstaetter-Fussenegger, F. (2012). Democratizing strategy: How crowdsourcing can be used for strategy dialogues. *California Management Review, 54*(4), 44–68.

15. Jeppesen, L., & Lakhani, K. (2010). Marginality and problem-solving effectiveness in broadcast search. *Organization Science, 21*(5), 1016–1033.
16. Harrison, D., & Klein, K. (2007). What's the difference? Diversity constructs as separation, variety, or disparity in organizations. *Academy of Management Review, 32*(4), 1199–1228.
17. Echterhoff, G., Higgins, E., & Levine, J. (2009). Shared reality: Experiencing commonality with others' inner states about the world. *Perspectives on Psychological Science, 4*(5), 496–521; Ensley, M., & Pearce, C. (2001). Shared cognition in top management teams: Implications for new venture performance. *Journal of Organizational Behavior: The International Journal of Industrial, Occupational and Organizational Psychology and Behavior, 22*(2), 145–160; Fiore, S. M., Salas, E., & Cannon-Bowers, J. A. (2001). Group dynamics and shared mental model development. In M. London (Ed.), *How People Evaluate Others in Organizations*, (pp. 309–336). Mahwah, NJ: Lawrence Erlbaum Associates; Hinds, P., & Mortensen, M. (2005). Understanding conflict in geographically distributed teams: the moderating effects of shared identity, shared context, and spontaneous communication. *Organization Science, 16*(3), 290–307; Lau, R., & Cobb, A. (2010). Understanding the connections between relationship conflict and performance: The intervening roles of trust and exchange. *Journal of Organizational Behavior, 31*(6), 898–917; Park, H. (2008). The effects of shared cognition on group satisfaction and performance: Politeness and efficiency in group interaction. *Communication Research, 35*(1), 88–108; Peterson, E., Mitchell, T., Thompson, L., & Burr, R. (2000). Collective efficacy and aspects of shared mental models as predictors of performance over time in work groups. *Group Processes & Intergroup Relations, 3*(3), 296–316; van Ginkel, W., & van Knippenberg, D. (2008). Group information elaboration and group decision making: The role of shared task representations. *Organizational Behavior and Human Decision Processes, 105*(1), 82–97.
18. Majchrzak, A., Jarvenpaa, S., & Hollingshead, A. (2007). Coordinating expertise among emergent groups responding to disasters. *Organization Science, 18*(1), 147–161.
19. Majchrzak, A., More, P., & Faraj, S. (2012). Transcending knowledge differences in cross-functional teams. *Organization Science, 23*(4), 951–970.
20. Harvey, S. (2014). Creative synthesis: exploring the process of extraordinary group creativity. *Academy of Management. The Academy of Management Review, 39*(3), 324–342.

21. Harrison, D., Price, K., & Bell, M. (1998). Beyond relational demography: Time and the effects of surface- and deep-level diversity on work group cohesion. *Academy of Management Journal, 41*(1), 96–107; Mohammed, S., & Angell, L. C. (2004). Surface-and deep-level diversity in workgroups: Examining the moderating effects of team orientation and team process on relationship conflict. *Journal of Organizational Behavior: The International Journal of Industrial, Occupational and Organizational Psychology and Behavior, 25*(8), 1015–1039; Harrison, D., Price, K., Gavin, J., & Florey, A. (2002). Time, teams, and task performance: Changing effects of surface-and deep-level diversity on group functioning. The *Academy of Management Journal, 45*(5), 1029–1045; Phillips, K. W., & Loyd, D. L. (2006). When surface and deep-level diversity collide: The effects on dissenting group members. *Organizational Behavior and Human Decision Processes, 99*(2), 143–160.

References

Baer, M., Dirks, K., & Nickerson, J. (2013). Microfoundations of strategic problem formulation. *Strategic Management Journal, 34*(2), 197–214.

Bayus, B. L. (2013). Crowdsourcing New Product Ideas over Time: An Analysis of the Dell IdeaStorm Community. *Management Science, 59*(1), 226–244.

Brabham, D. (2008). Moving the Crowd at iStockphoto: The Composition of the Crowd and Motivations for Participation in a Crowdsourcing Application. *First Monday*. Retrieved from https://firstmonday.org/article/%20view/2159/1969.

Carlile, P. (2004). Transferring, Translating, and Transforming: An Integrative Framework for Managing Knowledge Across Boundaries. *Organization Science, 15*(5), 555–568.

Cohen, W., & Levinthal, D. (1990). Absorptive Capacity: A New Perspective on Learning and Innovation. (Technology, Organizations, and Innovation). *Administrative Science Quarterly, 35*(1), 128–152.

Cronin, M., & Weingart, L. (2007). Representational Gaps, Information Processing, and Conflict in Functionally Diverse Teams. *The Academy of Management Review, 32*(3), 761–773.

Di, P., Wasko, M., & Hooker, R. (2010). Getting Customers' Ideas to Work for You: Learning from Dell How to Succeed with Online User Innovation Communities. *MIS Quarterly Executive, 9*(4), 213–228.

Dupont. (2015). Winners of the 2015 DuPont Safety and Sustainability Awards. Retrieved from http://www.dupont.com/dss/dss-awards-2015/winners-2015.html.

Echterhoff, G., Higgins, E., & Levine, J. (2009). Shared Reality: Experiencing Commonality with Others' Inner States About the World. *Perspectives on Psychological Science, 4*(5), 496–521.

Ensley, M., & Pearce, C. (2001). Shared Cognition in Top Management Teams: Implications for New Venture Performance. *Journal of Organizational Behavior: The International Journal of Industrial, Occupational and Organizational Psychology and Behavior, 22*(2), 145–160.

Fiore, S. M., Salas, E., & Cannon-Bowers, J. A. (2001). Group Dynamics and Shared Mental Model Development. In M. London (Ed.), *How People Evaluate Others in Organizations* (pp. 309–336). Mahwah, NJ: Lawrence Erlbaum Associates.

Firth, B., Hollenbeck, J., Miles, J., Ilgen, D., & Barnes, C. (2015). Same Page, Different Books: Extending Representational Gaps Theory to Enhance Performance in Multiteam Systems. *Academy of Management Journal, 58*(3), 813–835.

Frey, K., Lüthje, C., & Haag, S. (2011). Whom Should Firms Attract to Open Innovation Platforms? The Role of Knowledge Diversity and Motivation. *Long Range Planning, 44*(5), 397–420.

Füller, J., Jawecki, G., & Mühlbacher, H. (2007). Innovation Creation by Online Basketball Communities. *Journal of Business Research, 60*(1), 60–71.

Giaccardi, E., & Fischer, G. (2008). Creativity and Evolution: A Metadesign Perspective. *Digital Creativity, 19*(1), 19–32.

Goldschmidt, G. (2011). Avoiding Design Fixation: Transformation and Abstraction in Mapping from Source to Target. *Journal of Creative Behavior, 45*(2), 92–100.

Harrison, D., & Klein, K. (2007). What's the Difference? Diversity Constructs as Separation, Variety, or Disparity in Organizations. *Academy of Management Review, 32*(4), 1199–1228.

Harrison, D., Price, K., & Bell, M. (1998). Beyond Relational Demography: Time and the Effects of Surface- and Deep-Level Diversity on Work Group Cohesion. *Academy of Management Journal, 41*(1), 96–107.

Harrison, D., Price, K., Gavin, J., & Florey, A. (2002). Time, Teams, and Task Performance: Changing Effects of Surface-and Deep-Level Diversity on Group Functioning. *The Academy of Management Journal, 45*(5), 1029–1045.

Harvey, S. (2014). Creative Synthesis: Exploring the Process of Extraordinary Group Creativity. *Academy of Management. The Academy of Management Review, 39*(3), 324–342.

Hinds, P., & Mortensen, M. (2005). Understanding Conflict in Geographically Distributed Teams: The Moderating Effects of Shared Identity, Shared Context, and Spontaneous Communication. *Organization Science, 16*(3), 290–307.

Jeppesen, L., & Lakhani, K. (2010). Marginality and Problem-Solving Effectiveness in Broadcast Search. *Organization Science, 21*(5), 1016–1033.

Kohn, N., & Smith, S. (2011). Collaborative Fixation: Effects of Others' Ideas on Brainstorming. *Applied Cognitive Psychology, 25*(3), 359–371.

Lau, R., & Cobb, A. (2010). Understanding the Connections Between Relationship Conflict and Performance: The Intervening Roles of Trust and Exchange. *Journal of Organizational Behavior, 31*(6), 898–917.

Leimeister, J., Huber, M., Bretschneider, U., & Krcmar, H. (2009). Leveraging Crowdsourcing: Activation-Supporting Components for It-Based Ideas Competition. *Journal of Management Information Systems, 26*(1), 197–224.

Majchrzak, A., & Malhotra, A. (2013). Towards an Information Systems Perspective and Research Agenda on Crowdsourcing for Innovation. *Journal of Strategic Information Systems, 22*(4), 257–268.

Majchrzak, A., Jarvenpaa, S., & Hollingshead, A. (2007). Coordinating Expertise Among Emergent Groups Responding to Disasters. *Organization Science, 18*(1), 147–161.

Majchrzak, A., More, P., & Faraj, S. (2012). Transcending Knowledge Differences in Cross-Functional Teams. *Organization Science, 23*(4), 951–970.

Malhotra, A., Majchrzak, A., & Niemiec, R. (2017). Using Public Crowds for Open Strategy Formulation: Mitigating the Risks of Knowledge Gaps. *Long Range Planning, 50*(3), 397–410.

Massa, S., & Testa, S. (2008). Innovation and SMEs: Misaligned Perspectives and Goals Among Entrepreneurs, Academics, and Policy Makers. *Technovation, 28*(7), 393–407.

Michinov, N., Jamet, E., Metayer, N., & Le Henaff, B. (2015a). The Eyes of Creativity: Impact of Social Comparisons and Individual Creativity on Performance and Attention to Others' Ideas During Electronic Brainstorming. *Computers in Human Behavior, 42*(C), 57–67.

Michinov, N., Jamet, E., Métayer, N., & Le Hénaff, B. (2015b). The Eyes of Creativity: Impact of Social Comparison and Individual Creativity on Performance and Attention to Others' Ideas During Electronic Brainstorming. *Computers in Human Behavior, 42*(C), 57–67.

Miron-Spektor, E., Gino, F., & Argote, L. (2011). Paradoxical Frames and Creative Sparks: Enhancing Individual Creativity Through Conflict and Integration. *Organizational Behavior and Human Decision Processes, 116*(2), 229–240.

Mitchell, R., & Nicholas, S. (2006). Knowledge Creation in Groups: The Value of Cognitive Diversity, Transactive Memory and Open-Mindedness Norms. *The Electronic Journal of Knowledge Management, 4*(1), 67–74.

Mohammed, S., & Angell, L. C. (2004). Surface-and Deep-Level Diversity in Workgroups: Examining the Moderating Effects of Team Orientation and Team Process on Relationship Conflict. *Journal of Organizational Behavior: The International Journal of Industrial, Occupational and Organizational Psychology and Behavior, 25*(8), 1015–1039.

Montag, T., Maertz, C., & Baer, M. (2012). A Critical Analysis of the Workplace Creativity Criterion Space. *Journal of Management, 38*(4), 1362–1386.

Padgett, J. F., & Powell, W. W. (2012). The Problem of Emergence. In J. F. Padgett & W. W. Powell (Eds.), *The Emergence of Organizations and Markets* (pp. 1–29). Princeton, NJ: Princeton University Press.

Park, H. (2008). The Effects of Shared Cognition on Group Satisfaction and Performance: Politeness and Efficiency in Group Interaction. *Communication Research, 35*(1), 88–108.

Pertula, M., & Sipilä, P. (2007). The Idea Exposure Paradigm in Design Idea Generation. *Journal of Engineering Design, 18*(1), 93–102.

Peterson, E., Mitchell, T., Thompson, L., & Burr, R. (2000). Collective Efficacy and Aspects of Shared Mental Models as Predictors of Performance Over Time in Work Groups. *Group Processes & Intergroup Relations, 3*(3), 296–316.

Phillips, K. W., & Loyd, D. L. (2006). When Surface and Deep-Level Diversity Collide: The Effects on Dissenting Group Members. *Organizational Behavior and Human Decision Processes, 99*(2), 143–160.

Poetz, M., & Schreier, M. (2012). The Value of Crowdsourcing: Can Users Really Compete with Professionals in Generating New Product Ideas? *Journal of Product Innovation Management, 29*(2), 245–256.

Porter, A. J., Tuertscher, P., & Huysman, M. (2018). Saving Our Oceans: Tackling Grand Challenges through Crowdsourcing. In *34th European Group for Organizational Studies (EGOS) Colloquium: Surprise in and around Organizations: Journeys to the Unexpected*. EGOS.

Prpić, J., Shukla, P., Kietzmann, J., & Mccarthy, I. (2015). How to Work a Crowd: Developing Crowd Capital Through Crowdsourcing. *Business Horizons, 58*(1), 77–85.

Putnam, L., Fairhurst, G., & Banghart, S. (2016). Contradictions, Dialectics, and Paradoxes in Organizations: A Constitutive Approach. *The Academy of Management Annals, 10*(1), 65–171.

Schemmann, B., Herrmann, A., Chappin, M., & Heimeriks, G. (2016). Crowdsourcing Ideas: Involving Ordinary Users in the Ideation Phase of New Product Development. *Research Policy, 45*(6), 1145–1154.

Sio, U., Kotovsky, K., & Cagan, J. (2015). Fixation or Inspiration? A Meta-analytic Review of the Role of Examples on Design Processes. *Design Studies, 39*, 70–99.

Smith, G. (1989). Defining Managerial Problems: A Framework for Prescriptive Theorizing. *Management Science, 35*(8), 963–998.

Smith, S. (2003). The Constraining Effects of Initial Ideas. In *Group Creativity: Innovation Through Collaboration* (pp. 15–31). Oxford: Oxford University Press.

Smith, S., Linsey, J., & Kerne, A. (2011). Using Evolved Analogies to Overcome Creative Design Fixation. In *Design Creativity 2010* (pp. 35–39). London: Springer.

Solomon, M. (2006). Groupthink Versus the Wisdom of Crowds: The Social Epistemology of Deliberation and Dissent. *Southern Journal of Philosophy, 44*, 28–42.

Stieger, D., Matzler, K., Chatterjee, S., & Ladstaetter-Fussenegger, F. (2012). Democratizing Strategy: How Crowdsourcing Can Be Used for Strategy Dialogues. *California Management Review, 54*(4), 44–68.

Tsoukas, H. (2002). Introduction: Knowledge-Based Perspectives on Organizations: Situated Knowledge, Novelty, and Communities of Practice. *Management Learning, 33*(4), 419–426.

United Nations. (2017b). Goal 14: Conserve and Sustainably Use the Oceans, Seas, and Marine Resources. Retrieved from http://www.un.org/sustainabledevelopment/oceans/.

van Ginkel, W., & van Knippenberg, D. (2008). Group Information Elaboration and Group Decision Making: The Role of Shared Task Representations. *Organizational Behavior and Human Decision Processes, 105*(1), 82–97.

Viswanathan, V., & Linsey, J. (2013). Examining Design Fixation in Engineering Idea Generation: The Role of Example Modality. *International Journal of Design Creativity and Innovation, 1*(2), 109–129.

5

Practice 3: Amplify Creative Associations of Knowledge Fragments

In this chapter, we focus on the third of our five practices shown in Fig. 5.1: Practice 3: Amplify Creativity Associations. We were interested in understanding if there were any patterns to the posts that affected if an innovative idea emerged from the crowd. So, we took our trace data and worked backward from each of the 297 ideas rated by the executive for the innovativeness of the idea (calculated as a combination of ratings on the idea's novelty, usefulness, and implementability). The idea ratings vary from low to high so we could see if there were certain patterns of posts which were more likely to occur *before* those ideas which were rated as more innovative as compared to the absence of those patterns preceding those ideas that were rated as less innovative. We found that Innovative ideas were more likely to be preceded by creative associations than any other type of knowledge. Creative associations are personal experiences a participant might have had with a similar problem in a different context, or conflicting objectives a participant believes must be solved by any proposed solution. Creative associations have a twofold inspirational value. First, they inspire others to post their own creative associations, thus amplifying the number of creative associations available for anyone reading the posts. Second, they inspire the creation of innovative ideas by helping participants make connections in their own minds that spur creative discovery. This effect only works when the creative associations are present in the most recent five posts prior to the innovative idea; posts further back are ignored.

We refer to our findings as indicating the *inspirational power of others' posts* because we find that the more creative associations in the five posts immediately prior to a rated idea, the more innovative the idea. We refer to such posts as

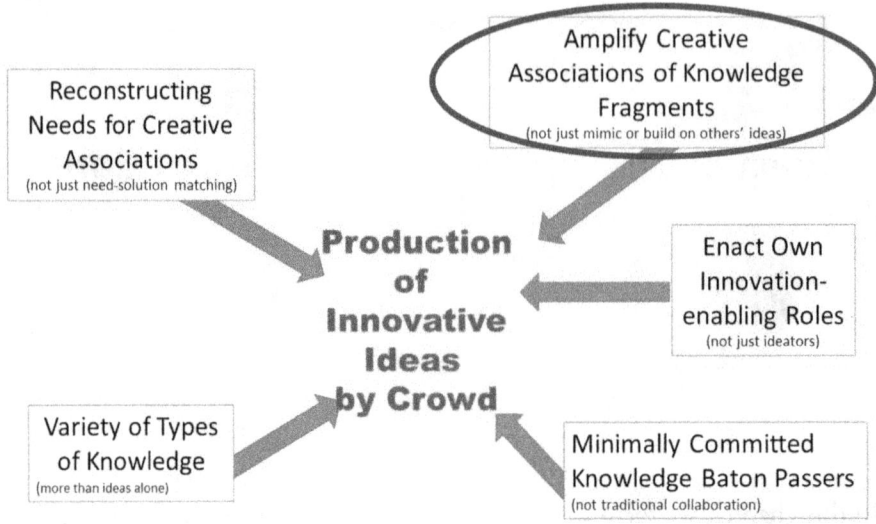

Fig. 5.1 Practices of Collective Production

inspiring others because the creative associations are *not* ideas; rather they contain knowledge content that helps others' draw associations in their memory when they think about the problem. The participant who then posts at the end of a trace containing such "inspiring" posts appears to be inspired by these associations to come up with an idea that is particularly innovative. The fact that this effect of creative associations occurred repeatedly across the 20 crowdsourcing events suggests this is not just a random occurrence. Moreover, this effect was *not* likely following older posts (traces that were prior to the most recent trace)—only the most recent posts inspire. Thus, it is the most recent knowledge fragments (in the trace that a participant is exposed to when arriving at the event's website) that act on participants to make "creative associations" which are the key ingredient in fostering innovation by the crowd.

In this chapter, we take the description of the creative association process above and explain it in more detail. We first (Sect. 5.1) present an anecdote to illustrate how creative associations can help a collective with its problem-solving. In Sects. 5.2, 5.3, and 5.4, we explain what we mean by creative associations in a collective. Then, in Sect. 5.5, we present evidence to support the importance of creative associations from our 20 field research. In the final sections, we discuss alignment with the literature and implications for practice and future research.

5.1 A Case of Creative Associations: A Story at Novell

A 90-person software development group at one of Novell's Network divisions was working on a new product for launch. Since they were geographically distributed, they used a wiki to record the group's work. They posted meeting minutes to the wiki like one might post changes to an article on Wikipedia. Everyone in the group posted to the sections in the wiki devoted to meeting minutes, announcements, status, open issues, and help wanted for fixing a particularly thorny problem. The wiki helped ensure the team's awareness of potential areas of knowledge overlap with others and also increase the chances that knowledge from others will be reused and built upon. As in all wikis, the wiki postings are essentially anonymous (with some tracking down of the poster possible).

The product the group developed was intended to secure the transport of digital messages even as messages needed to pass through several different networks to get from the source to the recipient. The group had a lot of the technical details down but couldn't put the product together in a strategically coherent manner. The Novell group's wiki was replete with discussions about trying to figure out how to package the various product features they had recently developed into a strategically coherent message so that documentation and marketing material could be created toward a single message. Several meetings ensued but frustration was building. The wiki posed an open issue to the team asking: "What is our singular vision for the customer?" Posts were being made by team members in response to the open issue. However, none of these posts seemed to coalesce any support for the open issue, nor did they seemingly inspire others to create that single statement of vision. One day, however, a post suggested that this new product seemed to be like hockey since the digital messages could be seen as the hockey puck, and the puck was kept moving forward to its recipient with each feature the team had developed serving as another hockey stick. This hockey metaphor strongly and immediately resonated with the rest of the group. The hockey metaphor helped the team focus their documentation efforts and helped the marketing team to finalize and describe the software in a strategically coherent way. The hockey metaphor was never used in the marketing messages but the metaphor ended up serving its purpose. After the metaphor was posted, it seemed to unleash the creativity of others on the team. In order to explore whether a so-called expert on the team had used their expertise to unlock the team's creativity, we followed the trace of posts to see who surfaced the hockey analogy. Much to our surprise, we found that it was a secretary whose role was to keep the status tables updated! Upon interviewing her, we found that she suggested the analogy because she was team mom of her son's hockey team and attended practices listening to the coach.

There are two morals to this story:

- *the power of creative associations*, and
- *a creative association to a problem can come from anywhere and anyone if the crowd is unmindcuffed.*

These two morals of the story set the stage for what we hope to accomplish in this chapter. First, we show that crowd-based problem-solving involves actors who never know which of their own knowledge can be useful to others. There have been a number of studies done on crowdsourcing examining the role of domain-relevant expertise, and it is generally found that those with less domain-relevant expertise are more likely to offer creative ideas.[1] However, we are saying something a bit different from these studies. We are suggesting that, because the problem is wicked, what is the relevant content defined for the domain that needs to be shared isn't known and therefore, it is not possible to know who has domain-relevant expertise or not. Therefore, the crowd needs to feel encouraged and enabled to contribute any and every knowledge they might think is pertinent, without really knowing its utility ex-ante. Second, the phrasing of one's knowledge as an analogy helped to stimulate others to be creative. Thus, during the Collective Production of innovative ideas, it is not the knowledge that one has that matters but how it is phrased so that others can be creatively inspired by it.

In what follows, we first explain why the initial statement of the problem as wicked can be the catalyst to start a creative association process if participants are allowed to freely share their knowledge. Then, as the crowd contributes knowledge, the knowledge accumulates to form digital traces that are constantly evolving in response to the creative associations being contributed constantly be the crowds. Sometimes, these digital traces contain certain patterns that lead to dead ends, but at other times the digital traces contain patterns that keep creativity going. When the patterns do sustain creativity, it leads to innovative ideas. These creative production paths of the crowds are what we uncover in this chapter.

5.2 Triggering the Start of a Creative Process with the Wicked Problem

The phrasing of a problem statement for the crowd as a wicked problem is key to starting a creative process in collectives such as crowds formed in response to an innovation crowdsourcing event. The wicked problem provides the starting gun. As we defined in Chap. 1, wicked problems are the kind of problems that are difficult or near impossible to solve by an individual or small group of individuals. Wicked problems are not well-understood and are uniquely context-dependent, with a myriad of interdependent considerations.

Framing the problem as a wicked problem stretches thinking, challenging the crowd. Wickedly framed problems also signal to the crowd a higher expectation and value of the crowd to the organization. The expectation and value signals are commonly talked about as conditions for encouraging creativity in groups.[2] The wicked problem in conjunction with the removal of constraints on how to share knowledge gives the crowd autonomy in how to solve the problem. This is another key condition for encouraging creativity. Finally, by creating time constraints on the problem-solving effort—such as short 5–10 day time windows in innovation crowdsourcing event—a sense of urgency and focus is created which also is a condition fostering creativity.[3]

Posing a wicked problem also signals to participants that individually generated ideas are unlikely to be of value because of the systemic, multi-faceted and complex nature of the problem.[4] Wicked problems allow participants the latitude for their own creative interpretations of the problem, causal models, and possible solutions because there is no obvious single correct solution.[5] This ability to creatively interpret the problem itself is a major mindcuff release. Further, facing wicked problems with no ex-ante known solutions, participants are free to develop alternative solutions. This reduces the likelihood of groupthink and cognitive fixation of any particular solution.[6]

The wickedness of a problem supports creativity since it fulfills a requirement suggested by creativity researchers: that creative teams be tasked with problems that require reflective reframing.[7] Since wicked problems involve so many different perspectives, participants cannot simply use their first thoughts about how to solve the problem which then makes reflective reframing of the problem a necessity to move forward to a solution.[8] Because a wicked problem has so many interdependent elements, no single individual has all the expertise on all of them, and no single individual can accurately forecast how the interdependencies affect each other. For example, if a bank posed the wicked problem of identifying new markets for its services, the interdependent elements include current competitors' offerings, millennials' current and future banking needs, possible partnerships, the future state of the economy, and the bank's current capabilities, constraints, and resources. To solve wicked problems requires the input of many different perspectives on the problem, inducing a creative process of learning from each other.[9] Therefore, the wickedness of the problem encourages humility on the part of any single individual, raising the importance of being open to others' knowledge.

Finally, the wicked problem inherently attracts people with any relevant knowledge about the problem and an interest in solving the problem.[10] For example, the secretary in the Novell anecdote was privy to the frustration experienced by the team and saw that the team was floundering for a solution. As she was sitting watching the hockey coach take her son and his team through practice, the connection between her software team's problem and hockey came into her mind.

5.3 What Are Creative Associations and How Can They Be Inspired?

Simply because knowledge is contributed by individuals in the collective does not mean it is understood and used for creativity.[11] Not all knowledge sharing is generative; knowledge that is shared may not necessarily inspire or stimulate creative cognitive processes.[12] Knowledge shared by the crowds, especially unmindcuffed crowds, can also become voluminous and evolve rapidly. The key to any trace (as we conceived traces and explained in Chap. 2) is that a trace represents the current moment's state of knowledge, not the entire opus of all knowledge created by the crowd. As a participant enters the Innovation Crowdsourcing event website, there is a trace that is uniquely available to that participant at that point in time. Assuming this participant posts, the trace will be different for the next participant.

As mentioned in Chap. 4, traces can be very long (i.e., the entire chronological sequence of posts from the start of the crowdsourcing event to the end) or much shorter. Since the websites only show on the front page the five most recent posts, these become the minimum "freshest" trace for each participant. A participant may also choose to click on these recent posts or look at entire discussions for each thread lengthening the trace available to the participant. By looking only at the most recent five-post trace, however, participants are freed up from having to process all knowledge shared by the entire crowd.

5 Practice 3: Amplify Creative Associations of Knowledge Fragments

They can focus on the knowledge that immediately precedes that point in time when they are looking at the crowd's posts. In that trace, then, there must be something posted that inspires creativity.

There are various obstacles that make understanding of others' knowledge difficult, especially in collectives attempting to creatively solve wicked problems. One approach to overcome these difficulties that we discussed in Chap. 4 is adapted from the theory of knowledge misrepresentation gaps in cross-functional teams.[13] The scholars who developed this theory argue that it is easier for members of the team to share and understand each other's knowledge when the knowledge is distinguished by its purpose in a problem-solving process. They distinguish different types of knowledge by the value the knowledge type can bring to a problem-solving process: goals, assumptions, ideas, and ways to implement the ideas. We demonstrated in Chap. 4 that the crowdsourcing events are more likely to generate innovative ideas when a larger variety of these knowledge types are shared by the crowd. Note that ideas are only one of several knowledge types and not prioritized over the others.

How might knowledge fragments in traces inspire and stimulate creative cognition in others? There is substantial research on creative cognition that may suggest an answer lies in the dual subconscious creative association processes of generation and exploration.[14] Each subconscious process works separately from the other—connected of course, but separate.

In the generation subconscious process, individuals use creative associations to link or search for existing knowledge from their own memory to identify solutions or components to solutions used in the past for analogically similar situations. For example, if the problem is to find a way to repair the biodiversity of an open area, suppose Sally thinks of her backyard and how some of the plants seemed to have drawn a few native butterflies. She has now generated an association. In the exploration subconscious process, individuals take those creative association they generated and then iteratively explore them in their mind—by rearranging, reassembling, and rotating the set of components in interesting and novel ways—until a creative discovery ensues. Continuing our example, Sally takes her creative association and starts thinking about how it might apply to an open area, the interdependencies among different plants, and the presence of different animal species. After rearranging her association and combining it with others, she has a creative discovery that maybe the reintroduction of certain predator species such as wolves may increase the production and distribution into the open area of certain prey species which spread and fertilize native plants.

Creative discoveries are never assured and when they don't emerge during subconscious exploration, the individual will seek new creative associations. Therefore, the continuous replenishment of creative associations is needed for those individuals in the crowd willing to engage in the subconscious exploration process.

There are a variety of ways that a crowd can stimulate an individual to engage in generating creative associations. Others' creative associations can stimulate creative associations in one's own memory; these associations may act as creative triggers for the next participant by reminding the participant of an object or word already in their memory. For example, if the wicked problem is to figure out how to describe a new software product to customers, participants could suggest not only hockey pucks but other associations to networking software such as security, value chains for packets, from here-to-there, and uninterrupted flow. None of these creative associations have to be the ones that an individual can use; these creative associations need only to inspire others to engage in the subconscious process of generating their own creative associations. Sometimes, though, a creative association offered by one person may have a direct generative effect on another person. For example, an individual might be reminded of several words or objects; when retrieved, these words or objects might now be associated in novel ways, as when a person reads someone's posts of "ball" and the word "hard", and then associates the two words to think about whether the software product is like a soft or hardball. Creative associations can also be inspired by asking participants to simply list creative associations to a problem.[15]

With creative associations in hand, the cognitive process of creative exploration starts in which the participant mentally rearranges, reassembles, and rotates the associations in interesting and novel ways to see if a creative discovery emerges.[16] For example, in a prior study one of us conducted, a team was observed which was responsible for designing a new facility layout with apparently contradictory objectives of giving employees privacy while fostering open collaboration and engagement.[17] The team started early on to draw potential employee desk-seating arrangements but these drawings did not lead to the creative discovery. It was not until the team started physically rotating the drawings in different ways that they were able to see creative ways to achieve both privacy and collaboration.

Creative associations can also be inspired by paradoxes. Paradoxes have been frequently demonstrated in research to stimulate an exploratory cognitive associative process. Paradoxes are "a real opposition of views, standpoints, or requirements",[18] a statement of objectives and requirements existing

5 Practice 3: Amplify Creative Associations of Knowledge Fragments

simultaneously, which are difficult or impossible to achieve simultaneously with current known solutions.[19]

Paradoxes are the identification of issues or conflicting requirements that are difficult or impossible to achieve simultaneously with current known solutions.	Examples of paradoxes: "How do we sell the software cheaply but don't lose our high-end market, how do we increase the revenue for maintenance and yet not lose clients."

Paradoxes between objectives establish a creative tension that forces more creativity to generate a solution solving both sides of the paradox.[20] When resolving the paradox becomes the goal to be achieved, this level of challenge has been shown to stimulate group creativity.[21] Paradoxes present "opportunities to discover different assumptions, shift perspectives, pose problems in fundamentally different ways".[22] In organizations, making latent paradoxes explicit can bring about changes that result in innovation.[23] Management of paradoxes in the form of strategic contradictions has been argued to be key for innovation-related cognitive processes in organizations.[24]

Therefore, we expected that when a crowd participant phrases knowledge of the problem as a paradox, this might serve to stimulate others' creativity. In discussions with our field crowds, we found that they were uncomfortable with the term of paradoxes but could easily offer creative associations when we relabeled paradoxes to the more concrete term, "tradeoffs". Perhaps it is because a "tradeoff" is easier to accomplish than solving a paradox since it acknowledges that neither apparently conflicting objective will be reached 100%.

Analogical transfer is another way in which creative associations might be generated. Analogies are descriptions of how a similar problem has been solved in other domains such that "assertions based in one source domain are placed into correspondence with assertions in a target domain, and further assertions true of the base domain are then inferred to be potentially true of the target".[25]

Analogies are statements about how similar problems may have been addressed or solved in another company/industry/context	Examples of analogies: "Over at company X they've been doing something like this for years that looks like …, could we follow the way that X does it …"

In analogical transfer, a concept in one context is transferred to another context.[26] The analogy might be created explicitly for the purpose of transfer, as was the case with the hockey puck metaphor used in the Novell anecdote described at the outset of this chapter. Alternatively, the analogy may be a simple example provided by one participant, to which the next participant uses the example to formulate another analogy of how that example might apply to another domain. Analogies simplify the transfer of tacit knowledge by allowing for "the functional operation of new concepts or systems to be explored by reference to things that are already understood."[27] Analogies play a powerful role in spurring associations in one's memory because they invoke a process of flexible thinking about the underlying mechanisms required to solve the problem.[28] Analogies are also a key trigger in associative reasoning processes for creative work,[29] as well as central to solving wicked design problems[30] because they allow for pattern-matching and abstraction.[31] Researchers have proposed that the use of analogies may spur creative idea generation in large collectives such as crowds.[32] Our discussions with the field crowds indicated that they did not resonate to the requests to offer their knowledge as "analogies" but were more comfortable presenting their knowledge in response to a request for examples of experiences they have had.

5.4 Summary of the Process of Creative Associations

In sum, we suggest that unmindcuffed crowds may engage in a process of creative associations. This process, as we have described it thus far, may unfold as shown in Fig. 5.2.

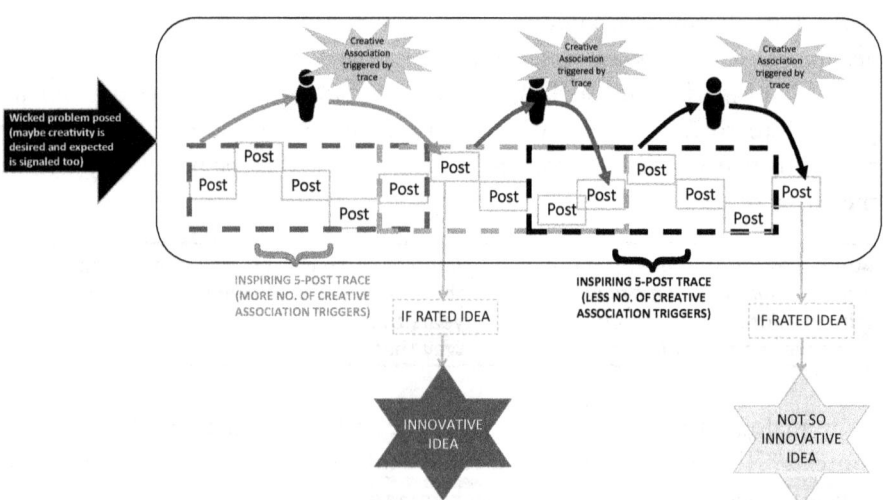

Fig. 5.2 A process of creative associations used by crowds

The process starts when a wicked problem statement announcement is offered by an organization which sets the context indicating that creativity is desired and expected by anyone and everyone. As individuals join (or rejoin) the crowd, they read the latest knowledge trace formed by the knowledge fragments recently shared by others in the crowd. The probability of inspiring more creative associations goes up when the traces contain knowledge fragments presented as creative associations since there will be more unusual parts of the problem conveyed, more analogies to draw on, more opportunities of finding components of the problem that hadn't been considered previously that can be mentally combined with other knowledge to mentally manipulate in new ways, and more possibilities of paradoxes arising which elevate the reflective reframing of the problem in new ways. Therefore, as participants post their knowledge about the wicked problem, whether they choose to share their knowledge as creative associations instead of as facts, ideas, social support, questions, or opinions may activate the shape of others' creative cognitive processes. With more associations, there is more to explore and thus the probability of a creative discovery increases. As participants read the most recent digital traces, they may become inspired to engage not simply in more generation of creative associations but in exploring those associations to create ideas. In sum, we propose that *as the number of creative associations in the most recent digital trace accumulates, an individual's propensity to offer more innovative ideas should increase.* In the next section, we test this proposal using the 20 field research crowdsourcing events.

5.5 What Is the Evidence for the Effects of Creative Associations on Innovativeness of Ideas?

To test our proposal—that the number of creative associations in the most recent trace will stimulate more innovative ideas—we coded the knowledge posts for whether the posts contained paradoxes or analogies, two forms of creative associations. We then counted backward from each of the 297 ideas rated for innovativeness to identify the five most recently posted knowledge fragments, and then counted the number of creative associations in each five-post trace. We then looked at whether a larger number of creative associations were more likely to be found prior to ideas rated by the executives as more innovative. To remind the reader, when executives were rating the ideas, they were not aware of the traces that preceded the idea they were rating.

The results of the analysis are italicized in Table 5.1. *The results indicate that the presence of a greater number of creative associations in a five-post trace is more likely to be followed by an idea that is more innovative.* This means that, as participants present their knowledge in terms of creative associations such as analogies and paradoxes, they are inspiring the next participant to generate and explore their associations for creative discoveries. Looking at the model fit statistics, it is clear that model that includes the most recent trace (model D in Table 5.1) shows the greatest fit to the data, that is, the best explanatory power in explaining the variation in the innovativeness of rated idea. In other words, the model with creative associations in the immediate prior trace shows a better fit compared to model A (controls only model), as it has smaller values of the negative log-likelihood or twice the negative log-likelihood (-2 log-likelihood). Akaike's Information Criterion (AICc) is another model fit indicator; the model that has the smallest AICc value indicates the better fit, that is, has better power to explain the variation in the dependent variable (innovativeness of an idea). A difference of 10 in AICc between models indicates they are significantly differentiable in their explanatory ability.[33]

5.6 Exploring If Other Alternative Explanations for Creative Association Influence Co-production of Innovative Ideas

We included control variables (model A in Table 5.1) as a baseline for comparison. These controls included, for each crowdsourcing event, the number of participants, whether the problem restricted participants to think about markets or particular product categories, and the number of total ideas that the executive had to rate. We also included controls at the knowledge trace level—the time order of the trace and the activity level of the participant in the crowd who posted the idea—just in case the effect of the trace on innovativeness was entirely due to these two variables. The results in Column A in Table 5.1 indicate that more innovative ideas emerge in events with more participants and more ideas emerge later in the event, and are more likely to be posted by more active participants. Even with these controls, innovative ideas are still influenced by the number of creative associations in the trace immediately prior to the rated idea.

To rule out effects that might negate the importance of most recent creative associations, we examined whether creative associations were still important in addition to ideas in the trace since there has been substantial research on

5 Practice 3: Amplify Creative Associations of Knowledge Fragments

Table 5.1 Results of patterns of knowledge traces and their relationship with innovativeness of ideas

DV = Innovativeness of the idea after a digital trace ($N = 297$)	Control model (A)	Most recent post effect model (B)	Past prior trace effect model (C)	Immediate prior trace effect model (D)
Controls:				
At event level:				
Number of participants	0.04*** (0.01)	0.4*** (0.01)	0.03*** (0.01)	0.03** (0.01)
Problem unrestrictiveness	−1.22** (0.46)	−1.30** (0.47)	−0.42 (0.55)	−0.75 (0.48)
Total rated ideas	0.16*** (0.04)	0.17*** (0.04)	0.16** (0.05)	0.16*** (0.04)
At trace level:				
Time order of the trace (log)	1.52* (0.65)	1.36* (0.61)	0.68 (0.44)	3.23* (1.61)
Activity level of crowd actor posting the idea	3.73* (1.74)	4.11* (2.05)	2.21 (1.19)	1.56* (0.65)
Alternative explanations explored:				
1. Whether last post of the immediate prior trace =				
…Idea		−0.14 (0.29)		
…Fact		0.46 (1.09)		
…Creative association		1.52 (1.15)		
…Social support		−0.25 (0.44)		
2. Past prior trace has larger number of…				
…Ideas			0.09 (0.13)	
…Facts			2.05 (1.41)	
…Creative associations			0.34 (0.33)	
…Social supports			−0.12 (0.08)	
Independent variable of interest				
No. of ideas in the immediate prior trace				0.16 (0.11)
No. of facts in the immediate prior trace				0.20 (0.16)
No. of creative associations in the immediate prior trace				*0.46* (0.22)*
No. of social supports in the immediate prior trace				−0.13*** (0.02)
Model fit				
−2 residual log-likelihood	1278.28	1256.02	1259.46	1243.75
−2 log-likelihood	1263.52	1241.19	1245.41	1228.96
AICc	1275.82	1261.97	1266.19	1249.77

*$p < 0.05$; **$p < 0.01$; ***$p < 0.001$

the effects of idea brainstorming on generating more innovative ideas.[34] One conclusion from this research is that exposure to others' ideas helps to activate one's own creative associations.[35] These activated associations can then "be used to generate [further] ideas by combining knowledge, forming new associations or applying knowledge to a new domain".[36] A completely opposite conclusion from this research has found that exposure to others' ideas depletes and saps one's creative energies. As others voice their ideas, this demotivates individuals if they think or receive any feedback to the effect that their ideas are not as good or are worried how others are evaluating ideas, especially theirs. This phenomenon has been referred to as personal fear of invalidity.[37] Moreover, others' ideas may block the production of one's own ideas by creating a fixation toward those ideas. Such creative fixation leads to a reduction in breadth of ideas.[38] Initial ideas and excessive focus on those ideas can have a severe constraining effect.[39] Individuals, when exposed to initial ideas, may tend to reproduce elements of the initial idea rather than finding new solutions.[40]

Sharing ideas over the internet called anonymous electronic brainstorming may overcome some of these production blocking problems but the value of presenting ideas as knowledge stimulating the innovativeness of others' ideas is not yet clear.[41] Therefore, we analyzed whether the number of ideas in the immediately prior trace affected innovativeness of the rated ideas. Note that there were hundreds of ideas but only 297 were rated because only those that were non-duplicates were rated. Therefore, there could be many ideas in a recent knowledge trace before the idea rated for innovativeness. Apparent from the results in Table 5.1 is that the number of ideas in the immediately prior trace did *not* affect the innovativeness of an idea. *Thus, the innovativeness of an idea is not simply a reflection of brainstorming.*

Next, we looked at whether facts conveyed about the problem affect innovativeness. We counted the number of posts with facts in the five-post trace immediately prior to the rated idea. Facts pertaining to the wicked problem might serve to stimulate innovativeness because they could be viewed as associations that one has about the problem—albeit not a particularly creative association such as perceived or objective information, data, statistics, charts, or established practices related to the problem statement. When traces contain factual knowledge, it makes others aware of the different assumptions of others, and it may motivate others to resolve these differences through creative exploration. Facts may also provide basic knowledge for combining in novel ways.[42] In sum, simply requesting that individuals articulate their own factual assumptions about a problem have been found to sometimes encourage creative thinking.[43] We wanted to make sure that creative associations are still related to the innovativeness of an idea even when facts are shared. Apparent from Table 5.1 is that the facts in the immediate prior trace did not affect the innovativeness of an idea. *Thus, it is not the content per se that matters as much (at least in terms of facts) for creating innovative ideas in crowds as to whether the knowledge is presented as creative associations.*

Another possible cause of innovativeness of rated ideas that we considered was the degree to which the crowd offered social support to others, such as agreements with a prior statement. Social support for one's contributions and ideas create what is called psychological safety to take risks.[44] This literature argues that people will be more willing to offer innovative ideas if they are supported by others in offering non-conformist ideas. This quells their evaluation apprehension and confirms the norm that what is desired by others is not simply ideas, but innovative ones. Simple ways of showing social support might be simple statements such as "Great idea", "I like the idea", and "I'd like to extend on this idea because it was so good". *Apparent from Table 5.1 is that the number of social support posts in the five-post immediate trace had a NEGATIVE effect on the innovativeness of the ideas—the opposite of what would be expected from the literature.* One possible reason might be that social support distracts participants from their internal cognitive processing of generating and exploring creative associations. Social support may also *not* create psychological safety as expected but instead remind participants that their ideas are being evaluated by others, which makes their evaluation apprehension more salient.

We also examined if it was the number of creative associations in a trace that matters or whether having the creative association in the most recent post was what mattered the most. Results of Table 5.2 (model B) indicate that *the presence of a single creative association immediately prior to the innovative idea did not significantly affect if the rated idea was innovative*. Therefore, it is clear that it is the pattern of posts by multiple participants in the crowd that matters.

Finally, we examined if older traces had the same effect as the most recent trace. If that is the case, then, we would question whether participants are really being affected by reading the most recent traces. Since all participants are unlikely to read *all* prior posts, and if older traces affect innovativeness of the idea, then our interpretation of traces inspiring participants may not be appropriate since one cannot be inspired by posts they don't read. It might be that people who read older posts are more likely to be creative because they are engaged more with the topic or more interested in what others have to say. We created an "older" trace composed of posts 6–10 (counting backward from the rated idea), and calculated the number of creative associations (as well as the number of ideas and social support and facts) in the trace. Apparent from the results in Table 5.1 is that the *older traces have no effect*, allowing us to maintain our interpretation of the findings.

In sum, *what matters for innovative ideas to be generated is the number of creative associations in the most recent trace—and NOT the number of social supports, number of facts, number of ideas, size of the crowd, time, and activity level during the event and by the poster. An innovative idea is more likely with more creative associations in the immediate prior trace. The number of creative associations has twice an effect on the innovativeness of ideas as the number of ideas and facts in the trace. Finally, this effect evaporates since there is no effect of older traces on the innovativeness of ideas.*

5.7 Is There Evidence for How Creative Associations Are Inspired?

Having demonstrated the importance of others' creative associations on the production of innovative ideas, we wondered what keeps participants posting creative associations. *Given the centrality to the process of posting creative associations, if participants stop posting creative associations, the Collective Production process will collapse.* Since there were no explicit requirements for participants to post creative associations (although we did offer suggestions to post any knowledge about the problem including ideas, facts, tradeoffs, and examples), we asked: how do these creative associations emerge and keep getting posted?

To answer this question, we considered that each of the 2428 posts could have been a creative association. We created 2428 five-post traces for each of the 2428 posts to see if the traces before a post affect whether the post is a creative association or not. The results of this analysis are shown in italics in Table 5.2.

After including the same control variables as before, Table 5.2 shows that the *presence of a creative association after the most recent five posts is due in large measure to the number of creative associations in those five posts.* This effect is nearly eight times more than the next important effect: the number of facts. This is not a simple mirroring, mimicry or copy-cat effect because the creative associations are never the same. That is, if three different people post analogies, the three analogies will reference three different contexts (if it's precisely the same and acknowledged as such, we coded it as social support). We call this an *amplification* effect since two creative associations beget a third, three creative associations beget a fourth, and so on.

In addition to the amplification effect of creative associations on more creative associations, we discover an effect of the number of facts and ideas on

5 Practice 3: Amplify Creative Associations of Knowledge Fragments

Table 5.2 Knowledge traces affecting posting of creative associations

DV = Contribution of creative association after a trace (N = 2428)	Control model (A)	Immediate prior trace effect model (B)
Controls:		
At event level:		
Crowd size	0.002*** (0.0005)	0.004*** (0.0003)
Problem unrestrictiveness	0.21*** (0.03)	0.09*** (0.03)
At trace level:		
Time order of the trace (log)	0.01* (0.003)	0.01** (0.005)
Activity level of crowd actor posting the idea	0.01* (0.005)	0.007* (0.003)
Independent variable of interest		
No. of ideas in the immediate prior trace		0.002* (0.001)
No. of facts in the immediate prior trace		0.02* (0.008)
No. of creative associations in the immediate prior trace		0.17** (0.05)
No. of social supports in the immediate prior trace		0.004 (0.002)
Model fit		
−2 residual log-likelihood	3419.85	1258.96
−2 log-likelihood	3399.96	1237.98
AICc	3409.98	1256.06

*$p < 0.05$; **$p < 0.01$; ***$p < 0.001$

posting a creative association next. We call this *a diffusion* effect since ideas and facts don't affect the innovativeness of the ideas directly but instead help to inspire additional creative associations, which then lead to more innovative ideas. Note that the number of social support posts does not help create an innovative idea. Also remember that the number of facts and ideas do *not* affect innovativeness of the idea rated; *therefore, the value of ideas and facts offered by the crowd is for their direct effect on inspiring creative associations, NOT for any direct effect on the creative discovery process that leads to innovative ideas.*

5.8 Summary of the Process of Creating and Using Creative Associations

We bring all these findings together here into a subprocess of the Collective Production process that focuses on how creative associations are created and used during the crowd's Collective Production process. This subprocess of creating and using creative associations *refers to a process in which participants inspire or stimulate other participants—not through direct statements such as "let's*

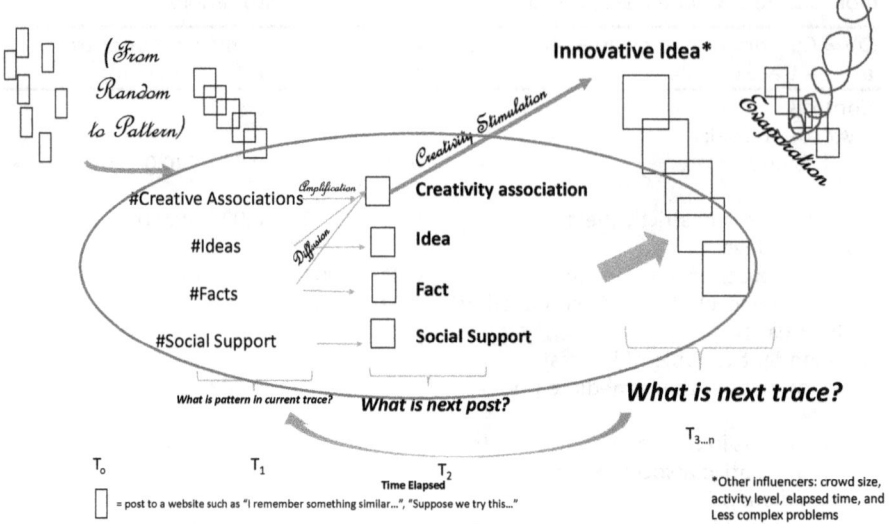

Fig. 5.3 Model of crowd's creative association process

be more creative", or knowledge fragments or ideas that are recombined—but by presenting their own knowledge in ways that both demonstrates their own creative thinking and provides cues to help others be more creative.

Figure 5.3 summarizes our findings into a model of the crowd's process.

The posts initially start in the upper left-hand corner of the figure as random posts from participants in response to the wicked problem statement. After the first five posts have been contributed, they together form the first trace, with each successive post creating a new trace. Eventually, the trace of the five most recent posts may contain a pattern that starts the collective creative process. To start the process, this pattern must be one which encourages posting more creative associations—such as by amplified posting of creative associations and diffused posting of ideas and/or facts. At some point, the five most immediately prior posts may contain a pattern primarily of creative associations. When this occurs, the idea that is posted next will be more innovative than ideas offered earlier.

To illustrate, let's count backward from a post a participant is about to make where post 1 is the more recent post the participant sees and 5 is the oldest post that the participant sees prior to offering her own post. Take a look at Table 5.3.

Jane sees a pattern of two social supports, two creative associations, and two ideas. Because the social supports are so salient, Jane is likely to post a non-innovative idea. Compare Jane to Lori who comes in after Pat. At the time that Lori logs in to look at the website for the crowdsourcing event, Lori sees

5 Practice 3: Amplify Creative Associations of Knowledge Fragments

Table 5.3 How patterns in posts influence participants

	Most recent post				Oldest post seen	So the person posts:
Jane sees	Creative association	Idea	Idea	Social support	Social support	Jane posts idea (that we predict will not be innovative)
Pat sees	Jane's idea	Creative association	Idea	Idea	Social support	Pat posts creative association
Lori sees	Pat's creative association	Idea	Creative association	Idea	Idea	Lori posts idea (that we predict will be innovative)

two creative associations, three ideas, and no social support. Consequently, Lori is more likely than Jane to post an innovative idea.

The effect of patterns—both influencing whether a creative association is offered, and whether an innovative idea is offered—in the digital traces is the essence of the collective creative association process. The patterns cannot be predetermined; they can only be identified when they occur, affecting the next behavior taken by the next participant. The more ideas, facts, analogies, and tradeoffs in the five-post trace, the more likely that the next post will be a creative association of either paradox or tradeoff. As more posts are added, the creative associations may begin to add up in a trace. This build-up of creative associations then sparks a participant to contribute an innovative idea from one's own associative memory. In other words, the Collective Production of innovative ideas is not mimetic, that is, prior amassing of ideas is not what yields an innovative idea from the masses. Nor is it the simple combination of others' ideas or knowledge.

The next set of valuable patterns is amplification as part of creating new creative associations. All creative associations in the trace foster the addition of a new creative association. Then, when enough creative associations accumulate, innovative ideas emerge.

The final pattern (shown in the figure) is one of evaporation. As our results clearly indicated, the 6–10 post trace does not show a relationship with the innovativeness of the idea emerging from the crowd at the end of the trace.

5.9 How Do Our Findings Contribute to Current Research on Online Crowds?

Our findings offer several specific contributions to existing research on online crowds. Our findings suggest that idea brainstorming has limited direct value to innovative idea generation, despite research to the contrary. Our findings suggest that social support has a negative direct value to innovative idea generation, despite scholarship to the contrary. Our findings suggest that facts offered by others are *not* integrated into innovative ideas, despite scholars suggesting otherwise. Our findings suggest that patterns (i.e., trends) in a trace have greater effect on the emergence of innovative ideas than the presence of any specific content in the trace, despite scholarship essentially ignoring the pattern-identification capability and influence within online crowds. Finally, our findings indicate that knowledge baton passing occurs because of the recency effect of patterns in traces, coupled with the fluidity of the participation, ensuring that evaporating traces are constantly replaced with recent ones.

All of these findings suggest that, given the central importance of the volume of creative associations generated by the crowd, an important research question to address is: *how does the crowd know to do this?* Is there some innate seduction of creative associations that draws crowds to offer these associations? Is there some underlying need met when a participant is able to offer a creative association that motivates this behavior? Is this a learned behavior from some societies and not found in other societies?

Finally, could these findings have implications for improvements in how teams innovate? Suppose teams were not told to solve a specific problem-solving process but told to share knowledge about the problem and that creative associations with the problem would help some people in generating and exploring for creative discoveries; would such teams perform better than those follow more traditional problem-solving processes?

5.10 What Do These Findings Mean for Practice?

There are many practical implications of the findings presented in this chapter. For managers interested in improving the innovativeness of their organization—its products, its reputation, its speed of innovation, the inventiveness of its employees, its culture—our findings offer the secret recipe: focusing on creative associations during conversations. Instead of simply offering discussion threads or having an idea-focused innovation crowdsourcing event, consider removing the mindcuffs and have employees share creative associations that lead to more innovative ideas. Doing this repeatedly for different topics important to management and employees can build up an internal capability since creative associations may not initially come naturally. Moreover, repeated crowdsourcing events can help participants practice mentally manipulating associations in the exploration of creative discoveries.

5 Practice 3: Amplify Creative Associations of Knowledge Fragments

How an R&D unit is managed should also be reconsidered as stage-gate models follow the old funnel model approach with the assumptions of distinctions between problem definition and problem-solving; between idea generation, selection, and implementation; and between managers doing one of these activities and participants doing another. The findings from this chapter suggest that these distinctions may not be the keys to innovation, and in fact may harm innovation since they emphasize social support (which we found harms innovativeness of ideas created). Creative associations—about paradoxes and examples are not exclusively about the problem nor about the solution. Creative associations are fostered not only by facts about the problem but also about solution-ideas. Therefore, the distinction between problem definition and solution doesn't apply. Moreover, innovativeness did not derive from the initial generation of ideas, followed by selection, and then consideration for implementation. Part of the value of the diversity in the crowd is to consider all issues—novelty, usefulness, and implementability—simultaneously rather than sequentially, which is possible when diverse people are brought together early in the problem-solving.[45] Finally, selection is never done by the crowd during Collective Production in order to focus on a single solution. Instead, the crowd is focusing on multiple definitions of the problem and solutions simultaneously.[46] In sum, the reflective R&D manager should look at these findings and consider reorienting the R&D unit around a new process—one of managed chaos of creative associations, the multiple considerations of all aspects of the problem simultaneously, and pursuing multiple solutions simultaneously. Obviously, there are timelines needed but they are oriented around critical path and options analysis, not a funnel process.

Another implication for the reflective practitioner is for the individual who is worried about what is referred to as the "silo effect" of knowledge sharing in society today in which AI tools, based on keyword analysis, only give people the knowledge that is associated with what they've shared previously. This is a criticism waged against Facebook and Twitter, for example. Applying the focus on creative associations to the silo effect problem suggests that AI tools should move beyond keyword analysis and suggest creative associations which will connect people who are equally concerned about a topic, but are exposed to creative ways to think about the topic. Then, when these people are brought together on a common forum to have a discussion, emphasizing the further generation of creative associations and their use in creative discoveries, they may help to break some of the societal stalemates of failing to talk and listen to the "other side".

Another implication concerns whether executives are using their top management teams in the most productive way possible. Most top management teams are often tasked to offer innovative solutions to wicked problems. They tend to use traditional idea-search methods to arrive at these solutions such as idea brainstorming, scenario-building, and occasionally "thinking out of the box".[47] As described in Chap. 3, our findings suggest that crowds using these traditional idea-search methods are less efficient at generating innovative ideas than crowds using Collective Production. If this applies to teams, then top management teams can be made more efficient at their innovative problem-solving if they follow the practices of Collective Production, one of which we describe in this chapter as creative associations.

Notes

1. Poetz, M. K., Schreier, M., (2012). The value of crowdsourcing: can users really compete with professionals in generating new product ideas? J. Prod. Innov. Manage. 29 (2), 245–256; Jeppesen, L., & Lakhani, K. (2010). Marginality and problem-solving effectiveness in broadcast search. Organization Science, 21(5), 1016–1033; Nishikawa, H., Schreier, M., Ogawa, S., (2013). User-generated versus designer-generated products: a performance assessment at Muji. Int. J. Res. Mark. 30 (2), 160–167.
2. Amabile, T. M., & Pratt, M. G. (2016). The dynamic componential model of creativity and innovation in organizations: Making progress, making meaning. Research in Org Behavior 36, 157–183.
3. Anderson, N., Nik, K. P & Zhou, J. (2014). Innovation and creativity in organizations: A state-of-the science review, prospective commentary and guiding framework. Journal of Management 40(5) 1297–1333; Amabile, T. M., & Pratt, M.G. (2016). The dynamic componential model of creativity and innovation in organizations: Making progress, making meaning. Research in Org Behavior 36, 157–183.
4. Van Bueren, E. M., Klijn, E. H., & Koppenjan, J. F. (2003). Dealing with wicked problems in networks: Analyzing an environmental debate from a network perspective. Journal of public administration research and theory, 13(2), 193–212.
5. Buchanan, R. (1992). "Wicked problems in design thinking". Design Issues, 8(2), 5–21; Rittel, H., & Webber, M. (1973). "Dilemmas in a general theory of planning". Policy Sciences, 4, 155–169.
6. Nijstad, B., Stroebe, W., Lodewijkx, H. (2002) Cognitive stimulation and interference in groups: Exposure effects in an idea generation task. J. Experiment. Soc. Psych. 38(6):535–544; Smith, S. (2003) The constraining effects of initial ideas. Paulus, P., Nijstad, B., eds. Group Creativity: Innovation Through Collaboration (Oxford University Press, Oxford, UK), 15–31.

7. Amabile, T. M., & Pratt, M. G. (2016). The dynamic componential model of creativity and innovation in organizations: Making progress, making meaning. Research in Org Behavior 36, 157–183; Anderson, N., Potočnik, K., & Zhou, J. (2014). Innovation and creativity in organizations: A state-of-the science review, prospective commentary, and guiding framework. Journal of Management, 40(5), 1297–1333.
8. Baer, M., Dirks, K. T., & Nickerson, J. A. (2013). Microfoundations of strategic problem formulation. Strategic Management Journal, 34(2), 197–214; Nickerson, J. A., Wuebker, R., & Zenger, T. (2017). Problems, theories, and governing the crowd. Strategic Organization, 15(2): 275–288.
9. Batie, S. (2008). Wicked problems and applied economics. *American Journal of Agricultural Economics, 90*(5), 1176–1191.
10. Brabham, D.C., (2013). Crowdsourcing. MIT Press, Cambridge, MA.
11. Dong, Y., Bartol, K. M., Zhang, Z. X., & Li, C. (2017). Enhancing employee creativity via individual skill development and team knowledge sharing: Influences of dual-focused transformational leadership. Journal of Organizational Behavior, 38(3), 439–458; Huang, X., Hsieh, J. J., & He, W. (2014). Expertise dissimilarity and creativity: The contingent roles of tacit and explicit knowledge sharing. Journal of Applied Psychology, 99(5), 816.
12. Avital, M., & Te'Eni, D. (2009). From generative fit to generative capacity: exploring an emerging dimension of information systems design and task performance. Information systems journal, 19(4), 345–367; Martinez, M. G. (2015). Solver engagement in knowledge sharing in crowdsourcing communities: Exploring the link to creativity. Research Policy, 44(8), 1419–1430.
13. Cronin, M. A., & Weingart, L. R. (2007). Representational gaps, information processing, and conflict in functionally diverse teams. Academy of Management Review, 32(3), 761–773.
14. Althuizen, N., & Reichel, A. (2016). The effects of IT-enabled cognitive stimulation tools on creative problem solving: A dual pathway to creativity. Journal of Management Information Systems, 33(1), 11–44; Finke, R. A., Ward, T. B., Smith, S. M. (1996) Creative Cognition: Theory, Research, and Applications. Cambridge: MIT Press; Nijstad, B. A., De Dreu, C. K., Rietzschel, E. F., & Baas, M. (2010). The dual pathway to creativity model: Creative ideation as a function of flexibility and persistence. European Review of Social Psychology, 21(1), 34–77.
15. Althuizen, N., & Reichel, A. (2016). The effects of IT-enabled cognitive stimulation tools on creative problem solving: A dual pathway to creativity. Journal of Management Information Systems, 33(1), 11–44.
16. Finke, R. A., Ward, T. B., Smith, S. M. (1996) Creative Cognition: Theory, Research, and Applications. Cambridge: MIT Press.
17. Majchrzak, A., More, P. H. B., Faraj, S. (2012) Transcending knowledge differences in cross-functional teams. Organization Science, 23: 951–970.
18. Dorst, K. (2006). Design problems and design paradoxes. Design issues, 22(3), 4–17.

19. Jay, J. (2013). Navigating paradox as a mechanism of change and innovation in hybrid organizations. Academy of management journal, 56(1), 137–159.
20. Miron-Spektor, Ella, Francesca Gino, and Linda Argote. "Paradoxical frames and creative sparks: Enhancing individual creativity through conflict and integration." Organizational Behavior and Human Decision Processes 116, no. 2 (2011): 229–240.
21. Gong, Y., Kim, T. Y., Lee, D. R., & Zhu, J. (2013). A multilevel model of team goal orientation, information exchange, and creativity. Academy of Management Journal, 56(3), 827–851; Harvey, S. (2014). Creative synthesis: Exploring the process of extraordinary group creativity. Academy of Management Review, 39(3), 324–343; Leonard-Barton, D. A. Wellsprings of Knowledge: Building and Sustaining the Sources of Innovation. Boston: Harvard Business School Press, 1995; Miron-Spektor, Ella, Francesca Gino, and Linda Argote. "Paradoxical frames and creative sparks: Enhancing individual creativity through conflict and integration." Organizational Behavior and Human Decision Processes 116, no. 2 (2011): 229–240.
22. Poole, M. S., & Van de Ven, A. H. (1989). Using paradox to build management and organization theories. Academy of management review, 14(4), 562–578.
23. Smith, W. K., & Lewis, M. W. (2011). Toward a theory of paradox: A dynamic equilibrium model of organizing. Academy of management Review, 36(2), 381–403.
24. Smith, W. K., & Tushman, M. L. (2005). Managing strategic contradictions: A top management model for managing innovation streams. Organization science, 16(5), 522–536.
25. Gentner, D., Brem, S., Ferguson, R. W., Markman, A. B., Levidow, B. B., Wolff, P., & Forbus, K. D. (1997). Analogical reasoning and conceptual change: A case study of Johannes Kepler. The journal of the learning sciences, 6(1), 3–40.
26. Biscaro, C. & Comacchio, A. (2018). Knowledge creation across worldviews: how metaphors impact and orient group creativity. Organization Science, 29(1): 58–79.
27. Nonaka, I. (1994). A dynamic theory of organizational knowledge creation. Organization science, 5(1), 14–37.
28. Burleson, W. (2005). Developing creativity, motivation, and self-actualization with learning systems. International Journal of Human-Computer Studies, 63(4–5), 436–451.
29. Goldschmidt, G. (2001). Visual analogy—A strategy for design reasoning and learning. In C. Eastman, W. Newsletter, & M. McCracken (Eds.), Design knowing and learning: Cognition in design education (pp. 199–219). New York: Elsevier.
30. Tseng, I., Moss, J., Cagan, J., & Kotovsky, K. (2008). The role of timing and analogical similarity in the stimulation of idea generation in design. Design Studies, 29, 203–221.

5 Practice 3: Amplify Creative Associations of Knowledge Fragments

31. Holyoak, K. J., Gentner, D., & Kokinov, B. N. (2001). Introduction: The place of analogy in cognition. The analogical mind: Perspectives from cognitive science, 1–19.
32. Lixiu Yu, Aniket Kittur, and Robert E. Kraut. (2014). Searching for Analogical Ideas with Crowds. In Proceedings of the SIGCHI Conference on Human Factors in Computing Systems (CHI '14), 1225–1234.
33. Symonds, M. R., & Moussalli, A. (2011). A brief guide to model selection, multimodel inference and model averaging in behavioural ecology using Akaike's information criterion. Behavioral Ecology and Sociobiology, 65(1):13–21.
34. Osborn, A. F. (1963). Applied imagination: Principles and procedures of creative thinking (2nd ed.). New York, NY: Charles Scribner's Sons.

    For a review of the literature see Paulus, P. B. & V. R. Brown. 2003. Enhancing ideational creativity in groups: Lessons from Research on brainstorming. In P. B. Paulus & B. A. Nijstad (Ed.) Group Creativity: Innovation Through Collaboration.
35. Gong, Y., Kim, T. Y., Lee, D. R., & Zhu, J. (2013). A multilevel model of team goal orientation, information exchange, and creativity. Academy of Management Journal, 56(3): 827–851; Giaccardi, E., & Fischer, G. (2008). Creativity and evolution: a metadesign perspective. Digital Creativity, 19(1), 19–32; Paulus, P. (2000). Groups, teams, and creativity: The creative potential of idea-generating groups. Applied Psychology, 49(2), 237–262.
36. Nijstad, B. A., & Stroebe, W. (2006). How the group affects the mind: A cognitive model of idea generation in groups. Personality and Social Psychology Review, 10(3), 145.
37. Rietzschel, E. F., De Dreu, C. K., & Nijstad, B. A. (2007). Personal need for structure and creative performance: The moderating influence of fear of invalidity. Personality and Social Psychology Bulletin, 33(6), 855–866.
38. Kohn, N. W., & Smith, S. M. (2011). Collaborative fixation: Effects of others' ideas on brainstorming. Applied Cognitive Psychology, 25(3), 359–371.
39. Smith, S. M. (2003). The constraining effects of initial ideas. Group creativity: Innovation through collaboration, 15–31.
40. Perttula, M., & Sipilä, P. (2007). The idea exposure paradigm in design idea generation. Journal of Engineering Design, 18(1), 93–102.
41. Dennis, A., M. Williams. (2003). Electronic brainstorming. P. Paulus, B. A. Nijstad, eds. Group Creativity: Innovation Through Collaboration 160–178; Smith, S. M. (2003). The constraining effects of initial ideas. Group creativity: Innovation through collaboration, 15–31.
42. Lubart, T. (2001). Models of the creative process: Past, present and future. Creativity Research Journal, 13:3–4, 295–308.
43. Harvey, S. (2014). Creative synthesis: Exploring the process of extraordinary group creativity. Academy of Management Review, 39(3), 324–343; Hender, J. M., D. L. Dean, T. L. Rodgers, J. F. Nunamaker. 2002 An examination of

the impact of stimuli type and GSS structure on creativity: Brainstorming versus non-brainstorming techniques in a GSS environment. J of Management Information Systems 18(4) 59–86.
44. Edmondson, A. (1999). Psychological safety and learning behavior in work teams. Administrative science quarterly, 44(2), 350–383.
45. Similar to design for manufacturability or design for sustainability in engineering.
46. Similar to R&D efforts which "ride multiple horses simultaneously"; there is no reason to downselect early or even later.
47. Senge, P. M. (2006). The fifth discipline: The art and practice of the learning organization. Broadway Business.

References

Althuizen, N., & Reichel, A. (2016). The Effects of IT-Enabled Cognitive Stimulation Tools on Creative Problem Solving: A Dual Pathway to Creativity. *Journal of Management Information Systems, 33*(1), 11–44.

Amabile, T. M., & Pratt, M. G. (2016). The Dynamic Componential Model of Creativity and Innovation in Organizations: Making Progress, Making Meaning. *Research in Organizational Behavior, 36*, 157–183.

Anderson, N., Potočnik, K., & Zhou, J. (2014). Innovation and Creativity in Organizations: A State-of-the-Science Review, Prospective Commentary, and Guiding Framework. *Journal of Management, 40*(5), 1297–1333.

Avital, M., & Te'Eni, D. (2009). From Generative Fit to Generative Capacity: Exploring an Emerging Dimension of Information Systems Design and Task Performance. *Information Systems Journal, 19*(4), 345–367.

Baer, M., Dirks, K. T., & Nickerson, J. A. (2013). Microfoundations of Strategic Problem Formulation. *Strategic Management Journal, 34*(2), 197–214.

Batie, S. (2008). Wicked Problems and Applied Economics. *American Journal of Agricultural Economics, 90*(5), 1176–1191.

Biscaro, C., & Comacchio, A. (2018). Knowledge Creation Across Worldviews: How Metaphors Impact and Orient Group Creativity. *Organization Science, 29*(1), 58–79.

Brabham, D. C. (2013). *Crowdsourcing*. Cambridge, MA: MIT Press.

Buchanan, R. (1992). Wicked Problems in Design Thinking. *Design Issues, 8*(2), 5–21.

Burleson, W. (2005). Developing Creativity, Motivation, and Self-Actualization with Learning Systems. *International Journal of Human-Computer Studies, 63*(4–5), 436–451.

Cronin, M. A., & Weingart, L. R. (2007). Representational Gaps, Information Processing, and Conflict in Functionally Diverse Teams. *Academy of Management Review, 32*(3), 761–773.

Dennis, A., & Williams, M. (2003). Electronic Brainstorming. In P. Paulus & B. A. Nijstad (Eds.), *Group Creativity: Innovation Through Collaboration* (pp. 160–178). Oxford: Oxford University Press.

Dong, Y., Bartol, K. M., Zhang, Z. X., & Li, C. (2017). Enhancing Employee Creativity Via Individual Skill Development and Team Knowledge Sharing: Influences of Dual-Focused Transformational Leadership. *Journal of Organizational Behavior, 38*(3), 439–458.

Dorst, K. (2006). Design Problems and Design Paradoxes. *Design Issues, 22*(3), 14.

Edmondson, A. (1999). Psychological Safety and Learning Behavior in Work Teams. *Administrative Science Quarterly, 44*(2), 350–383.

Finke, R. A., Ward, T. B., & Smith, S. M. (1996). *Creative Cognition: Theory, Research, and Applications*. Cambridge: MIT Press.

Gentner, D., Brem, S., Ferguson, R. W., Markman, A. B., Levidow, B. B., Wolff, P., & Forbus, K. D. (1997). Analogical Reasoning and Conceptual Change: A Case Study of Johannes Kepler. *The Journal of the Learning Sciences, 6*(1), 3–40.

Giaccardi, E., & Fischer, G. (2008). Creativity and Evolution: A Meta-Design Perspective. *Digital Creativity, 19*(1), 19–32.

Goldschmidt, G. (2001). Visual Analogy – A Strategy for Design Reasoning and Learning. In C. Eastman, W. Newsletter, & M. McCracken (Eds.), *Design Knowing and Learning: Cognition in Design Education* (pp. 199–219). New York: Elsevier.

Gong, Y., Kim, T. Y., Lee, D. R., & Zhu, J. (2013). A Multilevel Model of Team Goal Orientation, Information Exchange, and Creativity. *Academy of Management Journal, 56*(3), 827–851.

Harvey, S. (2014). Creative Synthesis: Exploring the Process of Extraordinary Group Creativity. *Academy of Management Review, 39*(3), 324–343.

Hender, J. M., Dean, D. L., Rodgers, T. L., & Nunamaker, J. F. (2002). An Examination of the Impact of Stimuli Type and GSS Structure on Creativity: Brainstorming Versus Non-brainstorming Techniques in a GSS Environment. *J of Management Information Systems, 18*(4), 59–86.

Holyoak, K. J., Gentner, D., & Kokinov, B. N. (2001). Introduction: The Place of Analogy in Cognition. In *The Analogical Mind: Perspectives from Cognitive Science* (pp. 1–19). Cambridge, MA: MIT Press.

Huang, X., Hsieh, J. J., & He, W. (2014). Expertise Dissimilarity and Creativity: The Contingent Roles of Tacit and Explicit Knowledge Sharing. *Journal of Applied Psychology, 99*(5), 816.

Jay, J. (2013). Navigating Paradox as a Mechanism of Change and Innovation in Hybrid Organizations. *Academy of Management Journal, 56*(1), 137–159.

Jeppesen, L., & Lakhani, K. (2010). Marginality and Problem-Solving Effectiveness in Broadcast Search. *Organization Science, 21*(5), 1016–1033.

Kohn, N. W., & Smith, S. M. (2011). Collaborative Fixation: Effects of Others' Ideas on Brainstorming. *Applied Cognitive Psychology, 25*(3), 359–371.

Leonard-Barton, D. A. (1995). *Wellsprings of Knowledge: Building and Sustaining the Sources of Innovation*. Boston: Harvard Business School Press.

Lubart, T. (2001). Models of the Creative Process: Past, Present and Future. *Creativity Research Journal, 13*(3–4), 295–308.

Majchrzak, A., More, P. H. B., & Faraj, S. (2012). Transcending Knowledge Differences in Cross-Functional Teams. *Organization Science, 23*, 951–970.

Martinez, M. G. (2015). Solver Engagement in Knowledge Sharing in Crowdsourcing Communities: Exploring the Link to Creativity. *Research Policy, 44*(8), 1419–1430.

Miron-Spektor, E., Gino, F., & Argote, L. (2011). Paradoxical Frames and Creative Sparks: Enhancing Individual Creativity Through Conflict and Integration. *Organizational Behavior and Human Decision Processes, 116*(2), 229–240.

Nickerson, J. A., Wuebker, R., & Zenger, T. (2017). Problems, Theories, and Governing the Crowd. *Strategic Organization, 15*(2), 275–288.

Nijstad, B., Stroebe, W., & Lodewijkx, H. (2002). Cognitive Stimulation and Interference in Groups: Exposure Effects in an Idea Generation Task. *Journal of Experimental Social Psychology, 38*(6), 535–544.

Nijstad, B. A., & Stroebe, W. (2006). How the Group Affects the Mind: A Cognitive Model of Idea Generation in Groups. *Personality and Social Psychology Review, 10*(3), 145.

Nijstad, B. A., De Dreu, C. K., Rietzschel, E. F., & Baas, M. (2010). The Dual Pathway to Creativity Model: Creative Ideation as a Function of Flexibility and Persistence. *European Review of Social Psychology, 21*(1), 34–77.

Nishikawa, H., Schreier, M., & Ogawa, S. (2013). User-Generated Versus Designer-Generated Products: A Performance Assessment at Muji. *International Journal of Research in Marketing, 30*(2), 160–167.

Nonaka, I. (1994). A Dynamic Theory of Organizational Knowledge Creation. *Organization Science, 5*(1), 21.

Osborn, A. F. (1963). *Applied Imagination: Principles and Procedures of Creative Thinking* (2nd ed.). New York, NY: Charles Scribner's Sons.

Paulus, P. (2000). Groups, Teams, and Creativity: The Creative Potential of Idea-Generating Groups. *Applied Psychology, 49*(2), 237–262.

Paulus, P. B., & Brown, V. R. (2003). Enhancing Ideational Creativity in Groups: Lessons from Research on Brainstorming. In P. B. Paulus & B. A. Nijstad (Eds.), *Group Creativity: Innovation Through Collaboration*. Oxford: Oxford University Press.

Perttula, M., & Sipilä, P. (2007). The Idea Exposure Paradigm in Design Idea Generation. *Journal of Engineering Design, 18*(1), 93–102.

Poetz, M. K., & Schreier, M. (2012). The Value of Crowdsourcing: Can Users Really Compete with Professionals in Generating New Product Ideas? *Journal of Product Innovation Management, 29*(2), 245–256.

Poole, M. S., & Van de Ven, A. H. (1989). Using Paradox to Build Management and Organization Theories. *Academy of Management Review, 14*(4), 564.

Rietzschel, E. F., De Dreu, C. K., & Nijstad, B. A. (2007). Personal Need for Structure and Creative Performance: The Moderating Influence of Fear of Invalidity. *Personality and Social Psychology Bulletin, 33*(6), 855–866.

Rittel, H., & Webber, M. (1973). Dilemmas in a General Theory of Planning. *Policy Sciences, 4*, 155–169.

Senge, P. M. (2006). *The Fifth Discipline: The Art and Practice of the Learning Organization.* New York: Broadway Business.

Smith, S. (2003). The Constraining Effects of Initial Ideas. In P. Paulus & B. Nijstad (Eds.), *Group Creativity: Innovation Through Collaboration* (pp. 15–31). Oxford: Oxford University Press.

Smith, W. K., & Lewis, M. W. (2011). Toward a Theory of Paradox: A Dynamic Equilibrium Model of Organizing. *Academy of Management Review, 36*(2), 381–403.

Smith, W. K., & Tushman, M. L. (2005). Managing Strategic Contradictions: A Top Management Model for Managing Innovation Streams. *Organization Science, 16*(5), 522–536.

Symonds, M. R., & Moussalli, A. (2011). A Brief Guide to Model Selection, Multimodel Inference and Model Averaging in Behavioural Ecology Using Akaike's Information Criterion. *Behavioral Ecology and Sociobiology, 65*(1), 13–21.

Tseng, I., Moss, J., Cagan, J., & Kotovsky, K. (2008). The Role of Timing and Analogical Similarity in the Stimulation of Idea Generation in Design. *Design Studies, 29*, 203–221.

Van Bueren, E. M., Klijn, E. H., & Koppenjan, J. F. (2003). Dealing with Wicked Problems in Networks: Analyzing an Environmental Debate from a Network Perspective. *Journal of Public Administration Research and Theory, 13*(2), 193–212.

Yu, L., Kittur, A., & Kraut, R. E. (2014). Searching for Analogical Ideas with Crowds. In *Proceedings of the SIGCHI Conference on Human Factors in Computing Systems (CHI '14)* (pp. 1225–1234).

6

Practice 4: Reconstructing Needs for Creative Associations

In this chapter, we focus on the fourth of our five practices shown in Fig. 6.1. We examine the participants' behaviors during a crowdsourcing event undertaken by a managed health-care insurance company. The executives conducted an internal crowdsourcing event to solicit from the claims professionals innovative ways to service customers. We found that those posts initially offering a specific need coupled with a specific solution garnered the most attention by participants, but did not necessarily lead to innovative solutions. What led to innovative solutions were participants peeling away the need, then reconstructing the need into a creative association only tangentially related to the initial need. Thus, innovation in crowds does not emerge from simply listing requirements for the solution, but rather, from needs being creatively reconstructed to inspire others to think of new solutions.

6.1 The Story of Optum Behavioral Health Care's Crowdsourcing for Innovation

United Health Care is the largest managed care company in the world. Within this large company is a division called Optum Speciality Networks, with about 1000 health-care specialists, including psychiatrists, chiropractors, mental disorder counselors, registered nurses, social workers, autism counselors, and substance abuse counselors focused on behavioral health. The 1000 specialists managed relationships with health-care clients (businesses) and individual members with health-care needs (employees of the businesses). The

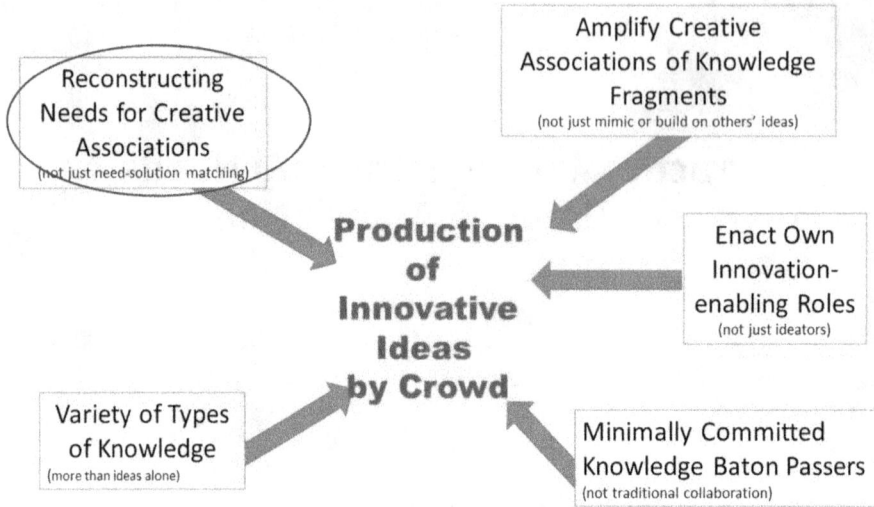

Fig. 6.1 Practices of Collective Production

Optum specialists were in customer-facing roles, spending time on the phone with customer organizations (those employing the people covered by health-care insurance) as well as individual members (those who are covered by health-care insurance). They were geographically dispersed, with small groups focused on specific types of customers in specific regions of the United States, with the specific state and local regulations that apply. As a consequence, the clinicians develop unique perspectives on the needs and service delivery options of the members they serve.

As managed care is becoming increasingly competitive, Optum, as an organization, must remain on top of the needs of the customers, repeatedly offering new innovative and efficiently delivered claims management products to their customer organizations and individual members. Optum top management realized that it had a wealth of knowledge among these licensed clinicians. The challenge was that the knowledge was being applied to quite different customer segments with different regulations, premiums, and benefits plans, and from different clinical specialties. Bringing together these diverse perspectives to build on them is foundational to innovating the health-care delivery process. Bringing 1000 specialists together to co-develop new claims management products was not feasible. Optum, therefore, turned to using an Innovation Crowdsourcing Event to bring together diverse perspectives to develop innovative products and services that meet customer needs. The following message was broadcast to all 1000 clinicians a week before the start of the Innovation Crowdsourcing Event:

As clinicians within Specialty Networks, you have held critical roles in driving our clinical vision, supporting our customers, providers, and members, upholding our ethical and quality standards while managing care on behalf of our customers and members. We are now looking to you to become more deeply involved in shaping our strategic clinical direction and innovations on a national level. I am pleased to announce this Innovation Challenge which will use the power of your talent and expertise to find new innovative solutions to make the service system work better for everyone by making it more engaging, effective and affordable. Since you span multiple time zones and many locations, we are using the power of online collaboration. We are asking you to go much further than just sharing your knowledge and ideas with management. We would like you to be the FIRST at OPTUM to build on your combined knowledge as a group, to create innovative solutions to key challenges. (William C. Bonfield M.D., M.P.H., Chief Medical Officer, Behavioral Solutions, Optum Specialty Networks)

This crowdsourcing event was run without the mindcuffs on and involved the clinicians only, with no managerial involvement. Such requirements were imposed on the event because of the nature of the clinicians: "*a tough crowd to engage because they are short on time, only wanting to give fragmented time; it's tough to get 10 of these people in a meeting, let alone participating in crowdsourcing*" (private communication with Chief Medical Officer).

Prior to the date of the start of the Innovation Crowdsourcing Event, the clinicians were informed of the problem statement:

How do we become more effective as a managed care company focusing on improving the member experience?

Figure 6.2 shows the front webpage for the Crowdsourcing Event.[1] Note that, for clinicians, it is made as simple as possible so they could spend little time making contributions and reading others' contributions.

Clinicians' participation was voluntary and anonymous. Over 13 days, 258 of the 1000 clinicians participated (26%) by either posting knowledge content, commenting on others' posts, or voting and created 10,000 views. Among the 258 participants, 99 either posted a topic starting a discussion thread or commented on an existing thread. By the end of the event, 75 separate discussion threads were created, plus comments for a total of 255 posts. Similar to the participants in the 20 innovation crowdsourcing events described in Chap. 3, participants were minimally committed to the event, contributing from one to three comments.

Optum executives considered the crowdsourcing event a success. This was the first challenge that was conducted on such a large scale, involving the

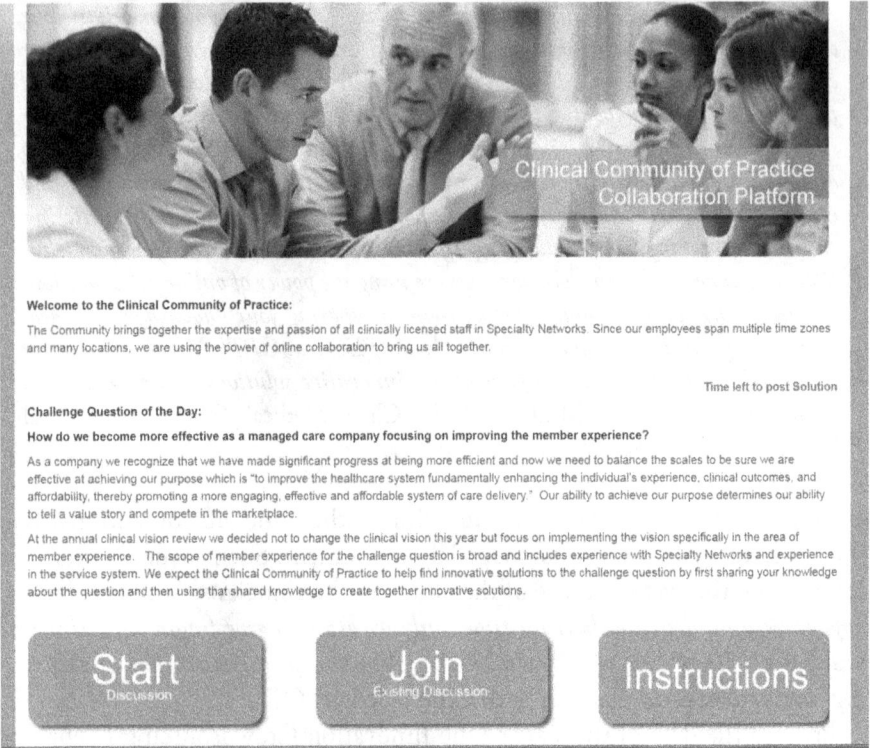

Fig. 6.2 Crowdsourcing event webpage

largest concentration of Optum clinicians, compared to the other 250 crowdsourcing events run by the parent organization over the last decade. In the words of one of the executives at Optum: "*The fact that we got the amount of participation from this group is a huge win.*" Another executive commented about how surprised he was at the depth, thoughtfulness, and breadth of the recommendations.

After the event ended, the sponsor at Optum organized the 255 posts into 17 different categories of similar topics. A senior executive steering committee focused on the seven topics receiving the most comments. The recommendations in all seven topics were implemented. The crowd received a short report indicating how their recommendations were implemented.

Initially, we reviewed the discussions posted and didn't see any indications of particularly interesting practices followed by the crowd of clinicians. But then, upon further examination, we noticed two characteristics of the discussions that peaked our interest to further analyze:

1. Some of the discussion starter posts had a lot of replies and some had none, as if there was something about the way in which a crowd participant posted information in the discussion starter post *that enticed other* participants to reply.
2. When there were replies, some of the replies seemed to offer creatively unique solutions that appeared on the surface to have nothing in common with the discussion starter posts.

These characteristics led us to want to learn more about how Optum employees collectively produced the innovative ideas that senior management thought were so powerful that they were implemented. Our quantitative trace data of the Optum crowdsourcing event (described in detail later) eventually led us to *suggest that what was unique about Optum was that the collective was engaged not simply in discussions about solutions that each were proposing, but rather, a very focused knowledge baton passing about problem-related needs and problem-related solutions. Moreover, this knowledge baton passing was not focused on discussing problem-related needs to understand them better, but rather, in reconstructing needs to be used as creative associations, which then appeared to release the creativity of the crowd to propose innovative solutions.*

6.2 Relevant Literature on How Discussion Threads Lead to Innovative Ideas

There is no existing literature specifically about how discussion threads unfold to lead to innovative ideas. Therefore, we looked at three literatures to see if they could address the two questions we had about the Optum discussions:

1. Was there something about the way in which the discussion topic was described that garnered attention from the crowd so that Collective Production could occur? and
2. Was there something about follow-on comments during Collective Production that led to innovative ideas?

The three literatures we looked at were the creativity literature (similar to what we examined for Chaps. 4 and 5), the literatures on internal crowdsourcing and employee voicing, and the literature on problemistic search.

We first looked at the internal crowdsourcing literature. Unfortunately, despite the promise of internal crowdsourcing producing high-quality ideas, several studies have found that the outcomes are often of lower quality than expected.[2] A survey of over 1000 firms using a range of employee knowledge-sharing tools, including crowd-based innovation platforms, showed that less than 25% reported increases in the number of successful innovations for new products or services despite an increased speed of access to each other's knowledge.[3] Another study of online enterprise-wide knowledge sharing found only half the employees interviewed used the knowledge of others to "recombine knowledge in ways that produced a product or process innovation".[4]

We then looked at the employee voicing literature because Optum's crowdsourcing event was composed of employees voicing their opinions to management, and they were explicitly asked to offer innovative improvements to the services they delivered to their clients.[5] Voicing is defined as communication by employees to managers regarding needs or concerns employees have about their work conditions. Voicing occurs in an effort to have management improve the conditions in an organization.[6] Voicing is an important characteristic of effective organizations[7] because it ensures that managers are aware of barriers to employees' work performance, learning from their employees, and in response, adapting organizational structures and processes.[8] Recent studies have shown that voicing is particularly effective in terms of changing work conditions when it is improvement-oriented[9] and customer-focused.[10]

In the voicing literature, employees are viewed as individual voicers, or voicers representing others. Via voicing, employees engage in (semi)private dialogues with management,[11] challenging the extant hierarchies or institutions[12] to eventually result in a bottom-up expression of will or discontent.[13] Most of the empirical work has studied the effect of voicing from the individual to managers in terms of how voicing is influenced by and influences an individual's self-efficacy,[14] promotion opportunities,[15] job satisfaction,[16] turnover,[17] visibility,[18] and favorable performance evaluations.[19] While there have been calls for research on how individuals' voices influence others' individual voices,[20] there is little substantial research on this topic as yet, and no research on how individual voices when shared on a collaborative forum will influence others' individual voices in developing innovative solutions to the voices. However, from this literature, we do know that individuals often share their voices as needs ("This is what I need") or complaints ("This is bad for my clients"), and will surface solutions to these needs if explicitly asked.[21]

We also looked at the problemistic search[22] literature that describes needs and solutions as two separate aspects of problem solving. From all four literatures, Table 6.1 describes these expectations from the literature that we garnered. As we will point out later, *none* of these expectations were met when examining how the collective "collectively voices" to produce innovative ideas.

Table 6.1 Expectations from literatures about what drives crowd attention to ultimately affect emergence of innovative ideas

• *Devolution of crowdsourcing into a sea of complaints*: Employees, when allowed the opportunity for large-scale interaction, may end up using crowdsourcing to complain rather than collectively producing an innovative solution.[a] • *Critique-based innovation*: Constructive critique of others' ideas or needs leads to the production of higher quality ideas.[b] • *Support effect*: Employees need support from peers to turn voicing into creativity.[c] • *Persuasion effect*: Persuasive word choices in posts draw crowd attention, and with more attention, there is a greater chance of innovative solution generation.[d] • *Clarification of a need without solution invites crowd attention*: Offering customer needs without solutions appears more welcoming of new ideas because the problem is not considered solved.[e] • *Constructive conflict leads to innovation*: Constructive conflict leads to greater surfacing of similarities and differences between the parties in conflict so that negotiations can be pursued, leading to more innovative ideas.[f]

[a]Burris, E. R., Detert, J. R., & Chiaburu, D. S. (2008). Quitting before leaving: the mediating effects of psychological attachment and detachment on voice. *Journal of Applied Psychology, 93*(4), 912; Ng, T. W., & Feldman, D. C. (2012). Employee voice behavior: A meta-analytic test of the conservation of resources framework. *Journal of Organizational Behavior, 33*(2), 216–234; MacKenzie, S. B., Podsakoff, P. M., & Podsakoff, N. P. (2011). Challenge-oriented organizational citizenship behaviors and organizational effectiveness: Do challenge-oriented behaviors really have an impact on the organization's bottom line? *Personnel Psychology, 64*(3), 559–592; McClean, E. J., Burris, E. R., & Detert, J. R. (2013). When does voice lead to exit? It depends on leadership. *Academy of Management Journal, 56*(2), 525–548

[b]Tausczik, Y. R., Kittur, A., & Kraut, R. E. (2014, February). Collaborative problem solving: A study of math overflow. In *Proceedings of the 17th ACM conference on Computer supported cooperative work & social computing* (pp. 355–367). ACM; Lovelace, K., Shapiro, D. L., & Weingart, L. R. (2001). Maximizing cross-functional new product teams' innovativeness and constraint adherence: A conflict communications perspective. *Academy of Management Journal, 44*(4), 779–793

[c]Malinen, S. (2015). Understanding user participation in online communities: A systematic literature review of empirical studies. *Computers in Human Behavior, 46*, 228–238; Zhou, J., & George, J. M. (2001). When job dissatisfaction leads to creativity: Encouraging the expression of voice. *Academy of Management Journal, 44*(4), 682–696

[d]Arguello, J., Butler, B. S., Joyce, E., Kraut, R., Ling, K. S., Rose, C., & Wang, X. (2006). Talk to me: Foundations for successful individual-group interactions in online communities. *Proc. SIGCHI conference on Human Factors in computing systems* (ACM), 959–968; Joyce, E., & Kraut, R. E. (2006). Predicting continued participation in newsgroups. *Journal of Computer-Mediated Communication, 11*(3), 723–747

[e]According to a solid body of literature (Arguello, J., Butler, B. S., Joyce, E., Kraut, R., Ling, K. S., Rose, C., & Wang, X. (2006). Talk to me: Foundations for successful individual-group interactions in online communities. *Proc. SIGCHI conference on Human Factors in computing systems* (ACM), 959–968; Burke, M., Joyce, E., Kim, T., Anand, V., & Kraut, R. (2007). Introductions and Requests: Rhetorical strategies that elicit response in online communities. Steinfield, C., Pentland, B. T., Ackerman, M., & Contractor, N., eds. *Communities and Technologies* (Springer, London), 21–39; Joyce, E., & Kraut, R. E.

(continued)

Table 6.1 (continued)

(2006). Predicting continued participation in newsgroups. *Journal of Computer-Mediated Communication, 11*(3), 723–747; Tausczik, Y. R., Kittur, A., & Kraut, R. E. (2014). Collaborative problem solving: A study of math overflow. *Proc.17th ACM conference on Computer supported cooperative work & social computing* (ACM), 355–367), the use of justifications for an argument can be counter-productive for follow-on creative discussion since it can lead to impressions of defensiveness rather than openness to others' opinions

fAmabile, T. M., & Pratt, M. G. (2016). The dynamic componential model of creativity and innovation in organizations: Making progress, making meaning. *Research in Organizational Behavior, 36*, 157–183; Anderson, N., Potočnik, K., & Zhou, J. (2014). Innovation and creativity in organizations: A state-of-the-science review, prospective commentary, and guiding framework. *Journal of Management, 40*(5), 1297–1333; Harvey, S. (2014). Creative synthesis: Exploring the process of extraordinary group creativity. *Academy of Management Review, 39*(3), 324–343

Given this literature, we then turned to the trace data collected from the Optum crowdsourcing to find out answers to our two questions: (1) How can discussions capture crowd attention to be potentially generative? and (2) Was there something about follow-on comments during Collective Production that led to innovative ideas?

6.3 How Can Discussions Capture Crowd Attention to Be Potentially Generative?

If there are no follow-on comments responding to a discussion thread started by a crowd participant, then obviously, no Collective Production can occur. Thus, for any discussion thread started, ideally, a discussion would ensue. To explore how discussions are initiated in crowds seeking solutions for the initial problem statement, we looked at the 75 discussion thread starters in the Optum crowdsourcing event. Discussion thread starting statements are the posts for which participants have indicated they are starting a new discussion thread (as opposed to the only other option to the participant is to post a reply on a discussion thread already started). We took the expectations from the literature as shown in Table 6.1 and created codes for whether the starting statement contains a complaint, a solution, a need, or a need-solution match. The coding instructions are shown in Table 6.2.

Apparent from the frequency of the different coded statements in the discussion thread starters is a contrast to the literature's warning of the possibility of negative voicing. We find instead that complaints in initial posts are few. We also find that only eight of the discussion thread starters were limited to

6 Practice 4: Reconstructing Needs for Creative Associations   173

Table 6.2 Coding of the 75 discussion thread starters

Content	Description	Example	# posts coded as
Starting statement includes complaint	A frustration or concern raised without specifying a particular solution for solving the complaint and without specifying a particular customer concern the complaint is serving[a]	Being a Care Advocate is extremely difficult. We are expected to have all the answers at the drop of a hat, to be professional and courteous, empathetic, and to provide information on accessing the right care at the right time. Throw in navigating KIT, iBAAG, PASS, filing complaints, submitting CAST requests, dealing with ABA requests, among crisis calls and constant troubleshooting, dealing with IT issues, we can sometimes be short. We are asked to treat every call of the day like it is our first call of the day. If you can tell me how I can become more energetic, happy, etc. and make that last all day long, I would be thrilled. Sometimes, our own lives get in the way too. And we aren't allowed any time off in January at all and because we're in a queue we have to bid on holidays time off. When the work/life balance is off, everything else in life will be off.	18
Starting statement includes solution-idea only, with no need specified	A solution-idea offered without specifying the particular customer need the idea is meant to meet	This recently published study concerns improving quality, service delivery, and patient experience in a musculoskeletal physiotherapy service in the UK. What was clearly evident in the results was that system changes, particularly multifaceted approaches, were vastly more successful than strategies designed to motivate individual clinicians to change their behavior. "This initiative showed the value of patient feedback in delivering services and driving change … It is essential that clinical services are viewed through the eyes of their users"	7

(continued)

Table 6.2 (continued)

Content	Description	Example	# posts coded as
Starting statement includes need only, with no solution-idea specified	Specification of a customer concern such as a negative experience by the customer by the participant	We are often being told to refer members to member services; however, we have no idea what that phone number is or the other departments are. The departments are very separate, medical, pharmacy, etc. I have had contact with another department, including medical teams who often report, "we can't accept this case" and have no interest in collaborating with behavioral health. One manager said, "The case loads are high" and the member is not on anyone's caseload. No further assistance or collaboration was provided. Medical and behavioral collaboration is so important, yet some teams are so hidden and others have no interest in collaboration.	8
Starting statement includes both solution and need	Solution-idea with justification typically based on a customer concern	Members and provider have considerable difficulty getting reads on claims issues. [Customer concern] … When a provider or member has a claims issue that is not resolved to their satisfaction, there needs to be an internal claims readings team with more training for escalation that can be accessed without the need for clinical care advocates and their team members to resolve the issues… [Solution-idea]…	52
Total # of codes assigned to starter posts; a starter post could have more than one code			85 codes

[a]Garner, J. T. (2009). When things go wrong at work: An exploration of organizational dissent messages. *Communication Studies, 60*(2), 197–218

just describing a customer need. Clearly, allowing clinicians to engage in a process of collaboratively developing innovative products and services for Optum does not devolve into a complaint-fest and demoralizing litany of problems that the company needs to solve.

6 Practice 4: Reconstructing Needs for Creative Associations

Table 6.3 Predictors of number of replies to a discussion thread starter (N = 75)

	DV = Number of replies to starter post	
	Control only Estimates (SD)	Full model Estimates (SD)
Control variables for starter post		
Time order	−0.02*** (0.003)	−0.02*** (0.003)
Poster of starter offered at least one comment later on	−0.17 (0.17)	−0.36 (0.18)
Poster posted earlier in the event	−0.18 (0.13)	−0.22 (0.13)
Number of other participants responding	−0.05 (0.03)	−0.04 (0.03)
Total words in starter	0.0005 (0.001)	−0.0007 (0.001)
Persuasiveness of word choice		
Clout manifest	0.002 (0.003)	0.001 (0.003)
Emotional tone	0.03 (0.02)	0.04 (0.02)
Authenticity	0.005 (0.003)	0.008* (0.003)
Independent variables describing content of starter		
Solution-need match		0.05** (0.17)
Complaint		0.23 (0.17)
Solution-only		−0.016 (0.001)
Model fit		
- log-likelihood (d.f.)	−250.95 (9)	−240.22 (12)
Residual deviance	351.39 (65)	329.93 (62)
Deviance Chi-Square difference (d.f.)		21.46*** (3)
AICc	519.90	504.44

*$p < 0.05$, **$p < 0.01$, ***$p < 0.001$

To address the question of how discussions are started, we looked at the number of replies each of the 75 discussion thread starters received. We then examined quantitatively if the content of the starter (as coded in Table 6.2) affected the number of replies. We included three of the four coded content: solution-need match, complaint, and solution-only (need-only was highly inversely correlated with solution-only, so was not needed in the analysis) The results are shown in Table 6.3.

Apparent from Table 6.3 is that *when discussion starters contain a Solution-Need Match, the starters solicit more replies from the crowd.*

6.3.1 Ruling Out Alternative Plausible Causes of Number of Replies

We looked at other factors that might affect the number of replies. As shown in Table 6.2, there is substantial research that suggests that the persuasive tone of the starter post might affect the number of replies. To show that persuasive tone was *not* the only reason why there were replies, we had to calculate how persuasive the tone of the starter post was. We show how we did this in

> **Box 6.1 Measuring Persuasive Tone of a Starter Poster**
>
> In order to objectively determine the persuasive tone of the initial post, we used a very commonly used methodology called Linguistic Inquiry and Word Count (LIWC). The LIWC software tool helps compare the words used in a text being analyzed against a dictionary of words to ascertain how many of the words in the pre-established dictionary representing a particular category are used in the text being analyzed. For our exploratory purpose, we use LIWC to calculate the persuasiveness of the words in the potential discussion starting post with regards to three categories: clout, emotion, and authenticity. Whereby, the higher the count in each category, the more persuasive is the post.
>
> The first dimension of persuasion is ***Clout*** that is an indicator of use of words that exhibit decisiveness and confidence. Clout score ranges from 0 to 100, whereby a high score means more decisiveness and confidence being expressed through words. The second dimension of persuasion is ***Authenticity***, which is an indicator of the words in the text that represent the writer in an authentic or honest way. In the LIWC dictionary, first-person pronouns, more "exclusive" words (e.g., but, except, and without), more evaluations, and judgment words (e.g., think, believe) are all associations with higher authenticity [54]. Authenticity score ranges from 0 to 100. The third and final dimension of LIWC that we use as representative of persuasion is the ***Emotional Tone*** expressed in the post. Emotional Tone score also ranges from 0 to 100, with a higher score representing a more positive tone with use of words such as happy, good, love, nice, and so on.

Box 6.1. Apparent from the results in Table 6.3 is that only one measure of persuasiveness—authenticity—had a very small effect on the number of replies, and that even with this effect, a solution-need match in the starter was still important.

In addition to the content and persuasiveness of the starter post, we also included the length of the post, the activity of the person making the post, and the time (chronological order) when the post was made. Apparent from Table 6.3 is that these alternative explanations for more replies do not overwhelm the importance of whether the post has a need-solution match. Thus, Collective Production doesn't simply start by posting ideas, but when the ideas are associated with an articulation of the need.

6.4 Was There Something About Follow-on Comments During Collective Production that Led to Innovative Ideas?

Earlier, we showed what starts a discussion that *could* lead to Collective Production: the presence of a need-solution match. Here, we are now interested in how this initial need-solution match led to creative changes by the

6   Practice 4: Reconstructing Needs for Creative Associations   177

Table 6.4 Example of need-solution match followed by a discussion supporting initial solution idea

Post Title: Better Tools + Better Member Decisions
Topic Post: How can we develop better tools to help members make informed treatment decisions? Can we develop a checklist or interactive tool that will help them decide which kind of treatment or provider is most likely to help them or a family member. This would be of huge value in the area of substance use disorders, where members and families are often subject to intense marketing efforts that do not represent the efficacy of treatment accurately.
Sample of reply comments
Reply 1: Members themselves may have an idea of what they need, but more specific guidelines (simplified) will give a clearer expectation of the levels of care they are actually meeting for.
Reply 2: We could develop an online checklist/survey for members and/or their family to complete to initially determine if they are experiencing a substance abuse versus dependence problem, which would then determine the best level of care. Then members could access a list of preferred providers (that Optum has developed) that members could contact. And members could call an Optum substance use disorder specialist care advocate for additional questions and assistance.
Reply 3: Companies that sell products routinely gather data from their customers to then design new products. Then, they test prototypes with focus groups. I think we should be able to provide tools to whatever age group is looking for them. I like the idea of an interactive tool, where the member responds to questions, the tool uses an algorithm to provide information about treatment with appropriate references. We could have live chat services with care advocates on the web. All this pales in comparison with the marketing efforts referenced earlier. We need to be able to manipulate social media and web search engines to put our message out there, rather than passively await a Live and Work Well visit
Reply 4: Love the idea of a live chat.

crowd. For example, in Table 6.4 is an example of a discussion that did *not* lead to the crowd generating different solutions than the initial one.

To see how discussions led to the emergence of new solutions, we created discussion progressions, which started with the initial need-solution pair[23] and ended with some statement about the initial solution such as an agreement (as in Table 6.4), conceptual expansion of the initial solution (i.e., modifying the initial solution), or solution reframing (offering an entirely new solution). As with others, we distinguish between conceptual expansion and reframing,[24] with the latter representing more creative thinking.[25] To do this, we coded each of the 266 replies to the discussion thread starters according to Table 6.5. Apparent from Table 6.5 is that about half of the replies (132) either conceptually reframe (new solutions) or conceptually expand (modified solution) on the initial solution in the starter. Moreover, for any discussion thread starter, there were multiple solutions posted—some of which were modified and some of which were new. This allowed us to com-

Table 6.5 Coding for changes to initial solution-ideas in replies

Type of post	Definition	Example	No. of replies coded as
A reply conceptually reframing starter solution	A reply-comment to initial solution-idea that offers a new perspective on the solution by changing its basic form and/or function[a]	In response to an initial solution-idea posted in the discussion thread starter to suggest a checklist for substance abuse members to know their treatment options: • "Maybe we have Optum substance use disorder specialist care advocates instead of just a checklist" • "We need to deliver psychoeducation that helps this population make their treatment decisions on facts, not emotions"	85
A reply conceptually expanding the starter solution	A reply-comment to initial solution-idea that adds new features to the solution without changing its basic form, function, or technology	In response to an initial solution-idea posted in the discussion thread starter to suggest a checklist for substance abuse members to know their treatment options: • "Maybe we have Optum substance use disorder specialist care advocates" • "We need to deliver psychoeducation that helps this population make their treatment decisions on facts, not emotions" "One-stop shopping for all the needs, including mental health, substance abuse, pharmacy, and eventually, medial"	47
Total number of coded replies in discussion threads, which were then aggregated as a count for the number of reframed solutions and number of expanded solutions (vis-à-vis initial solution-idea)			132

[a]Tsoukas, H. (2009). A dialogical approach to the creation of new knowledge in organizations. *Organization Science*, *20*(6), 941–957

pare what conversations ensued that led to new solutions versus modified ones.

To construct a sequence, we identified the series of posts that occurred between the initial need and initial solutions posts and the new solution or a modification of the initial solution in a discussion thread. All sequences started with the same initial need specification and initial solution. However, the posts within each sequence were unique to the sequence (occurred subsequent to the last new or modified solution). All sequences ended with a new

6 Practice 4: Reconstructing Needs for Creative Associations

solution or a modified solution. In such a way, there were 132 such sequences. In most sequences, there were only 1–5 (with average being 2.3) posts in any sequence. These sequences represent acts of Collective Production, whereby one or more participants take the initial starter need-solution match and carry it forward in some fashion. In addition, there were additional 46 sequences that ended in agreement with the initial solution. In total, there were 178 sequences in which some interaction occurred and one of the three outcomes was achieved: a new solution, a modification of initial solution, or an agreement with the initial solution. Finally, there were 25 instances in which no other post was made in the discussion thread, but no replies were made to the discussion thread starter.

To understand these acts of Collective Production, we then coded these sequences in terms of what was being discussed. Our codes for the sequences are shown in Table 6.6. There is quite a range of different knowledge content in these sequences, with the most frequently contributed knowledge being a support for the initial customer need, and those offering a new customer need.

Now, we were ready to see if the content of these Collective Production sequences affected the creation of a new solution. These results are shown in Table 6.7.

Table 6.6 Content discussed during Collective Production sequences

Type of post	Definition	Example	Number of replies coded as
Explore similarity of needs posted in starter to poster's context.	Replies that echo, restate, agree, or describe similarities between initial customer need offered in the starter post and the new poster's context.	Need to effectively communicate with members that may have behavioral health diagnoses and to take away the fears and the underlying stigma that many may have concerning these members (Initial Customer Concern). Inability to communicate effectively with behavioral health persons may be a contributing factor to increase in suicidal thought and actions (Support for Customer Concern).	69

(continued)

Table 6.6 (continued)

Type of post	Definition	Example	Number of replies coded as
Critique solution posted in starter.	Replies that provide a counterpoint or a flaw in logic associated with initial solution-idea offered in starter post.	Communicate to the providers through fax blasts and newsletters. (Initial Solution). I think fax blasts and newsletters would be helpful, albeit a little annoying if overloaded. I do think some transparency about the IFR template would be beneficial (Critique of Initial Solution).	14
Critique need posted in starter.	Replies that provide a counterpoint or a flaw in logic/ assumption associated with customer need offered in starter post.	Members and provider have considerable difficulty getting resolutions on claims issues. The issues tend to filter back to care advocacy and thus use their time and staff to assist in resolution (Initial Customer Concern). We currently do have a process much like what you described. If you search Clinical Claims Escalation on KIT, you will find a QRG that references this. However, not all managers/ supervisors may be aware of this and/or trained on this process (Critique of Initial Customer Concern).	14
Offer a need different from starter post.	Replies that offer a different customer need than the initial need offered in starter post.	There is a broader question (than just offering treatment options) and philosophical issues that need to be addressed, e.g., when it is appropriate for people to make their own treatment decisions and when is professional involvement important?"Members don't understand that partial hospital with boarding is NOT residential or inpatient."	50
Support for solution posted in starter.	Replies that echo, restate, and/or agree the initial solution-idea offered in starter post.	"I like the idea.""I agree."	46
Total number of codes allocated to 278 Collective Production sequence. A sequence can have more than one code (as there may be more than one post in the sequence).			193

6 Practice 4: Reconstructing Needs for Creative Associations

After including the same controls as before, Table 6.7 shows that (a) critiquing the initial solution or the initial need is not helpful (the insignificant β associated with the regression variable: number of replies critiquing the initial solution-idea), (b) supporting the initial customer need is more likely to lead to modified solutions, and (c) new needs that build on but reformulate the initial need are more likely to lead to a new solution.

Given the importance of "# of replies offering new customer need" in affecting whether a new solution is offered by the crowd, we read each of the 50 posts offering a different need. *We were surprised that many of the new needs*

Table 6.7 Determinants of new solutions during Collective Production

	DV = Does sequence end with conceptual reframing of initial solution?	
	Control only Estimates (SD)	Full model Estimates(SD)
Control variables for topic post		
Time order	−0.02 (0.01)	−0.02 (0.01)
Did topic poster comment on topic?	−0.23 (0.46)	−0.60 (0.46)
Did topic poster offer earlier comment?	−0.72 (0.46)	−0.85 (0.48)
Number of contributors responding to topic	0.01 (0.09)	0.05 (0.10)
Number of replies to topic	0.06 (0.05)	0.09 (0.05)
Total words in topic post	−0.01* (0.004)	−0.01** (0.004)
Persuasiveness of word choice		
Clout manifest	−0.01 (0.01)	−0.01 (0.01)
Emotional tone	−0.01 (0.008)	−0.01 (0.01)
Authenticity	0.03* (0.01)	0.03* (0.01)
Content includes customer care + solution	1.27 (0.68)	1.32 (0.74)
Independent variables describing knowledge in sequence of posts leading up the DV post		
# replies offering new customer need		2.15*** (0.54)
# replies exploring similarity to initial need		−1.12* (0.48)
#replied critiquing initial solution-idea		−0.14 (0.79)
# replies critiquing initial customer need		0.18 (0.81)
Model fit		
- log-likelihood (d.f.)	−113.5 (12)	−98.7 (28)
Deviance	226.99	197.39
Deviance Chi-Square difference (d.f.)		29.59* (16)
AICc	253.39	250.99
BIC	346.16	290.74

^Sequences (178 sequences ending with modified or new solution plus 25 sequences ending with agreements with the initial solution = 203); *$p < 0.05$, **$p < 0.01$, ***$p < 0.001$

Table 6.8 Coding for posts offering new customer needs

Making initial need more concrete (to apply very specifically to a very specific context): A reply regarding prior initial need that provides a concrete example in another participant's context.	In response to a starter need to help those with substance use disorders know their treatment options: • "However, we should primarily be focusing on helping the patient connect with their MD/APRN…" • "Family members call me and want the addicted individual to be sent to a freestanding facility and not grouped with mandated clients." • "Members don't understand that partial hospital with boarding is NOT residential or inpatient." • "Members with substance abuse going to the website are not able to identify the levels of care a facility offers, so they aren't empowered to make their own decisions."
Making initial need abstract: A reply regarding a prior initial need that describes a more general principle that a need should fulfill.	In response to a starter need to help those with substance use disorders know their treatment options: • "There is the broader questions and philosophical issues that need to be addressed, e.g., when is it appropriate for people to make their own treatment decisions and when is professional involvement important?" • "What benefit does human interaction offer in the assessment process?" "Don't all age groups (not just adults) need to know their treatment options?"

were explicitly inspirational in the manner of offering creative associations rather than direct extrapolations of more requirements than those of the initial needs. That is, as shown in Table 6.8, the new needs were either concrete examples about the initial need that provide analogies for creative associations or more abstracted principles that widen creative association possibilities.

Just to be sure that we were accurate, we removed the few cases in which the posts did not fall into one of these inspirational categories and did the analysis specifically to see if using these inspirational posts versus finding similarities to the need already posted would lead to more creative solutions. We used a multinomial linear regression model to assess if inspirational posts are more likely to lead to creative ideas than posts that explore similarities among needs (see Box 6.2 if you want to know more about multinomial linear regression).

Box 6.2 Multinomial Linear Regression

Multinomial logistic (MNL) regressions allow for more than two discrete outcomes. MNL models help predict the presence or absence of an outcome (usually, a group membership) based on a set of predictor variables (Cooper et al. 1991; Lee 2004). As compared to linear regression models, MNL models allow for dependent variables to be nominal and do not require a normal distribution (Maddala 1983). In addition, multinomial logistic regression relaxes several assumptions required in traditional regression analysis, including multivariate normality, equal variance-covariance matrices across groups, linear relationships between dependent and independent variables, interval-scaled independent variables, and normally distributed error terms (Bayaga 2010; Tabachnick et al. 2001).

In MNL analysis, the paramount interest is in how an explanatory variable X_k impacts the probability π_j that a sequence belongs to sequence group j. As such, the probabilities themselves are a non-linear function of explanatory variables. The results from the logit-form of the model are the log-odds of a sequence having an outcome *j* versus reference category *J* and are linear functions of the explanatory variable. Therefore, the standard MNL model is expressed as (Yamaguchi 2000):

$$\log\left(\pi_j \big/ \pi_J\right) = \alpha_j + \sum_{k=1}^{K} \beta_{jk} X_k.$$

A key decision in MNL is in the selection of the reference category against which other categories will be compared. For example, if there are four categories being compared, in MNL, one will be the reference case and the other three will be the comparison categories. The choice of reference case is left to the researchers. It is recommended that researchers choose the reference category as the one that makes the most interpretive sense.

Three categories of outcomes were distinguished: (1) no co-creation, (2) idea reframing, and (3) idea expansion. The reference category used was idea expansion, as the key distinction we wanted to explore was between co-creation dialogues that result in idea expansion versus those that result in idea reframing. The no-dialogue category was not included in this analysis (dropping the sample by 25) because it was not needed for this test. The two explanatory variables were included: the sequence was focused on identifying similarity of client needs versus sequence was focused on identifying creative associations from those initial needs. A few dialogues included both explanatory variables; instead of eliminating them from the sample, the relaxation of the requirement that independent variables be uncorrelated with MNL allowed for the inclusion of these few dialogues.

To test hypotheses with MNL models, one first examines the model fit of the MNL regression equation. The goodness of fit of the multinomial logistic regression model is determined by looking at the whole model chi-square test and the R^2 (Peng et al. 2002). Once the fit of the overall model is demonstrated, one examines the direction and significance of the estimates. The direction of the

(continued)

Box 6.2 (continued)

> estimate is always toward the non-reference category. Thus, if the estimate is positive and significant, the results indicate that the non-reference category has a higher probability of occurring with the explanatory variable than the reference category. If the estimate is negative and significant, the results indicate that the reference category has a higher probability of occurring with the explanatory variable than the non-reference category.

For the analysis, we included three potential outcomes: (1) worst case: the final post of the sequence simply supported the initial solution, signifying no Collective Production during that sequence, (2) idea modification, meaning that the initial idea was modified as a result of the sequence, and (3) the best case of a new idea being proposed as a result of the Collective Production in the sequence. The results are shown in Table 6.9.

The way to interpret Table 6.9 is that the negative value of −1.50 and −1.37 means that the more that participants in the sequence discuss the similarity of the initial need with their own contexts, the more likely they are to limit their Collective Production to modifications of the existing solution-idea. Inversely, the positive sign of 1.52 means that the more the participants

Table 6.9 Test for impact of need-solution pair start on DVs when dialogue occurs

Dependent variable Log Odds ($n = 178$)		
	New solution-idea vs. modification of initial solution-idea	Modification of initial solution-idea vs. no Collective Production of altered solution-ideas
Intercept	0.77 (0.49)	0.02 (0.54)
Independent variables		
Exploration of similarity of initial need across contexts	−1.50** (0.41)	−1.37** (0.45)
Describe needs in inspirational way	1.52** (0.49)	−0.03 (0.62)
Control variables		
Time order of initiating comment	0.01 (0.01)	0.03* (0.01)
Word length of initiating comment	−0.002 (0.002)	−0.001 (0.003)
Model fit		
Generalized R-square	0.22	
- log-likelihood	187.65	
Chi-Square	39.07**	

Note: This analysis does not include threads that had no replies
***$p < 0.001$, **$p < 0.01$, *$p < 0.05$

in the sequence offer creative associations (concrete examples or abstract principles), the more likely they are to offer a new creative discovery. *Thus, we conclude that innovative solutions are inspired by the crowd, rather than resulting from an increased set of need-based requirements.*

6.5 Summary of Findings of Practice 4

Our findings imply a step-through process of Collective Production where the discussion starter post must stimulate enough crowd members to pull in crowd attention (by having both a need and a solution), and then, the discussion that ensues must be focused on reconstructing the initial needs to inspire creative discovery. What the process does *not* do is to encourage inclusiveness of all requirements, support the initial need, argue against either the need or the solution, or complain. It is almost as if the crowd understands that unless it infuses the discussion with creative associations, such as specific concrete examples for analogies or abstract principles to broaden out the types of creative associations that could be considered, new solutions will not emerge.

Figure 6.3 shows a summary of our findings and illustrates the notion of a need-focused Collective Production process. This process is an extension of the collective creative process discussed in Chap. 5. Needs mentioned can serve as creative associations, provided there is some triggering for that to happen (i.e., by abstracting or making the needs initially presented in the starter more concrete).

This second form of collective creativity, shown in Fig. 6.3, reinforces the notion of creative association stimulation that underlies the process. We suggest that when crowds look at the pattern of recent knowledge evolution (manifest in traces and sequences) laid out in front of them prior to posting their own contribution, they will be creatively stimulated by whether the posts exhibit knowledge variety (as discussed in Chap. 4), amount of stimulation demonstrated previously (as in Chap. 5), or whether the solution-idea is coupled with an articulation of the need (as in this chapter). What is unexpected of this last finding is that need-solution matching might be expected to harm creativity because it provides a "complete package" of both the need and the solution. But the crowd appears to have no qualms in essentially separating out the need from the solution, ignoring the solution, not arguing about the need, and then, reformulating the need to be more inspirational.

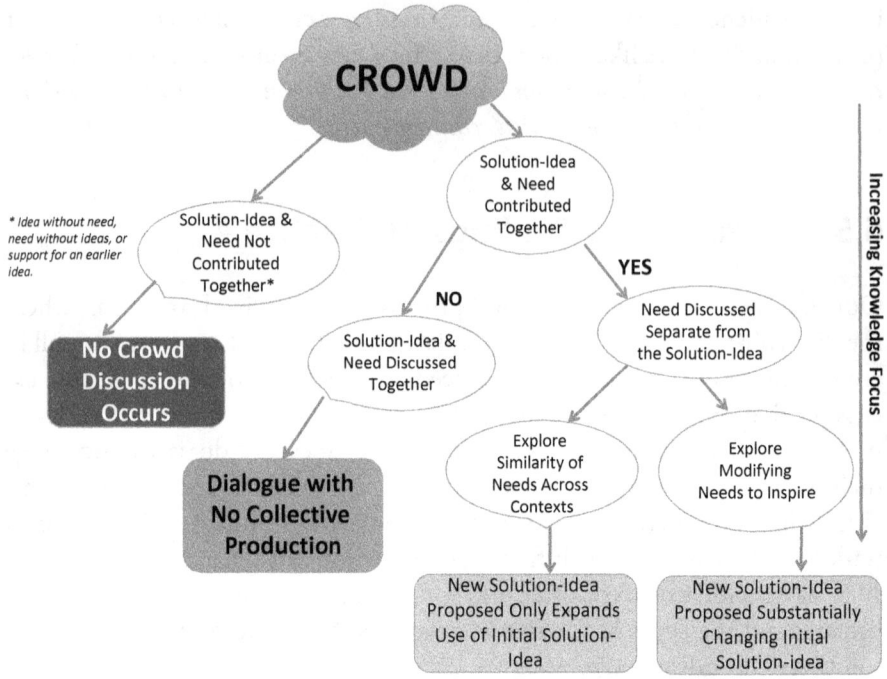

Fig. 6.3 Summary of second form of collective creativity

6.6 How Our Findings Align with Existing Research on Crowdsourcing

Table 6.10 shows the alignment with the existing literatures on voicing, problemistic search, and creativity. Apparent from the table is that there are substantial differences.

As new technologies such as virtual online workspaces (e.g., collaborative workspaces, social media, online forums, and crowdsourcing software) become commonplace in organizations, the nature of voicing may change. The new technologies provide the possibility of turning the *employee-management* voicing process to a *peer-to-peer* voicing as individuals are able to view each other's voice.[26] Enabled by technology platforms, individuals in organizations are able to translate their ideas and thoughts into digital traces. In doing so, participants do not simply post their own voices independent of others, as might occur in private employee-to-manager voicing, but can instead voice in response to others' prior voices.[27] As we have described here, such voicing in response to others' voices appears to create the possibility of an evolving progression of voices as knowledge sequences, affecting the cre-

Table 6.10 Expectations from literature and findings about what drives crowd attention and ultimately affects the emergence of innovative ideas

Expectations for crowdsourcing from the literature on voicing, creativity, and problemistic search	Findings from Optum's innovation crowdsourcing event	Speculations about why our findings might be so different from literature
• **Devolution of crowdsourcing into a sea of complaints**: Employees when allowed the opportunity for large-scale interaction may end up using crowdsourcing to complain rather than collectively producing innovative solution.[a]	• **The need-focus**: There were few complaints or statements about just needs, with most offering solution-ideas as asked for in the problem statement.	• Clinicians may be more likely to think in terms of needs to be served, not problems. • Focusing event on innovative solutions may reduce complaints.
• **Critique-based innovation**: Constructive critique of others' ideas or needs leads to production of higher quality ideas.[b]	• **Critiques are dead-ends**: When discussion threads were started with a constructive critique, they went nowhere.	• Critiques keep focus on the idea rather than inspire a different focus.
• **Support effect**: Employees need support from peers to turn voicing into creativity.[c]	• **Support is a dead-end**: When comments on others' posts focus on supporting others, the discussions do not progress further and rarely lead to generation of innovative solutions.	• This replicates our findings in Chap. 5: support hurts innovativeness.
• **Persuasion effect**: Persuasive word choices in posts draw crowd attention, and with more attention, there is a greater chance of innovative solution generation.[d]	• **Persuasion dead-ends**: Persuasive word choices do not draw more attention (i.e., more replies) to the post.	• The crowd is not interested in being "persuaded" about anything; they want to be inspired.
• **Clarification of a need without solution invites crowd attention**: Offering customer needs without solutions appears more welcoming of new ideas because the problem is not considered solved.[e]	• **Need must be with solution to capture crowd attention**: Posts that included both a need and a solution had more replies.	• Need without solution doesn't help since there are so many needs. • Solutions without needs do not help the crowd because the rationale for the solution isn't clear.

(continued)

Table 6.10 (continued)

Expectations for crowdsourcing from the literature on voicing, creativity, and problemistic search	Findings from Optum's innovation crowdsourcing event	Speculations about why our findings might be so different from literature
• **Constructive conflict leads to innovation**: Constructive conflict leads to greater surfacing of similarities and differences between the parties in conflict so that negotiations can be pursued, leading to more innovative ideas.[f]	• **Constructive conflict about needs in the need-solution pair hurt**: Conflict over the need that justified the solution leads to less innovative solutions.	• Arguing against the need puts attention of the crowd on negotiating to get a consensus on needs, and yet, there will never be agreement in a crowd about needs. • It also diverts crowd attention away from solution generation.
• **Predefined needs and solutions can find each other**: There are always a variety of needs and solutions floating around which can be matched for a particular context.[g]	• **Starting with, and reconstructing from a need inspires more innovative solutions**: When crowds take a need as given, but then use it to reconstruct new related needs, more innovative solutions arise.	• By starting with the need, the crowd is not denying the voice of the poster with the need. • By reconstructing the need to fit different contexts, the need becomes malleable, opening the crowd to new creative association possibilities.
• **Expanding problem needs leads to more innovative solutions**: Making needs or requirements of the problem broader for more inclusion of additional contexts will yield more innovative solutions since it requires new ways of thinking about how to have a solution that covers so many needs.[h]	• **Reconstructing needs to not expand but make them more concrete or more abstract leads to more innovative solutions**. Half of the time, innovative solutions occurred when a need posted by one participant was made more concrete by the next participant by providing specific examples. For the other half, innovative solutions followed when a need was made into a more abstract goal (such as from fixing a database to helping a customer find the right provider).	• Needs should be inspirational, not as specific requirements. Making needs more inclusive is just making requirements more broad which doesn't support creative thinking. Adding concrete examples serve as an analogy to support creative thinking. Offering more abstract goals helps to widen the creative associations that may be found in one's memory.

(continued)

Table 6.10 (continued)

[a]Burris, E. R., Detert, J. R., & Chiaburu, D. S. (2008). Quitting before leaving: the mediating effects of psychological attachment and detachment on voice. *Journal of Applied Psychology, 93*(4), 912; Ng, T. W., & Feldman, D. C. (2012). Employee voice behavior: A meta-analytic test of the conservation of resources framework. *Journal of Organizational Behavior, 33*(2), 216–234; MacKenzie, S. B., Podsakoff, P. M., & Podsakoff, N. P. (2011). Challenge-oriented organizational citizenship behaviors and organizational effectiveness: Do challenge-oriented behaviors really have an impact on the organization's bottom line?. *Personnel Psychology, 64*(3), 559–592; McClean, E. J., Burris, E. R., & Detert, J. R. (2013). When does voice lead to exit? It depends on leadership. *Academy of Management Journal, 56*(2), 525–548

[b]Tausczik, Y. R., Kittur, A., & Kraut, R. E. (2014, February). Collaborative problem solving: A study of math overflow. In *Proceedings of the 17th ACM conference on Computer supported cooperative work & social computing* (pp. 355–367). ACM; Lovelace, K., Shapiro, D. L., & Weingart, L. R. (2001). Maximizing cross-functional new product teams' innovativeness and constraint adherence: A conflict communications perspective. *Academy of Management Journal, 44*(4), 779–793

[c]Malinen, S. (2015). Understanding user participation in online communities: A systematic literature review of empirical studies. *Computers in Human Behavior, 46*, 228–238; Zhou, J., & George, J. M. (2001). When job dissatisfaction leads to creativity: Encouraging the expression of voice. *Academy of Management Journal, 44*(4), 682–696

[d]Arguello, J., Butler, B. S., Joyce, E., Kraut, R., Ling, K. S., Rose, C., & Wang, X. (2006). Talk to me: Foundations for successful individual-group interactions in online communities. *Proc. SIGCHI conference on HumanFactors in computing systems* (ACM), 959–968; Joyce, E., & Kraut, R. E. (2006). Predicting continued participation in newsgroups. *Journal of Computer-Mediated Communication, 11*(3), 723–747

[e]According to a solid body of literature (Arguello, J., Butler, B. S., Joyce, E., Kraut, R., Ling, K. S., Rose, C., & Wang, X. (2006). Talk to me: Foundations for successful individual-group interactions in online communities. *Proc. SIGCHI conference on Human Factors in computing systems* (ACM), 959–968; Burke, M., Joyce, E., Kim, T., Anand, V., & Kraut, R. (2007). Introductions and requests: Rhetorical strategies that elicit response in online communities. Steinfield, C., Pentland, B. T., Ackerman, M., & Contractor, N., eds. *Communities and Technologies* (Springer, London), 21–39; Joyce, E., & Kraut, R. E. (2006). Predicting continued participation in newsgroups. *Journal of Computer-Mediated Communication, 11*(3), 723–747; Tausczik, Y. R., Kittur, A., & Kraut, R. E. (2014). Collaborative problem solving: A study of math overflow. *Proc.17th ACM conference on Computer supported cooperative work & social computing* (ACM), 355–367), the use of justifications for an argument can be counter-productive for follow-on creative discussion since it can lead to impressions of defensiveness rather than openness to others' opinions

[f]Amabile, T. M., & Pratt, M. G. (2016). The dynamic componential model of creativity and innovation in organizations: Making progress, making meaning. *Research in Organizational Behavior, 36*, 157–183; Anderson, N., Potočnik, K., & Zhou, J. (2014). Innovation and creativity in organizations: A state-of-the-science review, prospective commentary, and guiding framework. *Journal of Management, 40*(5), 1297–1333; Harvey, S. (2014). Creative synthesis: Exploring the process of extraordinary group creativity. *Academy of Management Review, 39*(3), 324–343

[g]von Hippel, E., & von Krogh, G. (2016). Crossroads—Identifying viable "need–solution

(continued)

Table 6.10 (continued)

pairs": Problem solving without problem formulation. *Organization Science, 27*(1), 207–221; Posen, H. E., Keil, T., Kim, S., & Meissner, F. D. (2018). Renewing research on problemistic search—A review and research agenda. *Academy of Management Annals, 12*(1), 208–251

[h]In the problemistic search literature, Posen, H. E., Keil, T., Kim, S., & Meissner, F. D. (2018). Renewing Research on Problemistic Search—A Review and Research Agenda. *Acad. of Management Annals 12*(1), 237: "Taking the problem and problem-definition search as the starting point, we consider organizational action as exploratory, not on the basis of solution novelty, but rather, on the basis of the novelty of the problem definition (i.e., its distance from prior problem definitions). A recent body of work argues that the 'problem' is a critical unit of analysis (Nickerson, J. A., & Zenger, T. R. (2004). A knowledge-based theory of the firm—The problem-solving perspective. *Organization Science, 15*(6): 617–632; Nickerson, J. A., Yen, C. J., & Mahoney, J. T. (2012). Exploring the problem-finding and problem-solving approach for designing organizations. *The Academy of Management Perspectives, 26*(1), 52–72. O'Reilly, C. A., & Tushman, M. L. (2004). The ambidextrous organization. *Harvard Business Review, 82*(4): 74–83. Extending this logic, a central dimension of novelty in organizations reflects the novelty of the problem being solved." In addition, in the creative teams literature: Hargadon and Bechky (2006) speak of the reflective reframing stage of collective creativity in which the problem definition is itself reframed to incorporate the frames of others. They argue: "In these interactive moments, by mindfully considering the possibility that past knowledge may have alternative meanings, problem solvers maintained the flexibility to see new connections between their past experiences and the current projects others faced. This flexibility enabled them to explore a range of interpretations of any given situation and, from this range, collectively consider and pursue possibilities that might not have emerged otherwise (Hargadon and Bechky 2006; p 492)". When collections of creatives become creative collectives: A field study of problem solving at work. *Organization Science, 17*(4): 484–500. Tsoukas H (2009) A dialogical approach to the creation of new knowledge in organizations. *Organization Science, 20*(6): 941–957 says something quite similar in his discussion of how conceptual reframing of problems occur. Finally, from the creativity literature, Mumford et al. (1993) is quoted as saying: "more original or creative products would be obtained when people were asked to combine diverse categories" (p. 6) and "because creative thought calls for the combination and reorganization of extant categories" (p. 128). Mumford, M. D., Costanza, D. E, Threlfall, K. V, Baughman, W. A., & Reiter-Palmon, R. (1993). Personality variables and problem construction activities: An exploratory investigation. *Creat. Res. J. 6*: 365.

ation of innovative ideas by turning purely voicing behavior into constructive problem-solving behavior.[28]

However, there may be negative effects of transparent voicing. As others contribute to many-to-many persistently visible discussions, complaints initially surfaced may be amplified, leading to lowered morale and increased employee detachment from the organization,[29] resulting in a negative organizational climate.[30] These negative effects deserve study as they may interfere with the ability of a collective to innovatively create new ideas.

6.7 What Does This Mean for Future Research?

One implication for future research is that innovative ideas come from the freedom to generate multiple problem definitions and that need-focus may be the way to understand how problem definition and redefinition occurs. Further research, field and experimental, can explore if indeed need modification is seen as—and implies—a new vision of the initial problem. Our work also suggests that more ideas are not necessarily better, but only ideas that are coupled with a clear articulation of need that others can then reconstruct for inspiration. That is, need-solution pairs in discussion starting posts are better as they serve as catalysts, not end points. Future research can take this alternative perspective on initial solutions and explore it further.

Second, innovation occurs through not just ideating and making others' solution-ideas better, but from taking needs and thinking expansively or concretely based on those needs. Our findings related to crowd Collective Production may be applied to that of small innovation groups, that is, need extraction can yield innovation and not just idea refinement. More research is needed on explicit ways in which the crowd can be motivated to extract and modify needs. Can crowds be instructed to do so or is it an emergent process that can be amplified by drawing attention to it when it occurs? What are the catalysts for need extraction—if it is other incongruent needs, can this be moderated by adding more needs or will that cause need overload? Going back to Chap. 5, tradeoffs are opposite needs. We found in Chap. 5 that tradeoffs inspire creative discovery. Here, in Chap. 6, we find that needs do not always have to be posed as tradeoffs; instead, they can be reformulated to be more concrete or more abstract, stimulating creative discovery as well. As suggested in Chap. 5, the amplification process is key. What amplified need extraction and modification might apply when needs are reformulated? Is there a limit to the reformulation such that the new reformulated need becomes too distant from the initial need, losing the interest of the crowd?

Another implication for research is that our research suggests that simple modifications of needs are not as generative as reformulating for inspiration. This is quite a different finding from past research. Does this apply in small groups? Does this apply in dyads? Or is the fact that this is performed over an internet constrain this finding to that context?

A final implication for research is that problem-need extraction may not be as important as need extraction and reformulation, despite the research arguing for separating out problem descriptions from solutions.[31] Does this inspirational quality of the reformulated need in the problem description depend on organization contexts to stimulate innovation? Is past research wrong simply because it focused on the separation—rather than the reformulation—of needs? Are there other qualities for a reformulated need that makes it inspirational other than abstraction and concrete examples?

6.8 What Does This Mean for Practice?

Internal crowdsourcing innovation events, such as the one described in the opening quote, refer to an online practice used increasingly in large geographically dispersed organizations such as IBM, United Health, Mattel, and British Telecom.[32] In this practice, frontline employees from the various regions and customer segments in the company are engaged in offering innovative ideas to improve customer service throughout the company, not just to help individual customer segments serviced by each employee.[33]

To improve these internal crowdsourcing events, practitioners should consider motivating, moderating, and modeling the explication and exploration of hidden needs. They should encourage needs underlying solutions to be extracted and abstracted. When employees submit solutions with unexplicated needs, they should be encouraged to go back and explicate the underlying needs. But they are being asked to do this not because this is part of an individualized suggestion system and stage-gate innovation process in which employees prepare a market need report for their idea. Instead, they are being asked to do this so that this becomes part of a discussion that inspires innovation. The concept is to help employees and managers recognize that innovation derives not by a single individual developing a detailed proposal for change, but rather, by offering up needs and solution-ideas for others to use to generate creative associations leading to creative discoveries.

Notes

1. Used with permission of Optum.
2. Kesting, P., & Parm Ulhøi, J. (2010). Employee-driven innovation: Extending the license to foster innovation. *Management Decision*, *48*(1), 65–84.
3. McKinsey Quarterly (2009). How companies are benefiting from Web 2.0: McKinsey global survey results. *Business Technology Office* (Accessed 12 September 2017). http://www.mckinsey.com/business-functions/digital-mckinsey/our-insights/how-companies-are-benefiting-from-web-20-mckinsey-global-survey-results.

4. Leonardi, P. M. (2014). Social media, knowledge sharing, and innovation: Toward a theory of communication visibility. *Information Systems Research, 25*(4), 810.
5. Kesting, P., & Parm Ulhøi, J. (2010). Employee-driven innovation: Extending the license to foster innovation. *Management Decision, 48*(1), 65–84; Majchrzak, A., & Malhotra, A. (2016). Effect of knowledge-sharing trajectories on innovative outcomes in temporary online crowds. *Information Systems Research, 27*(4), 685–703; Zuchowski, O., Posegga, O., Schlagwein, D., & Fischbach, K. (2016). Internal crowdsourcing: Conceptual framework, structured review, and research agenda. *Journal of Information Technology, 31*(2), 166–84; Bishop, L., Levine, D.I., 1999. Computer-mediated communication as employee voice: a case study. *Industrial & Labor Relations Review 52*(2), 217.
6. E.g., Hirschman, A. O. (1970). *Exit, voice, and loyalty: Responses to decline in firms, organizations, and states.* Cambridge, MA: Harvard University Press; Liang, J., Farh, C. I., & Farh, J. L. (2012). Psychological antecedents of promotive and prohibitive voice: A two-wave examination. *Academy of Management Journal, 55*(1), 71–92.
7. Detert, J. R., Burris, E. R., Harrison, D. A., & Martin, S. R. (2013). Voice flows to and around leaders: Understanding when units are helped or hurt by employee voice. *Administrative Science Quarterly, 58*(4), 624–668; Morrison, E. W., & Milliken, F. J. (2000). Organizational silence: A barrier to change and development in a pluralistic world. *Academy of Management Review, 25*(4), 706–725.
8. Morrison, E. W., & Milliken, F. J. (2000). Organizational silence: A barrier to change and development in a pluralistic world. *Academy of Management Review, 25*(4), 706–725; Morrison, E. W., & Milliken, F. J. (2003). Speaking up, remaining silent: The dynamics of voice and silence in organizations. *Journal of Management Studies, 40*(6), 1353–1358.
9. Burris, E. R. (2012). The risks and rewards of speaking up: Managerial responses to employee voice. *Academy of Management Journal, 55*(4), 851–875; Fast, N. J., Burris, E. R., & Bartel, C. A. (2014). Managing to stay in the dark: Managerial self-efficacy, ego defensiveness, and the aversion to employee voice. *Academy of Management Journal, 57*(4), 1013–1034; Detert, J. R., & Treviño, L. K. (2010). Speaking up to higher-ups: How supervisors and skip-level leaders influence employee voice. *Organization Science, 21*(1), 249–270; Maynes, T. D., & Podsakoff, P. M. (2014). Speaking more broadly: An examination of the nature, antecedents, and consequences of an expanded set of employee voice behaviors. *Journal of Applied Psychology, 99*(1), 87–112; Van Dyne, L., Ang, S., & Botero, I. C. (2003). Conceptualizing employee silence and employee voice as multidimensional constructs. *Journal of Management Studies, 40*(6), 1359–1392.

10. Lam, C. F., & Mayer, D. M. (2014). When do employees speak up for their customers? A model of voice in a customer service context. *Personnel Psychology, 67*(3), 637–666.
11. E.g., Burris, E. R., Detert, J. R., & Romney, A. C. (2013). Speaking up vs. being heard: The disagreement around and outcomes of employee voice. *Organization Science, 24*(1), 22–38.
12. Hambrick, D. C., Geletkanycz, M. A., & Fredrickson, J. W. (1993). Top executive commitment to the status quo: Some tests of its determinants. *Strategic Management Journal, 14*(6), 401–418; Redding, W. C. (1985). Rocking boats, blowing whistles, and teaching speech communication. *Communication Education, 34*, 245–258.
13. See also Burris, E. R. (2012). The risks and rewards of speaking up: Managerial responses to employee voice. *Academy of Management Journal, 55*(4), 851–875; LePine, J. A., & Van Dyne, L. (1998). Predicting voice behavior in work groups. *Journal of Applied Psychology, 83*(6), 853–868.
14. E.g., Fast, N. J., Burris, E. R., & Bartel, C. A. (2014). Managing to stay in the dark: Managerial self-efficacy, ego defensiveness, and the aversion to employee voice. *Academy of Management Journal, 57*(4), 1013–1034.
15. E.g., Dutton, J. E., & Ashford, S. J. (1993). Selling issues to top management. *Academy of Management Review, 18*(3), 397–428.
16. E.g., Detert, J. R., & Burris, E. R. (2007). Leadership behavior and employee voice: Is the door really open?. *Academy of Management Journal, 50*(4), 869–884.
17. E.g., Milliken, F. J., & Morrison, E. W. (2003). Shades of silence: Emerging themes and future directions for research on silence in organizations. *Journal of Management Studies, 40*(6), 1563–1568.
18. E.g., Stamper, C. L., & Van Dyne, L. (2001). Work status and organizational citizenship behavior: A field study of restaurant employees. *Journal of Organizational Behavior, 22*(5), 517–536.
19. E.g., Bashshur, M. R., & Oc, B. (2015). When voice matters a multilevel review of the impact of voice in organizations. *Journal of Management, 41*(5), 1530–1554.
20. Morrison EW (2011) Employee voice behavior: Integration and directions for future research. *The Academy of Management Annals, 5*(1): 373–412.
21. Morrison EW (2011) Employee voice behavior: Integration and directions for future research. *The Academy of Management Annals, 5*(1): 373–412.
22. Posen HE, Keil T, Kim S, Meissner FD (2018) Renewing Research on Problemistic Search—A Review and Research Agenda. *Acad. of Management Annals 12*(1): 208–251.
23. Sometimes, the starter post actually consisted of two posts where the first post was the solution and the second post by the same person was the need. We treated these as the same starter post.
24. Tsoukas, H. (2009). A dialogical approach to the creation of new knowledge in organizations. *Organization Science, 20*(6), 941–957.

25. Biscaro, C. & Comacchio, A. 2018. Knowledge creation across worldviews: How metaphors impact and orient group creativity. *Org Sci, 29*(1), 58–79.
26. Faraj, S., Jarvenpaa, S. L., & Majchrzak, A. (2011). Knowledge collaboration in online communities. *Organization Science, 22*(5), 1224–1239.
27. Faraj, S., Jarvenpaa, S. L., & Majchrzak, A. (2011). Knowledge collaboration in online communities. *Organization Science, 22*(5), 1224–1239.
28. Baralou, E., & Tsoukas, H. (2015). How is new organizational knowledge created in a virtual context? An ethnographic study. *Organization Studies, 36*(5), 593–620; Faraj, S., Jarvenpaa, S. L., & Majchrzak, A. (2011). Knowledge collaboration in online communities. *Organization Science, 22*(5), 1224–1239; Van Osch, W., & Avital, M. (2009). Collective generativity: the emergence of IT-induced mass innovation. *Sprouts: Working Papers on Information Systems, 9*(54), 1–33; Wasko, M. M., & Faraj, S. (2000). "It is what one does": why people participate and help others in electronic communities of practice. *The Journal of Strategic Information Systems, 9*(2), 155–173.
29. Burris, E. R., Detert, J. R., & Chiaburu, D. S. (2008). Quitting before leaving: the mediating effects of psychological attachment and detachment on voice. *Journal of Applied Psychology, 93*(4), 912; Ng, T. W., & Feldman, D. C. (2012). Employee voice behavior: A meta-analytic test of the conservation of resources framework. *Journal of Organizational Behavior, 33*(2), 216–234.
30. E.g., MacKenzie, S. B., Podsakoff, P. M., & Podsakoff, N. P. (2011). Challenge-oriented organizational citizenship behaviors and organizational effectiveness: Do challenge-oriented behaviors really have an impact on the organization's bottom line? *Personnel Psychology, 64*(3), 559–592; McClean, E. J., Burris, E. R., & Detert, J. R. (2013). When does voice lead to exit? It depends on leadership. *Academy of Management Journal, 56*(2), 525–548.
31. Nickerson J, Yen CJ, Mahoney JT (2012) Exploring the Problem-Finding and Problem-Solving Approach for Designing Organizations. *Acad. of Management Perspectives* 26(1): 52–72; Nickerson JA, Wuebker R, Zenger T (2017) Problems, theories, and governing the crowd. *Strategic Organization* 15(2): 275–288; Nickerson JA, Zenger TR (2004) A Knowledge-Based Theory of the Firm: The Problem-Solving Perspective. *Organ. Sci.* 15(6): 617–632; von Hippel E, von Krogh G (2016) CROSSROADS—Identifying Viable "Need–Solution Pairs": Problem Solving Without Problem Formulation. *Organ. Sci.* 27(1): 207–221; Baer, M., Dirks, K. T., & Nickerson, J. A. (2013). Microfoundations of strategic problem formulation. *Strategic Management Journal, 342*: 197–214.
32. Bjelland OM, Wood RC (2008) An inside view of IBM's 'Innovation Jam'. *MIT Sloan Management Review, 5*(1): 32–40; Kesting PJ, Ulhøi P (2010) Employee-driven innovation: extending the license to foster innovation. *Management Decision, 48*(1): 65–84; Stieger D, Matzler K, Chatterjee S, Ladstaetter-Fussenegger F (2012) Democratizing strategy: How crowdsourc-

ing can be used for strategy dialogues. *California Management Review, 54*(4): 44–68; Zuchowski O, Posegga O, Schlagwein D, Fischbach K (2016). Internal crowdsourcing: conceptual framework, structured review, and research agenda. *Journal of Information Technology, 31*(2): 166–184.
33. Karlsson J, Skålén P (2015) Exploring front-line employee contributions to service innovation. *European Journal of Marketing, 49*(9/10): 1346–1365; Santos-Vijande ML, López-Sánchez JÁ, Rudd J (2016) Frontline employees' collaboration in industrial service innovation: Routes of co-creation's effects on new service performance. *Journal of the Academy of Marketing Science, 44*(3): 350–375.

References

Amabile, T. M., & Pratt, M. G. (2016). The Dynamic Componential Model of Creativity and Innovation in Organizations: Making Progress, Making Meaning. *Research in Organizational Behavior, 36*, 157–183.

Anderson, N., Potočnik, K., & Zhou, J. (2014). Innovation and Creativity in Organizations: A State-of-the-Science Review, Prospective Commentary, and Guiding Framework. *Journal of Management, 40*(5), 1297–1333.

Arguello, J., Butler, B. S., Joyce, E., Kraut, R., Ling, K. S., Rose, C., et al. (2006). Talk to Me: Foundations for Successful Individual-Group Interactions in Online Communities. In *Proceedings of the SIGCHI Conference on Human Factors in Computing Systems* (pp. 959–968). New York, NY: ACM.

Baer, M., Dirks, K. T., & Nickerson, J. A. (2013). Microfoundations of Strategic Problem Formulation. *Strategic Management Journal, 342*, 197–214.

Baralou, E., & Tsoukas, H. (2015). How Is New Organizational Knowledge Created in a Virtual Context? An Ethnographic Study. *Organization Studies, 36*(5), 593–620.

Bashshur, M. R., & Oc, B. (2015). When Voice Matters a Multilevel Review of the Impact of Voice in Organizations. *Journal of Management, 41*(5), 1530–1554.

Biscaro, C., & Comacchio, A. (2018). Knowledge Creation Across Worldviews: How Metaphors Impact and Orient Group Creativity. *Organization Science, 29*(1), 58–79.

Bishop, L., & Levine, D. I. (1999). Computer-Mediated Communication as Employee Voice: A Case Study. *Industrial & Labor Relations Review, 52*(2), 217.

Bjelland, O. M., & Wood, R. C. (2008). An Inside View of IBM's 'Innovation Jam'. *MIT Sloan Management Review, 5*(1), 32–40.

Burke, M., Joyce, E., Kim, T., Anand, V., & Kraut, R. (2007). Introductions and Requests: Rhetorical Strategies That Elicit Response in Online Communities. In C. Steinfield, B. T. Pentland, M. Ackerman, & N. Contractor (Eds.), *Communities and Technologies* (pp. 21–39). London: Springer.

Burris, E. R. (2012). The Risks and Rewards of Speaking Up: Managerial Responses to Employee Voice. *Academy of Management Journal, 55*(4), 851–875.

Burris, E. R., Detert, J. R., & Chiaburu, D. S. (2008). Quitting Before Leaving: The Mediating Effects of Psychological Attachment and Detachment on Voice. *Journal of Applied Psychology, 93*(4), 912.

Burris, E. R., Detert, J. R., & Romney, A. C. (2013). Speaking Up vs. Being Heard: The Disagreement Around and Outcomes of Employee Voice. *Organization Science, 24*(1), 22–38.

Detert, J. R., & Burris, E. R. (2007). Leadership Behavior and Employee Voice: Is the Door Really Open? *Academy of Management Journal, 50*(4), 869–884.

Detert, J. R., & Treviño, L. K. (2010). Speaking Up to Higher-Ups: How Supervisors and Skip-Level Leaders Influence Employee Voice. *Organization Science, 21*(1), 249–270.

Detert, J. R., Burris, E. R., Harrison, D. A., & Martin, S. R. (2013). Voice Flows to and Around Leaders: Understanding When Units Are Helped or Hurt by Employee Voice. *Administrative Science Quarterly, 58*(4), 624–668.

Dutton, J. E., & Ashford, S. J. (1993). Selling Issues to Top Management. *Academy of Management Review, 18*(3), 397–428.

Faraj, S., Jarvenpaa, S. L., & Majchrzak, A. (2011). Knowledge Collaboration in Online Communities. *Organization Science, 22*(5), 1224–1239.

Fast, N. J., Burris, E. R., & Bartel, C. A. (2014). Managing to Stay in the Dark: Managerial Self-Efficacy, Ego Defensiveness, and the Aversion to Employee Voice. *Academy of Management Journal, 57*(4), 1013–1034.

Garner, J. T. (2009). When Things Go Wrong at Work: An Exploration of Organizational Dissent Messages. *Communication Studies, 60*(2), 197–218.

Hambrick, D. C., Geletkanycz, M. A., & Fredrickson, J. W. (1993). Top Executive Commitment to the Status Quo: Some Tests of Its Determinants. *Strategic Management Journal, 14*(6), 401–418.

Hargadon, A. B., & Bechky, B. A. (2006). When Collections of Creatives Become Creative Collectives: A Field Study of Problem Solving at Work. *Organization Science, 17*(4), 484–500.

Harvey, S. (2014). Creative Synthesis: Exploring the Process of Extraordinary Group Creativity. *Academy of Management Review, 39*(3), 324–343.

Hirschman, A. O. (1970). *Exit, Voice, and Loyalty: Responses to Decline in Firms, Organizations, and States.* Cambridge, MA: Harvard University Press.

Joyce, E., & Kraut, R. E. (2006). Predicting Continued Participation in Newsgroups. *Journal of Computer-Mediated Communication, 11*(3), 723–747.

Karlsson, J., & Skålén, P. (2015). Exploring Front-Line Employee Contributions to Service Innovation. *European Journal of Marketing, 49*(9/10), 1346–1365.

Kesting, P., & Parm Ulhøi, J. (2010). Employee-Driven Innovation: Extend-ing the License to Foster Innovation. *Management Decision, 48*(1), 65–84.

Kesting, P. J., & Ulhøi, P. (2010). Employee-Driven Innovation: Extending the License to Foster Innovation. *Management Decision, 48*(1), 65–84.

Lam, C. F., & Mayer, D. M. (2014). When Do Employees Speak Up for Their Customers? A Model of Voice in a Customer Service Context. *Personnel Psychology, 67*(3), 637–666.

Leonardi, P. M. (2014). Social Media, Knowledge Sharing, and Innovation: Toward a Theory of Communication Visibility. *Information Systems Research, 25*(4), 810.

LePine, J. A., & Van Dyne, L. (1998). Predicting Voice Behavior in Work Groups. *Journal of Applied Psychology, 83*(6), 853–868.

Liang, J., Farh, C. I., & Farh, J. L. (2012). Psychological Antecedents of Promotive and Prohibitive Voice: A Two-Wave Examination. *Academy of Management Journal, 55*(1), 71–92.

Lovelace, K., Shapiro, D. L., & Weingart, L. R. (2001). Maximizing Cross-Functional New Product Teams' Innovativeness and Constraint Adherence: A Conflict Communications Perspective. *Academy of Management Journal, 44*(4), 779–793.

MacKenzie, S. B., Podsakoff, P. M., & Podsakoff, N. P. (2011). Challenge-Oriented Organizational Citizenship Behaviors and Organizational Effectiveness: Do Challenge-Oriented Behaviors Really Have an Impact on the Organization's Bottom Line? *Personnel Psychology, 64*(3), 559–592.

Majchrzak, A., & Malhotra, A. (2016). Effect of Knowledge-Sharing Trajectories on Innovative Outcomes in Temporary Online Crowds. *Information Systems Research, 27*(4), 685–703.

Malinen, S. (2015). Understanding User Participation in Online Communities: A Systematic Literature Review of Empirical Studies. *Computers in Human Behavior, 46,* 228–238.

Maynes, T. D., & Podsakoff, P. M. (2014). Speaking More Broadly: An Examination of the Nature, Antecedents, and Consequences of an Expanded Set of Employee Voice Behaviors. *Journal of Applied Psychology, 99*(1), 87–112.

McClean, E. J., Burris, E. R., & Detert, J. R. (2013). When Does Voice Lead to Exit? It Depends on Leadership. *Academy of Management Journal, 56*(2), 525–548.

McKinsey Quarterly. (2009). *How Companies Are Benefiting from Web 2.0: McKinsey Global Survey Results*. Business Technology Office. Retrieved September 12, 2017, from http://www.mckinsey.com/business-functions/digital-mckinsey/our-insights/how-companies-are-benefiting-from-web-20-mckinsey-global-survey-results.

Milliken, F. J., & Morrison, E. W. (2003). Shades of Silence: Emerging Themes and Future Directions for Research on Silence in Organizations. *Journal of Management Studies, 40*(6), 1563–1568.

Morrison, E. W. (2011). Employee Voice Behavior: Integration and Directions for Future Research. *The Academy of Management Annals, 5*(1), 373–412.

Morrison, E. W., & Milliken, F. J. (2000). Organizational Silence: A Barrier to Change and Development in a Pluralistic World. *Academy of Management Review, 25*(4), 706–725.

Morrison, E. W., & Milliken, F. J. (2003). Speaking Up, Remaining Silent: The Dynamics of Voice and Silence in Organizations. *Journal of Management Studies, 40*(6), 1353–1358.

Mumford, M. D., Costanza, D. E., Threlfall, K. V., Baughman, W. A., & Reiter-Palmon, R. (1993). Personality Variables and Problem Construction Activities: An Exploratory Investigation. *Creativity Research Journal, 6,* 365.

Ng, T. W., & Feldman, D. C. (2012). Employee Voice Behavior: A Meta-Analytic Test of the Conservation of Resources Framework. *Journal of Organizational Behavior, 33*(2), 216–234.

Nickerson, J. A., & Zenger, T. R. (2004). A Knowledge-Based Theory of the Firm—The Problem-Solving Perspective. *Organization Science, 15*(6), 617–632.

Nickerson, J., Yen, C. J., & Mahoney, J. T. (2012a). Exploring the Problem-Finding and Problem-Solving Approach for Designing Organizations. *Academy of Management Perspectives, 26*(1), 52–72.

Nickerson, J. A., Yen, C. J., & Mahoney, J. T. (2012b). Exploring the Problem-Finding and Problem-Solving Approach for Designing Organizations. *The Academy of Management Perspectives, 26*(1), 52–72.

Nickerson, J. A., Wuebker, R., & Zenger, T. (2017). Problems, Theories, and Governing the Crowd. *Strategic Organization, 15*(2), 275–288.

O'Reilly, C. A., & Tushman, M. L. (2004). The Ambidextrous Organization. *Harvard Business Review, 82*(4), 74–83.

Posen, H. E., Keil, T., Kim, S., & Meissner, F. D. (2018). Renewing Research on Problemistic Search—A Review and Research Agenda. *The Academy of Management Annals, 12*(1), 208–251.

Redding, W. C. (1985). Rocking Boats, Blowing Whistles, and Teaching Speech Communication. *Communication Education, 34*, 245–258.

Santos-Vijande, M. L., López-Sánchez, J. Á., & Rudd, J. (2016). Frontline Employees' Collaboration in Industrial Service Innovation: Routes of Co-creation's Effects on New Service Performance. *Journal of the Academy of Marketing Science, 44*(3), 350–375.

Stamper, C. L., & Van Dyne, L. (2001). Work Status and Organizational Citizenship Behavior: A Field Study of Restaurant Employees. *Journal of Organizational Behavior, 22*(5), 517–536.

Stieger, D., Matzler, K., Chatterjee, S., & Ladstaetter-Fussenegger, F. (2012). Democratizing Strategy: How Crowdsourcing Can Be Used for Strategy Dialogues. *California Management Review, 54*(4), 44–68.

Tausczik, Y. R., Kittur, A., & Kraut, R. E. (2014, February). Collaborative Problem Solving: A Study of Math Overflow. In *Proceedings of the 17th ACM Conference on Computer Supported Cooperative Work & Social Computing* (pp. 355–367). New York, NY: ACM.

Tsoukas, H. (2009). A Dialogical Approach to the Creation of New Knowledge in Organizations. *Organization Science, 20*(6), 941–957.

Van Dyne, L., Ang, S., & Botero, I. C. (2003). Conceptualizing Employee Silence and Employee Voice as Multidimensional Constructs. *Journal of Management Studies, 40*(6), 1359–1392.

Van Osch, W., & Avital, M. (2009). Collective Generativity: The Emergence of IT-Induced Mass Innovation. *Sprouts: Working Papers on Information Systems, 9*(54), 1–33.

von Hippel, E., & von Krogh, G. (2016). Crossroads—Identifying Viable 'Need–Solution Pairs': Problem Solving Without Problem Formulation. *Organization Science, 27*(1), 207–221.

Wasko, M. M., & Faraj, S. (2000). 'It Is What One Does': Why People Participate and Help Others in Electronic Communities of Practice. *The Journal of Strategic Information Systems, 9*(2), 155–173.

Zhou, J., & George, J. M. (2001). When Job Dissatisfaction Leads to Creativity: Encouraging the Expression of Voice. *Academy of Management Journal, 44*(4), 682–696.

Zuchowski, O., Posegga, O., Schlagwein, D., & Fischbach, K. (2016). Internal Crowdsourcing: Conceptual Framework, Structured Review, and Research Agenda. *Journal of Information Technology, 31*(2), 166–184.

7

Practice 5: Allowing the Crowd to Play Any Innovation-Enabling Roles They Choose

In traditional Idea-Sharing crowdsourcing, crowds are told what role to play: they are to be either ideators (offering Ideas) or Idea Commenters and Refiners (offering comments to help others' idea be refined). People who don't have ideas, but just have thoughts, personal experiences, and assumptions about the nature of the problem are left *out*, without a voice. But such people are the bedrock of innovation in crowdsourcing since they provide the creative associations. In unmindcuffed crowds, some participants just offer facts while others just offer creative associations, and others just offer ideas. This allows everyone to have a voice. In this chapter, we discuss the last of the five practices that unmindcuffed crowds organically follow (Fig. 7.1).

Crowds who are told to offer ideas are, unsurprisingly, tied to the role of either Ideators (offering Ideas) or Idea Commenters and Refiners (offering comments to help others' idea be refined). But when crowds are unmindcuffed, we find new and different roles are taken on by some participants. Not all of them take on all roles. As long as enough people take on the range of roles, then the crowd surfaces innovative ideas. In this chapter, we'll look at some of the roles that are played by different participants in different unmindcuffed crowdsourcing events.

We believe that, in a sense, this is the heart of the democratization of the Collective Production process. Not everyone has to have an idea. Not everyone has to know a great deal about the problem. Not everyone has to have had enough personal experience with the problem to know that there are paradoxical objectives needing to be met. Each participant can contribute what s/he feels most capable of contributing. Everyone's voice can be heard, not simply because each person may have a different opinion, but more importantly,

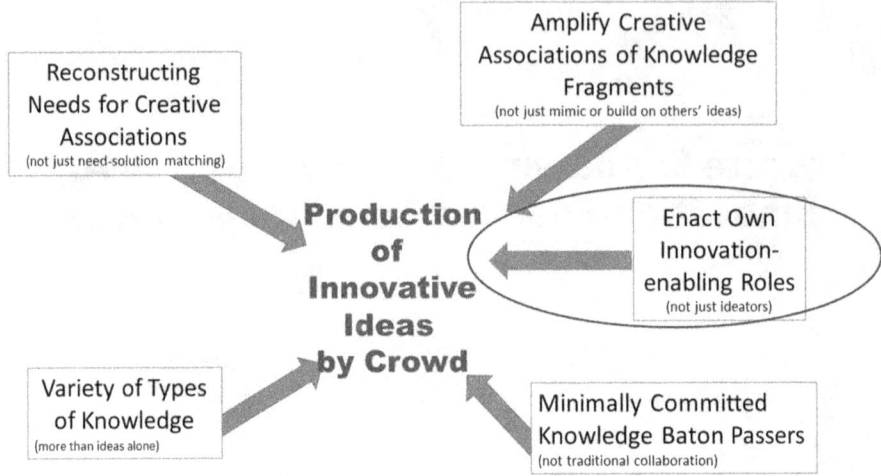

Fig. 7.1 Practices of Collective Production

because each person plays a different role in helping the crowd collectively innovate.

In this chapter, we first describe what we believe a role means to a crowd. We then look in-depth at one innovative crowdsourcing event to see what roles were played. We then see if the same sets of roles were played across our 20 field crowdsourcing events and find a consistent pattern of roles. We discuss what these roles mean for future research and practitioners. Finally, we are ready to summarize what we've learned about the practices unmindcuffed crowds use to collectively produce innovative ideas.

7.1 What Is a Role to a Crowd?

Roles are a set of tasks that people engage in repeatedly to accomplish an objective. Motherhood is a role, for example. Roles can be imposed by society or the workplace, or they can be self-created (also called "enacted").[1] A mother who is the CEO of a large corporation has self-created the role that might be called: "executive with family" or "working mother" or "balanced senior executive". What makes it a role, rather than just a characteristic of a hard-working woman is that more than one person does it.[2] Almost all crowds have roles. In Wikipedia, there is the formally imposed role of editor. There are also roles that participants self-create, such as one called "shaper" in which participants reorganize a Wikipedia article so that it makes logical sense and fits with Wikipedia's stringent citation standards.[3] These self-created roles are not predefined or performed in perpetuity. Rather, individuals define their role in real time by performing a set of actions they choose to. Further, they also decide as to when and how long to perform their roles, easily stopping as soon as they desire to.[4]

It appears that these self-created roles are triggered in some way by the dynamics of the group or context. For example, a participant in Wikipedia appears to take on the role of article shaper when there is some indication that the article might be nominated to be a "best article". Or, a person seeing a conflict between two people is triggered to take on the role of conflict manager.

Since crowdsourcing is primarily following Idea-Sharing, it is perhaps not a surprise that most of the roles discovered thus far are either that of an ideator, or that of a commenter who refines others' ideas.[5] Do we find this when crowds are un-mind-cuffed? We answer this question first by looking at one crowdsourcing event and just examining the actions taken by the participants. We find that un-mind-cuffed participants also ideate and comment on others, thus not providing much enlightenment about how roles help. Then, we look at our 20 crowdsourcing events in which we have coded the knowledge content and find that, by looking more closely at the knowledge content shared, we discover much more nuanced roles that help to explain crowds' innovativeness production.

7.2 A Story About Different Roles Played by Crowd Participants in the Predator-Free New Zealand Challenge

> *Vertebrate pests, such as possums, rats, and stoats pose a serious threat to the survival of New Zealand's native biota, yet there are vast areas across the country where these pests are not being managed. The future of vertebrate pest management in New Zealand will need to involve scientific research and monitoring, but also careful consideration of economic and social factors. We need your ideas that creatively integrate technological, social, economic and legal recommendations. Here at Landcare Research, we believe the best way to come up with these ideas is to enable diverse New Zealand citizens to use their creativity and ingenuity to work together online to come up with recommendations for this important conservation challenge for the future of pest management.*

With that wicked problem statement, a 10-day nationwide online collaboration to develop recommendations for a Predator-Free New Zealand was underway. Instructions on the crowdsourcing website unconstrained the crowd, encouraging them to post their knowledge such as facts, examples, and tradeoffs about the problem, as well as their "wild idea seeds" to solve the wicked problem facing New Zealand's citizens.

A total of 252 stakeholders registered for the event. Of those, 89 actively participated in the event. A survey was completed by most of them, indicating that they represented a wide diversity of the populace, including businesses related to conservation, non-government organizations such as Pūkaha National Wildlife Centre and Predator-Free New Zealand, members of the government's Department of Conservation, researchers with Landcare Research (one of seven Crown Research Institutes in New Zealand) as well as from a number of other research institutes, college students, ecology consultants, individuals working in the farming and forestry industries, a project manager for wastewater treatment, a software developer, field operations for wilderness services, lumber exporters, New Zealand's Department of Internal Affairs, Christchurch city council, Ministry for the Environment, private citizens, homemakers, and retirees, educators, pest control manager, private landowners, subsistence farmers, restoration volunteers, members of the Royal Society of New Zealand, Ministry of Business, Innovation and Employment, healthcare workers, workers in the construction industry, and a broadcaster.

The 89 participants started 104 discussions! Further, 430 comments were posted in response to the discussion (thread) starters—an average of six comments per person. This is a much higher engagement than the typical minimal engagement for innovation crowdsourcing discussed in Chap. 3 as our first practice. The increased engagement may be due to the passion exercised by a subset of the New Zealand population.

Participants discussed a range of topics, as indicated by the semantic cloud shown in Fig. 7.2. Apparent from the cloud is that toxins were of concern, as were effects of feral cats on native fauna, and the possibility of trying new pest management techniques on one of New Zealand's islands. Less frequently discussed, but easily as interesting, was the possibility of using drones, and genetic engineering for predator cannibalism. There were also discussions about the need to expand the definition of pests beyond vertebrate pests to include insects such as wasps that are damaging biomass of the forests. These different foci for discussion led us to consider the possibility that different participants played different roles. That is, we wondered if some people posted only some content and others posted different content.

We sought out roles by looking simply at whether they posted on discussion threads started by others. This led us to group the 89 participants into 3 distinct roles being played in the crowd. We used cluster analysis to do the

7 Practice 5: Allowing the Crowd to Play Any Innovation-Enabling... 205

Fig. 7.2 Topic cloud of posts from the Predator-Free New Zealand innovation crowdsourcing

grouping. Here, we provide examples of the underlying actions associated with each of these emergent enacted roles in the crowd.

Ideators. 20 of the 89 participants played this role, starting a discussion (threads) on the website, which contained any idea of theirs. These people are playing the traditional ideator role seen in the Idea-Sharing process. Further, half of them extended their participation by defending their ideas later in the thread, when others questioned the ideas or asked for explanations. None of these ideators contributed to discussion threads started by others. As an example:

> "Wes" starts a discussion thread with an idea: "*I suggest a clock, similar to the one in Times Square which gives the estimated cost of full eradication and the cost of*

noneradication, with the costs going down with improvements in technology and up with another pest incursion. The clocks should be located at the airports, in cities, on the internet." "Mr. T" then responds with a concern related to the idea: "*There may be a danger of thinking the price would be higher than it really is and thereby put people off*". "Wes" defends his initial idea rather than waiting to see how others respond, saying: "*I think being able to estimate the cost goes hand in hand with having a coordinated plan*". "Wes" didn't post in any other discussion threads.

<u>Other-Focused Reactives</u>. Most of the participants—48—enacted this role. They reacted to the posts of others by offering comments. As an example: "Mike" posted four times in four different discussion threads, none of which he started. In his first post, he responded to an idea of someone else's to "*convince the world that possum testes are an aphrodisiac*" by saying: "*not a silly idea at all. We managed to convince fisherman on Mauritius not to eat a wayward elephant seal by expressing surprise and saying you don't want to eat that*".

<u>Knowledge Extenders</u>. 21 participants played this role. They started new discussion threads, typically to introduce a new direction to the discussion. They also commented on other discussion threads. As an example, "Paul", a retired economist and restoration volunteer, offered a new discussion thread with "*The roads and railways provide corridors not only for people and goods but rats, mice, stoats, and other pests. Setting and checking traps along these corridors would be relatively easy*", as well as two posts on other discussion threads about where to set trapping lines, and the "*need for a regional 'gamekeeper' to oversee and coordinate all our efforts*".

From this categorization, we learn that the first two are continuations of what has been found in Idea-Sharing crowdsourcing events: there are those who post ideas, and there are those who comment on others' ideas. That is, despite the crowd being un-mind-cuffed, fully two-thirds of them enacted the same two roles as are found in Idea-Sharing events. One additional role was discovered, used by about a fourth of the participants. In this role, the participants didn't offer a new idea but rather offered new information to the discussion. Note that these comments on other posts are not necessarily to refine another's idea, but rather to reflect on issues raised in others' discussion threads.

In the next section, we turn to an analysis of all the participants in all 20 crowdsourcing events to see if the roles are similar to those we found in New Zealand, or a new set of roles.

7.3 Collective Production Roles Found Across the 20 Field Crowdsourcing Events

With the first four (out of the 20) crowdsourcing events we conducted, we published results indicating that there were a much richer set of roles than just the three found in the New Zealand Challenge and the simple two found in Idea-Sharing crowds. In that analysis, we again focused on the actions that participants took, not the content of their knowledge. We found the existence of four distinctive roles.[6]

1. "Drive-by Ideator", a participant posting only one idea and never commenting on or adding to others' threads, and leaving the event completely.
2. "Convenience Generative", a participant posting her own ideas and *only* commenting on others' knowledge discussion threads at the precise time that the person has logged in to check to see if others' have posted on her discussion thread.
3. "Knowledge Benefactor", a participant who exclusively posts to help others.
4. "Cheerleader", a participant who exclusively offers social support and nothing else.

This analysis suggested that when un-mind-cuffed, crowds coalesce around four roles which had not been described previously. Drive-by posters appear to have no interest in how others react to ideas they post nor in how useful the idea is to the collective. It is almost as if the drive-by poster has an idea that needs to be shared, and once shared, the drive-by poster's interest in the crowdsourcing event dissipates. The Convenience Generative, on the contrary, is willing to help others out, but only during the few times when she reenters the event and responds to comments that others make to her idea. It is almost as if this participant is demonstrating how little time she has for the event. The Knowledge Benefactor is equivalent to Commenters in Idea-Sharing Events. Finally, there the cheerleaders; given the significant negative effect that social support has on innovation idea generation, cheerleaders create a negative pull on the crowd.

In this next analysis, we wanted to drill down into the actual knowledge content that contributors shared. We had a large dataset of all participants across the 20 innovation crowdsourcing events. While there were 1720 registered participants across the 20 events, only 603 were active participants (however, 16 participants were only active in terms of voting for posts, but did not post anything themselves). Therefore, we clustered the remaining 583 who posted something (even if it was only once) according to the knowledge types they posted. We use those actions that we have discussed from earlier chapters that contribute to the Collective Production of innovative ideas, including creative associations (either examples or tradeoffs), facts, as well as ideas since these contributions have been demonstrated in the earlier chapters to foster Collective Production. We did not include, for example, social support posts since these were more likely to harm Collective Production (see results in Chap. 5). We included questions asked since some questions may be helpful.

We calculated the proportion of the five behaviors they could have engaged in: posting creative associations, posting facts about the problem, asking others questions, starting a top-level post with their own idea, and offering an idea when commenting on others' discussion threads. The five behaviors were used to drive the clusters. We conducted a hierarchical cluster analysis using Wards method to obtain six clusters of behaviors shown in Table 7.1. The number of clusters was determined by inspection of the Dendrogram as well as by taking into consideration the Cubic Clustering Criterion (CCC). Inspecting the distance graph of the Dendrogram indicated that either a five- or a six-cluster solution would better represent demarcations in the behaviors. We also looked at the CCC, which showed the biggest peak (CCC jumped from 14 to 24) when going from five to six clusters. Therefore, we decided to pursue a six-cluster solution. Crowd participants were exclusively one or the other clusters. In other words, the clustering method assigned every individual exclusively to one role (one cluster).

Role 1: Generalists. This was the most common role assumed by participants. In this role, participants did a little of everything to help the process along: posting creative associations to stimulate others, offering facts about

Table 7.1 Roles enacted by participants in the 20 crowdsourcing events

	Cluster	Count	Proportion of facts posted	Proportion of creative associations posted	Proportion of questions posted	Proportion of ideas posted	Proportion of ideas posted on others' threads
Generalists	1	228	0.12	0.15	0.05	0.18	0.29
Collaborative ideators	2	39	0.00	0.00	0.00	0.87	1.00
Creative associators	3	27	0.00	1.00	0.17	0.00	0.00
Fact sharers	4	30	1.00	0.00	0.00	0.00	0.00
Questioners	5	61	0.22	0.10	0.77	0.10	0.17
Drive-by-ideators	6	198	0.00	0.00	0.00	1.00	0.00

the problem, questioning to help surface more knowledge, and offering ideas both on own discussion threads and in response to others' posts. They help to keep the Collective Production process moving forward by making all types of knowledge sharing central to and prominent in their process. Thus, our expectation that individuals specialize into roles is not found for most of the participants.

Role 2. *Collaborative Ideators*. The 39 people who enacted this role posted their ideas on threads started by others as well as their own. Participants playing this role keep the Collective Production process moving forward by demonstrating to others that their ideas were in response to others' knowledge. By "burying" their ideas in discussion threads started by others, they are clearly indicating that their ideas are created in collaboration with others. Also, by burying their ideas in others' discussion threads, they are indicating that they are less concerned with getting recognition for their idea by elevating it to a topic starter, than in co-producing an idea based on the development of the new knowledge (ideas) building on others' knowledge.

Role 3. *Creative Associators*. 27 participants enacted this role. Such role players offer either analogies or tradeoffs to the crowd about the problem. As described in Chap. 5, creative associations are absolutely essential to the Collective Production process. Such knowledge is not only essential for stimulating new innovative ideas, but it also serves the role of simultaneously reconceptualizing the problem itself. As can be observed from Table 7.1, this is the least frequently played role. The low number of people exclusively serving in this role highlights that it is not the number of people who provide creative associations that matter, but whether such associations are provided at all.

Role 4. *Fact Sharers*. The 30 participants who enacted this role spent their time almost exclusively offering facts about the problem. They helped to move Collective Production forward by ensuring factual information about the problem was shared, so that the problem could be redefined, if need be. As shown in earlier chapters, the posting of factual assumptions can trigger the posting of creative associations (such as tradeoffs and examples). Even though factual assumptions do not directly lead to innovative ideas, they serve an important amplification role.

Role 5. *Questioners*. The 61 participants who enacted this role spent most of their time asking others questions and occasionally offering ideas. This implies that they were reading others' knowledge posts when introducing their own ideas. Questioners may keep the Collective Production process moving forward by drawing attention to others' knowledge. By the very act of questioning for clarification, instead of just posting their own ideas, questioners attach importance to others' knowledge, demonstrating to others that the knowledge may matter for the Collective Production process. It also sends a signal to the participant being questioned that their contribution matters to someone. The questions were rarely answered, however. But in many ways, that is not the point. If someone else could answer the question, or if the question stimulated a crowd participant to think in a new way, the question serves its purpose as a creative stimulant.

Role 6: Drive-by Ideators. This was the second most common role taken by the participants: posting their own idea as a discussion topic starter and not posting again. They did not defend their idea, participate in any way in others' threads, or offer any new knowledge besides their own idea in their own thread. Their ideas may or may not have been the culmination of reading others' ideas; there is no way of knowing. These ideators were distributed throughout the events, not just at the beginning. In other words, drive-by ideators come and go as they please, at a time convenient to them, and then, only post their own idea as a new thread, never to return again to contribute in any other way. This role was the closest to what would be expected if a collective is asked to generate ideas using the Idea-Selecting process. In the Collective Production process we observed through our research and discussed in Chaps. 5 and 6, participants who only ideate do serve an important role as their ideas can spark creative associations in others, which lead to innovative ideas.

Each of the six roles is interesting in their own right, but also as a set. There appear to be participants who specialize in roles (such as drive-by ideators) and participants who don't (generalists). There are a small number of participants who provide the creative associations that the crowd needs, and there are others who provide the ideas, facts, and questions that the creative associators may use. There are selfish people (drive-by ideators) and collaborative participants (collaborative ideators).

Allowing a diversity of roles, then, appears to be critical to capture the diversity of preferences expressed in these roles. Since these roles are self-created, instructions cannot specify that, for example, every second person should take on a fact sharer role or every fourth person should take on a drive-by ideator role. Crowd actors organically choose to play whichever role they want to play when they choose to participate in a crowdsourcing event. This organic choice allows participants to play to their strengths and interests, and yet, still make a contribution. Not everyone is an ideator or should be. Crowd participants seem to perform a role that they are most comfortable with.

Do these roles correspond to the ability of unmindcuffed crowds to generate more innovative ideas? Table 7.2 shows the differences between the two

7 Practice 5: Allowing the Crowd to Play Any Innovation-Enabling…

Table 7.2 Distribution of roles played in Idea-Sharing versus Unmindcuffed events

		Generalists	Collaborative ideators	Creative associators	Fact-sharers	Questioners	Drive by ideators
Idea sharing ($n = 7$)	Raw count	56	20	3	2	18	51
	Total %	9.61	3.43	0.51	0.34	3.09	8.75
	% in the process	37.33	13.33	2.00	1.33	12.00	34.00
Collective production ($n = 13$)	Count	172	19	24	28	43	147
	Total %	29.50	3.26	4.12	4.80	7.38	25.21
	% in the process	39.72	4.39	5.54	6.47	9.93	33.95

types of events in terms of the number of participants playing different roles. We used a contingency analysis to determine if there was a difference. Both the Likelihood Ratio (Chi-square = 23.15, $p < 0.001$) and the Pearson tests (Chi-square = 22.67, $p < 0.001$) were significant, showing that there were significant contingency differences.

The table shows that, for both Idea-Sharing or unmindcuffed events, there are about the same proportion of drive-by ideators and generalist participants; thus, the proportion playing each role doesn't affect the innovativeness of the ideas generated. Moreover, the high percentage of collaborative ideators in the Idea-Sharing events may be indicative of the traditional idea-refinement process seen in Idea-Sharing crowdsourcing, suggesting that collaborative ideators are not the differentiators in fostering innovative ideas in unmindcuffed events. Instead, *what seems to differentiate the two types of events is that Collective Production events had three times as many creative associators than in the Idea-Sharing events (6% vs. 2%), and five times more fact sharers than in the Idea-Sharing events (6.5% vs. 1.5%).*

In sum, unmindcuffed crowds engage in Collective Production in part by having larger numbers of participants playing the roles of fact sharers and creative associators, both of which prior chapters have shown are essential to the innovative production process.

Finally, we looked at whether specific role playing led to more innovative ideas. Interestingly, we found that with creativity associators, when they post ideas, those ideas tend to be lower rated (Difference = 1, $t = 2.32$, $p < 0.05$). It implies that these role players are better served just by posting creative associations rather than by engaging in idea generation.

Below, we summarize our findings by overlaying the six roles onto the Collective Production process we described in Chap. 6. This is shown in Fig. 7.3. Creative Associators, for example, provide the creative associations that are needed in the last five posts to stimulate an innovative idea. Fact shar-

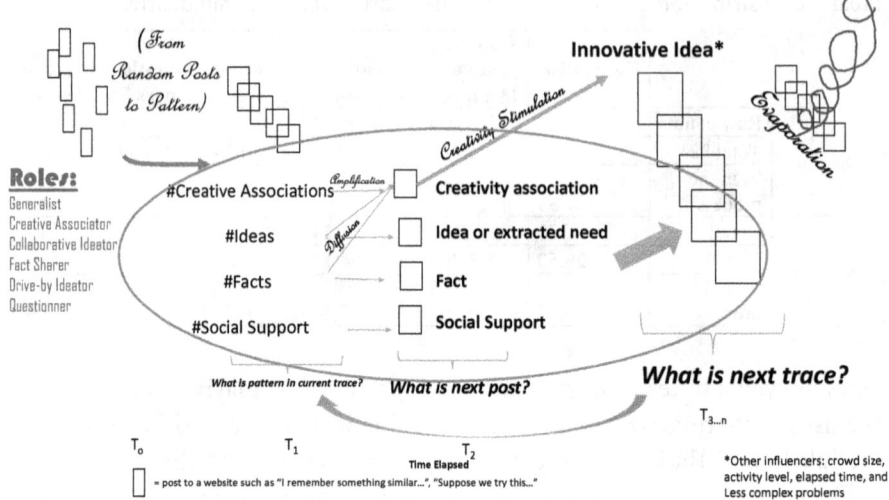

Fig. 7.3 Roles placed in the collaborative production process

ers are needed to generate the facts that provide the information through which creative associations can be discovered. Then, as with all crowdsourcing events, collaborative ideators, drive-by-ideators, questioners and generalist players provide additional information, create norms that comments are permitted on other discussion threads, and that ideas can be offered buried within discussions.

7.4 How Do the Roles We Find Align with Existing Research?

Since there is no prior research on roles enacted during innovation crowdsourcing using the Collective Production process, the closest research is on roles enacted in innovation crowdsourcing using the Idea-Sharing process and roles enacted within Wikipedia.

Using Wikipedia data, there are two studies looking at roles and both show the dynamism of the roles. In another study,[7] researchers found that article preparation required a variety of different roles to be played, including what they called article shapers, idea champions, and content defenders. This is similar to our findings that a variety of roles are needed for the Collective Production of innovative ideas, although the specific types of roles needing to be played are different.

In another study[8] of 200,000 distinct participants offering 700,000 edits to 1000 articles, they found that across the articles, there were both a consistent set of roles that were played and an inconsistent set of people playing the roles, that is, the people who played those roles changed often. Our findings are similar in this respect. That is, whether the crowdsourcing event in New Zealand was about making the country pest-free, or about new business models for a technology hardware company, the same types of roles were needed, although the people playing those roles were different.

There have been a few studies describing the presence of roles in Idea-Sharing Innovation Crowdsourcing contests. In one study,[9] the posts of 320 participants were given the option to comment on others' ideas as well as to post their own ideas. The researchers found that some comments were cooperative and others were competitive. They also found that 25% of the participants contributed only competitive behavior, 11% contributed only cooperative behavior, and most (57%) contributed both, what they called "communition" behavior. They suggested that communitators were more likely to win the contest. In our analysis, the multi-role players did not differentiate Idea-Sharing from unmindcuffed crowds. Clearly, more research on this is needed.

In another study,[10] the researchers examined the trace data of participants who engaged in an Idea Search innovation competition for designing jewelry. More than 1700 participants created more than 3000 designs of jewelry and commented on others' designs. The researchers found six different roles played by the participants. Most participants played the role of passive commentators, who mainly provided motivational statements of social support or played the role of idea generators offering ideas of low quality. The remainder minority played either the role of providing constructive feedback or generating high-quality ideas. Most interesting, they found that idea generators—whether they offered poor or high quality—attracted little follow-on attention from the crowd, failing to lead to Collective Production. The only ones who attracted attention were the 1% high-quality idea generators, who also spent significant time providing support and motivation to others. In this chapter, we have also highlighted more specifically what constructive feedback in crowds looks like—posting of questions, facts, and creative associations. This is also what a large portion of the roles in our sample do. Provision of feedback then, as highlighted by us, is critical to attention drawing and stimulating and amplifying in the Collective Production process.

Finally, another study suggests that in Idea Search crowdsourcing events, each role corresponds to a different motivation of the participant. That is, participants enter the crowdsourcing with premeditated role preferences based on their different motivations to participate, and then, simply play that role when they post.[11] For example, an individual motivated to participate in order to win the competition will only post ideators while an individual interested in helping others to learn will post on others' discussion threads. We question whether the roles are (1) premeditated and (2) based on different motivations.

We suggest that instead of considering roles as premeditated based on motivations, the roles represent a unique time-by-skill-gap match. That is, during Collective Production, when facts have been only sparsely contributed, a gap is implicitly identified: the need for more facts. Then, assuming that the crowd is unmindcuffed from just offering ideas, someone in the crowd who has factual knowledge about the problem will perceive this implicit need and offer facts. In a similar fashion, when there is a dearth of creative associations offered, someone in the crowd will fill the gap and offer creative associations. Since these self-created roles emerge during the process, rather than a priori, it is not clear if incentives specifically geared to specific participants with specific motivations and specific role preferences are either feasible or desirable. While some people may be better at certain roles than others, it is not clear that people are sufficiently aware of their skill capabilities before seeing how the Collective Production process unfolds. In other words, it is not the incentives that lead to premeditated roles; rather, it is how the dynamic knowledge-sharing process of the crowd unfolds that then inspires participants to play a role that they are comfortable with, in response to the unfolding of others' contributions.

Consequently, if Collective Production is to occur, participants cannot be mandated nor incentivized to play particular roles because that would violate the process whereby the unfolding knowledge-sharing gaps determine which roles need to be played, not whether someone is incentivized to play a particular role. Incentives for particular roles are likely to have participants playing those roles at inappropriate points in time during the dynamic knowledge-sharing process, thus harming Collective Production. Instead, we suggest that the crowd simply be informed of the need for the different roles to be played; keep them informed of knowledge gaps unfolding and encourage anyone to fill in that gap.

In sum, the existing research aligns with our findings, indicating that people engage in crowdsourcing events using multiple different self-created roles. We extend that research by finding that two particular roles distinguish between Idea-Sharing and Collective Production: the presence of creative associators and the presence of fact sharers.

7.5 What Does This Mean for Future Research?

One area of research for which our findings in this chapter have implications concerns how duties are separated during the innovation process. As we explained in Chap. 1, much of that research centers on a predefined separation of duties in which crowds only offer ideas and managers select the ideas they think are most likely to work (with the possible voting suggestions by the crowd). The findings in this chapter suggest that predefined separation of duties is likely to be counterproductive for innovation since roles need to be allowed to emerge from the process so that participants can dynamically enact a role they feel will help the collective. For example, some[12] have suggested that the role of the broker or boundary spanner or technology scout is needed to foster innovation. These are process roles, helping to ensure that knowledge is exchanged between two groups. We suggest, instead, that when a crowd is allowed to share their knowledge, such process roles are not needed and should be replaced with content roles. The content roles focus on a provision of facts or creative associations. Further, each of the content role is needed only on an ad-hoc dynamically unique basis. There is no single individual designated the technology scout for example; instead, everyone who has any knowledge about technology is expected to share their knowledge. Thus, research is needed on how to reconceptualize traditional innovation research around the possibility that it is the crowd participants playing self-created roles who are more effective at stimulating creative discoveries.

Our analysis found that the roles of fact sharer and creative associator were particularly important since they distinguished between the Idea-Sharing and the unmindcuffed events. How important are the other roles since they create a context for new knowledge to be shared? Moreover, if a role is not being enacted early on in the event, would the enactment of the missing role later in the event help foster Collective Production of innovative ideas?

How many people are needed to play these roles? Much research is needed to understand whether a critical mass of role players is needed or having only one person playing each role will suffice as long as the role is played well? If it is the number of people playing a role that matters, then the roles may serve as a normative control on the potential chaos of the crowd. Or, it may be that having only one person playing the role is particularly important since it makes the role behaviors more unique relative to other behaviors and therefore more salient to others in encouraging Collective Production. Still, another alternative might be that it is not how many participants play the role but rather how well the role is played that matters for Collective Production. For example, if a number of Assumption Sharers simply toss out facts about the problem without explaining how the facts might affect the conceptualization of the problem, this might be a lower-quality role enactment than a single Assumption Sharer explaining how a particular fact might redirect problem conceptualization. This also brings attention to the need to study how the knowledge (of different types) is presented—to see its efficacy for the Collective Production process. Does the linguistics matter? Is it the choice of words that implicitly signal emotive tone, authority, and credibility that leads to the role (as played out by the type of knowledge being contributed) that drives the utility of the role and associated knowledge contribution?

7.6 What Does This Mean for Practice?

- Keep a lookout for harmful roles, such as argumentative ones, or ones that have complaints and no needs or ideas. Or, ones that take a negative tone, rather than a positive tone.
- Use trace data in-process during the event to find roles that are not being enacted and suggest participants that they enact them (and perhaps even unobtrusively model to the participants what role behaviors would be appropriate).
- Encourage role enactment in the instructions with examples of possible roles participants could play.
- Ask leading questions to encourage others to take on those roles, for example, "Are there any companies in other industries that might have solved a similar problem?." Or, "Remember when Ford thought of a fuel-efficient car?" Or, "Does this toy have to be fun as well as educational?" Or, "Why did Fidget Spinners become so viral as a toy?"
- Keep a lookout for people who like to enact the roles we identified in other contexts (such as small innovation teams, skunkworks groups, etc.) and suggest they become involved in the crowdsourcing event as well as become involved in enacting these roles during in-person innovation teamwork.

7.7 Summary of Our Practices

We have now completed describing the five practices that we discovered in our research that compose the Collective Production process taken by crowds to create innovative ideas. We find that when the design of platform and process "un-mind-cuffs" the crowd from a focus on Idea-Sharing, the ideas such crowds collectively produce are more innovative and produced more efficiently compared to those produced by crowds restricted to an Idea-Sharing crowdsourcing process. A deep analytical examination of the trace data left by the 20 crowds led us to find 5 practices the crowds engaged in, which explain how crowds produce innovative ideas when they are "unmindcuffed". These five practices make it possible for crowd participants to learn about all the various issues involved in solving the wicked problem by sharing bite-sized fragments and creative associations easily consumable and useful as inspirations by others. The five practices are:

7.7.1 Practice 1: Minimally Committed Knowledge Baton Passers

A crowd that isn't limited to simply posting ideas and refining others' ideas through a drawn-out dialogic process does not "collaborate" in a traditional sense. Such crowds do not engage in extensive socialization and back-and-forth "person addressed" communication as they would in a traditional team or in an online community. Rather, crowds collaborate by passing bits of knowledge as batons, with each baton adding inspiration to others. In our data, an individual participant on average offers less than two posts, with virtually no dialogue, and spends little time in social niceties like posting how wonderful others' ideas are. Yet, as a whole, the crowd ends up producing innovative ideas.

7.7.2 Practice 2: Sharing a Variety of Knowledge Types Matters More Than any Specific Knowledge Shared

We coded the traces for a variety of different types of knowledge shared about the problem description and solution. The types we looked at were facts about the problem, examples of how the problem may have been solved in other contexts, paradoxical objectives to consider in solving the problem, and ideas for solving the problem. We then analyzed if it was the specific types of knowledge sharing mattered or it was the overall variety which preceded an innovative idea. We found that variety mattered more than any other single specific type of knowledge, including ideas. In other words, more ideas do not breed better solutions, which is what most of the literature emphasizes. Nor was this variety related to the actual content; it was the variety of types of knowledge that matters.

7.7.3 Practice 3: Amplification of Others' Creative Associations

Just mimicking others' ideas does not make the crowd more likely to innovate. Instead, participants use the creative associations shared by others as jumping off points, to think about other associations they might have in their own memory about the problem. Individuals then post these associations, which serve to inspire others to post associations, which starts a positive feedback loop providing more fodder for creative discovery.

7.7.4 Practice 4: Reformulating Problem-Associated Needs to Spark Creative Associations

The crowd cannot simply accept needs or solutions offered by others if the crowd wants to collectively produce innovative solutions. If they simply accepted others' professed needs, the best the crowd could do would be to generate a solution that is more expansive or inclusive of those needs. That is counterproductive as all that this accomplishes is that new solutions suggested by the crowd are merely a refinement and broadened version of earlier solutions. Instead, Collective Production of innovation requires that the crowd reformulates the initial needs to spark others to explicate their creative associations. The crowd reformulates others' initial professed needs either by offering personalized and concrete examples of the need in a different context to create an analogy for others to build upon or to abstract the initial need to apply to societal issues and corresponding human action. This then, in turn, inspires others in the crowd to strive to achieve solutions that address new, more value-based goals.

7.7.5 Practice 5: Crowd Enacts Self-selected Innovation-enabling Roles

We find that the ideal crowd is composed of not just mere ideators. Rather, in more innovation-producing crowds, individuals perform a range of other innovation-enabling roles. Some individuals engage in need elicitation, others offer need reframing, others offer creative associations, and yet others offer basic knowledge-like facts. Then, there are those individuals who generate new solutions specifically by using (integrating or reshaping) the knowledge provided by others. Different roles involve different skills and allow for a wide variety of individuals from the crowd to participate in the Collective Production process, rather than be constrained by the high bar of participation, that is, producing ideas only.

Where do we go now? In the next chapter, we talk about Implementation: implementing these ideas into future research, implementing these ideas into the design of new technologies supporting crowdsourcing, and implementing this work, as a practitioner, into one's next innovation crowdsourcing event.

Notes

1. Faraj, S., Jarvenpaa, S., & Majchrzak, A. (2011). Knowledge collaboration in online communities. *Organization Science, 22*(5), 1224–1239; Kane, G., Johnson, J., & Majchrzak, A. (2014). Emergent life cycle: The tension between knowledge change and knowledge retention in open online coproduction communities. *Management Science, 60*(12), 3026–3048.
2. Biddle, B. (1979). *Role theory: Expectations, identities, and behaviors.* New York: Academic Press; Katz, D., & Kahn, R. (1978). *The social psychology of organizations* (2nd ed.). New York: Wiley.

    Parsons, T. (1951). *The social system.* Glencoe, IL: Free Press; for a review of this traditional literature on roles, see Sluss, D. M., van Dick, R., & Thompson, B. S. (2011). Role theory in organizations: A relational perspective. *APA Handbook of Industrial and Organizational Psychology, 1,* 505–534.
3. Goffman, E. (1959). *The presentation of self in everyday life.* Garden City, NY: Doubleday.
4. Faraj, S., Jarvenpaa, S., & Majchrzak, A. (2011). Knowledge collaboration in online communities. *Organization Science,* 22(5), 1224–1239.
5. Füller, J., Hutter, K., Hautz, J., & Matzler, K. (2014). User roles and contributions in innovation-contest communities. *Journal of Management Information Systems, 31*(1), 273–308.
6. Malhotra, A., & Majchrzak, A. (2014). Managing crowds in innovation challenges. *California Management Review, 56*(4), 103–123.
7. Kane, G., Johnson, J., & Majchrzak, A. (2014). Emergent life cycle: The tension between knowledge change and knowledge retention in open online coproduction communities. *Management Science, 60*(12), 3026–3048.
8. Arazy, O., Daxenberger, J., Lifshitz-Assaf, H., Nov, O, & Gurevych, I. (2016). Turbulent stability of emergent roles: The dualistic nature of self-organizing knowledge coproduction. *Information Systems Research, 27*(4), 792–812.
9. Hutter, K., Hautz, J., Fuller, J., Mueller, J., & Matzler, K. (2011). Communitition: The tension between competition and collaboration in community-based design contests. (Report). *Creativity and Innovation Management, 20*(1), 3–21.

10. Füller, J., Hutter, K., Hautz, J., & Matzler, K. (2014). User roles and contributions in innovation-contest communities. *Journal of Management Information Systems, 31*(1), 273–308.
11. Leimeister, J., Huber, M., Bretschneider, U., & Krcmar, H. (2009). Leveraging crowdsourcing: Activation-supporting components for IT-based ideas competition. *Journal of Management Information Systems, 26*(1), 197–224.
12. Burt, R. (2009). *Structural holes: The social structure of competition.* Cambridge, MA: Harvard University Press; Levina, N., Fayard, A-L. (2018). Tapping into diversity through open innovation platforms: The emergence of boundary-spanning practices. In Christopher L. Tucci, Allan Afuah, and Gianluigi Viscusi (eds.), *Creating and Capturing Value through Crowdsourcing.* Oxford: Oxford University Press; Allen, T. (1977). *Managing the flow of technology: Technology transfer and the dissemination of technological information within the R&D organization.* Cambridge, MA: MIT Press.

References

Allen, T. (1977). *Managing the Flow of Technology: Technology Transfer and the Dissemination of Technological Information Within the R&D Organization.* Cambridge, MA: MIT Press.

Arazy, O., Daxenberger, J., Lifshitz-Assaf, H., Nov, O., & Gurevych, I. (2016). Turbulent Stability of Emergent Roles: The Dualistic Nature of Self-Organizing Knowledge Coproduction. *Information Systems Research, 27*(4), 792–812.

Biddle, B. (1979). *Role Theory: Expectations, Identities, and Behaviors.* New York: Academic Press.

Burt, R. (2009). *Structural Holes: The Social Structure of Competition.* Cambridge, MA: Harvard University Press.

Faraj, S., Jarvenpaa, S., & Majchrzak, A. (2011). Knowledge Collaboration in Online Communities. *Organization Science, 22*(5), 1224–1239.

Füller, J., Hutter, K., Hautz, J., & Matzler, K. (2014). User Roles and Contributions in Innovation-Contest Communities. *Journal of Management Information Systems, 31*(1), 273–308.

Goffman, E. (1959). *The Presentation of Self in Everyday Life.* Garden City, NY: Doubleday.

Hutter, K., Hautz, J., Fuller, J., Mueller, J., & Matzler, K. (2011). Communitition: The Tension Between Competition and Collaboration in Community-Based Design Contests (Report). *Creativity and Innovation Management, 20*(1), 3–21.

Kane, G., Johnson, J., & Majchrzak, A. (2014). Emergent Life Cycle: The Tension Between Knowledge Change and Knowledge Retention in Open Online Coproduction Communities. *Management Science, 60*(12), 3026–3048.

Katz, D., & Kahn, R. (1978). *The Social Psychology of Organizations* (2nd ed.). New York: Wiley.

Leimeister, J., Huber, M., Bretschneider, U., & Krcmar, H. (2009). Leveraging Crowdsourcing: Activation-Supporting Components for IT-Based Ideas Competition. *Journal of Management Information Systems, 26*(1), 197–224.

Levina, N., & Fayard, A.-L. (2018). Tapping into Diversity Through Open Innovation Platforms: The Emergence of Boundary-Spanning Practices. In C. L. Tucci, A. Afuah, & G. Viscusi (Eds.), *Creating and Capturing Value Through Crowdsourcing* (pp. 204–235). Oxford: Oxford University Press.

Malhotra, A., & Majchrzak, A. (2014). Managing Crowds in Innovation Challenges. *California Management Review, 56*(4), 103–123.

Parsons, T. (1951). *The Social System*. Glencoe, IL: Free Press.

Sluss, D. M., van Dick, R., & Thompson, B. S. (2011). Role Theory in Organizations: A Relational Perspective. *APA Handbook of Industrial and Organizational Psychology, 1*, 505–534.

Part III

What's Next: Implications for Research, Technology Platforms, and Managers

In Part III, it is time for action. We describe the next steps that can be taken by researchers, technology developers, and the managers who want to be able to manage the crowds. Each chapter is devoted to a different audience.

In Chap. 8, we tie together our findings into a theory of Collective Production of innovative ideas that disrupts current theories about how crowdsourcing works. We use this theory to describe possible research questions for the future.

In Chap. 9, we describe our eight principles for the design of crowdsourcing platforms that support Collective Production. These principles are:

- Incentivizing "Coopetition" for sharing and reusing knowledge
- Fostering creative abrasion
- You can't make crowds do anything, but prime them and some will follow
- Encouraging surfacing different problem descriptions
- Making knowledge sharing easier
- Enhancing crowd's knowledge evolution transparency
- Crowds need to share ideas first (even if they are of limited value)

In addition, Chap. 9 describes principles for the design of the technology platform for a new wave of organizations, referred to as crowd-powered. In these organizations, crowds are able to regularly influence an organization as it moves forward, not just for one-off events. These design principles include:

- Design for fast event spinups
- Maintain history despite the fluidity

- Manage the nuanced need to share sensitive information
- Use performance assessment for multiple, non-people, purposes.

In Chap. 10, we provide specific guidance for helping managers with an apparent paradox: how can practitioners manage crowds that should not be mindcuffed? We answer this paradox with guidance on the following issues:

- Who should be the sponsor?
- How should crowdsourcing be sold to internal constituents in an organization?
- What types of wicked problems should be posed to the crowd?
- What is the role of the planning committee?
- How should crowds be identified and encouraged to participate?
- Should crowds be monitored and moderated? If so, how?
- What criteria should be used to select the innovative ideas?
- What should be done with the best solutions?

In Chap. 10, we also move beyond managing crowdsourcing, to helping managers change the way they manage innovation in organizations.

We close our book with Final Words meant to inspire you to see that this book is not about crowdsourcing. It never was. It is about the future of work and how organizations and workers of the future will find common ground so that organizations are able to learn from the crowd and the crowd is able to provide the solutions to the wicked problems of the world that organizations can implement. We no longer see the world divided into those within an organization and outside of it; rather, we believe it is time to find ways to leverage all of our minds—collectively, creatively, and practically—no matter where we are.

8

Tying It All Together: A Theory of Collective Production of Innovation to Inspire Future Research

Since we are interested in progressing research, we present a scholarly version of our theory of Collective Production of innovation in which innovating crowds consist of some participants willing to use their scant two posts to disaggregate their knowledge into creative associations of knowledge batons and others willing to take those knowledge batons and co-mingle them to stimulate creative discoveries. The disaggregation occurs as people break down their causal models, their coherent perspectives, their proposals of need-solution pairs into factual assumptions, short statements of ideas, and creative associations. Since crowds spend so little time contributing to the wicked problem, the more effective the crowd can be at eliciting each other's disaggregated knowledge in a way that stimulates creative thought in a virtuous cycle, the more likely that the crowd will successfully produce an innovative solution. The implications for a new direction for research on innovation and new organizational forms are discussed.

As we explained in Chap. 1, there are two existing theories of Collective Production of innovative solutions—both of which we find inadequate for explaining how crowds can collectively produce innovative solution-ideas.[1] One theory is the variation, selection, retention evolutionary model. In this theory, the crowd is expected to provide sufficient variation that a great idea is provided for a well-defined problem, the idea is found and selected by the management, and the idea is retained as it moves through the various stage gates of the innovation process. In Chap. 2, we demonstrated that this theory doesn't work, especially when the problem being addressed is a wicked one.

The second existing theory for Collective Production of innovative solutions which we discussed in Chap. 1 is that of a cross-functional team col-

© The Author(s) 2020
A. Majchrzak, A. Malhotra, *Unleashing the Crowd*,
https://doi.org/10.1007/978-3-030-25557-2_8

lectively producing a solution. The knowledge that is being used in this process is the perspectives of the individuals in the team. The perspectives contain the need as seen by the individual and the paired solution that the individual's background suggests will work, based on disciplinary assumptions about cause-and-effect relationships. The perspective is an internally coherent thought world, as embedded in the individual's experience. The challenge for the team is to solicit each person's thought world in a way that is understood by others. To weave perspectives together to resolve tensions and integrate synergies requires immense cognitive effort (and common social context), which is best done within a team. To elicit these perspectives requires the team members to generally explain what they know to each other, engage in a back-and-forth process of dialectics and constructive questioning to help reframe and create a consensus about the problem that attempts to integrate each other's knowledge, and then, engage in a process of creative problem-solving in which divergent ideas are discussed, criteria for evaluating solutions are agreed upon, and a consensus on the solution gradually materializes.

Our theory is different from both existing theories of innovation production.

8.1 Theory of Collective Production of Innovation

In developing our theory, we have drawn from two streams of research literature to explain why this process of comingling fragmented knowledge successfully leads to innovative solutions. One of the streams is that of creative cognition.[2] From this theory, we draw on the fact that creativity involves individuals first creating associations in their own memory, inspired by the knowledge fragments of others. Then, additional knowledge fragments from others are used to delink and link associations until they spark a creative discovery of a solution.

A second stream we draw from is the theory of creativity in context.[3] In this theory, creativity is likely to emerge from individuals who are given challenging problems, individual autonomy in how to solve those problems, and a norm supporting creativity. In our theory, the challenging problem is the wicked problem. Autonomy is exemplified in our theory by not specifying in the theory who offers what knowledge in what order. Finally, implicit norms seem to have emerged in the crowd, supporting a process of associative fragmentation and associative amplification.

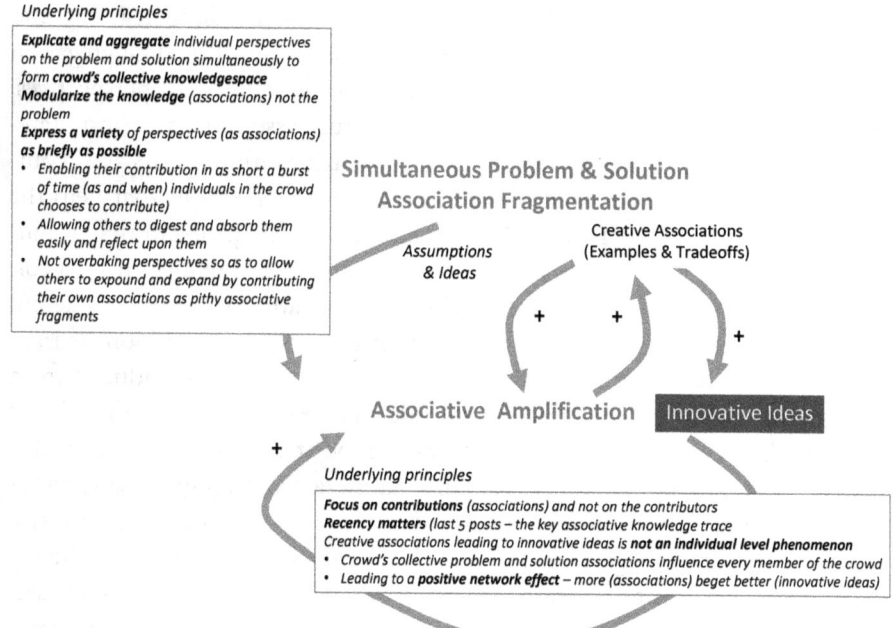

Fig. 8.1 Theory of Collective Production of innovative ideas by crowds

Figure 8.1 graphically depicts our theory of fragmented associations and associative amplification.

Our theory differs from existing theories in the following ways:

1. The participants do not need to spend significant time in the innovation process to make an important contribution, and that time is not spent in dialectical back-and-forth conversations to understand each other.
2. Instead of attempting to understand each other's perspective, the participants take their perspectives and break them down into short creative associations and statements of facts and wild ideas. Therefore, no single person's complete perspective matters as much as a varied collage of pieces or fragments of perspectives shared.
3. The fragments are for both the problem and the solution simultaneously. That is, there is no consensus reached about the problem definition prior to solutions being offered. As such, solution-ideas can cause creative associations about problem definitions that may have not been considered previously.
4. Creative associations form the heart of the process since they stimulate others to amplify the creative associations leading to a positive network effect on the production of innovative ideas.

Our theory of Collective Production is paradoxically disaggregating and reaggregating in a way that is collectively productive. The disaggregation occurs as people break down their causal models, their coherent perspectives, their proposals of need-solution pairs into factual assumptions, short statements of ideas, and creative associations. The reaggregation occurs as a "comingling" of the different fragments from different perspectives that help the collective appreciate the many issues associated with the problem that a solution will need to address.[4] Instead of searching and selecting ideas from a collection of ideas, and instead of working in a team to create a coherent perspective, a crowd's Collective Production centers on the notion of fragmenting and creatively associating knowledge. Our theory—induced from our findings—is that crowds spend so little time contributing to the wicked problem that the more effective the crowd can be at eliciting each other's disaggregated knowledge in a way that stimulates creative thought in a virtuous cycle, the more likely that the crowd will successfully produce an innovative solution. The knowledge that is desired from the crowd is not "individually constructed" coherent perspectives of needs with solutions, and causal models of assumptions. Rather, what is needed to help the crowd innovate is to disaggregate cause-effect models, so they can be reconsidered creatively, and offer fragments of knowledge phrased as creative associations. This knowledge is then attended to not to create an aggregated integration, but rather, as short reflective interpretations, with particular attention paid to the creative patterns in the most recent knowledge traces.

8.2 Time for a New Perspective to Understanding Online Innovation

We found that out of the four types of knowledge content explored, only trace patterns emphasizing creative associations are strongly related to the innovativeness of the ideas posted after the trace and those emphasizing social support harm innovativeness. This result is in contrast to research suggesting the importance of social support and shared understanding for innovation.[5] Trace patterns that surfaced factual assumptions had no effect on idea innovativeness even though the teams' literature suggests the importance of surfacing factual assumptions.[6] Trace patterns that emphasized ideas also had no effect on idea innovativeness despite the literature on online brainstorming[7] emphasizing the important effect that others' ideas have on the creation of innovative ideas.

We also found that no single knowledge post had an effect on the innovativeness of ideas, despite the extensive literature on digital artifacts arguing for the important value of a digital artifact.[8] We found that the knowledge posts needed to be strung together for participants to observe patterns across the posts before innovative ideas emerged. While metaphorical boundary objects might explain the importance of creative associations,[9] there is nothing in this literature that indicates that a single metaphor is inadequate, requiring multiple creative associations to be stimulating.

We found that only the most recent trace has an important effect on innovative ideas compared to past prior traces. Since traces change with each post, the effect is fleeting.

Finally, we also find that creative associations are more likely to be posted if, in the immediately previous trace, there is a greater number of facts, ideas, and creative associations. This suggests that facts and ideas seem to serve the role of *sustaining* the innovation potential of the crowd not by directly stimulating innovative ideas, but by keeping the crowd continuing to offer creative associations.

These findings suggest that the knowledge posts are not boundary objects serving as a point of shared understanding, as some have suggested.[10] Knowledge posts are also not as individually stimulating as the extensive focus in the literature on boundary objects would suggest. Instead, knowledge posts are worthwhile because of the series (i.e., trajectories, direction, and patterns) of posts that accumulate over time.

Theories that focus on patterns of posts accumulated over time are missing from research on innovation production in general and crowdsourcing in particular[11]; our findings clearly indicate the importance of using these traces of multiple posts strung together as fodder for understanding how innovation evolves. While research on team and collective innovation have failed to appreciate the importance of traces of multiple posts strung together, there is a recently developed theory in cognitive behavior that innovation researchers should become aware of—which does attempt to characterize patterns in traces and their effects on human behavior. We describe this perspective in order to stimulate more theorizing and research on how patterns of traces of individual posts might influence innovation in ways that may extend beyond our theory of Collective Production.

This perspective on how traces of multiple posts affect human behavior is referred to as "cognitive stigmergy", a meta-theory combining complex adaptive systems theory, chaos theory, and distributed cognition to explain behaviors of humans in large complex forms of organizations.[12] The theory has been described by these authors as having possible implications for a variety of online phenomena[13] but has not yet been comprehensively applied as a possible explanation of how crowds come to offer innovative ideas. Cognitive stigmergy is distinctive from the simpler form of entomology (insect-based) coordinative stigmergy that has been applied to describe some of the coordination mechanisms that occur in Wikipedia[14] and open source software development.[15] Cognitive stigmergy overcomes criticized constraints of entomology stigmergy by recognizing that humans have interpretive and creative capabilities and that human actors respond to stimuli to do more than simply coordinate.[16]

The underlying theoretical context assumptions of cognitive stigmergy provide an excellent fit to the context of an open crowd, as shown in Table 8.1. For example, in cognitive stigmergy, actors communicate by the objects they leave in their environment and are not centrally controlled; similarly, with un-mindcuffed crowds, participants communicate solely through the knowledge posts and are not centrally controlled by anyone, including the sponsoring organization, because they can leave at any point.

In Table 8.2, we compare our findings with theoretical explanations of cognitive stigmergy, discovering that all the findings are fully consonant with cognitive stigmergy. For example, the finding that social support has a negative effect on the emergence of innovative ideas is explainable in cognitive stigmergy as a violation of the self-organizing principles of stigmergic systems[30] since expressions of social support put greater importance on certain posts over other posts, which violate the self-organizing principles of all posts having equal weight, causing the system to collapse. As another example, the finding that patterns in immediately prior traces are more influential than older traces is explainable by the cognitive stigmergy principle of evaporation—where the effects of stimuli are reduced over time.

Another indication that cognitive stigmergy provides a useful interpretation of the findings is that processes of cognitive stigmergy are explainable, based on a few simple rules describing the types of stimuli needed in emergent patterns in traces as well as types of feedback needed between traces.[36] With relatively little effort, we are able to identify those simple rules from our findings:

1. **Creative Association Rule**: The more creative associations shared by the crowd in a trace, the greater the likelihood that innovative ideas by crowds will be generated.
2. **Amplification Rule**: Creative associations posted by multiple people encourage others to post new creative associations, not mimic the precise nature of the creative association.

Table 8.1 Comparison of open crowd conditions and cognitive behavior of stigmergic actors

Assumptions from cognitive stigmergy about how actors behave	How assumptions fit with basic characteristics of an open crowd
• Actors don't wait for others; they are engaged in large-scale parallel participation.[17]	• Actors can post in multiple threads simultaneously.[18]
• Actors "communicate" only in a broadcast mode where they leave objects which modify their local environment and any other actor may be stimulated by that modification in some way; there are no other means of communication.[19]	• Virtual objects posted on a virtual workspace are the primary mechanism for communication.[20]
• Actors only see the state of their immediate surroundings (called "local environment"), no single actor has all information, they only contribute briefly to that state, not explicitly directing others' behaviors.[21]	• Minimal individual effort desired by collaborative crowdsourcing actors since collective outcomes result from the aggregation of the individual behaviors; example: "drive-by" posters.[22]
• Actors are not centrally controlled, but act in a distributed fashion influenced by traces left by others.[23]	• Crowd actors can choose whether and how to participate, influenced by traces left by others.[24]
• Actor characteristics are less important than the actions taken.[25]	• In a crowd, there is "a lack of salience of individual differences; general equality characterizes its crowd".[26]
• Process starts by actors randomly depositing stimuli on the environment, referred to as cognitive trails.[27]	• Crowd actors begin by contributing knowledge content in the form of digital texts in their virtual workspace.
• Self-organization must be allowed to occur; there must not be any external hierarchy or imposed process, rules, or limitations.[28]	• In collaborative/coopetitive crowds, crowd actors are allowed (and often encouraged) to share what knowledge they want in whatever way they prefer.[29]

3. **Diffusion Rule**: Sharing of ideas and assumptions by open crowds stimulates the production of more creative associations, not innovative ideas.
4. **Evaporative Traces Rule**: Recency of knowledge contained in traces dampens.
5. **Isocracy Rule**: When attention is diverted away from the content of digital traces to social hierarchy, the effect of the process on innovative ideas is harmed.

Our Collective Production theory briefly described here, then, contains five simple abstract rules about how the content shared by open crowds leads

Table 8.2 Comparison of findings with explanations by cognitive stigmergy

Exploratory questions and related findings	Cognitive stigmergy explanation
Q1: What content shared (as digital artifacts) by open crowds is related to the emergence of innovative ideas by the crowds? Findings: Creative associations (+) Shared understanding (−) Factual assumptions (not significant) Ideas (not significant)	• Stimuli represent either means to the goal (called markers), or the evidence of the goal itself (called sematectonic), with each type having different effects.[31] Creative associations appear to be the markers. • Shared understanding imposes a non-self-organizing effect of hierarchy, harming the innovative outcome.[32] • Others' assumptions and ideas do not provide useful markers because another's view of the problem is less relevant than how one can think creatively about the problem.[33]
Q2: What are the knowledge-sharing patterns that affect the emergence of innovative ideas in open crowds? Findings: • Patterns in traces of multiple digital artifacts are more important than any single artifact. • The explicit pattern of having more creative associations increases the likelihood of an innovative idea generated.	• An initial trace emerges from accumulated stimuli, based on either qualitative or quantitative counts of the stimuli.[34] • Accumulated digital texts, rather than the last single text, affect the next action.
Q3: How do such innovation-related knowledge-sharing patterns emerge and sustain themselves in crowds? Findings: • The more the creative associations in a trace, the more likely it is that the next digital text contribution is a creative association. • Effect of a pattern is reduced over time. • The number of ideas and assumptions diffuse to increase the emergence of creative associations.	• The probability of the patterned traces continuing depends on balancing positive feedback loops (amplification and diffusion) with negative feedback (evaporation, saturation, competition for attention).[35] So, each of these findings is explained by principles of feedback loops: • **Amplification** (not mimicry): the more creative associations in the pattern, the greater the probability that the next post is a new creative association. • **Evaporation**: only the most recent 5-post traces affected innovativeness. • **Diffusion**: The number of ideas and assumptions affected the emergence of creative associations although they didn't affect innovativeness directly.

to innovative ideas. In brief, as shown in Fig. 8.1, the process appears to be one of the crowds beginning their process by randomly posting knowledge, with some of that knowledge falling into the four types: shared understanding, factual assumptions, creative associations, and ideas. At some point, enough of a single knowledge type accumulates in traces of five posts or more. When enough factual assumptions or ideas or creative associations accumulate, then the crowd begins to amplify its creative associations (Rules 2 and 3). Crowd actors essentially ignore anything older than five posts as well as any single post, which helps to avoid information overload (Rule 4). The crowd also ignores any expressions of social support because the social hierarchy created from such posts would give preferential ordering to certain posts, which would make innovative ideas less likely (Rule 5). Eventually, an actor views accumulated creative associations, which stimulate an idea, which is later assessed to be innovative (Rule 1). Since the crowd is not aware of which ideas are more innovative, they keep posting, using the latest idea as just another post accumulating in a trace. It is this repeated process that keeps the process sustained in an open crowd.

We suggest, provocatively, that this may be a performative routine[37] in that these are the specific actions by specific actors at specific times in specific forms of open crowds that make the emergence of innovative ideas in open crowds "routine". Therefore, we offer the following proposition for future testing: *in an open crowd that follows this process, there is a higher probability of emergence of innovative ideas compared to an open crowd that does not follow this process, and that any communicative activities that essentially disrupt this process, such as expressions of social support, will harm the process.* Building from cognitive stigmergy,[38] this process is emergent in the sense it derives from the accumulation of individual actions rather than inputs such as characteristics of individual actors or size of the crowd, although as shown in the analysis, both variables exerted an influence. *Thus, in contrast with much of the research on crowdsourcing that focuses on establishing initial conditions of crowd sizes and diversity,[39] we suggest that such initial inputs may be less important than initially thought.*

Identifying such simple rules can accelerate the evolution of a science of crowd innovation capital.[40] Such simple rules can be implemented into simulations so that a wide range of additional potential factors can be assessed for the complex interactive effects on the production of innovative ideas. Such simple rules can also be implemented into crowd governance research.[41] Finally, such simple rules are hypotheses to assess against plausible alternative hypotheses, such as comparing the importance of sharing ideas, assertions about shared understanding, and the importance of factual assumption-based knowledge sharing.

8.3 Implications of Our Theorizing for Research on Innovation

The five simple rules, and our Collective Production process, raise a number of questions for future research on innovation. Some of these questions are specifically about crowdsourcing. Most of these questions, however, are about research on innovation in general.

Do Characteristics of Actors Affect Innovative Outcomes? The role of the individual actors in open crowds—and possibly in innovative teams—should be reconsidered. There has been substantial research devoted to arguing for increasing the number of actors in a crowd, the diversity of the crowd, and the expertise in a crowd.[42] In contrast, our Collective Production theory focuses on the stigmergic qualities of the knowledge posts left by any actor, irrespective of the actor's status, reputation, expertise, or experience. It may be that research has inadvertently given individual reputation far more importance than it deserves. While the assumption has been that reputable actors should be given attention, such attention violates isocracy[43] that is foundational for a stigmergic system to yield innovative outcomes.[44] However, simply because expertise and reputation may not be important doesn't mean that characteristics of actors have no impact on Collective Production. This process may require individuals who do not need social support.[45]

If R&D teams were treated as crowds, would innovative ideas be generated more efficiently and with higher quality results as problems emerged? Research is needed on how the traditions of managing R&D teams could be changed to managing R&D as crowds. Since we have been able to demonstrate that crowds are able to innovate through the dual process of associative fragmentation and amplification, could R&D units do the same? Such a process would allow R&D teams to breakdown functional distinctions quicker so that new cross-functional perspectives can be developed. Such a process would encourage radical rethinking rather than incremental fixes. The process would also allow anyone to participate including suppliers and customers, taking any participative role they want, rather than having their role constrained to participating in focus groups. Lastly, the new crowd view of R&D process would change the R&D unit, not into solution seekers as some have suggested,[46] but rather into a crowd of really bright people willing to step in and help solve any problems that arise without devoting substantial time to any single issue.

Should any and all problem-solving teams be treated as a crowd? Increasingly, problem-solving teams have fuzzy memberships[47] in the sense that internet-enabled communication tools allow any expert on a certain subtopic of the problem the team is solving to be drawn into the team's deliberations for short spurts or sprints.[48] This ability to acquire the "most able", not simply "the most available"[49] ensures that the team engages in a problem-solving effort with the right knowledge. This way of working in teams—where expertise is pulled in as needed with even core team members rotating as the problem proceeds down the stage-gate path—sounds increasingly like a crowd, where each incarnation of the crowd is focused on a different aspect of the problem being solved. If a team is a crowd, then the literature on team creativity will benefit a new set of practices which allow the team to act as a crowd, and yet, still produce innovative solutions: by disaggregating knowledge into fragmented associations, and amplifying these associations. For example, the tenet of team problem-solving processes to use constructive conflict dialogue during back-and-forth conversations[50] is replaced with participants engaged in reflective personalized dialogue with the post, not the person. As another example, the tenet that problem definition should precede problem resolution[51] is replaced with disaggregating knowledge about solutions and problems into a collage of knowledge, all of which are contributed simultaneously, rather than in sequence.

We do not know the role of anonymity in Collective Production of innovation. In our research, as explained in Chap. 2, we speculated that anonymity is important for Collective Production because it allows participants to ignore social cues, which might otherwise have led to domination by certain individuals over others, as well as to ignore social support from others, which might have otherwise constricting participants offering risky ideas. Anonymity is relatively easy to maintain online. But in collocated teams where anonymity is impossible, these restraints on the negative effects of social influence on innovation are reinstated. As future research applies our Collective Production theory to collocated teams, practices to overcome social influence may need to be adopted. For example, in one study[52] on three highly innovative collocated teams, it was found that all three used a practice of creating a collage of knowledge written on Post-It notes, which dissociated the note from the person who wrote it. The authors conclude that this practice helped to trigger creativity since everyone could focus on the same set of knowledge, regardless of who had contributed that knowledge.

We do not know the make-up of the ideal crowds. Diversity of expertise in crowds has always been suggested as important for all sorts of problems, and particularly for ill-structured problems.[53] We have suggested that diversity of knowledge types (diverse fragments) are equally or more critical. But there surely must be a threshold level of knowledge variety, which is needed in the crowd for the crowd to be able to process the knowledge to provide useful solutions. It is also possible that beyond a certain threshold, the increasing knowledge variety has a deleterious impact on Collective Production of innovation due to information overload. Therefore, research about the minimum thresholds of diverse knowledge types to be shared is needed. A similar future research question arises with the consideration of technical problems. Can a crowd really solve cancer if all crowd participants do not have scientific knowledge of the human genome as long as a few experts do?

We do not have a solution to the exploitation paradox of crowdsourcing for innovation. This paradox is that, on the one hand, to ask the crowd to share their knowledge without payment is a form of exploitation since the organization sponsoring the crowdsourcing event is intending to obtain revenue from the very best ideas generated. The paradox is that, simultaneously, participants are volunteers and can leave if they feel exploited, but they do not do so. We see more and more instances of voluntary crowds that attempt to solve organizations' most wicked problems. Research is needed on the various mechanisms for managing this paradox in a manner that feels equitable to the participants in the long run. Does the fact that participants are only contributing fragmented knowledge rather than well-developed proposals reduce perceptions of exploitation? Does the fact that participants are only participating one or two times reduce perceptions of exploitation? Does the fact that participants can choose to offer ideas, or facts, or creative associations affect perceptions of exploitation? When blockchain is used in the future to track which contributions led to the most innovative solution, will that affect perceptions of exploitation?

How do we increase a crowd's innovative capability? Not all crowds in our sample had the ability to offer innovative solutions. They did not have enough creative associations generated, not enough needs separated from solutions and reformulated, and they had so many people offering social support that the social support posts drowned out the creative associations. How do we help the crowd gain their innovative capability when participants make less than two posts? The Open Ocean Challenge[54] spent significant time during in-person workshops to train the crowd participants. This limits the breadth of crowd participation. How do we prepare them online? Is training a critical missing element of a successful Collective Production process? Moreover, what, in fact, is the mechanism that explains the causal relationship between the number of creative associations and the production of an innovative idea? Is it the increased possible access points into people's memories so that new elements for a solution are surfaced to be recombined? Or could it be the "mood" of the crowd that is created through "un-mind-cuffing", in which the crowd feels freer to be creative than anyone of them individually would feel? Or could it be that by unmindcuffing, the crowd is receiving a message of respect, which triggers the kind of cognitive engagement needed for creativity?[55]

What are the temporal implications for Collective Production of innovation? Most of the Collective Production events in our sample were 7–10-day bursts.[56] The question still remains as to how to time-splice these events to increase the probability of innovative ideas being produced? Should these events be longer than 7–10 days to allow participants more opportunity to engage? But would the increased time reduce the perceived urgency to post immediately? There may also be another downside to allowing events to go on too long. For example, do perpetual user innovation communities lose their Collective Production ability because the attention of participants is lost over time? Moreover, third-party innovation intermediaries sometimes suggest multiple stages for a crowdsourcing event—such as a first stage for independent research, followed by a stage of offering ideas, followed by a stage of focused development on a limited set of ideas.[57] These stages force participants to disaggregate their perspectives on the problem and the solution. However, as we have demonstrated such decoupling of perspectives does not occur naturally in unmindcuffed events as they do not follow the staged approach. The question then is, could such a staged model of innovation hurt the innovation potential of the crowd?

8.4   Implications of Our Theorizing for Innovation Potential of New Organizational Forms

The research presented in this book on the microfoundations of crowd innovation has implications for new organizational forms including emergent forms,[58] heterarchical forms,[59] forms incomplete by design,[60] catalyst organizations,[61] and boundaryless organizations.[62] These new organizational forms meet the needs for continuous innovation in markets which are environmentally turbulent, hypercompetitive, and replete with technological disruptions, globalization, zero-cost of information exchange, and virtuality of work.[63]

Common among these is that there is *no* longer the expectation that "the work of generative recombination requires intense interaction and deeply familiar access to knowledge bases and productive resources",[64] "intense relational engagement … to gain … emergent intersubjectivity and a shared new sensibility",[65] and consensus.[66] Crowds "interact" through an information commons by stringing together digital artifacts into constantly changing traces, identifying patterns in those traces, and reacting to those patterns.

Such digital "interactions" deserve scrutiny in future research on managing these new organizational forms for innovation.

Research on organizational governance of such crowd-based interactions is needed. What types of actors need to be recruited to efficiently innovate in new crowd-based organizational forms? While having actors with diverse experiences[67] are likely to be important requirements, they are unlikely to be sufficient conditions. Is there a particular skill for framing one's knowledge about a problem as a paradox or analogy that is easily understood by others? Is there a particular skill for reading patterns in traces and being willing to behave in accordance with those patterns without human interaction or expressions of shared understanding? Can these skills be taught or encouraged in real time? One way to address these questions may be to view those who contribute creative associations as boundary-spanners in practice.[68]

The effect of feedback in the process suggests that traces with less stimulating patterns (such as ones with only ideas or only factual assumptions) need to be replaced on a continuous basis with more stimulating traces as old ones evaporate and stimulating artifacts are amplified. Such feedback loops governed by evaporation, amplification, and diffusion, however, do not align well with governance approaches which split a crowd's innovation process into multiple stages.[69] There is no guarantee that those crowd actors able to frame their knowledge in stimulating ways will have joined the crowd at the appropriate stage. Research is needed on participation architectures, which are less based on stages than on encouraging feedback loops and participation of the right actors at the right time.

An important area of fruitful research is the extension to intertwining internal and external crowds.[70] Innovative ideas may not be implemented in organizations accustomed to old ways of thinking and working.[71] The extent to which this process may overcome the not-invented-here syndrome is worthy of research. By having the dialogue focused on artifacts as boundary objects that quickly emerge and evaporate, the process may foster the self-distanciation[72] critical for considering new ideas in dialogues. By learning how to convey tacit knowledge as analogies and paradoxes, an organization may also be able to preserve intellectual property, a significant concern when involving internal and external crowds together.[73]

8.5 Conclusion About the Research Implications

In conclusion, our book raises knowledge fragments that are intended as the start of a theory of Collective Production of innovation. We hope that the readers will be stimulated to form their own creative associations. The need is clearly there to understand more about how innovation occurs in post-bureaucratic organizational forms, such as crowd-powered catalyst organizations,[74] distributed innovation organizations,[75] and organizations designed for incompleteness[76] since such forms are completely dependent on innovations not only in the product but in the organizational process as well. Will Collective Production make organizations of the past redundant and make only those organizations able to design innovation platforms to support Collective Production the ones that survive into the future?

Notes

1. Please see endnotes for Chap. 1, which contains the references supporting these statements.
2. Finke, R.A., Ward, T.B., Smith, S.M. (1996) Creative Cognition: Theory, Research, and Applications. Cambridge: MIT Press.
3. Amabile, T. M. 1996. Creativity in Context: The Social Psychology of Creativity. Boulder, CO: Westview.
4. Scott Page in his Academy of Management Perspective article discusses the concept of superadditivity, when multiple perspectives are engaged so that new perspectives are created. The result is not integration or synthesis in the sense of simply accommodating to different perspectives, but rather, the creation of a new perspective. We do not use Page's words of superadditivity and prefer co-mingling to avoid any confusion that the issues raised simply add up to a new perspective. Page, S. E. (2007). Making the difference: Applying a logic of diversity. Academy of Management Perspectives, 21(4), 6–20.
5. Bechky, B. A. 2003. Sharing meaning across occupational communities: The transformation of understanding on a production floor. *Organization Science*, 14(3): 312–330; Carlile, P. R. 2004. Transferring, translating, and transforming: An integrative framework for managing knowledge across boundaries. *Organization Science*, 15(5): 555–568; Levina, N., & Vaast, E. 2005. The emergence of boundary spanning competence in practice: implications for implementation and use of information systems. *MIS Quarterly*: 335–363; Star, S. L., and J. R. Griesemer. 1989. Institutional ecology, translations' and boundary objects: Amateurs and professionals in Berkeley's Museum of Vertebrate Zoology, 1907–39. *Social Studies of Science* 19.3 (1989): 387–420.
6. Cronin and Weingart (2007); Harvey, S. (2014). Creative synthesis: Exploring the process of extraordinary group creativity. Academy of Management Review, 39(3): 324–343.
7. Reviewed by Dennis, A., & Williams, M. 2003. Electronic brainstorming. In P. B. Paulus & B. A. Nijstad (Eds) Group creativity: Innovation through collaboration: 160–178.

8. Bechky, B. A. 2003. Sharing meaning across occupational communities: The transformation of understanding on a production floor. Organization Science, 14(3): 312–330; Carlile, P. R. 2004. Transferring, translating, and transforming: An integrative framework for managing knowledge across boundaries. Organization Science, 15(5): 555–568; Levina, N., & Vaast, E. 2005. The emergence of boundary spanning competence in practice: implications for implementation and use of information systems. MIS Quarterly: 335–363; Star, S. L., and J. R. Griesemer. 1989. Institutional ecology, translations' and boundary objects: Amateurs and professionals in Berkeley's Museum of Vertebrate Zoology, 1907–39. Social Studies of Science 19.3 (1989): 387–420.
9. Biscaro, C., & A., Comacchio. 2018. Knowledge creation across worldviews: how metaphors impact and orient group creativity, Organization Science, 29: 58–79; Koskinen, K. U. (2005). Metaphoric boundary objects as co-ordinating mechanisms in the knowledge sharing of innovation processes. *European Journal of Innovation Management*, 8(3): 323–335.
10. For example, Biscaro, C., & A., Comacchio. 2018. Knowledge creation across worldviews: how metaphors impact and orient group creativity, Organization Science, 29: 58–79; Levina, N. & Fayard, A. L. 2018. Tapping into diversity through open innovation platforms: The emergence of boundary-spanning practices. In Tucci, C. L., Afuah, A., & Viscusi, G. (Eds.) Creating and Capturing Value through Crowdsourcing, Oxford University Press; Howison, J., & Crowston, K. 2014. Collaboration through open superposition. MIS Quarterly, 38(1): 29–50.
11. Majchrzak, A. and Malhotra, A. 2016. Effect of Knowledge-sharing Trajectories on Innovative Outcomes in Temporary Online Crowds, Information Systems Research, 27(4): 685–703 are one exception to this.
12. Cognitive stigmergy is most comprehensively described by Christensen, L. R. 2013. Stigmergy in human practice: Coordination in construction work. Cognitive Systems Research, 21: 40–51; Marsh, L., & Onof, C. 2008. Stigmergic epistemology, stigmergic cognition. Cognitive Systems Research, 9(1–2): 136–149; Dipple, A., Raymond, K., & Docherty, M. 2014. General theory of stigmergy: Modelling stigma semantics. Cognitive Systems Research, 31: 61–92 and Ricci, A., Omicini, A., Viroli, M., Gardelli, L., & Oliva, E. 2006. Cognitive stigmergy: Towards a framework based on agents and artifacts. In D. Weyns, H.V.D. Parunak & F. Michel (Eds). International Workshop on Environments for Multi-Agent Systems (pp. 124–140). Springer, Berlin, Heidelberg.
13. Heylighen, F. 2016. Stigmergy as a universal coordination mechanism I: Definition and components. Cognitive Systems Research, 38: 4–13.
14. Elliott, M. A. 2016. Stigmergic collaboration: A framework for understanding and designing mas collaboration. U. Cress et al. [Eds.] Mass Collaboration and Education, Springer.

15. Bolici, F., Howison, J., & Crowston, K. 2016. Stigmergic coordination in FLOSS development teams: Integrating explicit and implicit mechanisms. Cognitive Systems Research: 38, 14–22.
16. Dipple, A., Raymond, K., & Docherty, M. 2014. General theory of stigmergy: Modelling stigma semantics. Cognitive Systems Research, 31: 61–92.
17. Heylighen, F. 2016. Stigmergy as a universal coordination mechanism I: Definition and components. Cognitive Systems Research, 38: 4–13.
18. Tapscott, D., & Williams, A. 2006. Wikinomics: How mass communication changes everything. Penguin Group, NY.
19. Wilson, E.O. 2000. Sociobiology: The New Synthesis, Twenty-Fifth Anniversary Edition 2nd Edition. Harvard University.
20. Majchrzak, A. and Malhotra, A. 2016. Effect of Knowledge-sharing Trajectories on Innovative Outcomes in Temporary Online Crowds, Information Systems Research, 27(4): 685–703.
21. Parunak, H.V.D. 2006. A survey of environments and mechanisms for human-human stigmergy In D. Weyns, H.V.D. Parunak & F. Michel (Eds). International Workshop on Environments for Multi-Agent Systems (pp. 124–140). Springer, Berlin, Heidelberg.
22. Malhotra, A., & Majchrzak, A. 2014. Managing crowds in innovation challenges. California Management Review, 56(4): 103–123; Ranade, G., & Varshney, L. R. 2018. The role of information patterns in designing crowdsourcing contests. In C. Tucci, A. Afuah and G. Viscusi (Ed) Creating and Capturing Value Through Crowdsourcing. Oxford Scholarship Press.
23. Marsh, L., & Onof, C. 2008. Stigmergic epistemology, stigmergic cognition. Cognitive Systems Research, 9(1–2): 136–149.
24. Füller, J., Hutter, K., Hautz, J., & Matzler, K. 2014. User roles and contributions in innovation-contest communities. Journal of Management Information Systems, 31(1): 273–308.
25. Heylighen, F. 2015. Stigmergy as a universal coordinaton mechanisms: components, varieties and applications. In T. Lewis and L. Marsh (Eds) Human Stigmergy: Theoretical Developments and New Applications. Springer.
26. Viscusi, G. & Tucci, C.L. 2018. Three's a Crowd. In Tucci, C. L., Afuah, A., & Viscusi, G. (Eds.) Creating and capturing value through crowdsourcing, Oxford University Press, p. 42.
27. Theraulaz, G. 2014. Embracing the creativity of stigmergy in social insects. Architectural Design 84(5): 54–59.
28. Dipple, A., Raymond, K., & Docherty, M. 2014. General theory of stigmergy: Modelling stigma semantics. Cognitive Systems Research, 31: 61–92.
29. Majchrzak, A. and Malhotra, A. 2016. Effect of Knowledge-sharing Trajectories on Innovative Outcomes in Temporary Online Crowds, Information Systems Research, 27(4): 685–703.
30. Heylighen, F. 2016. Stigmergy as a universal coordination mechanism I: Definition and components. Cognitive Systems Research, 38: 4–13; Parunak,

H.V.D. 2006. A survey of environments and mechanisms for human-human stigmergy In D. Weyns, H.V.D. Parunak & F. Michel (Eds). International Workshop on Environments for Multi-Agent Systems (pp. 124–140). Springer, Berlin, Heidelberg.
31. Parunak, H.V.D. 2006. A survey of environments and mechanisms for human-human stigmergy In D. Weyns, H.V.D. Parunak & F. Michel (Eds). International Workshop on Environments for Multi-Agent Systems (pp. 124–140). Springer, Berlin, Heidelberg.
32. Heylighen, F. 2016. Stigmergy as a universal coordination mechanism I: Definition and components. Cognitive Systems Research, 38: 4–13.
33. Dipple, A., Raymond, K., & Docherty, M. 2014. General theory of stigmergy: Modelling stigma semantics. Cognitive Systems Research, 31: 61–92.
34. Dipple, A., Raymond, K., & Docherty, M. 2014. General theory of stigmergy: Modelling stigma semantics. Cognitive Systems Research, 31: 61–92.
35. Ricci, A., Omicini, A., Viroli, M., Gardelli, L., & Oliva, E. 2006. Cognitive stigmergy: Towards a framework based on agents and artifacts. In D. Weyns, H.V.D. Parunak & F. Michel (Eds). International Workshop on Environments for Multi-Agent Systems (pp. 124–140). Springer, Berlin, Heidelberg.
36. Dipple, A., Raymond, K., & Docherty, M. 2014. General theory of stigmergy: Modelling stigma semantics. Cognitive Systems Research, 31: 61–92; Parunak, H.V.D. 2006. A survey of environments and mechanisms for human-human stigmergy In D. Weyns, H.V.D. Parunak & F. Michel (Eds). International Workshop on Environments for Multi-Agent Systems (pp. 124–140). Springer, Berlin, Heidelberg.
37. This builds on the discussion of routines in Feldman, M. S., & Pentland, B. T. 2003. Reconceptualizing organizational routines as a source of flexibility and change. Administrative Science Quarterly, 48(1): 94–118.
38. And, using the defenition of emergence from Mittal, S. 2013. Emergence in stigmergic and complex adaptive systems: A formal discrete event systems perspective. Cognitive Systems Research, 21: 22–39.
39. Afuah, A. 2018a. Crowdsourcing: A Primer and Research Framework. In Creating and capturing value through crowdsourcing. In Tucci, C. L., Afuah, A., & Viscusi, G. (Eds.), *Creating and Capturing Value through Crowdsourcing*, Oxford University Press, pp. 39–57.
40. Viscusi, G. & Tucci, C.L. 2018. Three's a Crowd. In Tucci, C. L., Afuah, A., & Viscusi, G. (Eds.) *Creating and capturing value through crowdsourcing*, Oxford University Press, pp. 39–57.
41. Nickerson, J. A., Wuebker, R., & Zenger, T. 2017. Problems, theories, and governing the crowd. *Strategic Organization*, *15*(2): 275–288.
42. For example, Afuah, A. 2018a. Crowdsourcing: A Primer and Research Framework. In Creating and capturing value through crowdsourcing. In Tucci, C. L., Afuah, A., & Viscusi, G. (Eds.), *Creating and Capturing Value through Crowdsourcing*, Oxford University Press, pp. 39–57; Dahlander, L.,

Piezunka, H., & Jeppesen, L. 2018. How organizations manage crowds: Define, broadcast, attract and select. In J. Sydow and H. Berends (eds.) *Managing Inter-organizational collaborations – Process View.* Part of a series: Research in the Sociology of Organizations; Jeppesen, L. B., & Lakhani, K. R. 2010. Marginality and problem-solving effectiveness in broadcast search. *Organization Science*, 21(5): 1016–1033.
43. Isocracy (countable and uncountable, plural isocracies): A form of government where all citizens have equal political power (Wikipedia); Kazamias, A. M. (1961). Meritocracy and Isocracy in American Education: Retrospect and Prospect. In *The Educational Forum* (Vol. 25, No. 3, pp. 345–354). Taylor & Francis Group.
44. Theraulaz, G. 2014. Embracing the creativity of stigmergy in social insects. *Architectural Design* 84(5): 54–59.
45. Thank you to John Wentworth for this wonderful idea.
46. Lifshitz-Assaf, H. (2018). Dismantling knowledge boundaries at NASA: The critical role of professional identity in open innovation. Administrative science quarterly, 63(4), 746–782.
47. Mortensen, M., & Hinds, P. (2002). Fuzzy teams: Boundary disagreement in distributed and collocated teams. Distributed work, 284–308.
48. A. Cockburn, Agile software development, Reading, MA, USA: Addison-Wesley, 2002.
49. Malhotra, A., Majchrzak, A., Carman, R., & Lott, V. (2001). Radical innovation without collocation: A case study at Boeing-Rocketdyne. MIS quarterly, 229–249.
50. Lovelace, K., Shapiro, D. L., & Weingart, L. R. (2001). Maximizing cross-functional new product teams' innovativeness and constraint adherence: A conflict communications perspective. Academy of management journal, 44(4), 779–793.
51. Baer M, Dirks KT, Nickerson JA. 2013. Microfoundations of strategic problem formulation. Strategic Management Journal 34: 197–214.
52. Majchrzak, A., More, P. H., & Faraj, S. (2012). Transcending knowledge differences in cross-functional teams. Organization Science, 23(4), 951–970.
53. Page, S. E. (2007). Making the difference: Applying a logic of diversity. Academy of Management Perspectives, 21(4), 6–20.
54. Saving Our Oceans: Tackling Grand Challenges Through Crowdsourcing by Amanda J. Porter, Philipp Tuertscher, & Marleen Huysman, to be published in Journal of Management.
55. Thank you to John Wentworth for this interesting idea.
56. This notion of the burstiness of the crowd was raised by Riedl, C., & Woolley, A. W. (2017). Teams vs. crowds: A field test of the relative contribution of incentives, member ability, and emergent collaboration to crowd-based problem solving performance. *Academy of Management Discoveries*, 3(4), 382–403.

57. Lakhani, K.R., Fayard, A. L., Levina, N., & Pokrywa, S. H. (2012). OpenIDEO. Harvard Business School Technology & Operations Mgt. Unit Case (612-066).
58. Garud, R., Kumaraswamy, A., & Sambamurthy, V. 2006. Emergent by design: Performance and transformation at Infosys Technologies. *Organization Science*, 17(2): 277–286.
59. Stark, D. 1999. Heterarchy: Distributing intelligence and organizing diversity. In J.H. Clippiner & E. Dyson (Eds.) *The Biology of Business: Decoding the natural laws of enterprise*, SF: Jossey-Bass. 153–179.
60. Garud, R., Jain, S., & Tuertscher, P. 2008. Incomplete by design and designing for incompleteness. *Organization Studies*, 29(3), 351–371.
61. Majchrzak, A., Griffith, T., Reez, D., Alexy, O. 2018. Organizations Designed for Grand Challenges: Generative Dilemmas and Implications for Organization Design Theory. *Academy of Management Discoveries*, 4(4): 472–496.
62. Ashkenas, R., Ulrich, D., Jick, T., & Kerr, S. 2015. *The Boundaryless Organization: Breaking the chains of organizational structure*. John Wiley & Sons.
63. Altman, E. J., Nagle, F., & Tushman, M. 2014. Innovating without information constraints. Organizations, communities, and innovation when information costs approach zero. In C. Shalley, M. A. Hitt, & J. Zhou (Eds.), *The Oxford handbook of creativity, innovation, and entrepreneurship*: 353–384. Oxford Handbooks Online.
64. As suggested by Vedres, B., & Stark, D. 2010. Structural folds: Generative disruption in overlapping groups. *American Journal of Sociology*, 115(4): 1150–1190.
65. As suggested by Tsoukas, H. 2009. A dialogical approach to the creation of new knowledge in organizations. *Organization Science*, 20(6): 941–957.
66. As suggested by Nickerson, J. A., Wuebker, R., & Zenger, T. 2017. Problems, theories, and governing the crowd. *Strategic Organization*, 15(2): 275–288.
67. Dahlander, L., Piezunka, H., & Jeppesen, L. 2018. How organizations manage crowds: Define, broadcast, attract and select. In J. Sydow and H. Berends (eds.) Managing Inter-organizational collaborations – Process View. Part of a series: Research in the Sociology of Organizations; Jeppesen, L. B., & Lakhani, K. R. 2010. Marginality and problem-solving effectiveness in broadcast search. Organization Science, 21(5): 1016–1033.
68. Kane, A. A., & Levina, N. 2017. 'Am I Still One of Them?': Bicultural Immigrant Managers Navigating Social Identity Threats When Spanning Global Boundaries. *Journal of Management Studies,* 54(4): 540–577; Levina, N., & Vaast, E. 2005. The emergence of boundary spanning competence in practice: implications for implementation and use of information systems. *MIS Quarterly*: 335–363.

69. E.g., Dahlander, L., Piezunka, H., & Jeppesen, L. 2018. How organizations manage crowds: Define, broadcast, attract and select. In J. Sydow and H. Berends (eds.) Managing Inter-organizational collaborations – Process View. Part of a series: Research in the Sociology of Organizations; Levina and Fayard (2018).
70. Malhotra, A., Majchrzak, A., & Niemiec, R. M. 2017. Using public crowds for open strategy formulation: mitigating the risks of knowledge gaps. *Long Range Planning*, 50(3): 397–410; Malhotra, A., Majchrzak, A., Kesebi, L., & Looram, S. 2017. Developing innovative solutions through internal crowdsourcing. *MIT Sloan Management Review*, 58(4): 73.
71. Levina, N. & Fayard, A. L. 2018. Tapping into diversity through open innovation platforms: The emergence of boundary-spanning practices. In Tucci, C. L., Afuah, A., & Viscusi, G. (Eds.) *Creating and Capturing Value through Crowdsourcing*, Oxford University Press.
72. That Tsoukas, H. 2009. A dialogical approach to the creation of new knowledge in organizations. *Organization Science*, 20(6): 941–957 argues.
73. Afuah, A., & Tucci, C. L. (2012). Crowdsourcing as a solution to distant search. *Academy of Management Review*, 37(3): 355–375; Dahlander, L., Piezunka, H., & Jeppesen, L. 2018. How organizations manage crowds: Define, broadcast, attract and select. In J. Sydow and H. Berends (eds.) Managing Inter-organizational collaborations – Process View. Part of a series: Research in the Sociology of Organizations.
74. Majchrzak, A., Griffith, T., Reez, D., Alexy, O. (2018) Organizations Designed for Grand Challenges: Generative Dilemmas and Implications for Organization Design Theory. Academy of Management Discoveries, 4(4), 472–496.
75. Lakhani KR and Panetta JA (2007) The principles of distributed innovation. Innovations 2(3): 97–112; Kornberger, M. (2017). The visible hand and the crowd: Analyzing organization design in distributed innovation systems. Strategic Organization, 15(2), 174–193.
76. Garud, R., Jain, S., & Tuertscher, P. (2008). Incomplete by design and designing for incompleteness. Organization studies, 29(3), 351–371.

References

Afuah, A. (2018). Crowdsourcing: A Primer and Research Framework. In Creating and Capturing Value through Crowdsourcing. In C. L. Tucci, A. Afuah, & G. Viscusi (Eds.), *Creating and Capturing Value through Crowdsourcing* (pp. 39–57). Oxford University Press.

Afuah, A., & Tucci, C. L. (2012). Crowdsourcing as a Solution to Distant Search. *Academy of Management Review, 37*(3), 355–375.

Altman, E. J., Nagle, F., & Tushman, M. (2014). Innovating without Information Constraints Organizations, Communities, and Innovation When Information Costs Approach Zero. In C. Shalley, M. A. Hitt, & J. Zhou (Eds.), *The Oxford Handbook of Creativity, Innovation, and Entrepreneurship* (pp. 353–384). Oxford Handbooks Online.

Amabile, T. M. (1996). *Creativity in Context: The Social Psychology of Creativity*. Boulder, CO: Westview.

Ashkenas, R., Ulrich, D., Jick, T., & Kerr, S. (2015). *The Boundaryless Organization: Breaking the Chains of Organizational Structure*. John Wiley & Sons.

Baer, M., Dirks, K. T., & Nickerson, J. A. (2013). Microfoundations of Strategic Problem Formulation. *Strategic Management Journal, 34*, 197–214.

Baralou, E., & Tsoukas, H. (2015). How Is New Organizational Knowledge Created in a Virtual Context? An Ethnographic Study. *Organization Studies, 36*(5), 593–620.

Bechky, B. A. (2003). Sharing Meaning across Occupational Communities: The Transformation of Understanding on a Production Floor. *Organization Science, 14*(3), 312–330.

Biscaro, C., & Comacchio, A. (2018). Knowledge Creation across Worldviews: How Metaphors Impact and Orient Group Creativity. *Organization Science, 29*, 58–79.

Bolici, F., Howison, J., & Crowston, K. (2016). Stigmergic Coordination in FLOSS Development Teams: Integrating Explicit and Implicit Mechanisms. *Cognitive Systems Research, 38*, 14–22.

Carlile, P. R. (2004). Transferring, Translating, and Transforming: An Integrative Framework for Managing Knowledge across Boundaries. *Organization Science, 15*(5), 555–568.

Christensen, L. R. (2013). Stigmergy in Human Practice: Coordination in Construction Work. *Cognitive Systems Research, 21*, 40–51.

Cronin, M. A., & Weingart, L. R. (2007). Representational Gaps, Information Processing, and Conflict in Functionally Diverse Teams. *Academy of Management Review, 32*(3), 761–773.

Dahlander, L., Piezunka, H., & Jeppesen, L. (2018). How Organizations Manage Crowds: Define, Broadcast, Attract and Select. In J. Sydow & H. Berends (Eds.), *Managing Inter-organizational Collaborations – Process View* (Part of a series: Research in the Sociology of Organizations). Bingley: Emerald Publishing Limited.

Dennis, A., & Williams, M. (2003). Electronic Brainstorming. In P. B. Paulus & B. A. Nijstad (Eds.), *Group Creativity: Innovation through Collaboration* (pp. 160–178). Oxford University Press.

Dipple, A., Raymond, K., & Docherty, M. (2014). General Theory of Stigmergy: Modelling Stigma Semantics. *Cognitive Systems Research, 31*, 61–92.

Elliott, M. A. (2016). Stigmergic Collaboration: A Framework for Understanding and Designing Mas Collaboration. In U. Cress et al. (Eds.), *Mass Collaboration and Education*. Springer.

Feldman, M. S., & Pentland, B. T. (2003). Reconceptualizing Organizational Routines as a Source of Flexibility and Change. *Administrative Science Quarterly, 48*(1), 94–118.

Finke, R. A., Ward, T. B., & Smith, S. M. (1992). *Creative Cognition*. MIT Press.

Füller, J., Hutter, K., Hautz, J., & Matzler, K. (2014). User Roles and Contributions in Innovation-Contest Communities. *Journal of Management Information Systems, 31*(1), 273–308.

Garud, R., Kumaraswamy, A., & Sambamurthy, V. (2006). Emergent by Design: Performance and Transformation at Infosys Technologies. *Organization Science, 17*(2), 277–286.

Garud, R., Jain, S., & Tuertscher, P. (2008). Incomplete by Design and Designing for Incompleteness. *Organization Studies, 29*(3), 351–371.

Harvey, S. (2014). Creative Synthesis: Exploring the Process of Extraordinary Group Creativity. *Academy of Management Review, 39*(3), 324–343.

Heylighen, F. (2015). Stigmergy as a Universal Coordinaton Mechanisms: Components, Varieties and Applications. In T. Lewis & L. Marsh (Eds.), *Human Stigmergy: Theoretical Developments and New Applications*. Springer.

Heylighen, F. (2016). Stigmergy as a Universal Coordination Mechanism I: Definition and Components. *Cognitive Systems Research, 38*, 4–13.

Howison, J., & Crowston, K. (2014). Collaboration through Open Superposition. *MIS Quarterly, 38*(1), 29–50.

Jeppesen, L. B., & Lakhani, K. R. (2010). Marginality and Problem-Solving Effectiveness in Broadcast Search. *Organization Science, 21*(5), 1016–1033.

Kane, A. A., & Levina, N. (2017). 'Am I Still One of Them?': Bicultural Immigrant Managers Navigating Social Identity Threats When Spanning Global Boundaries. *Journal of Management Studies, 54*(4), 540–577.

Kazamias, A. M. (1961). Meritocracy and Isocracy in American Education: Retrospect and Prospect. *The Educational Forum, 25*(3), 345–354.

Kornberger, M. (2017). The Visible Hand and the Crowd: Analyzing Organization Design in Distributed Innovation Systems. *Strategic Organization, 15*(2), 174–193.

Koskinen, K. U. (2005). Metaphoric Boundary Objects as Co-ordinating Mechanisms in the Knowledge Sharing of Innovation Processes. *European Journal of Innovation Management, 8*(3), 323–335.

Lakhani, K. R., & Panetta, J. A. (2007). The Principles of Distributed Innovation. *Innovations, 2*(3), 97–112.

Lakhani, K. R., Fayard, A. L., Levina, N., & Pokrywa, S. H. (2012). *OpenIDEO*. Harvard Business School Technology & Operations Mgt. Unit Case (612-066).

Levina, N., & Fayard, A. L. (2018). Tapping into Diversity through Open Innovation Platforms: The Emergence of Boundary-Spanning Practices. In C. L. Tucci, A. Afuah, & G. Viscusi (Eds.), *Creating and Capturing Value through Crowdsourcing*. Oxford University Press.

Levina, N., & Vaast, E. (2005). The Emergence of Boundary Spanning Competence in Practice: Implications for Implementation and Use of Information Systems. *MIS Quarterly, 29*, 335–363.

Lifshitz-Assaf, H. (2018). Dismantling Knowledge Boundaries at NASA: The Critical Role of Professional Identity in Open Innovation. *Administrative Science Quarterly, 63*(4), 746–782.

Lovelace, K., Shapiro, D. L., & Weingart, L. R. (2001). Maximizing Cross-functional New Product Teams' Innovativeness and Constraint Adherence: A Conflict Communications Perspective. *Academy of Management Journal, 44*(4), 779–793.

Majchrzak, A., & Malhotra, A. (2016). Effect of Knowledge-Sharing Trajectories on Innovative Outcomes in Temporary Online Crowds. *Information Systems Research, 27*(4), 685–703.

Majchrzak, A., More, P. H., & Faraj, S. (2012). Transcending Knowledge Differences in Cross-functional Teams. *Organization Science, 23*(4), 951–970.

Majchrzak, A., Griffith, T., Reez, D., & Alexy, O. (2018). Organizations Designed for Grand Challenges: Generative Dilemmas and Implications for Organization Design Theory. *Academy of Management Discoveries, 4*(4), 472–496.

Malhotra, A., & Majchrzak, A. (2014). Managing Crowds in Innovation Challenges. *California Management Review, 56*(4), 103–123.

Malhotra, A., Majchrzak, A., Carman, R., & Lott, V. (2001). Radical Innovation without Collocation: A Case Study at Boeing-Rocketdyne. *MIS Quarterly, 25*, 229–249.

Malhotra, A., Majchrzak, A., Kesebi, L., & Looram, S. (2017a). Developing Innovative Solutions through Internal Crowdsourcing. *MIT Sloan Management Review, 58*(4), 73.

Malhotra, A., Majchrzak, A., & Niemiec, R. M. (2017b). Using Public Crowds for Open Strategy Formulation: Mitigating the Risks of Knowledge Gaps. *Long Range Planning, 50*(3), 397–410.

Marsh, L., & Onof, C. (2008). Stigmergic Epistemology, Stigmergic Cognition. *Cognitive Systems Research, 9*(1–2), 136–149.

Mittal, S. (2013). Emergence in Stigmergic and Complex Adaptive Systems: A Formal Discrete Event Systems Perspective. *Cognitive Systems Research, 21*, 22–39.

Mortensen, M., & Hinds, P. (2002). Fuzzy Teams: Boundary Disagreement in Distributed and Collocated Teams. In *Distributed Work* (pp. 284–308). Cambridge, MA: MIT Press.

Nickerson, J. A., Wuebker, R., & Zenger, T. (2017). Problems, Theories, and Governing the Crowd. *Strategic Organization, 15*(2), 275–288.

Page, S. E. (2007). Making the Difference: Applying a Logic of Diversity. *Academy of Management Perspectives, 21*(4), 6–20.

Parunak, H. V. D. (2006). A Survey of Environments and Mechanisms for Human-Human Stigmergy. In D. Weyns, H. V. D. Parunak, & F. Michel (Eds.), *International Workshop on Environments for Multi-Agent Systems* (pp. 124–140). Berlin, Heidelberg: Springer.

Ranade, G., & Varshney, L. R. (2018). The Role of Information Patterns in Designing Crowdsourcing Contests. In C. Tucci, A. Afuah, & G. Viscusi (Eds.), *Creating and Capturing Value Through Crowdsourcing*. Oxford Scholarship Press.

Ricci, A., Omicini, A., Viroli, M., Gardelli, L., & Oliva, E. (2006). Cognitive Stigmergy: Towards a Framework Based on Agents and Artifacts. In D. Weyns, H. V. D. Parunak, & F. Michel (Eds.), *International Workshop on Environments for Multi-Agent Systems* (pp. 124–140). Berlin, Heidelberg: Springer.

Riedl, C., & Woolley, A. W. (2017). Teams vs. Crowds: A Field Test of the Relative Contribution of Incentives, Member Ability, and Emergent Collaboration to Crowd-Based Problem Solving Performance. *Academy of Management Discoveries, 3*(4), 382–403.

Star, S. L., & Griesemer, J. R. (1989). Institutional Ecology, Translations' and Boundary Objects: Amateurs and Professionals in Berkeley's Museum of Vertebrate Zoology, 1907–39. *Social Studies of Science, 19*(3), 387–420.

Stark, D. (1999). Heterarchy: Distributing Intelligence and Organizing Diversity. In J. H. Clippiner & E. Dyson (Eds.), *The Biology of Business: Decoding the Natural Laws of Enterprise* (pp. 153–179). San Francisco: Jossey-Bass.

Tapscott, D., & Williams, A. (2006). *Wikinomics: How Mass Communication Changes Everything*. NY: Penguin Group.

Theraulaz, G. (2014). Embracing the Creativity of Stigmergy in Social Insects. *Architectural Design, 84*(5), 54–59.

Tsoukas, H. (2009). A Dialogical Approach to the Creation of New Knowledge in Organizations. *Organization Science, 20*(6), 941–957.

Vedres, B., & Stark, D. (2010). Structural Folds: Generative Disruption in Overlapping Groups. *American Journal of Sociology, 115*(4), 1150–1190.

Viscusi, G., & Tucci, C. L. (2018). Three's a Crowd. In C. L. Tucci, A. Afuah, & G. Viscusi (Eds.), *Creating and Capturing Value through Crowdsourcing* (pp. 39–57). Oxford University Press.

Wilson, E. O. (2000). *Sociobiology: The New Synthesis* (Twenty-Fifth Anniversary Edition) (2nd ed.). Harvard University.

9

Designing Technology Platforms for Collective Co-Production: Advice When Selecting Crowdsourcing Platforms

How should the technology platform look like in order to "unmindcuff" the crowd in a way that Collective Production occurs? Since our initial search for technology platforms did not turn up any platforms that unmindcuffed the crowd, we describe the crowdsourcing platform interface which should be in place, which can make the difference between a less productive Idea-Sharing crowd and a crowd with the capability of collectively producing innovative ideas. We frame our guidance in terms of design principles, that is, guidelines for ensuring that the platform will promote Collective Production.

In this chapter, we are focused on turning all of our findings into a very practical reality: what should the technology platform look like in order to unmindcuff the crowd in a way that Collective Production occurs. Since our initial search for technology platforms that we described in Chap. 2 did not turn up any platforms that unmindcuff the crowd, reflective managers and system developers need guidance about what the platform should look like. *If an organization sponsoring a crowdsourcing event simply implements existing crowdsourcing platforms as configured by third-party vendors, the organizations will be simply implementing Idea-Sharing crowdsourcing. If the organizations want the gains we have demonstrated from Collective Production, they will need to reconfigure the third-party vendor's software themselves, insist that third-party vendors make the changes, or some combination of both.* In this chapter, we have created design principles as a set of minimum qualifications for a collectively producing crowdsourcing platform. Use these design principles to assess platforms and then as requirements for the customization of the platform. These design principles are meant to empower managers desiring to start down the path of having crowds collectively innovate. We had one manager who had to almost fight the IT department in his organization to get them to reconfigure the crowdsourcing software for Collective Production; with these design principles, the fights may be more easily won. We also had vendors who need more clarity about the changes required to their existing software to make it more supportive of Collective Production; these design principles are meant to provide that clarity. Hopefully, vendors will use our research to design and promulgate better software using the improved results we have documented as a selling point for their products.

While crowdsourcing for innovation is generally run as episodic events, increasingly we are finding organizations that continuously look to crowds for advice, input, and solutions. As such, the platform technology needs to be designed away from a focus on individual events to the continuous involvement of the crowd—even as the crowd participants change often. Correspondingly, there are two major sections in this chapter: Sect. 9.1 Technology Platform Design Principles for Innovation Crowdsourcing Events, and Sect. 9.2 Technology Platform Design Principles for crowd-based organizations. What we outline in this chapter is the design of the platform and the instructions so that participants can be collectively productive.

9.1 Designing Technology Platforms for Collective Production in Innovation Crowdsourcing Events

Since innovation platforms provided by third-party platform providers are continuously evolving, we do not specifically suggest that vendors simply reconfigure their interfaces with the three features we discussed in Chap. 2. As research on crowdsourcing—especially Collective Production crowdsourcing—advances, new enabling features (some AI-based and others based on machine learning) are likely to emerge. Therefore, in this chapter, we discuss the underlying design principles that should be implemented through the design of the software to support Collective Production, regardless of the particular user interface used by the third-party platform providers. We discussed some of these principles in an earlier article, as what we called a *participation architecture* for crowd-generative information systems platforms.[1] In this chapter, we use the 20 field crowdsourcing events and case studies to provide a deeper understanding of these initial design principles. The design principles we present here were derived from the findings we have discussed in prior chapters about how crowds collectively produce their innovative ideas. We offer six design principles that cover how to use the platform to *motivate* people to share and reuse knowledge, allow for *easier* sharing and reuse of knowledge, make *evolving* knowledge (and not people in the crowd) central to the process of emerging innovative ideas.

9.1.1 Design Principle 1: You Can't Make Crowds Do Anything, But Prime Them and Some Will Follow

Crowds, especially unmindcuffed crowds, are composed of truly autonomous individuals who can be asked to contribute certain things in certain ways, but cannot be forced to do so. Throughout the 20 crowdsourcing events, the crowds did not always follow explicit instructions. Sometimes the lengths of the subject titles of their posts were longer than 142 characters, some participants posted ideas when they were explicitly asked not to, some just asked a lot of questions despite a request to offer personal knowledge about the problem, and some did not refer to prior posts they were building upon despite being asked to do so.

We knew that the crowd had a free will and could not be mandated to do anything it did not want to. If we forced them to, through the platform design or through enforcement action, the individuals would choose to stop participating and leave.[2] When we were designing our 20 field crowdsourcing events, we struggled with the balance between unmindcuffing the crowds so as to allow them maximum autonomy and at the same time encourage and guide them on how to contribute their knowledge. We found that, in the end, autonomy is *required* to obtain participation, but that *guidance* is needed as well, to help participants understand what is expected of as part of the Collective Production process. What we found, in addition, is that not everyone needs to follow the guidance to achieve desired outcomes, as long as enough participants play the different roles required to produce innovative ideas.

Therefore, we suggest that the suggestions we posted on the front webpage to serve as the inspiration of the knowledge-sharing opportunities be made available to them, rather than instructions they must follow. For example, we suggested different types of knowledge such as paradoxes and examples that a participant could post, but did not enforce the posting by type of knowledge.

9.1.2 Design Principle 2: Incentivizing "Coopetition" for Sharing and Reusing Knowledge

Participants in the Collective Production of innovation events for solving wicked problems are motivated by the impact that they can personally have on problem-solving and learning rather than for financial reward.[3] To track behaviors that might indicate impact, some platforms offered by third-party vendors give points for certain participant behaviors, such as posting an idea or posting a comment. These platforms then highlight those who follow such behaviors with a "leaderboard" on the front webpage with the intent that others in the crowd can be motivated to follow similar behaviors. This can have the obvious effect of incentivizing certain behaviors (such as posting an idea) over other behaviors. Figure 9.1 shows an example of a Leaderboard.

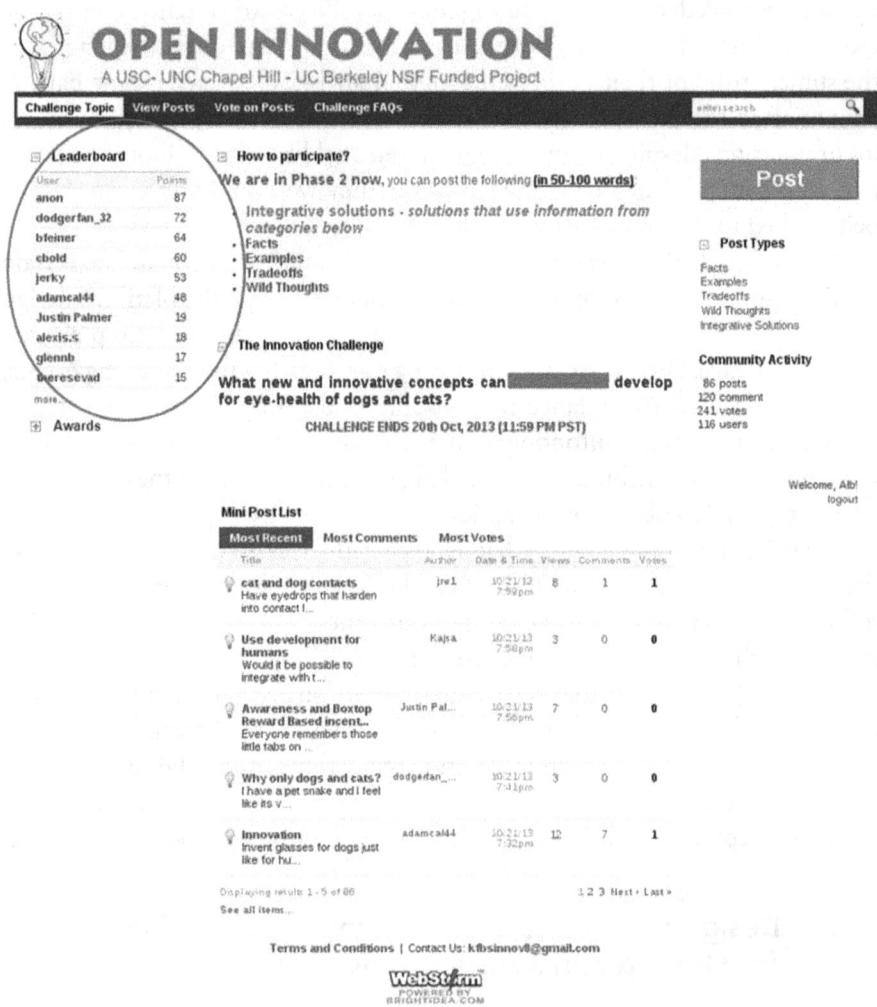

Fig. 9.1 Leaderboard

The presence of a leaderboard, however, does not mean that the behaviors associated with a Collective Production approach to innovation are highlighted. In fact, most third-party vendors set the defaults for the leaderboards to give points only for behaviors associated with Idea-Sharing, such as sharing an idea. For example, many third-party vendors will assign two or more points for each idea to a participant who offers a new idea, and one point for commenting on others' ideas. This ends up motivating participants to offer more and more ideas in order to become highest on the Leaderboard. As we have discussed in previous chapters, the simple production of more ideas is not the hallmark of Collective Production behaviors.

In order to promote behaviors more congruent with a Collective Production process, a different use of the Leaderboard should be followed. Participants should be given points if they offer creative associations, if their ideas are inspired by prior knowledge, and if they offer facts. Negative points can be given for behaviors not conducive to Collective Production such as social support posts.

Unfortunately, existing third-party vendor platforms are quite unsophisticated and will only be able to give points to behaviors that are easy to measure. Therefore, with current platforms, participants would need to indicate if they are offering a creative association, for example, in order for the system to give them points for creative associations. This is clearly inadequate since participants can game the system and say that everything they contribute is a creative association. Instead, real-time natural language processing should be incorporated into the Leaderboard point system so that the points are allocated based on an automatic determination of a creative association or fact or social support or inspiration from prior posts. The use of any automated processing should of course be to assign points accordingly and perhaps even flag the appropriate knowledge to draw attention to it. However the leaderboard functionality is implemented, it should be clearly explained to the crowd. Small prize incentives such as the opportunity to join an inner circle of contributors for future invited events can be attached to the Leaderboard.

We found that allowing the crowd to vote does not seem to play a significant role in whether a knowledge post was reused in later posts. We found that voting was actually detrimental to the entire process of Collective Production since voting makes certain posts more permanent and does not support an evolutionary model of inspiration. We also found that voting appeared to have a similar negative effect as the social support posts: they redirected the crowd's attention away from a collective creativity purpose to an individualized popularity purpose.

In addition to the Leaderboard in terms of points allocated to Collective Production behaviors, the innovativeness of the ideas proposed should be assessed and the crowd informed about the top 10% of the ideas (top 10% is sufficient rather than rank-ordering all ideas). Our experience is that the crowd should *not* be informed in real time about the innovativeness of the ideas since that will demobilize others from contributing. In a Collective Production model, how the contribution to the most innovative ideas is determined becomes quite difficult because individuals are assumed to have been influenced by the prior posts. We suggest that vendors should incorporate blockchains of contribution assignments so that the past posts that appear to have contributed to the most innovative solution-ideas can be recognized; until then, the contributor of an idea might be asked to flag prior posts that were inspirational for the creative discovery described.

9.1.3 Design Principle 3: Surface Differences

Instead of the simple discussion forums organized by ideas, which is the generic functional format of most crowdsourcing platforms, differences in assumptions, personal experiences, and objectives[4] need to be fostered. Consequently, instead of simple discussion forums, user interfaces should be considered in which there is a "backstage" where task-based generative disagreements and deliberations occur and a "front stage" where the current state of creative results resides.[5] For example, in Wikipedia, there are the "talk pages" on which participants in the article-writing process share and work out their disagreements if need be, and the article itself which displays the current state of the knowledge.[6] In a similar vein, platforms supporting Collective Production could allow for a "talk page" (or a separate "room" where debates and disagreement can occur) and then automatically move from the talk page to a "front page" of sorts, which may list the current state of the solution-ideas being offered.

An alternative approach to surfacing differences is to have contributors encouraged to look for differences and post them in the form of tradeoffs, which might then trigger others to creatively consider solutions to such tradeoffs. Asking that some in the crowd should provide tradeoffs, others provide examples of how these tradeoffs have been addressed in other domains, and still others provide partial solutions to each specific tradeoff that may provide a constructive way for the crowd to manage abrasions creatively.

9.1.4 Design Principle 4: Encourage Surfacing Different Problem Descriptions

A particularly salient distinction between the Idea-Sharing and the Unmindcuffed crowds is the way in which participants are encouraged and guided to share their perspectives on and knowledge related to the problem posed by the sponsoring organization. Idea-Sharing crowds are typically not guided to share any knowledge about the problem. Unmindcuffed crowds truly excel when they share individually held knowledge about the problem representing their individual experiences because personal experiences are easier to hear because they are less didactic and imperious; they appear more truthful, requiring that the crowd accommodate to them. The unmindcuffed crowds shared this knowledge about the problem in a variety of ways, such as contributing facts and creative associations, as we have outlined in earlier chapters. Rather than argue about different problem definitions, unmindcuffed crowds surface and consider different definitions in parallel. As a result, most of the emergent innovative ideas draw from more than one problem definition to discover solutions that more comprehensively encompass the differences.[7] Suggestions in the platform that encourage participants to post their individualized interpretations of the problem should be provided.

9.1.5 Design Principle 5: Making Knowledge-Sharing Easier

As we have found from our research and emphasized in our prior chapters, Collective Production requires that participants, with their minimal time commitment, feel encouraged to share knowledge with as little effort as possible. Allowing for easier sharing and reuse of knowledge entails designing the crowdsourcing platform to be as simple and straightforward as possible. Any crowd participant should be able to view any knowledge previously posted, even be alerted to the most recent knowledge and be given every way to combine and modify any knowledge they deem useful for producing innovative ideas.

To ensure ease of viewing and reuse of others' knowledge, we recommend that, at a minimum, the platform should foster the sharing of knowledge in a way that is concise, easily noticeable, and conveniently usable. This can be done by encouraging a 142-character suggested limit on the length of a post, which allows participants to more easily skim others' posts. The platform should clearly display, front and center, the last five posts as these are the ones that influence the participants. The platform should also make it easy to see a listing of types of knowledge that were posted since this might help participants to see the pattern in prior posts.

The focus on the last five posts is needed at this juncture because designs of crowdsourcing platforms offer only rudimentary attention-drawing features. In an ideal world, participants would be able to digest all of the crowd's knowledge, but with these rudimentary features, it is impossible. Moving forward with the next-generation platform design, personal assistants for the participant should be considered. A next-generation personal assistant approach would tag the content of each knowledge post and then have knowledge posts with similar content displayed as the participant starts typing based on the "smart" keywords match. A slightly more sophisticated personal assistant may also be able to display previously posted knowledge (examples, tradeoffs, etc.) related to a participant's current knowledge post, to encourage other participants to draw connections building on previous knowledge. An even more sophisticated computerized personal assistant could display creative associations as a participant starts typing her own post.

9.1.6 Design Principle 6: Enhance Crowd's Knowledge Evolution Transparency

Knowledge evolution transparency is essential since the crowd must be able to observe patterns, such as the emergence of creative associations following the posting of facts and ideas, which increases the participant's propensity to offer an innovative idea. As we described in Chap. 1, innovation platforms in use are often not configured to even allow the crowd to see what others post, so at a minimum, this needs to be changed. For Collective Production, others' knowledge, especially creative associations, are often inspirational in producing new knowledge—setting off the amplification process we have described earlier. Ideally, a graphical interface should be provided which shows trends over time such as word clouds and relationships between posts changing over time. An example of an evolution of the word cloud for the New Zealand Predator-Free Innovation is shown in Fig. 9.2,[8] where each figure represents a semantic network of the relationships between words (e.g., words used more closely together create larger clouds) drawn from first, second, and third sets of contributions made during the event.

> A number of different interpretations could be made from the evolution. One possible interpretation is that over time, the crowd became resigned to the fact

9 Designing Technology Platforms for Collective Co-Production...

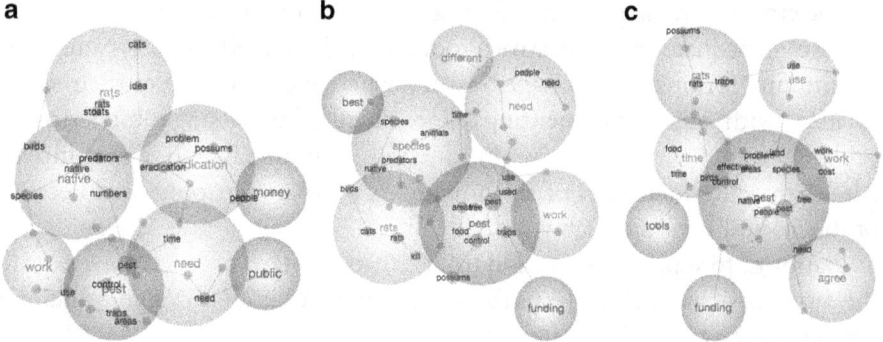

Fig. 9.2 Semantic network for first, second, and third of contributions for NZ Pest Event. (**a**) First third of contributions. (**b**) Second third of contributions. (**c**) Final third of contributions

that complete *eradication* would be too difficult (since that word went away), that some scoping was needed (such as just on rats instead of on *species*, which became less of a focal point in the network), and a variety of *tools* would be needed to be offered, not just a single one. Platforms should incorporate these word clouds to allow for easy identification of changing words and knowledge. Instead of simply indicating that a word is used frequently, the increasing use of certain words in conjunction with others may help to inspire new creative associations and discoveries.

9.2 Designing a Platform for a Crowd-Powered Organization

Much of this book has focused thus far on crowdsourcing structured as individual events. However, organizations are increasingly using crowdsourcing for innovation as a continuous activity of the organization, such as with user innovation communities (e.g., companies with active user innovation communities include Lego, Starbucks, Threadless, Thingiverse, and Dell) and open source software development communities. While these communities often modularize the work (such as asking new participants to fix bugs), innovation at a grander scale through continuous Collective Production is possible. For example, Hyperloop Transportation Technologies, Inc. has used the crowd to identify engineering solutions to complex engineering challenges such as safety controls, levitation and propulsion, and vacuuming the air out of the tubes so that the hyperloop capsule can levitate.[9]

The crowdsourcing platforms for many of these user innovation communities are inadequate for Collective Production. They tend to be organized as community forums and message boards[10] where individuals offer their needs or ideas with others commenting. Since there is not a single higher-order problem statement, Collective Production is minimal and disorganized. Alternative interpretations of an individual's need are not promoted because problems and ideas are highly individualized.

Platforms to support innovation from crowd-powered organizations require the same six design principles as those for events. Additional design principles are needed, however. These are:

- Design for fast event spinups
- Maintain history despite the fluidity
- Manage the nuanced need to share sensitive information
- Use performance assessment for multiple, non-people, purposes

9.2.1 Design Principle 7: Design for Fast Event Spinups

The crowd-powered organization's platform incorporates suggestions for when the crowdsourcing events should be spun-up for crowdsourced innovation, and then, provides a quick way to get the event started as a Collective Production approach. Templates for problem description to ensure that the problem is wicked enough for Collective Production, leaderboard point allocation, knowledge type descriptions are provided. In addition, since there are likely to be many events that could draw on the crowd's attention, the events should be given a priority based on the critical path dependencies associated with innovative solutions. This does not mean that the crowd should not pursue events of low priority; only that the lower priority ones do not need to be addressed as rapidly. Finally, for problems that are not sufficiently wicked for Collective Production (such as a call for people to help fix a bug or do research), or ideas that people have which are currently disconnected from any particular need of the organization, an alternative platform should be provided so those potential opportunities for crowd input can be fostered as well.

9.2.2 Design Principle 8: Maintain History Despite Fluidity

The fluidity of participants in a crowd-based organization means that history is often lost as participants leave. A good organization system does not work since organizing information is dependent on the context needs at the moment. Instead, context-dependent search capabilities using community-evolving folksonomies rather than structured ontologies are needed. An ontology is a structure describing the relationships between words, such as an index. A folksonomy is an ontology created dynamically by those who are in the crowd. For example, if someone several years ago prepared an interesting visualization of the organization chart for the crowd-powered organization, but that chart was not needed, a search of the workspace should surface that organization chart when others might need it. Sophisticated meta-tagging of the documents should be automatically suggested by smart tools. A personal assistant should be able to monitor a participant working in the community's workspace to recommend relevant historical information. Such a design principle ensures that the next innovative act builds on preexisting knowledge, avoiding reinvention of the wheel.

9.2.3 Design Principle 8: Manage the Nuanced Need to Share Sensitive Information

Many crowd-powered organizations are not in the open creative commons movement, carefully guarding trade secrets (e.g., Hyperloop Transportation Technologies, Inc., for example, competes with several other non-crowd powered companies). They are synchronously open and not open. This need to protect intellectual property creates a need for an onion-layered approach to Knowledge-Sharing. In the center of the onion are those crowd participants with greater commitment, accepting more responsibility and time for turning ideas into implemented outcomes. At the outside of the onion are those with less commitment, engaging in a traditional Collective Production approach of two or fewer posts to help solve a wicked problem during a crowdsourcing event. Those contributors (be they people or companies) in the center gain the intellectual property. Distinctions in enterprise social media (such as Slack and Facebook's Workplace) between public and private workspaces allow for segmenting participants into those groups permitted to have certain information. Creating rules for deciding what knowledge is permitted to cross over layers of the onion is a carefully constructed strategic activity of all crowd members. Moreover, the ability for participants to move between layers needs to be considered as well. The platform, then, must be designed to automatically follow the rules for knowledge segmentation and participant cross-layer moves.

9.2.4 Design Principles 9: Use Performance Assessment for Multiple, Non-people, Purposes

In crowd-powered organizations, not only is visibility of the knowledge needed, but the visibility of the people generating the knowledge is needed as well. In Hyperloop Transportation Technologies, Incl., Lucy is a tool that mines weekly email sent, indicating the number of hours worked, the projects worked on, and the blockers and accomplishments on the project thus far. Lucy initially was expected to serve as a roll-up of work activities for senior management. It became quickly apparent that a significant use of the tool was for everyone in the team to notice the issue (which they call blocker) that arose over time that prevented work from being done, thereby notifying management for the need to resolve the issue as soon as possible.

9.3 Conclusion

The design principles discussed in this chapter call out for further research. There has been no research that systematically turns on and off each of these principles—one at a time—to determine if they are all needed. For now, they serve as a requirements list that worked for our 20 crowdsourcing field events and describes the technology features used by the crowd-powered organizations. For the manager, take this list to your third-party vendors and IT departments and tell them to explain how these requirements are being met. Help them to understand that you need their help to move beyond Idea-Sharing software in support of crowds successfully and collectively producing innovative solutions.

Notes

1. Majchrzak, A., Malhotra, A. (2013) Towards an information systems perspective and research agenda for open innovation crowdsourcing. *Journal of Strategic Information Systems.* 22(4), 257–268
2. Martinez, M. G. (2015). Solver engagement in knowledge sharing in crowdsourcing communities: Exploring the link to creativity. *Research Policy*, 44(8), 1419–1430.

    Martinez, M. G. (2017). Inspiring crowdsourcing communities to create novel solutions: Competition design and the mediating role of trust. *Technological Forecasting and Social Change, 117*, 296–304.

3. Leimeister, J. M., Huber, M., Bretschneider, U., & Krcmar, H. (2009). Leveraging crowdsourcing: activation-supporting components for IT-based ideas competition. *Journal of management information systems*, 26(1), 197–224.
4. Leonard-Barton, D. A. Wellsprings of Knowledge: Building and Sustaining the Sources of Innovation. Boston: Harvard Business School Press, 1995 speaks of creative abrasion, but not in terms of arguing and fighting, but in terms of understanding that differences exist and each are valid.
5. Faraj, S., Jarvenpaa, S.L., Majchrzak, A. (2011) Knowledge collaboration in online communities. *Organization Science*, 22(5), 1224–1239.
6. Kane, G., Johnson, J., Majchrzak, A. (2014) Emergent lifecycle: The tension between knowledge change and knowledge retention in open online co-production communities. Management Science. 60(12): 3026–3048.
7. The importance of encouraging parallel problem definitions has also been raised in the context of social software by Von Krogh, G. (2012). How does social software change knowledge management? Toward a strategic research agenda. The Journal of Strategic Information Systems, 21(2), 154–164.
8. Sun, Y. (2019) Crowdsourcing For Integrative And Innovative Knowledge: Knowledge Diversity, Network Position, And Semantic Patterns Of Collective Reflection, PhD Dissertation, University of Southern California.
9. Majchrzak, A., Griffith, T., Reez, D., Alexy, O. (2018) Organizations Designed for Grand Challenges: Generative Dilemmas and Implications for Organization Design Theory. Academy of Management Discoveries, 4(4), 472–496.
10. Von Krogh, G. (2012). How does social software change knowledge management? Toward a strategic research agenda. *The Journal of Strategic Information Systems*, 21(2), 154–164.

References

Faraj, S., Jarvenpaa, S. L., & Majchrzak, A. (2011). Knowledge Collaboration in Online Communities. *Organization Science, 22*(5), 1224–1239.

Kane, G., Johnson, J., & Majchrzak, A. (2014). Emergent Lifecycle: The Tension between Knowledge Change and Knowledge Retention in Open Online Co-production Communities. *Management Science, 60*(12), 3026–3048.

Leimeister, J. M., Huber, M., Bretschneider, U., & Krcmar, H. (2009). Leveraging Crowdsourcing: Activation-Supporting Components for IT-Based Ideas Competition. *Journal of Management Information Systems, 26*(1), 197–224.

Leonard-Barton, D. A. (1995). *Wellsprings of Knowledge: Building and Sustaining the Sources of Innovation*. Boston: Harvard Business School Press.

Majchrzak, A., Griffith, T., Reez, D., & Alexy, O. (2018). Organizations Designed for Grand Challenges: Generative Dilemmas and Implications for Organization Design Theory. *Academy of Management Discoveries, 4*(4), 472–496.

Majchrzak, A., & Malhotra, A. (2013). Towards An Information Systems Perspective and Research Agenda on Crowdsourcing for Innovation. *The Journal of Strategic Information Systems, 22*(4), 257–269.

Martinez, M. G. (2015). Solver Engagement in Knowledge Sharing in Crowdsourcing Communities: Exploring the Link to Creativity. *Research Policy, 44*(8), 1419–1430.

Martinez, M. G. (2017). Inspiring Crowdsourcing Communities to Create Novel Solutions: Competition Design and the Mediating Role of Trust. *Technological Forecasting and Social Change, 117*, 296–304.

Von Krogh, G. (2012). How Does Social Software Change Knowledge Management? Toward a Strategic Research Agenda. *The Journal of Strategic Information Systems, 21*(2), 154–164.

Sun, Y. (2019). *Crowdsourcing for Integrative And Innovative Knowledge: Knowledge Diversity, Network Position, and Semantic Patterns of Collective Reflection.* PhD Dissertation, University of Southern California.

10

Unleashing the Crowd: Overcoming the Managerial Challenges

This chapter focuses on the major decisions that need to be made by the managers in organizations that sponsor crowds to solve the organization's wicked problems. *Fundamentally, leveraging unmindcuffed crowds requires solving a paradox: how to manage a crowd that prospers when unmanaged.* We break this paradox into five specific challenges managers need to overcome to have a successful crowdsourcing event. We offer specific suggestions for overcoming each challenge.

In the first part of this chapter, we focus on the challenges that arise when implementing crowdsourcing, the right questions to ask to overcome these challenges, and the subsequent action steps to take in order to overcome the challenges. Within each section, we refer to challenges related to both crowdsourcing with internal (to the organization) participants and crowdsourcing that engages external parties. In the second part of this chapter, we focus on the implications of what we've learned about Collective Production for managing organizations more generally.

Based on our five in-depth case studies as well as the 20 organizations we worked with for the crowdsourcing events, we raise several questions that need to be asked by organizations in order to run effective Collective Production crowdsourcing events. In addressing these questions through our observation and research findings, we detail clear action steps for managing crowds—whether they are internal or external to the organization that is running the crowdsourcing event.

Of course, when conceiving an organization as an open crowd, there are a lot of challenges that can lead to the crowd participating, but only offering incremental ideas—failing to take advantage of their collective knowledge to generate disruptively innovative ideas. In Table 10.1, we have identified sev-

Table 10.1 Managerial challenges in conducting collectively productive crowdsourcing challenges and steps for overcoming challenges

Internal crowdsourcing advantages	Challenges that can hamper emergence of innovative ideas from internal crowdsourcing	The questions to ask to overcome the challenges	Action steps to overcome the challenges
Signaling: that the company wants to be innovative and is looking for ways to be innovative by solving the most challenging wicked problems.	**Internal myopia**: forced by the wrong sponsor level inside the organization and the pressures of internal interests can lead to posing a question that is not really wicked and focuses the crowd on incremental short-term "burning fires" problems (process improvement) rather than solving strategically critical wicked problems.	1. Who should be the Sponsor to signal the importance of crowdsourcing? How should crowdsourcing be sold to internal constituents in an organization? 2. Who should be on the Planning Committee to establish the right process that signals all the right things? 3. What type of Wicked Problem signals the importance of crowdsourcing inside and outside the sponsoring organizations?	• **Establish the innovation ground by** getting the right level of executive sponsor, signaling the importance of the crowdsourcing event internally and focusing on wicked problems with long-term implications. • **Establish a planning committee to craft an all inclusive innovation process** that puts into place actions pre-, during, and post-crowdsourcing to go from selling the process (inside and outside the organization), to Collective Production of solutions, selection of solution, and then, implementation of the chosen solutions.

Column 1	Column 2	Questions	Recommendations

Morphing: in a way that stresses that collaboration (without regard to experience, expertise and location) without significant time commitment to any wicked problem and choosing which wicked problems to work on will be the way of work.	**Collaboration disincentives**: focus attention on "individual ideas" over Collective Production of "innovative solutions" for most strategic wicked problems
	
	Grandstanding: leads to some in the crowd wanting to just pose their under-developed ideas rather than work with others to collectively develop innovative solutions and create learning opportunities for all involved.
		1. How should individuals who might be interested in being crowd participants be identified?
		
		2. What kind of behaviors should the participants be encouraged to display? And, what participation structures should be put in place to enable participants to exhibit the right behaviors?
			• **Identify where to find individuals** "passionately engaged" with the wicked problem or "deeply impacted" by the wicked problem. Broadcast an open call attracting such individuals to participate in a Collective Production process to solve the open wicked problem.
			• **Promote Collective Production of innovation by:**
			  – Emphasizing need to consider others' knowledge contributions
			  – Stress variety of knowledge perspectives to be shared, rather than just ideas
			  – Use dual incentives—top solutions and top collaborators—to reward and recognize contributors
			• **Create psychological safety through anonymous participation**
			  – Focus on individuals' knowledge rather than individuals (their organizational status)
			  – Make everyone feel valued by encouraging them to share any and every perspective they might have related to the wicked problem

(continued)

Table 10.1 (continued)

Internal crowdsourcing advantages	Challenges that can hamper emergence of innovative ideas from internal crowdsourcing	The questions to ask to overcome the challenges	Action steps to overcome the challenges
Opening: the boundaries of innovation so as to engage everyone rather than restricting innovation as a functional role of "experts" in the organization.	**Domination by "experts"**: inside or outside the company (those with resources and "experience") to "crowd out" those who are not "experts", but may have the real knowledge to make a difference (because of their market-facing day-to-day roles).	1. Should crowds be monitored and moderated? If so, how?	• **Include "experts", but as another voice or for their on-demand expertise** – Anonymous posting allows "innovation experts" in the organization to participate without overwhelming the crowd with their "expertise" authority – The role of "experts" may be on-demand background knowledge. Crowd given background information from "experts" on an "as-asked" basis – "Internal experts" trained for the moderation role rather than ideation role.
Meaningfully engaging participants so as to increase their contribution impact and also providing them opportunities to learn.	**Outcome uncertainty**: How will the best solutions be determined? What happens to those solutions in the organization? These concerns tend to keep individuals from participating and contributing their knowledge.	1. Who should evaluate crowd's solutions? Based on what criteria? 2. What should be done with the best solutions?	• **Post-crowdsourcing Follow-up plan** (inform the crowd at beginning of the event of the follow-up plan with these elements): – Steering committee of implementers and decisionmakers to review solutions – Criteria for reviewing solutions should be 3: novelty, usability (e.g., contribute to competitive advantage or helpful for problem), and implementability; recognize that weighting of the 3 criteria may differ for different steering committee members and for different types of wicked problems – Winners won't be announced like a contest, but rather a report will be prepared indicating what the steering committee learned from reviewing all the solutions and their next steps

eral of those challenges and associated action steps organizations can take to overcome these challenges and to execute a crowdsourcing event as a source of innovation to solve wicked problems of organizations through the Collective Production process.

10.1 Action Steps to Overcome the Challenge of Myopic Incremental Improvement Focus

One of the major challenges in managing a Collective Production crowdsourcing event is myopia: posing a question that is not really wicked which focuses the crowd on incremental short-term "burning fires" problems (process improvement), rather than comprehensively solving a significant problem of strategic importance to the organization. To overcome this myopia, we suggest that the sponsoring organizations address four questions related to signaling the innovation importance of crowdsourcing to organizational decisionmakers before the crowdsourcing event is planned: (1) Who should be the internal sponsor of crowdsourcing event? (2) How should the crowdsourcing be positioned internally? (3) How can a planning committee be constituted to manage the crowdsourcing event? (4) What wicked question should be asked to unmindcuff the crowd? In this section, we describe specific action steps that address each of these questions and overcome the internal myopia challenge.

10.1.1 Who Should Be the Sponsor of the Crowdsourcing Event?

While this may sound like a trivial question, it is quintessential to the success of the crowdsourcing event. The sponsor should be the CEO (if it is a medium-to-small-size company) or Chief Innovation Officer (if it is a large-size company). In other words, the sponsor should be the strategic decisionmaker for the organization, not the marketing officer, not the information system director, and not R&D. Chief marketing officers are not the right sponsors because they are focused on offering products, and if the crowd decides that what is really needed is a change in the organization's culture or priorities, this is not within the purview of the CMO position. R&D is not the right sponsor because the crowd may decide on solutions that require strategic decisions such as mergers or acquisitions, or new areas of development where R&D does not currently have capabilities. Often, crowd's ideas are treated by R&D

as non-novel because R&D may have already considered the idea; in Collective Production, the ideas generated by the crowd tend to imply a more systemic solution than R&D can often implement, such as changes not only to a product, but changes in how the product is coupled with services and processes that require internal modifications to non-R&D aspects of the organization. Who is the sponsor should be specified on the crowdsourcing event webpage since crowds want to know who will listen to them? Unmindcuffed crowds will tend to test if the sponsor is serious enough about listening to the crowd. They will intentionally insert some negativity about the company to see if company moderators remove posts. While the crowd is willing to have the most egregious posts removed, anything short of that seriously harms the willingness of the crowd to collectively co-produce because the crowd no longer believes that the organization really wants them to innovate in unexpected ways.

When a crowdsourcing event is run exclusively for internal employees, it is also important that employees believe they are engaged in an exercise where their collective ideas are going to be implemented. Otherwise, employees will treat the crowdsourcing event as simply a vehicle for complaints, dragging down morale or superficially considered solutions which drag down the crowd's willingness to be creative. Having the chief innovation officer or CEO sponsoring the crowdsourcing signals to the crowd that important strategic change resulting from crowd creativity is desired, and therefore, employees should make the effort to participate. When senior executives champion the crowdsourcing event, there is a sense that ideas will be "heard" and implemented. Rather than just another organizational exercise, employees perceive the strategic importance of the event to the organization and therefore offer their knowledge more willingly. Having the CEO be the sponsor also attaches a special significance to the strategic implications of the problem itself.

An additional benefit of CEO sponsorship is that the crowdsourcing event can help the CEO get a view of the raw pulse of the market and/or employees. Instead of filtered ideas and opinions being brought to senior executive, CEOs are able to use a well-managed innovation crowdsourcing event as a first-hand source of multiple previously unheard perspectives.

10.1.2 How Should the Innovation Crowdsourcing Event Be Sold Internally?

The distinction between the idea-search crowdsourcing approach and one of unmindcuffed Collective Production crowdsourcing is not commonly spoken in practice or even seen by executives in organizations or by the public as different. Most in-practice implementations of crowdsourcing events are of the idea-search type. Correspondingly, most vendors provide websites for crowdsourcing that only foster the idea-search approach. When organizations decide to implement crowdsourcing events that subscribe to the "Collective Production" view that we have presented in this book, the senior executives who sponsor this event will need to expend time internally selling the collection production type of crowdsourcing, convincing others that this is not crowdsourcing as they know it. Collective Production type crowdsourcing creates a very different expectation (vis-à-vis idea-search type of crowdsourcing) of how it will be managed, implemented, and managed. For example, for idea-search crowdsourcing, large incentives are the norm for engaging the crowd since participants are expected to spend considerable time in individually solving the problem, and the marketing department might be a sponsor because crowdsourcing events are seen as public relations events rather than events strategically important to the top management team—actions that are the opposite of what is needed for Collective Production crowdsourcing.

Since Collective Production innovation crowdsourcing events follow none of the practices of Idea-Sharing crowdsourcing event, senior executives must avoid the temptation that Collective Production is simply a rebranding of a typical idea-search type of crowdsourcing. They have to think through how to market the event internally for support as well as externally for participation. The open call messaging for Collective Production types of crowdsourcing must signal that this event is different from Idea-Sharing events (and in these early days as Collective Production crowdsourcing is just becoming popularized, even explicitly draw differences from idea-search crowdsourcing). The message should clearly indicate that the intent, the process, and outcomes are quite different than what participants may have experienced routinely.

While some organizations may want to call the Collective Production crowdsourcing event simply an innovation discussion forum, we strongly advise against it. First, discussion threads rarely move toward a few key solutions[1] and often get off-track with high social content, rather than knowledge content. Second, Collective Production is not a consensus-based discussion of innovation because there is no consensus in the crowd. In fact, signaling or mandating consensus when broadcasting the open call will drive away creative crowds. Collective Production crowdsourcing is also not a discussion nor are there feelings of social support expressed. It is not a popularity contest since voting is not often used. The crowds who respond are unlikely to form a community because they come together on an ad hoc basis for an ephemeral duration to solve a wicked problem. Selling a community view as a discussion thread may signal prolonged commitment and may focus the process on social bond building rather than sharing knowledge with minimal commitment without regard to social support requirements—a hallmark of Collective Production.

IBM's effort for the Collective Production type of crowdsourcing was called Innovation Jam. This label worked for IBM since it was understood that knowledge was to be exchanged, diverse knowledge was needed to keep IBM from imploding, and strategic initiatives were the expected outcome of the time-constrained process.[2] The IBM Innovation Jam differs in important ways from what we observe unmindcuffed crowds doing since the crowds in our field research preferred anonymity while IBM does not, there aren't rewards for being picked by the CEO to implement the strategic initiative as there are with IBM; short knowledge fragments of different types of knowledge weren't encouraged by IBM; and many different knowledge types weren't encouraged as well. Nevertheless, at least IBM did not call it a discussion forum.

10.1.3 What Types of Wicked Problem Should Be Posed to the Crowd?

Let's take a step back and reiterate the central aspect of an innovation crowdsourcing event, that is, the problem statement. Crafting the wicked problem statement is still an evolving art. Before we summarize what we have observed about best problem statements, it is important to remember that the initial problem statement is only a starting point, one that unmindcuffed crowds iteratively change and develop. Thus, spending too much time in crafting a problem statement may not be expeditious. The risk also of overbaking the initial problem statement is that it may itself constrain the crowds (even though that is not the intent). The best problem statements are brief, sufficiently informative, and open. The problem statements we have seen work signal the strategic criticality of the wicked problem. Problem statements that attract engagement do not bound the participants to only suggest what they believe are easily implementable solutions since feasibility is only one of three criteria for evaluation. Finally, organizations must remember that the initial problem statement is just a starting point.

We have described throughout the book many examples of wicked problems that organizations can offer. There are many to choose from. We suggest that the sponsors make a selection based on (1) is it a problem for which prior solutions which have been tried have not been successful, (2) is it a problem that a broad swath of the population would have something to say about, and

(3) is the problem one for which multiple perspectives, multiple parallel solutions, and multiple ways to innovate exist?

In addition, there is a way to signal to the crowd how creatively you want them to think. This can be done by indicating if you want the solution to be in the same or different markets than what the current organization serves, and whether new or different product lines are desired. When the organization indicates to the crowd that it wants new product lines for new markets, more creativity will be assumed. If the problem is too narrowly defined and closed, it will tend to encourage the crowds to produce incremental improvement ideas rather than innovations. Consequently, they will acquiesce to what they believe the sponsor wants to hear and pretend to support the crowdsourcing initiative. On the other hand, if the problem is too broadly defined, it can lead to the crowd being engaged primarily in problem definition, with very little effort directed toward generating solutions. An example of too broad a problem statement is: How can we solve global warming? Instead, a more well-balanced question would provide some boundary, yet allow for the statement to be refined and the problem to be redefined by the crowd. The problem would be open to interpretation and redefinition, but not too open to lead to the crowd being hung up on just defining what exactly the problem to be solved should be. Therefore, a better question would be: "What can individual state governments in the U.S. do to have emissions cut in half 10 years from now?" Posing the question as a future focus helps to encourage creativity. Similarity, posing the question in this medium-broad nature ensures that the knowledge shared will not be too scattered into too many components of the problem while inspiring creativity.

We recommend that pilots be conducted once a wicked problem is drafted. The pilots can be conducted with a carefully selected group of employees or business partners who were not involved in any of the planning and can act as if they were crowd participants. The pilots can help ascertain reactions to the problem statement, types of knowledge naturally posted in response to the problem statement, and whether the problem statement is taken as a given or does the pilot crowd exercise effort to discuss and reframe the problem.

Once the wicked problem is decided upon, a communications expert should craft an open call, which signals to participants that their ideas are being sought for the future ideal state. Email messages and pitch videos can explain the importance of the open call so that employees understand that constraints on the strategic wicked problem are, for the time being, ignored. With the open call framed in this way, the organization signals that short-term fixes are not of interest and instead are interested in systemic, meaningful, long-lasting solutions. This then allows participants to focus on unmindcuffed possibilities that might be more novel.

10.1.4 What Is the Role of the Planning Committee in Managing the Crowdsourcing Event?

The planning committee plays the role of crafting an open call message that will be used to attract participants and signal clear expectations and outcomes associated with a Collective Production approach to crowdsourcing. The other, and equally important, use of the message is its use for internal purposes indicating the significance of the event to the organization. The planning committee should consist of a core of staff responsible for communications, IT liaison, project management, and human resources.

The communications expert should be in charge of messaging before, during, and after the event. In our observations in the field, the most well participated in and the best outcomes are from crowdsourcing events which have a significant "build-up" to them. Generating excitement regarding the wicked problem and possible outcomes is key to the build-up. Potential participants should be made to feel that it is a "big deal" to the organization and it is a "rare event" bringing together the best knowledge available. USAID's highly successful three-day crowdsourcing event required months of detailed planning, several tiers of increasingly involved stakeholders and contacts with over 1000 organizations around the world, each of which was asked to create their own videos, pamphlets, and marketing blitzes to convince their own stakeholders to become participants in the event. A strong communications person is needed even for internal crowdsourcing events since employees, just as external stakeholders, need to become convinced that participating is worth their time—no matter how minimal the time they can commit.

As we have also pointed out earlier, most platforms (and vendors) will tend to have an "off-the-shelf" solution that will calcify the event into an Idea-Sharing approach. Therefore, the planning committee will also need to include an IT person who can design, plan for, and supervise the reconfiguration of the crowdsourcing platform to enable Collective Production, following the design principles described in Chap. 9. Planning committee members, especially the IT liaison, will have to conduct several pilots to further customize the platform and adjust instructions for participants so they feel that they feel encouraged to easily engage in an unmindcuffed event.

Another key role of the planning committee is that of the project manager. This core planning committee member keeps things moving and thinks through all the potential implementation and feasibility issues that may need to be addressed. Some of the specific issues that the project manager needs to address for Collective Production crowdsourcing events is obtaining agreement on how and when ideas will be selected, when enough pilots have been conducted, which knowledge types will be suggested, which participants to invite, how to convince the audience to participate, whether there is moderation, how long the event will last, whether messages will be sent to participants during the event, and what the nonmonetary rewards will be, and how they will be allocated.

The human resources role will also need to be on the core planning committee, especially if the event is with employees. This role needs to ensure that employees have time and access to participate in the event. If anonymity is guaranteed, this role must make sure that obligations are met. This person should engage with the CEO and Chief Innovation Officer in deciding which ideas are selected and how the selected ideas are conveyed to the participants and the larger community. This person should monitor the content to ensure that basic rules of engagement during the crowdsourcing are followed. If the event is external, the human resources role needs to ensure that all participants are treated with dignity by others.

Beyond the core team, there is a need for legal representation on the planning committee. Since an idea may become so well implemented that it could serve as an important source of revenue for the organization, intellectual property issues need to discussed and resolved in advance. If the crowd feels that their rights are not respected, they will not participate. Organizations use a variety of approaches to providing the crowd with intellectual property, ranging from insisting that the organization has all the rights to all posts, to providing participants with rights to everything they post.

10.2 Action Steps to Overcome the Challenges of Collaboration Disincentives and Grandstanding in the Crowdsourcing Event

Two salient challenges emerge from the choice of incentives. The first is that the incentives focus on individually produced ideas rather than the Collective Production of solutions. We refer to this as collaboration disincentives. The second challenge is one where the incentives lead to a few advocating their ideas to appear as "experts" rather than participate in the Collective Production of solutions. We refer to this as grandstanding. To overcome the challenges of collaboration disincentives and grandstanding during the crowdsourcing event, organizations should ask and address two questions related to getting the right crowds wanting to engage in Collective Production and encouraging them to exhibit the right Collective Production behaviors: (1) How should individuals who might be interested in being crowd participants be identified? (2) What kind of behaviors should the participants be encouraged to display? And, what should be put in place to enable participants to exhibit the right behaviors? In this section, we describe specific action steps that address each of these questions and overcome the challenges that keep Collective Production from occurring during crowdsourcing events.

10.2.1 How Should Crowds Be Identified and Encouraged to Participate in Crowdsourcing Events?

It is important to invite people who will are likely to be "passionately engaged" with the wicked problem or are "deeply impacted" by the wicked problem. Sharing their passion and experiences with others is more likely to encourage them to engage in a Collective Production process to solve the wicked problem. It is important that crowdsourcing participants have faced the problem, but not too deeply entrenched in the context so as to not be fixated on a commonly accepted perspective on the problem as "experts" might be. Previous research has shown that most innovative ideas are brought to bear not by so-called experts, but rather, by those with marginal expertise.[3] Further, in Collective Production, the crowd needs to bring diverse and sometimes divergent perspectives (especially knowledge related to tradeoffs).

By "passionately engaged" with the problem, we mean people who have already been involved in discussions with others about either the exact same problem or a problem analogous to the problem posed to the crowd. As such, by being previously devoted to the same or similar problem, the crowdsourcing event will be seen as a natural extension for these passionate people: one that does not require a lot of start-up effort and one that can be addressed with minimal time commitment. Such passionate people can be found inside or outside the organization. When considering outside sources to invite potential candidates for participation, the sponsoring organization should begin by considering individuals from the sponsor's ecosystem, such as listserves who discuss the problem in public forums, universities, suppliers, small business owners, detractors, competitors, donors, fans, organizations in adja-

10 Unleashing the Crowd: Overcoming the Managerial Challenges 277

cent industries, professionals, complementors, and some customers (avoid having too many current customers since their perspective may be too similar to each other). As one senior executive remarked to us: "Ideas are everywhere and everyone can (and should) access them, competitive advantage comes to being first to market with these ideas."

Once the above-mentioned sources have been tapped for potential members for the crowd, one can extend the net to find others on the Internet who have shown an attachment to the same or similar problem. Such individuals can be identified from their contributions to articles on Wikipedia or through the comments they make on discussion forums. For example, for a problem statement related to US health care, there is a message board devoted to health-care insurance, healthinformaticsforum, blogs and forums on mednettech, forums on cafepharma, a doctors' hangout, and a mdhealthforum—all of which provide potential participants for a crowdsourcing event.

One can also reach out to members of professional associations or conference attendees related to associations and conferences that are impacted by and associated with the domain of the problem statement that the sponsoring organization is posing. Sometimes, it is as simple as reaching out to customers and those who follow the organization on social media. Such individuals have already explicitly indicated their affinity for the organization and its communication. Increasingly, organizations are using such customers and fans as part of the co-production of value.[4] Advertising in listservs and discussion groups or offering a video on Youtube tagged with a wide range of keywords can be another productive way to find people passionately engaged with or deeply impacted by a similar wicked problem.

A caveat is that organizations need to know that it is not always easy to find those who are passionate about a topic. It requires marshaling ideas from inside the company and an exploration of the internet. It may also require the sponsor organizations to create pre-events to drum up interest and increase awareness. These pre-events can also help to filter the desired participants. Ideally, an existing community of people passionately interested in the topic that have differing opinions or experiences should be invited. Make sure to consider customers, suppliers, other functions within the company, and so on. Ideally, 1000 or so people need to be invited in order to get a critical mass of about 100 participants. When targeting online avenues (discussion forums and online communities), ensure that the participants in those avenues are the right targets to solve the chosen wicked problem.

Let's take the case of Hyperloop Transportation Technologies, Inc (HyperloopTT). Their long-term wicked problem is to change the world of transportation so that it is inexpensive, fast, comfortable, and sustainable. Engineering, marketing, project management, and business operations professionals offer their time to support HyperloopTT's efforts. Contributors find out about how to help HyperoopTT in a number of different ways. Many have read about HyperloopTT in *Popular Science* Magazine as well as the general press. Some contributors learn about the organization as members of regional small business associations, supply chain associations, and railway associations looking at future transportation options. Some are space and flight enthusiasts and learn about them through their fellow enthusiasts. Others are involved in Digg discussions on a particular topic (such as levitation), where they hear about HyperloopTT when it is mentioned in the context of the discussions. Many hear about HyperloopTT when they attend the talks given by either the CEO or the Chairman of the Board in conferences and for associations. Finally, HyperloopTT makes it easy to be followed on Twitter, Facebook, and other forms of social media such that now the organization has about 60,000 followers.

Organizations may also need to create pre-event in-person means to drum up participation and get the participants excited about the upcoming crowdsourcing event. As an example, USAID engaged in the following activities to obtain a crowd of 6700 participants from 150 countries for a 3-day crowdsourcing event to generate ideas addressing the global challenges of human development, entrepreneurship, science and technology, and innovation.[5] In anticipation of the event, USAID conducted a planning workshop among a large diverse participant base early in the process, identified partner organizations from which to draw individuals based on the workshop. They invited individuals in partner organizations to take key roles, conducted conference calls with partner organizations and targeted USAID missions, and created a master guest list of over 1000 organizations. USAID also asked the partner organizations to develop creative and personalized approaches to inviting their constituents (such as videos, blogs). Further, USAID used a variety of social media channels, including Facebook badges indicating who registered before the start of the event, so as to encourage the laggards but interested to register for the event. Dozens of volunteer facilitators were also recruited to play key roles during the event, such as moderators, hosts, featured guest-experts in their field to lend credibility to the seriousness. We will delve deeper into the moderation of crowdsourcing events later in this chapter.

10.2.2 What Incentives Encourage the Crowd to Collectively Produce Innovative Solutions?

If the incentives (even simple nonmonetary rewards and recognition) are provided for only the best ideas, it can lead to the negative effects of competitive gamification and turn crowdsourcing into an individuals' "idea search" process. Such a situation leads to the negativity brought about by collaboration disincentives as the participants in the crowd perceive the crowdsourcing event to be another search for best "individually conceived" ideas. At worst, if the incentives do not stress the Collective Production nature of the crowdsourcing event, a few in the crowd will begin to throw out as many half-baked ideas as they can to win the reward or be recognized as the "expert". This is what we referred to as the grandstanding challenge. Most others who do not have ideas, but have very relevant knowledge and perspective that can lead to innovative ideas, will not feel the value in sharing their knowledge, as they may be perceived that there are incentives for doing so. The crowd of many perspectives will turn into the crowd of few ideators.

To avoid the challenges of grandstanding and collaboration disincentives, organizations should decide on the rewards and recognition that draw in participants and signal the collective nature of the awards. To effectuate the Collective Production process, the rewards should indicate the need to share knowledge and build on others' knowledge. Care should be taken so as to not frame the event in a way that encourages the crowd to think the crowdsourcing event is the traditional competitive Idea-Sharing event. Awards and recognitions do not need to be substantial or be exclusively of cash value since the value for participants should be the impact on the sponsoring organization. Example rewards include an opportunity to discuss winning solutions with senior executive(s), receiving a product from the company, and recognition in a company newsletter.

To avoid the challenges of collaboration disincentive and grandstanding, Collective Production needs also to be emphasized and recognized. As an example, for one crowdsourcing event sponsored by a large industrial products company, the names of the top three collaborators to all participants were sent out every day during the crowdsourcing event. Top collaborators were identified by aggregating points for contributing a wide array of knowledge (including creative associations). The list (and scoring for top collaborators) emphasized the importance of collaborative knowledge. To avoid competition among collaborators, the awards for idea contributors as well as top collaborators were kept low ($50 gift cards for each of the top three collaborators and for three contributors whose ideas were most voted-on ideas). Having both outcome-based and process-behavior based incentives encourages participants to take whichever role they prefer, and be rewarded accordingly.

Anonymity is important for encouraging employees to voice minority opinions or provide their invaluable personal perspectives (especially if they are not part of the in-group of "experts" or if their personal perspectives are not consistent with those of their manager). When participants are not allowed to be anonymous, they might simply espouse the formal positions of their organization or state perspectives that are more in line with their bosses'. In this vein, they might also be hesitant to offer knowledge as examples of how things work in their context since it might make other units not using those practices look bad. Anonymity frees participants from the desire or ability to seek "individual" status. They are much more likely to contribute their knowledge for altruistic reasons, to help others in the organization, regardless of who is being helped and whether they might get ahead. It is the problem and the Collective Production process that is attractive not the search for individual status.

The organizations we studied emphasized anonymity. This frees employees to share the knowledge that they might not share if they feel any pressure to advocate on behalf of the internal unit they represent. This reduces the roadblock related to grandstanding and competing instead of collectively producing innovation often time with other "non-experts open to listening". If participants use their real names, especially those who would be considered subject matter experts in the organization, they would feel the need to represent their unit's positions during the event. As such, their knowledge positions could not change over time and they could not offer wild idea seeds. With anonymity, the employees who are not the so-called experts would feel less intimidated to post their perspective or even half-baked ideas that others can build on. They would feel unmindcuffed to share examples of how they might have solved the wicked problem (or part of) in their own unit. Crowds can then contribute the knowledge beneficial to the innovation opportunity at hand without regard to "status" in the company or "functional location". With anonymous contributions, no one in the crowd knows what prior specific expertise any member of the crowd has about the innovation opportunity being addressed. As one employee from Li & Feng reported: "*Confidentiality was important to allow a free flow of information. Actually asking for input regarding challenges and solutions was impressive, encouraging.... For my entire tenure at Li & Fung, I have experienced that management does not want to discuss challenges and certainly does not want input. This challenge was refreshing. Thank you.*"

10.3 Action Steps to Overcome the Challenge of Domination by Experts

Even in unmindcuffed crowds encouraged to collectively produce innovation to solve wicked problems, there is a challenge of subsuming individual interests for the sake of the greater good. A few in the crowd can dominate the knowledge of the majority by interjecting themselves as experts in the process of Collective Production. To overcome the challenges of domination of knowledge exchange by a few "experts" during the crowdsourcing event, organizations should ask and address the question: Should crowds be monitored and moderated? If so, how? In this section, we describe specific action steps that address this question and help overcome the challenges that keep Collective Production from occurring during crowdsourcing events due to domination by a few experts.

For crowdsourcing events to result in innovative outcomes—whether they are internal or external—the crowd needs to be comprised of a healthy mix of so-called experts (with deep functional experience) and others that may be marginal to the problem in terms of expertise (whose routine job is not related to innovation). However, the challenge is that the presence of experts may cause others to be hesitant to participate. And in the worst case, experts may drown the "others" in the crowd, being too vocal about their suggestions.

At New Zealand LandCare, the senior sponsors of the crowdsourcing event at first decided to keep the R&D employees from participating. However, as the challenge progressed, participants explicitly asked for research evidence on certain scientific aspects of pest control and asked that experts address the scientific questions that arose. The experts were careful not to comment on the value of any particular idea, just provide additional knowledge, if asked. This knowledge-based contextual involvement of experts encouraged the discussion to continue, which otherwise might have stalled.

Beyond just regulating or having rules around the engagement of the experts and nonexperts together during the crowdsourcing, organizations must also ask whether having such a mix of expertise and diverse experiences may require moderation to ensure that a few experts do not dominate the process of knowledge exchange during the Collective Production process. It is to address this aspect that we turn to next.

10.3.1 Should Crowds Be Monitored and Moderated? If So, How?

Moderators can watch out and tone down any participants that are wanting to hijack conversations. This type of moderation can be tricky, as you don't want to shut down any creative abrasion. Perhaps, the clear signal of this may be one person hogging up most of the bandwidth in a discussion. In such a case, moderators may want to engage others by asking them for any counter opinions or tradeoffs or examples of when a forcefully proposed solution (by someone trying to force their own ideas) may not have worked elsewhere. Moderators can also monitor for questions that may need to be answered, any problems that may arise such as software glitches, and provide general support for the process by answering any questions participants may have related to the process.

All crowdsourcing events need some critical mass of knowledge to get started. One can rely on crowds to organically generate this knowledge. However, moderators may also be trained to keep an eye out for whether this organic growth of knowledge is naturally occurring. If not, moderators may themselves seed some knowledge (which may have been already scripted by the planning committee to cater for such a contingency or contributed during pilots). Moderators may also identify early who the particularly engaged people are and then ask them for their help in seeding knowledge of different types. In preparation for Optum's Behavioral Health innovation crowdsourcing event, 12 individuals who had been most vocal about ideas to change the organization and create new offerings were invited to be part of the pilot group for the event. The sponsor had to contact each of the 12 individually to assure them that this was a genuine effort to find ways to meet their concerns. The pilot group ran a short crowdsourcing event over a several-hour period to offer feedback on the user interface. The comments that the pilot group offered during the crowdsourcing were then used to "seed" the actual event. The authors of each comment were asked to repost their comments again early on in the actual event. This was done for two purposes: first, to convince others that the event was credible, and second, to establish a norm of the type of considered comment that would help foster Collective Production.

Similar steps can be taken to turn some members of external crowds into seeding moderators to help moderators avoid being overbearing. Note that there were *no* moderators in any of our 20 field crowdsourcing events. In contrast, the USAID Global Pulse Challenge explicitly asked people who were at a recognized high level in government or USAID positions to act as moderators. Yet, a third alternative was demonstrated in the New Zealand Predator-Free crowdsourcing event, in which a few individuals from the sponsoring organization acted as moderators during the early stages of the event. These moderators were instructed primarily to answer scientific questions from the public.

Readers contemplating moderating the crowdsourcing events they sponsor should note that none of the forms of moderation we have outlined are very "heavy-handed". In a nutshell, this is key to any moderation of crowdsourcing, if moderation is implemented. Collective Production is a fragile process in that any "in your face" effort to dictate behaviors, push a particular process agenda, or emphasize a particular suggestion can lead to the breakdown of the whole crowdsourcing event. As an example, in a couple of crowdsourcing events, we asked participants to separate their knowledge-sharing actions into two distinct phases. In Phase I, the participants were instructed to only share their knowledge about the problem. They were told that in Phase II, they would integrate the knowledge shared in Phase I to create integrative solutions. However, the crowd, in a very organic matter, ignored our instructions and integrated when they wanted and posted knowledge about the problem when they wanted. An unmindcuffed crowd will do what it wants to. The learning from our research is that mandated or heavy-handed process moderation do not generate as innovative as ideas when the crowd is allowed to share knowledge the way they want and how they want.

Moderation of internal crowdsourcing has similar caveats. Heavy-handed moderation may lead employees to feel demoralized. At worst, the crowdsourcing event instructions can create an impression that the organization only wants to hear the voices they want to hear rather than hearing all voices. If the moderators are posed as the "experts", it may also engender a feeling in the crowd that the process favors certain classes of workers ("other experts") over others ("non-R&D employees"). If the moderators are managers, the crowd, fairly or unfairly, may feel there is a hidden agenda which is forcing the crowd to focus on the small problems when employees want to impact the bigger wicked problems. Organizations may also need to develop an FAQ page on the crowdsourcing platform. The FAQ can complement the role of moderators and can include answers to anticipated and fundamental questions. The FAQ may also contain answers to the questions that may have come up during prototyping.

In sum, there are many ways to moderate an innovation crowdsourcing event for Collective Production, some of which will help—as we have detailed earlier—and some of which will hurt when they are too heavy-handed. We have elaborated some of those options, with the most important issue for sponsors contemplating moderation is that the participants do not feel manipulated by the sponsoring organization. For example, if moderation involves removing any posts that disagree with the organization, participants will stop participating. If moderation involves moderators pretending that they are not with the organization and guiding participants in a particular direction, participants will stop participating. If moderation involves favoring some participants over others, participants will leave. If participants feel that the organization has not ensured that voting is done fairly, the participants will simply manipulate the voting. So, above all else, ensure fairness, participant protection, and openness to participants so they know their individual voices genuinely matter.

10.4 Action Step to Overcome the Challenge of Outcome Uncertainty

The final challenge that needs to be overcome in order to effectuate a crowdsourcing event, especially a Collective Production-focused one, is related to outcome uncertainty. In our observations, two aspects related to outcomes keep participants from engaging in the crowdsourcing event. The first is related to how the best solutions will be determined, especially when those solutions are collectively produced by the crowd. The second is related to what will happen to the best solutions collectively produced by the crowds. In order to overcome the challenge related to outcome uncertainty, organizations should ask and address two questions: Who should evaluate the crowd's solutions, and, based on what criteria? What should be done with the best solutions? We address these two questions next and provide action steps related to overcoming outcome uncertainty.

10.4.1 What Criteria Can Be Used to Select the Innovative Solutions Posed by the Crowd?

Crowd participants can be engaged in and signaled for innovation creation by using the right criteria for judging the solutions. Our observations of various crowdsourcing events in practice, as well as the ones that are part of our sample, show that three distinct criteria for reviewing solutions that can have the desired innovation effects are: novelty, usability (e.g., contribute to competitive advantage or helpful to the problem), and implementability. These three criteria tend to be well balanced in terms of focusing attention on the crowd to the newness and practicality of collectively produced solutions. Organizations must recognize that weighting of the three criteria may differ for different steering committee members and for different types of wicked problems. So, the choice of what weight to give the different criteria is dependent on the context of the organization. However, no one criteria should be overly weighted or be the single criteria. Further, organizations may want to add additional criteria to suit their context; for example, they may choose to have a social impact or international feasibility when leveraging crowds to solve globally impactful, but locally implementable innovations for societal wicked problems. Having stated criteria (that are shared with the participants at the start of the event and are obtained from steering committee) will allow multiple individuals in a sponsoring organization to become involved in the evaluation and can also be used to circle back with participants.

We would like to offer caveats related to the criteria for selecting innovative solutions. First of all, different individuals in a sponsoring organization may prefer to focus on different criteria for evaluating the solutions. Having ideas that are novel and useful is the holy grail of innovation initiatives.[6] However, both novelty and usefulness are highly subjective criteria. Is novelty new to the company or new to the industry or new to the market? Is usefulness for external competitive advantage? Does a useful idea also have to be easily implementable, that is, using current capabilities and assets? Is an idea useful because it leads to cost reduction for the sponsor or faster production than before? One toy company wanting ideas for a new product line felt that usefully novel ideas were suggested by crowds when the crowd came up with a line of girl-focused STEM toys that can evolve as girls grow and particularly help girls overcome the negative perception of math jock and nerd profiles. USAID achieved useful novelty with ideas from the crowd for sponsoring concerts that showcased women singers, singing about politically charged issues, and providing role models to participants. Some sponsors may not care about the implementability of solutions; rather, focusing on the long-term value of ideas from the crowd. As an example, innovation in the New Zealand Landcare crowdsourcing was considered achieved when participants suggested genetically engineering pests to cannibalize—not because the organization was planning to implement the idea, but because the organization had started to discuss genetic engineering for the future when there were better safeguards in place but had no idea how the public would react.

Assessing the implementability of an idea can be difficult as well, as we discovered in the case of Optum's Behavioral Health Crowdsourcing event. Their case is an interesting one because their participants—internal clinicians—shared enough knowledge to generate ideas that the sponsoring executive felt that the ideas were incredibly systemic and thus likely to have important repercussions for the organization. Unfortunately, the senior executive realized that no single functional head was initially willing to take on any of the suggestions offered by the participants. It was not until the sponsor realized that there was a set of cross-functional improvement projects which had been funded at the beginning of the fiscal year which could each benefit from related systemic suggestions. The fit of the ideas suggested with existing projects was then added as a criterion to evaluate crowd ideas. Potential judges should understand the wicked problem and the context well enough to assess the innovativeness and feasibility of the ideas that will be posted.

While criteria for evaluating crowd ideas will vary from organization to organization based on their specific needs and context, our suggestion is that these criteria be established by the planning committee in advance of the crowdsourcing event. Then, the broadcast open call to potential participants should contain the criteria. How many criteria are enough and how many are too many? This is again a highly contextual question. At the minimum, ideas should be usefully novel and therefore need to communicate what they mean by (and how they will measure) usefulness and novelty. As an example, LG established four criteria (and evaluation weights for each criterion) for their own crowdsourcing event: (1) 40% for need fulfillment—customers are desirous of the idea and will pay for it, (2) 30% for creativity/originality—the idea was unique such that LG had not explored it in the past, (3) 20% for feasibility—the idea was technologically feasible without facing any hurdles, and (4) 10% for polish and appeal—the idea was easy to understand and had used cases for it.

For our sample of 20 crowdsourcing events, we used the 3 criteria of novelty, usability, and implementability. We sifted out the unique ideas and then presented them in a spreadsheet for sponsoring executives to rate on three criteria: novelty, implementability, and potential for providing a competitive advantage. The executives were easily able to rate the unique ideas from their crowdsourcing events (in many cases, there 20+ ideas to be evaluated), finding the evaluation process to be pretty straightforward. In several organizations, we asked multiple stakeholders representing a different perspective to rate each idea—such as R&D and marketing for a company, and government, constituents, and dwellers of the land for the New Zealand pest challenge. We found the ratings between the stakeholders to be quite different, and we did not feel comfortable simply averaging these opinions. We finally decided that many of the ideas could be implemented by different stakeholders and thus obtaining a single consensus on the ratings might not be needed in all cases. In other words, we ended up parallelizing the idea evaluation process, allowing diverse perspectives to remain.

10.4.2 What Should Be Done with the Best Solutions?

As we have emphasized earlier, participants in the crowdsourcing event are desirous of knowing what will be done with the chosen best solutions. As a clear action step, organizations, especially the planning committee, must have an implementation plan in place before the start of the crowdsourcing event. First of all, it should be made clear to the crowd that winners won't be announced like a contest, but rather, a report will be prepared, indicating what the steering committee learned from reviewing all the solutions and their next steps. This announcement plan is crucial in signaling to the crowd that this is a Collective Production process with serious implications for the organization sponsoring the crowd. Another critical element of the plan is to obtain a budget for prototyping and implementing the chosen solution(s). The budget is key and the sponsor must control the budget. Related to this aspect is a formal and public written sign off by the CEO about the plan and budget. This is essential and makes the sponsor own it in every way.

Ideally, some members of the steering committee designated to choose the best solutions should also be part of the implementation team (at least as champions). Organizations may also want to form implementation teams to include those from the crowd who collectively produced the solutions. At Li & Fung, those in the crowd who were engaged in the collective development of the solutions were given funds from the implementation budget to prototype, test, and further develop the collectively developed solution-ideas. However, at Optum, the physicians made it quite clear that the last thing they wanted was to become project managers of the solutions they recommended! Organizations must also have in the implementation plan the ways in which the chosen solutions will be highlighted and shared within the organization after the solutions have been chosen from the crowdsourcing events.

The specifics of the implementation plan should then be included in the open call for participants to engage in the crowdsourcing event. As an example, as part of a 19-point communiqué sent to employees in preparation for the internal crowdsourcing event, Optum established clarity about post-crowdsourcing follow-up. The crowd was told that within one week after the completion of the crowdsourcing event, the project team would send out a detailed report by the executive review team about the crowd recommendations, followed by a Town Hall meeting. In addition to pre-crowdsourcing messages to the crowd, post-crowdsourcing feedback is needed, especially for internal crowds or external participants who might be involved in future crowdsourcing. Examples of knowledge fragments that constitute the chosen solutions and who contributed them should be highlighted as it is particularly helpful in setting the grounds for future participation.

To summarize the action steps discussed in this section of the chapter, Table 10.2 summarizes our guidance about crowdsourcing planning committees.

Table 10.2 Checklist for actions to be taken by organizations using crowdsourcing to solve wicked problems

Pre-launch
- Scope and then craft the wicked problem question.
- Decide on the rewards and recognition that draw in participants, signal the collective nature of the awards.
- Upfront choice of judge(s) from the organization.
- Collectively gather a target—potential participants—pool (email list, contact information database, etc.).
- Create an open call broadcast plan and any follow-on in-person events to get participants ready for the crowdsourcing event.
- Create an Anonymity Preservation Plan as to how anonymity will be protected.
- Iteratively develop a set of brief instructions that you may want to use to guide the participants.
- You may also need to develop a FAQ page on the crowdsourcing platform.
- Consider a "what will we do with the ideas" plan—which ideas were chosen, why and how will they be implemented.

Launch the crowdsourcing events
- Broadcast your open call to various forums and communities where most passionate and engaged may be found.
- Start to build a sense of excitement. Have a countdown clock on the platform and also rebroadcast open call just prior to start.
- After some time has elapsed in the crowdsourcing event (usually hours), do one last open call broadcast blitz to get more registrants, telling them of what's exciting about what's been posted thus far and how many others are already participating.

After the crowdsourcing event
- At the close of the crowdsourcing event, remind the judge that you'll be sending them a list of ideas to evaluate.
- Filter out the collectively produced solutions that emerge (many times, inside the discussion threads) during the crowdsourcing events.
- Ask the judges to determine the winners based on a pre-established and publicized list of criteria. An objective scoring sheet (including all the criteria and weights) should be used.
- Close the loop with the participants by sharing with them a report containing the chose solutions and the implementation plan.

10.5 How to Manage Innovation in Organizations: Learning from Crowdsourcing

To end the chapter, in this part, we want to turn attention to what can be learned from crowdsourcing regarding managing innovation in organizations and instilling a culture of innovation within organizations. According to Gallup,[7] a whopping 87% of employees do not feel engaged in their work.

Our observations from internal and external crowdsourcing events have given us some insights as to how organizations can engage employees in innovation. While ad hoc ephemeral crowdsourcing events generate excitement due to their short-lived high attention nature, they unearth something more profound. People want the freedom to use their minds to better their worlds, to collaborate with others, to feel the satisfaction and excitement of intellectually engaging with another person. Instead of putting a high bar on these people that requires them to generate ideas as their primary contribution, people should be allowed to share any knowledge at any time they desire about a topic that grabs their passion.

In this vein, when crowdsourcing is turned internally as a primary means to generate innovation in an organization, the crowdsourcing events are no longer one-off events, but may occur often in response to difficult problems being encountered by anyone anywhere in the organization. Instead of creating swat teams to solve these problems, flash crowds are called to action. Anyone is welcome to join in as and when they want or to leave when they want. At Li&Fung, which conducts many internal crowdsourcing events, such a philosophy is manifest in the numerous crowdsourcing events they conduct, through the voices in the crowd. A survey of 313 employees[8] who participated in a crowdsourcing event at Li & Fung, which asked what they gained from participating, clearly points to intrinsic motivation at play. The results of the survey are shown in Fig. 10.1.

Apparent from Fig. 10.1 is that internal crowdsourcing as a manifestation of an innovation process is a way of engaging employees by letting them know that everyone's knowledge is valuable to the organization. It also sends a signal to employees that the organization is committed to continually innovating and that everyone's role is to innovate. By being part of an organization-wide process, employees are exposed to the diverse work experiences of other employees. This exposure, in itself, heightens the awareness of the organization that solving wicked problems innovatively requires integration of diverse work experiences and knowledge anywhere in the organization. Internal crowdsourcing for innovation also provides a much-needed complement to open organizations. Employees who are asked to participate in such crowdsourcing no longer ask why the management feels the need to go outside the organization when there are perfectly good ideas from non-R&D staff within the organization. It also affords an opportunity to collaborate with others in developing innovations to solve wicked problems—an opportunity that many employees are often not given because they are tied to phones, tied to conventional assembly line production processes, or otherwise overwhelmed at work

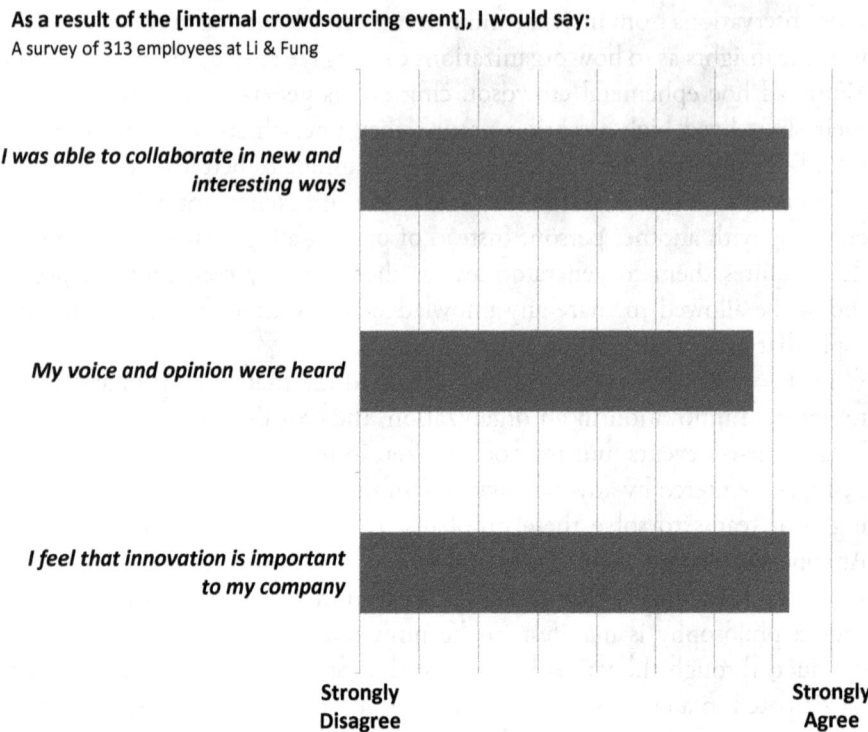

Fig. 10.1 Value of internal crowdsourcing for employees

fighting day-to-day fires. As an example, when asked what they saw as benefits for themselves as participants in open unmindcuffed innovation crowdsourcing, we received confidential anonymous surveys back from 105 Optum employees. Apparent from Fig. 10.2 is that the employees clearly indicated that freedom to be creative and personal learning were key benefits of either participating or just observing the event.

Remember that employees are given only about two posts at the crowdsourcing event. Apparent from Fig. 10.2 is that the internal crowd are able to, even with everyone's minimal contribution, learn a lot. To be able to achieve immense learning benefits with only two posts, on the average, becomes an important new way of thinking about how to help employees learn: a process we refer to as *maximal organizational impact with minimal individual commitment*. Organizations using such a process appear to be able to reap the benefits of the sum of the fragments of knowledge drawn from isolated islands being larger than the knowledge considered alone.

Wellness initiatives or satisfaction surveys are not crowdsourcing, as crowds (a set of internal employees) are not solving a wicked problem. Asking

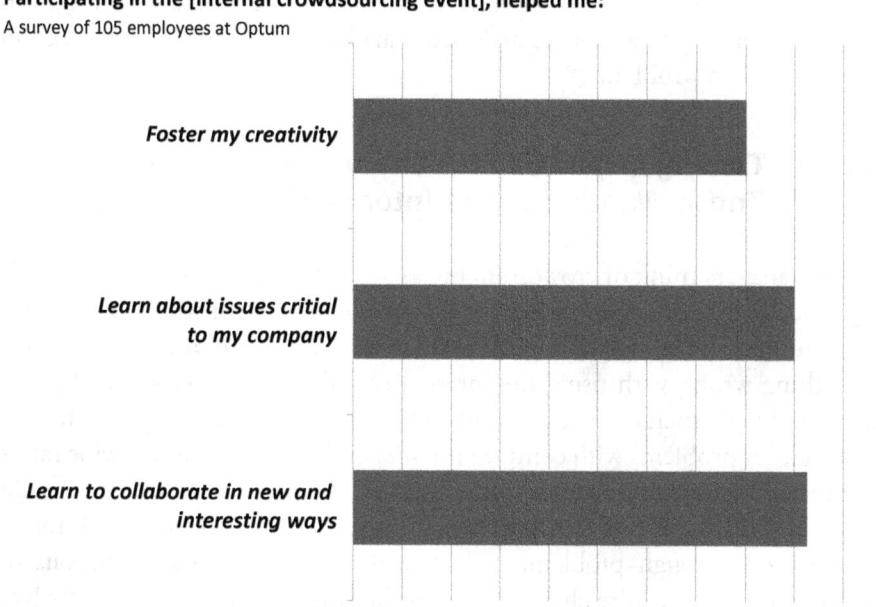

Fig. 10.2 Personal benefits from the crowdsourcing event at Optum

employees to voice their opinions on how to improve morale is also not the kind of wicked problem-solving crowdsourcing we are talking about in this book. Traditionally, even when organizations have opened themselves up to hearing from the employees, the employees are often asked for solutions. In the worst-case scenario, crowds then fail to engage their creative cognition because they feel that upper management has no intention of implementing any of the suggested solutions and they are just trying to let employees "blow off some steam".

Instead, engaging employees through crowdsourcing is about asking how new products can be developed to better serve existing customers or an underserved set of customers. Employee crowdsourcing then takes advantage of their personal knowledge with customers and constructively focuses the problem away from an us-versus-them to a "we" issue. From becoming traditional "suggestion boxes", innovation-based Collective Production crowdsourcing becomes a way to leverage an organization's vast reservoir of often geographically-dispersed knowledge. This form of crowdsourcing can open up new ways to learn about the organization and collaborating with others, as well as serving as an inspiration to use one's own creativity in solving problems. As such, collective crowdsourcing teaches managers to manage their organization as an open learning collaborative organization solving wicked problems.

10.5.1 Closing Inspiration for Executives (Especially Those Wanting to Use Internal Crowdsourcing)

Most managers think of crowdsourcing as a way to get individuals to provide good ideas for an organization to a relatively well-defined problem. This underutilizes the crowd, failing to see them as a vast ocean of expertise. There is nothing wrong with using the internal crowd to solve well-defined problems, and with such cases, the use of Idea-Search crowdsourcing may be just fine. But for problems with complex interdependencies that need a wide range of expertise brought to bear and cannot be reduced to pieces, managers should move beyond the use of top management teams or hand-selected task forces to work on a tough problem, and instead, consider crowds. Solutions to wicked problems require challenging age-old assumptions, sacred cows, silver bullets, internal politics, and singular objectives. In the words of Bill Bonfield, the sponsor for the Optum Behavioral Health Innovation Crowdsourcing Event:

> *Line staff coming together to create better solutions. This is totally foreign. This is a culture shift that would become inherent over time. I believe that consensus decision-making is very powerful, but it requires groups trained in consensus decision-making, and they're not nimble and efficient. This building on each other's knowledge in an iterative way is a new way of involving line staff in decision-making. There is a strategy and tactic to achieving this change. It may take some time. It won't happen by itself.*

Notes

1. Steiger, D., Matzler, K., Chatterjee, S., Ladstaetter-Fusseneger, F. (2012). Democratizing strategy: How crowdsourcing can be used for strategy dialogues. *California Management Review*, 54(4), 44–68.
2. Bjelland, O., & Wood, R. (2008). An inside view of IBM's "Innovation Jam". *MIT Sloan Management Review*, 50(1), 32–40.
3. Jeppesen, L., & Lakhani, K. (2010). Marginality and problem-solving effectiveness in broadcast search. *Organization Science*, 21(5), 1016–1033.
4. Sawhney, M., Verona, G., & Prandelli, E. (2005). Collaborating to create: The Internet as a platform for customer engagement in product innovation. *Journal of Interactive Marketing*, 19(4), 4–17.

5. Ferguson, D.A. (2010) Global Pulse 2010: Insights and Ideas from Around the World. Washington, DC, United States Agency for International Development.
6. Amabile, T. (1996). *Creativity in context: Update to the social psychology of creativity.* Boulder, CO: Westview Press.
7. http://www.gallup.com/services/190118/engaged-workplace.aspx.
8. *These results were shared with us by executives at Li & Fung as part of their post-event report related to their internal crowdsourcing event called The Kitchen.*

References

Amabile, T. (1996). *Creativity in Context: Update to the Social Psychology of Creativity.* Boulder, CO: Westview Press.

Bjelland, O., & Wood, R. (2008). An Inside View of IBM's "Innovation Jam". *MIT Sloan Management Review, 50*(1), 32–40.

Felin, T., & Zenger, T. R. (2011). Information Aggregation, Matching and Radical Market–Hierarchy Hybrids: Implications for the Theory of the Firm. *Strategic Organization, 9*(2), 163–173.

Ferguson, D. A. (2010). *Global Pulse 2010: Insights and Ideas from Around the World.* Washington, DC: United States Agency for International Development.

Jeppesen, L., & Lakhani, K. (2010). Marginality and Problem-Solving Effectiveness in Broadcast Search. *Organization Science, 21*(5), 1016–1033.

Sawhney, M., Verona, G., & Prandelli, E. (2005). Collaborating to Create: The Internet as a Platform for Customer Engagement in Product Innovation. *Journal of Interactive Marketing, 19*(4), 4–17.

Steiger, D., Matzler, K., Chatterjee, S., & Ladstaetter-Fusseneger, F. (2012). Democratizing Strategy: How Crowdsourcing Can Be Used for Strategy Dialogues. *California Management Review, 54*(4), 44–68.

West, J., & Lakhani, K. (2008). Getting Clear About Communities in Open Innovation. *Industry & Innovation, 15*(2), 223–231.

11

What's the Future? Managing Organizations as Crowds Enabled by Super-Connectivity and Big Data

The management and study of crowds has implications for how innovation should be managed. By using crowds to solve the most wicked problems, society and organizations are not dependent on the brilliance (or negatively impacted by the lack) of any single individual. Moreover, as organizations become increasingly opened and networked, and the overwhelmingly difficult wicked problems we are facing as a global society become more urgent, scholars can no longer trust that their traditional organizational and management principles are helpful. There is an increasing urgency to turn to nontraditional organizational forms to learn from them; examining how crowds innovate gives us insight into how these new organizational forms will need to function to maintain their innovative edge and to begin to solve the wicked problems we all face.

Moreover, as organizations increasingly rely on big data and intensively connective technologies, any employee, employer, partner, contractor, supplier, or customer can be anywhere in the world, be connected to each other seamlessly, and be able to exchange knowledge without friction. As needs of a company emerge, the company will be able to use technology-based intensive connectivity to initiate a crowd in real time through an open call for innovation broadcasted using omnipresent connective technologies. The coupling of connective technologies with the power of big data and artificial intelligence to analyze big data to identify patterns and trends will enable "spur of the moment" or "flash" crowds—wicked problem enthusiasts who come together for a brief period of time—for any and all organizations, regardless of size.

This connectivity and the access to data gives humans the power to use their knowledge to solve whichever wicked problem they are interested in, and join whichever flash crowd that suits their fancy. They may solve multiple problems simultaneously, being part of multiple crowds simultaneously. They will be enabled with easy access to big data, powerful search engines, and knowledge-sharing platforms. For example, any crowd member is now able to quickly sift through hundreds of thousands of designs on Thingiverse to find the right piece of hardware to solve a specialized manufacturing problem. They may have little need for formal organizations to do their work and make a living when, once they sniff out a market opportunity, they can find their own suppliers by using platforms such as Baidu, and connecting with customers directly through app platforms, giving rise to an on-demand entrepreneurship mindset. Will the flash crowds which temporarily form around problems and opportunities, then, be ad hoc ephemeral organizations, connecting with each other and constructing value chains in real time, coming together to address a nascent and ephemeral need in the market? The question of who should decide what ideas from the crowd are implemented begins to sound irrelevant, even archaic. Crowds of the future will extend beyond Eric von Hippel's lead user communities and define the opportunity, collectively produce the solutions, and then, decide which ones to take to market and how to market without the need for an organization.

Super-connectivity will allow crowds of opportunity-seekers to be highly fluid in their mobility to earn livelihoods. Software engineers can work open source projects as long as they feel attracted to the project until they are hired full-time by a software house or leave for other projects. As they are today, workers of the future can be freelancers, joining in and exiting crowds in real time, performing knowledge work they desire based on their interests and goals. The difference for the future is the magnitude and the flashness; that is, a janitor can sweep the floor one day, offer ideas to his CEO for new consumer goods another day, and offer another day his personal experiences to a flash crowd attempting to offer innovative solutions to a localized migration problem.

All this has huge impacts on organizations of the future. While, theoretically, organizations can easily find the right "Innovation Workers" anywhere in the world for the various innovation tasks they encounter, those workers may not be interested to work for stodgy archaic organizational forms in the future. This increases the value for the organization to spend more attention in leveraging a currently underutilized internal workforce as a crowd of people. The internal workforce is a crowd of people with many different skills, many different interests, and motivated by desires to challenge their mind, provided their efforts are listened to. As artificial intelligence increasingly frees all workers from repetitive knowledge work and menial tasks, employees in an organization are freed to explore and use their creative talent. Managers must find ways to absorb and leverage this "freed up" creative talent. Why can't the receptionist or the machinist or the dock worker who practices yoga and has three young kids who play with toys be the one to provide a toy design company's R&D unit with the suggestions for the design of yoga-based games and associated equipment as a new line of products? Or why can't the secretary be the one to bring a vision to a software development team, as we described earlier for Novell?

Managing an organization as a crowd of passionate interested people raises the bar for management to ensure that passion and interest is maintained in the organization's purpose and practices. Managing a crowd in this way raises the need to use big data and ever-evolving connective and collaborative technologies not just to produce new products for customers, but more critically, to produce new forms of transparency so that the crowd is made aware when a problem surfaces and can swarm to help.

Organizations in the future then will need to learn to foster Collective Production, whether the collectives are within or outside the organization. In the spirit of understanding fundamental behaviors of organizations and their members, researchers will also benefit from looking at workers of tomorrow not as passive recipients of a future workplace, but rather as actively and emergently engaging in new forms of dynamic interactions with artifacts, tools, data, and emergent collective behaviors, making Collective Production performed outside of any formal structure viable, interesting, and innovative.

Index[1]

A

Advantages of internal crowdsourcing
　meaningfully engaging, 268
　morphing, 267
　opening, 268
　signaling, 266
Amplification, 150, 153
Analogies, 143–146, 150, 153
Anonymity, 58–61, 235
Association fragmentation, 226, 234
Associative amplification, 226, 227, 234

B

Backstage, 256

C

Climate CoLab, 6, 112
Cognitive stigmergy, 229, 230, 232, 233
Collaboration, 96, 97, 100–101
　redefined for collective production, 96
Collaborative ideators, 209–212
Collective production
　comparison to idea searching, 29
　definition, 28
　theory, 28
Collective production practices
　amplification of others' creative associations, 81
　enact own innovation-enabling roles, 81
　Minimally Committed Knowledge Baton Passers, 80
　reformulating needs for creative associations, 81
　variety of knowledge types, 80–81
Comparison of collective producing crowds to
　online communities, 99, 100
　teams, 99, 100
Conceptually expanded solutions, 178
Coopetition, 253–256

---

[1] Note: Page numbers followed by 'n' refer to notes.

© The Author(s) 2020
A. Majchrzak, A. Malhotra, *Unleashing the Crowd*,
https://doi.org/10.1007/978-3-030-25557-2

Creative associations
  definition, 155
  effect on innovativeness of ideas, 155
  how inspired, 140–145, 150–151
  started by wicked problems, 139, 145
Creative associators, 209–211, 214, 215
Crowd, 83–103
  definition, 5
  redefined for collective production, 99
  temporary crowds, 4, 9
Crowd autonomy, 253
Crowd innovation capability, 237
Crowdsourcing for innovation, 3–28
  definition, 10, 11

D

Diffusion, 151
Discussion thread, 84, 85, 88, 89, 98, 100
Discussion thread starters, 172–175, 177, 179
Drive-by Posters, 91–92
Drive-by-ideators, 212

E

Efficiencies of unmindcuffed crowds, 91, 101
Expertise, 110, 112, 113, 120, 121, 123, 124, 126
  redefined for collective production, 120
Exploitation paradox, 236

F

Fact sharers, 209–212, 214
Field Research Study
  analysis method, 62, 64
  how field events assigned to different conditions, 56
  instructions for control *vs.* treatment conditions, 55, 56
  results, 63
  similar contexts between two conditions, 59
Follow-up plans, 268
Front stage, 256
Funnel model, 11–13

G

Generalists, 208, 210

H

Hyperloop Transportation Technologies, Inc, 52, 259, 261, 262

I

Idea brainstorming, 148, 153, 156
Idea Commenters, 201
Idea-Sharing
  assumptions, 3, 10–14, 18
  definition, 11
  dimensions of growth, 15
  evidence for, 3, 16, 19–23, 28
  evidence against, 3
  history, 14–18
  traditional website, 7–10, 25–27
Ideators, 201, 203, 205, 207, 209–212, 214, 218
Incentives, 255, 271, 275, 279, 280
Innovative solutions, 3, 5, 8, 16, 19, 25, 26, 28
  criteria for judging used in research, 62
  definition, 62
  who did judging in research, 62
Internal crowdsourcing, 165, 169, 192, 196n32, 274, 283, 287, 289, 290, 292
Internal R&D, 6, 11

K

Knowledge baton passing, 84, 92, 98, 100
Knowledge diversity
  definition, 121
  evolution, 122
  redefined for Collective Production, 125
Knowledge extenders, 206
Knowledge fragments, 78, 80, 83, 85, 101, 124
Knowledge production communities, 51
Knowledge type variety
  definition, 110
  effect on innovativeness of ideas, 109, 119–120
  measurement, 116

L

Leaderboard, 254–256, 260
Li&Fung, 52, 287, 289

M

Managerial challenges
  collaboration disincentives, 275–280
  domination by experts, 281–284
  grandstanding, 275–280
  internal myopia, 269
  outcome uncertainty, 284–288
Minimal time commitment, 84

N

Need-solution match, 172, 176, 177, 179, 185
New organizational forms
  boundaryless, 237
  catalyst, 237, 239
  emergent, 237
  heterarchical, 237
  incomplete by design, 235

New Zealand Landcare Research Inc, 52
Novell, 137–138, 143

O

Obstacles to understanding others' knowledge, 141
Optum, 165–170, 172, 174, 177, 287, 290, 291
Optum Behavioral Health Care, 52
Other-focused reactives, 206
Our Oceans Challenge, 6, 110–113

P

Paradoxes, 142, 143, 145, 146, 155
Peer-to-peer voicing, 186
Persistent visibility, 58–61
Persuasiveness, 176
Pilot, 273–275, 282
Planning committee
  action steps, 286, 287
  composition, 272
Platform design, 48
  comparing collective production to Idea-searching, 56
Principles, 230
Problem decomposability, 3
Problem elaboration, 115
Problemistic search, 169, 170, 186
Psychological safety, 267

Q

Questioners, 209, 210, 212

R

R&D, 234, 269, 270, 281, 286
Refiners, 201
Reflective reframing, 139, 145
Representation gaps, 113–115
Roles, 201–219
  enacted, 208, 212

Rules
  amplification, 230
  creative association, 230
  diffusion, 231
  evaporative traces, 231
  isocracy, 231

S

Shared understanding, 122, 123
  not needed for collective production, 122
Single expert fallacy, 77
Social support, 83, 93–95, 99, 101
Sponsorship, 270

T

Teams (*vs.* crowds) for solving ill-structured problems, 3, 26
Technology platform design principles
  crowd-based organizations, 252
  for innovation crowdsourcing events, 252–259
Technology platforms, 251–262
Theory of collective production, 225–239
Third-party innovation platform vendors, 49, 50
Topic cloud, 205
Trace data
  definition, 49
  example use to find patterns of paradoxes, 66
  how constructed, 49, 64–65

U

United States Agency for International Development, 52
Unmindcuffing, 47–67
USAID, 85–90, 274, 278, 282, 285
User innovation communities, 50

V

Variance-selection-retention theory of innovation
  definition, 12
  use in practice, 13
  use in research, 13
Vendors, 251, 252, 254–256, 262
Voicing, 169–172, 186, 190

W

Wicked problems, 3–5, 10, 17–19, 21, 24–28, 47, 48, 50–55, 60, 62, 65, 66, 69n1, 265, 269, 271–274, 276, 277, 280, 281, 283–286, 288–290, 292

GPSR Compliance

The European Union's (EU) General Product Safety Regulation (GPSR) is a set of rules that requires consumer products to be safe and our obligations to ensure this.

If you have any concerns about our products, you can contact us on

ProductSafety@springernature.com

In case Publisher is established outside the EU, the EU authorized representative is:

Springer Nature Customer Service Center GmbH
Europaplatz 3
69115 Heidelberg, Germany

www.ingramcontent.com/pod-product-compliance
Lightning Source LLC
LaVergne TN
LVHW020327260326
834688LV00037B/905